Bhagavad Gītā

Home Study Course

(Text in Sanskrit with transliteration, word-to-word and verse meaning, along with an elaborate commentary in English based on Śaṅkara-bhāṣyam)

Volume 4

Chapters 4 & 5

Swami Dayananda Saraswati
Arsha Vidya

Arsha Vidya
Research and Publication Trust
Chennai

Published by :
Arsha Vidya Research and Publication Trust
4 'Srinidhi' Apts 3rd Floor
Sir Desika Road Mylapore
Chennai 600 004 INDIA
Tel : 044 2499 7023
Telefax : 2499 7131
Email : avrandpt@gmail.com
Website: www.avrpt.com

ISBN : 978-93-80049-33-5
ISBN : 978-93-80049-39-7 (Set of 9 Volumes)

New Edition & Format :	July	2011	Copies : 1200
1st Reprint :	July	2012	Copies : 1000

Design & Layout :
Graaphic Design

Printed at :
Sudarsan Graphics
27, Neelakanta Mehta Street
T. Nagar, Chennai 600 017
Email : info@sudarsan.com

Preface

I am very happy that the 'Bhagavad Gītā Home Study Course' will now be available in nine compact volumes so that one can carry a given volume while travelling. As I said in my foreword for the last edition, I want the readers to be aware that these books do not constitute another set of books on the *Bhagavadgītā*. They are different in that they are edited transcript-pages of classroom discussions; they are presented to the reader as a program for self-study. If this is borne in mind, while reading, one can enjoy the same attitude of a student in the classroom, making oneself available to the whole process of unfoldment of the content of the words of Bhagavān. The study will then prove to be as rewarding as directly listening to the teacher. This attitude would prove to be *ātma-kṛpā*. Once this *kṛpā* is there, the other two, *śāstra-kṛpā* and *īśvara-kṛpā* would follow.

The enormous job of patient editing of the pages, thousands of them, and presenting them, retaining the original words and content without any compromise, was done by Dr. Martha Doherty. These books have created a number of committed students of the *Bhagavadgītā*, thanks to Martha's invaluable contribution to the teaching tradition of Vedanta. I also congratulate the staff of our Publication division ably led by Ms. K. Chandra, a dedicated student of Vedanta.

Swami Dayananda Saraswati
Arsha Vidya
June 19 2011

Key to Transliteration and Pronunciation of Sanskrit Letters

Sanskrit is a highly phonetic language and hence accuracy in articulation of the letters is important. For those unfamiliar with the *Devanägari* script, the international transliteration is a guide to the proper pronunciation of Sanskrit letters.

अ	*a*	*(but)*
आ	*ā*	*(father)*
इ	*i*	*(it)*
ई	*ī*	*(beat)*
उ	*u*	*(full)*
ऊ	*ū*	*(pool)*
ऋ	*ṛ*	*(rhythm)*
ॠ	*ṝ*	*(marine)*
लॅ	*ḷ*	*(revelry)*
ए	*e*	*(play)*
ऐ	*ai*	*(aisle)*
ओ	*o*	*(go)*
औ	*au*	*(loud)*
क	*ka*	*(seek)* 1
ख	*kha*	*(blockhead)**1
ग	*ga*	*(get)* 1
घ	*gha*	*(log hut)**1
ङ	*ṅa*	*(sing)* 1
च	*ca*	*(chunk)* 2
छ	*cha*	*(catch him)**2
ज	*ja*	*(jump)* 2
झ	*jha*	*(hedgehog)**2
ञ	*ña*	*(bunch)* 2
ट	*ṭa*	*(true)**3
ठ	*ṭha*	*(anthill)**3
ड	*ḍa*	*(drum)**3
ढ	*ḍha*	*(godhead)**3
ण	*ṇa*	*(under)**3
त	*ta*	*(path)**4
थ	*tha*	*(thunder)**4
द	*da*	*(that)**4
ध	*dha*	*(breathe)**4
न	*na*	*(nut)**4
प	*pa*	*(put)* 5
फ	*pha*	*(loophole)**5
ब	*ba*	*(bin)* 5
भ	*bha*	*(abhor)**5
म	*ma*	*(much)* 5
य	*ya*	*(loyal)*
र	*ra*	*(red)*
ल	*la*	*(luck)*
व	*va*	*(vase)*
श	*śa*	*(sure)*
ष	*ṣa*	*(shun)*
स	*sa*	*(so)*
ह	*ha*	*(hum)*

ं	*ṁ*	*anusvāra*	(nasalisation of preceding vowel)
:	*ḥ*	*visarga*	(aspiration of preceding vowel)
*			No exact English equivalents for these letters

1.	Guttural	–	Pronounced from throat
2.	Palatal	–	Pronounced from palate
3.	Lingual	–	Pronounced from cerebrum
4.	Dental	–	Pronounced from teeth
5.	Labial	–	Pronounced from lips

The 5th letter of each of the above class – called nasals – are also pronounced nasally.

Contents

Verse 22

Chapter 4

ज्ञान-कर्मसंन्यास-योगः

Jñāna-karmasannyāsa-yogaḥ

Topic of renunciation of action through knowledge

The origins of karma-yoga

In the first three verses of the fourth chapter, Kṛṣṇa sums up the subject matter of *karma-yoga* by indicating to Arjuna that it is not something new. Kṛṣṇa, as the Lord, had initiated it in the beginning of creation and, since then, *karma-yoga* has been handed down from generation to generation, even though it has not always been well preserved.

To become a *sannyāsī* requires a mature and contemplative disposition. You cannot simply decide to be mature or contemplative. Either you are or you are not. What you can do, however, is to live your life in such a way that you can gain a contemplative disposition. This is *karma-yoga.*

In order to gain self-knowledge, which is *mokṣa*, liberation, you have to recognise your nature as being free from action, as that which is the very centre of the entire creation, the reality of everything. For this recognition to take place, you can live a life of *sannyāsa* or a life of *karma-yoga. Karma-yoga* is engaging yourself in activities with the proper attitude, *pravṛtti-lakṣaṇaḥ yogaḥ.* And *sannyāsa* or *jñāna-yoga* is the renunciation of all activities, *nivṛtti lakṣaṇaḥ sannyāsaḥ.* So, *nivṛtti lakṣaṇa-jñāna-yoga* is for the *sannyāsīs* and *pravṛtti-lakṣaṇa-yoga, karma-yoga,* is for everyone else.

This two-fold *yoga* is intended to be unfolded throughout the *Gītā*. In fact, Kṛṣṇa had already completed the teaching in the second and third chapters. Knowing that he had taught all that had to be taught, Kṛṣṇa now praises this *yoga*, telling Arjuna that what he had taught him was something very old, introduced by himself, as Īśvara, in the very beginning, meaning in the Veda.

From teacher to student – sampradāya

In order to convey that this knowledge is something that is to be gained from a teacher by a student, who in turn hands it down to another student, a story is told. In understanding realities, it really does not matter who told whom; nevertheless, certain names are mentioned. The flow downward, from one generation to another, is called *sampradāya*. The *sampradāya* is important because this teaching has to be handled by someone who knows what it is all about. Therefore, the *sampradāya* is always introduced, either in the beginning or at the end of the text.

Verses 1-3

Kṛṣṇa presents the sampradāya and praises the knowledge

श्रीभगवानुवाच ।
इमं विवस्वते योगं प्रोक्तवानहमव्ययम् ।
विवस्वान्मनवे प्राह मनुरिक्ष्वाकवेऽब्रवीत् ॥ १ ॥

एवं परम्पराप्राप्तमिमं राजर्षयो विदुः ।
स कालेनेह महता योगो नष्टः परन्तप ॥ २ ॥

śrībhagavān uvāca

imaṁ vivasvate yogaṁ proktavān aham avyayam
vivasvān manave prāha manurikṣvākave'bravīt (1)

evaṁ paramparāprāptam imaṁ rājarṣayo viduḥ
sa kāleneha mahatā yogo naṣṭaḥ parantapa (2)

śrībhagavān – Śrī Bhagavān; *uvāca* – said;

aham – I; *vivasvate* – to Vivasvān; *imam* – this; *avyayam* – imperishable; *yogam* – *yoga*; *proktavān* – taught; *vivasvān* – Vivasvān; *manave* – to Manu; *prāha* – taught; *manuḥ* – Manu; *ikṣvākave* – to Ikṣvāku; *abravīt* – taught; *evam* – in this way; *paramparā-prāptam* – handed down from generation to generation; *imam* – this; *rājarṣayaḥ* – the kings who were sages; *viduḥ* – knew; *parantapa* – (Arjuna) the scorcher of foes!; *iha* – in this world; *saḥ* – that; *yogaḥ* – *yoga*; *mahatā kālena* – with the long lapse of time; *naṣṭaḥ* – has declined

Śrī Bhagavān said:

I taught this imperishable *yoga* to Vivasvān, Vivasvān taught it to Manu, (and) Manu taught it to Ikṣvāku.

Handed down from generation to generation in this way, the kings who were sages knew it. (But) with the long lapse of time, Arjuna, the scorcher of foes! this *yoga* has declined in the world.

Here, Kṛṣṇa tells Arjuna that he was the one who had introduced this knowledge in the Vedas in the beginning itself, along with the creation, through Vivasvān, the head of the solar clan, *sūrya-vaṁśa*. There was also another clan, the lunar clan, *candra-vaṁśa*. The *Mahābhārata* was an epic about the lunar clan and the *Rāmāyaṇa* was about the solar clan. Vivasvān also is a name given to the sun as a deity, the Lord Sun.

Kṛṣṇa is saying here that this knowledge has come down from Īśvara alone, referring to himself as the Lord. It is not something that is created by a given intellect, nor is it mere speculation. It is the knowledge that comes down from Īśvara along with the creation itself.

The difference between this knowledge and the other revealed bodies of knowledge is that it is something to be recognised. It is the knowledge that, 'I am the whole.' Any other form of revelation requires you to believe something. Some kind of a promise is always given, with reference to an after-life. However, in the knowledge, 'I am the whole,' there is no promise involved.

The statement, '*tat tvam asi*, you are that,' is not a promise. That you are Brahman is a simple statement of fact, just as the statement, 'Water is H_2O and it boils at 100° Centigrade at atmospheric pressure' is a fact and not a promise. 'You are Brahman' is a statement of fact and is something that is to be understood.

A statement of fact is verifiable knowledge. It is not something to be believed like in other forms of revealed bodies of knowledge. We must know, however, that these other revelations are also talking about the same reality. Thus, there is no problem; it is the Lord's knowledge. Because knowledge is not something that belongs to any one particular person or culture, we say that it is Īśvara's knowledge.

This two-fold *yoga, sannyāsa* and *karma-yoga,* was initiated by Lord Kṛṣṇa in the beginning, through Vivasvān, the head of the solar clan. Therefore, he says, *vivasvate aham proktavān.* Lord Sun is introduced here to convey the idea that this particular knowledge comes from Īśvara. Then, by the grace of Lord Sun, it was handed over to his son, Manu, who was the first king, the lawgiver for humanity. Manu taught his own son, Ikṣvāku, in turn.

Self-knowledge does not go away

What kind of *yoga,* knowledge is it? This knowledge is *avyaya-yoga* because it gives you that which does not die, meaning *mokṣa,* liberation. *Mokṣa* does not go away because it is identical with the *ātmā,* which is eternal. It is knowledge of the *ātmā. Mokṣa* gained is gained forever.

In his commentary on this verse, Śaṅkara says that *mokṣa,* the result of this *yoga,* is in the form of clear vision of the *ātmā* – *saṁyag-darśana-niṣṭhā* – for which there is no death, *vyaya,* at all. Once the knowledge is gained, it is gained. *Mokṣa* is not something from which you come back, like the experience of *nirvikalpa-samādhi,* because with this knowledge, the *jīvatva,* the notion of being a limited individual is destroyed. Once gained, there is no coming back, which is why the knowledge is called *avyaya.*

In the second verse, addressing Arjuna as *parantapa,* the destroyer of enemies, Kṛṣṇa says, 'In this way, the knowledge has been coming down through the families of kings, as well as through the families of sages, *ṛṣis.*' So, there are two types of flow through which this knowledge is transmitted from one generation to the other.

Because of this knowledge alone, Śaṅkara says that kings like Janaka were able to perform their duties well without abusing the royal powers entrusted to them. Power and understanding should go together, along with certain contentment. The more powerful a person is, the more informed he or she should be. Otherwise, those who come within his or her realm had it! Thus, this knowledge was introduced by Īśvara to give the kings the strength, *bala-ādhānāya*, needed to rule the world properly, there being no greater strength than *ātma-bala*, the strength of understanding oneself.

Not only the heads of royal families had this knowledge and passed it down from father to son, the sages living in the forest also had it. They taught it to their students who, in turn, taught it to their students throughout the generations.

Kṛṣṇa could see the wonder in Arjuna's eyes as he was unfolding this knowledge to him. It was as though Arjuna was asking, 'How is it that I did not know this before? Why did I not receive this knowledge while I was growing up? I was taught archery. I was taught what is right and wrong, but this, I was not taught. Why?'

When a person hears this knowledge for the first time, he or she often expresses the same wonder, 'How could I have missed something so obvious!' Although great sages like Vyāsa and Śuka lived in Arjuna's time, this knowledge that Kṛṣṇa had given to Arjuna was not readily available. Since only a few people knew it, it was as though lost. People were busy with many things. The Duryodhanas of the world were too numerous and people had no time for the knowledge. Though this knowledge sounded new and strange to Arjuna, Kṛṣṇa tells him, 'It has been around since the beginning, the same good old wisdom, and I am merely presenting it to you today as it has always been. It seems strange to you only because you have not yet had the occasion to listen to it.'

Kṛṣṇa anticipates that Arjuna's next question would be, 'Why did you choose to teach me today and not before?' Therefore, he says:

स एवायं मया तेऽद्य योगः प्रोक्तः पुरातनः ।
भक्तोऽसि मे सखा चेति रहस्यं ह्येतदुत्तमम् ॥ ३ ॥

sa evāyaṁ mayā te'dya yogaḥ proktaḥ purātanaḥ
bhakto'si me sakhā ceti rahasyaṁ hyetad uttamam (3)

me - my; *bhaktaḥ* – devotee; *sakhā* – friend; *ca* – and; *asi* – you are; *iti* – therefore; *mayā* – by me; *saḥ eva ayam* – that same; *purātanaḥ* – ancient; *yogaḥ* – *yoga; adya* – today; *te* – to you; *proktaḥ* – has been told; *hi* – indeed; *etat* – this; *uttamam* – profound; *rahasyam* – secret

> Today, that same ancient *yoga* has been told to you by me because you are my devotee and my friend. This is indeed a profound secret.

The vision of the Veda is that you are *paraṁ-brahma* and you are the cause of the whole creation. You are not a created being. Because this is said in the *Gītā*, it is said to be the essence of the Veda. Gaining this knowledge is the sole destiny of human life. Until you have this knowledge, you are bound to a life of *saṁsāra,* pleasure and pain, joy and sorrow, birth and death.

The Veda, true to its vision, gives you a two-fold way, *mārga,* to accomplish this destination. The destination is gaining the knowledge of the self being Brahman, a knowledge that is unlike any other knowledge. Any knowledge requires certain preparedness. For the knowledge of oneself, one requires emotional maturity. Mere intellectual accomplishment is not enough for a person to be emotionally mature. For instance, the greatest scientist in any discipline of knowledge can be emotionally immature. This person may feel that he or she is not respected, not recognised by peers and other members of the society. Such a person can have lot of regrets and become quite desperate.

On the other hand, you may be mature and not be intellectually accomplished. When you are able to live with yourself relatively happy and contemplative, you become matured and attain certain completeness. For such a person, a life of *sannyāsa,* renunciation, is advocated by the Veda, wherein the person is formally and completely released from all previously enjoined duties. The Veda that enjoins various duties also releases you from them, providing you with the sanction to live a life of a renunciate, so that you can pursue knowledge of the self to the exclusion of every other pursuit.

Or, if you need to gain this inner maturity, you can live a life of *karma-yoga,* pursuing the same self-knowledge that the *sannyāsī* pursues. This is the essence of all the Vedas.

When the word '*yoga*' is used in the *Gītā*, it refers to *jñāna-yoga* for a *sannyāsī*, and *karma-yoga* for one who is not a *sannyāsī*. Both of these include the pursuit of self-knowledge.

Although this knowledge remains in the royal families and with the sages, the people do not necessarily receive it. This point is addressed by Śaṅkara in his introduction to this verse. He says that the knowledge is as though lost when it reaches people whose minds are scattered – *durbalān ajitendriyān prāpya naṣṭam yogam*. Thus, it is lost, *naṣṭa*, due to the condition of the people, not because it is not available. It reaches people who have no inner strength, *durbalāḥ*, people who are not together, whose minds are scattered, *ajitendriyāḥ*. Reaching such people, this *yoga* also gets scattered, meaning that the knowledge has no hold on them. Therefore, it is as though lost.

In this verse, Kṛṣṇa acknowledges that this knowledge had always existed when he uses the expression '*sa eva*,' meaning 'that *yoga* alone, that knowledge alone,' the two-fold knowledge that is never new, *purātana*. No knowledge is ever new; it is always ancient, perennially eternal. Whatever is discovered may seem new, but, in fact, it has always been there. It seems new because no one knew of it before. Like we did not know that the sun does not move relative to the earth. Even so, the earth has always travelled around the sun and the sun has always been stationary. This is a fact that will always remain, whether one knows it.

So too, this knowledge is never new; it is *purātana*, ancient. Knowledge is always as true as the object is. If *ātmā* is eternal, then knowledge of *ātmā* is equally eternal. Nothing new is created here. The *yoga*, the knowledge, which was initiated by Kṛṣṇa in the beginning, is eternal, perennially eternal, *purātanaḥ*.

There are two types of eternity, perennial and absolute eternity. Absolute eternity has nothing to do with time and is called *pāramārthika-nityatva*, whereas perennial eternity is that which keeps on coming with every creation, every *kalpa*, and is called *pravāha-nityatva*. The Veda has *pravāha-nityatva*, being not eternal in the sense of timelessness. Although the knowledge that is the Veda keeps on coming with every creation, it is still time bound. Thus, the Veda is considered to be eternal in the perennial sense only.

Moreover, why had this perennially eternal knowledge not been given to Arjuna before? Kṛṣṇa had not held it back all along due to a lack of enthusiasm and only today became inspired to talk to Arjuna about it. The only reason Kṛṣṇa did not teach him earlier was that, until today, Arjuna had not asked for this knowledge. As soon as Arjuna asked for it, Kṛṣṇa teaches him, although they were in the middle of the battlefield!

Those who study the *Gītā*, usually take some months to study the second and third chapters in which Kṛṣṇa unfolded the knowledge. But Kṛṣṇa taught to Arjuna in one day according to Vyāsa's presentation, as Kṛṣṇa himself says, '*te adya proktaḥ*, it was told to you today.' After all, it takes only three hours to repeat the entire *Gītā*! We must remember, also, that it is not Kṛṣṇa who is actually talking in this particular verse form; it is Vyāsa. There was no necessity for Kṛṣṇa to put this knowledge into verse form. Vyāsa composed Kṛṣṇa's message in the form of verses as part of the *Mahābhārata*.

Being informed enough about the Veda, Vyāsa was qualified to present its essence in the *Gītā*. He did not need to have Kṛṣṇa say anything. Even if Kṛṣṇa were not there, we would still read Vyāsa's *Gītā*, just as we read his *Brahmasūtras*. Vyāsa, himself, is good enough for us to read because we are reading the Veda, not Kṛṣṇa or some philosopher like Kant,[1] Schopenhauer,[2] or Hegel.[3] There is no Kṛṣṇa philosophy. There is only the Veda, the knowledge that comes down to us from the *ṛṣis*.

People often say, having been given some good advice, 'Why did you not tell me this before? I have spent so many sleepless nights over it!' In fact, one may not be capable of seeing the wisdom of the advice until sleepless nights have been spent! Arjuna may have felt like chastising Kṛṣṇa for not giving him this knowledge in the days when they were in the

---

1 Kant, Immanuel (1724-1804), German idealist philosopher who argued that reason is the means by which the phenomena of experience are translated into undestanding. His classic works include 'Critique of pure Reason' (1781) and 'Critique of Practical Reason' (1788) in which he put forward his system of ethics based on the categorical imperative.

2 Schopenhauer, Arthur (1788-1860), German philosopher who believed that the will to live is the fundamental reality and that this will, being a consant striving, is insatiable and ultimately yields only suffering.

3 Hegel, George Wilhelm Friedrich (1770-1831), German philosopher who proposed that truth is reached by a continuing dialectic. His major works include 'Encyclopedia of the philosophical Sciences' (1817) and 'The Philosophy of Right' (1821)

forest and had so much time to sit and talk. Instead, here they were on the battlefield, caught between the two forces and surrounded by all the noise, dust, and confusion of war horses, chariots, elephants, infantry, conches, drums and orders being bellowed everywhere, definitely not a very conducive time or place for talking about Vedanta, about the infinite.

You should talk about the infinite only when you have infinite time, when you can sit leisurely on the bank of a river with nothing else to do, or when you are retired and no longer have to go to the office. The Pāṇḍavas had just returned from thirteen years of exile, twelve of which had been spent in the forest. Surely, Arjuna must have thought that it would have been the right time for Kṛṣṇa to teach him. He could have gained this knowledge in those twelve years.

Twelve years is a good period of time for any knowledge to take place. Even Jupiter, whose influence is said to be important in gaining knowledge, takes twelve years to come back to a given house in the zodiac. It is said that in order to master any discipline of knowledge, you must stay with it for twelve years. Such a period of time was given to Arjuna on a platter; he had a God sent banishment. That was when Kṛṣṇa should have said to him, 'Please sit down and listen to me! I have something to tell you. You grieve for those who should not be grieved for, *aśocyān anvaśocyastvam*, and so on.'

Self-knowledge is the greatest secret

In response to Arjuna's unspoken question about why Kṛṣṇa did not teach him when the surroundings were more conducive, Kṛṣṇa says in this verse that this particular knowledge is a secret, *rahasya*, and not an ordinary secret at that. The word '*Upaniṣad*' also has taken on the meaning of 'secret,' self-knowledge being the ultimate secret among all secrets, *uttamaṁ rahasyam*. Even if you share it with someone a hundred times, that person may still ask the question, 'What is *ātmā*?'

There are two types of secrets. One is a secret that is kept away from you, not because it is something that you cannot understand, but because it is kept away from your perception – from your ears and eyes. You are kept from coming to know of it by something other than yourself. The other type of secret is seen by you, it is available to be known by you, but still you do not understand. Therefore, it remains *rahasya*. The *rahasya* of Vedanta is both. For want of Vedanta, the truth of yourself remains a secret. But then, even when Vedanta is available, it remains a secret for want of preparedness on the part of the listener.

The reality revealed by Vedanta is not easy to understand by those who are conditioned into thinking that they are useless and limited, a conviction that is often confirmed by everyone around them. If a person, who thinks in this way, is told that he or she is *satya*, *jñāna*, *ananta*, *sarvakāraṇa*, *pūrṇa*, and so on, the person will become totally confused. He or she will have a new problem, 'If I am *satya*, why do I feel so useless? I must be even more useless than I thought!' The new problem is also brought about because *ātmā* is not easy to understand.

This knowledge can be misunderstood as well, which is why it was generally kept away from the majority of people.

Moreover, even if it is made available, it is not understood. For example, those who study the Veda, and are able to recite it, including the *Upaniṣads*, do not usually understand what they are reciting. For such people, the words revealing the truth are available, but not the knowledge thereof. Therefore, it is *uttama-rahasya*, the greatest secret. Thus, either due to its non-availability or due to non-understanding, the knowledge remains *uttama-rahasya*, the ultimate secret.

This knowledge should be given only to the one who wants to know

In Arjuna's case, the knowledge was not given to him because Kṛṣṇa knew that Arjuna was not interested in it before. Even if he had taught him, the knowledge would not have meant anything to Arjuna. Such knowledge should only be given to someone who wants to know.

Unless a person recognises that there is a problem, it is useless to offer a solution. We can give the person a hint by saying that there is a fundamental problem that he or she does not recognise. However, only when the person recognises that there is a problem, is the solution of any interest to him or her.

Arjuna also had to recognise that there was a problem. He had been brought up in a certain way at a time when Vyāsa and Śuka were household names. Such people were always walking in and out of the palaces where Arjuna, his brothers and their cousins were growing up. Naturally, then, Arjuna had many opportunities to hear about this knowledge, but as a prince, he was concerned with acquiring the skills, accomplishments and laurels of a prince, all of which were good and also necessary.

Even during his twelve year exile, Arjuna's main concern was the acquisition and maintenance of missiles and various skills in order to win back the kingdom. For Arjuna, this was an one pointed commitment, *ekāgratā*, an obsession. Therefore, he had neither the time nor the interest to pursue this knowledge. Now, in the battlefield, all his other interests melted away. Even his accomplishments appeared useless to him because he saw they were all meant only for destruction.

Arjuna had lived a life of *dharma*. He had the necessary *viveka* to be able to distinguish between right and wrong. He also had compassion because of which, when he saw how destructive the battle would be, he no longer wanted to fight. He was like a boxer who trains himself for the world championship. For six months, every day, all day, he runs, eats the proper food, exercises, works out with punching bags, and wears out several sparring partners as well. He also spends half a million dollars to achieve his end. On the day when the bout is to take place, he climbs into the ring, applauded by the enthusiastic fans that have come to watch. Then, looking at his opponent, he suddenly becomes sympathetic and walks out!

This may be the proper thing to do, but his opponent is not going to see it this way. Instead, he will brag, 'The poor fellow took one look at me and ran away!' Everyone else, including his own manager, will say the same thing, and his opponent will become the champion by default.

This was exactly Arjuna's problem. He did not want to fight, not out of fear, but out of compassion. Naturally, then, he had to decide whether he should fight or not. He was cornered, so to speak, and had to make a decision.

Whenever you have to make a decision that involves the consideration of several factors, it is always helpful to have the opinion of someone else who is not involved in the issue. The mind of such a person will very likely be more objective than yours with reference to the particular issue you are attempting to resolve.

Kṛṣṇa was someone Arjuna could talk to. Having seen the meaninglessness of all his previous pursuits and victories, Arjuna wanted to know the meaning of life, not the meaning of victory – 'What am I going to gain out of this victory? Why should I gain anything at all?' It is a question about life itself and was the essence of Arjuna's question. And now that Arjuna had asked the question, Kṛṣṇa could give him the knowledge.

For the asking, this knowledge may be given, but it does have to be asked for. This was how it was kept away from the people. Vedanta was almost unheard of until recently. Only during the past one hundred years has it been more widely available. And many of the translations that are presently in circulation contain erroneous concepts resulting in further confusion about Vedanta.

Vedanta is not a common subject matter. It is kept away from people either because it is so easily misunderstood or because people are not interested in it. In fact, it is better to listen to Vedanta without any background whatsoever than to have already been wrongly initiated into it. Otherwise, you have to recast your understanding, which is not easy and can be very painful, as well.

Deliberately keeping Vedanta away from people can be a problem because it prevents them from knowing it is there. Yet, a person who has this knowledge may have a conflict about talking publicly about Vedanta because the people who come to listen may not really want to know or even need to know. They may come to the talk thinking they are going to get something out of it without really knowing what is going to be taught. Moreover, if they already know what is being taught, they do not need to come. Whether it will help those who do not know is anyone's guess.

Also, after the teaching has taken place, it can be very easily misconstrued by those who are not ready, as evidenced by the kind of questions that are asked and the comments made. In such cases, it seems to be a waste not only with reference to the people themselves, but also in terms of the erroneous notions that they pass to those to whom they talk. This is why many teachers talk only to those who come to them and not to the public.

However, if no one talks to the public, how are people going to know? There is a saying in Tamil that is very appropriate here. In India, the month before the northern solstice begins is considered to be a very important time for prayers and other religious activities. During this period, one person of a particular family is appointed to go to each house in several villages between four and five every morning and blow a conch. Then, during the following month, which is harvest time, he will go to everyone and collect enough rice to last him for the whole year.

Although this person is supposed to blow the conch at each house just before dawn, he has so many villages to cover that he must begin in the first village at eleven at night! He then has to walk to all the other villages, which are approximately one hour apart, so, he arrives at the other villages at twelve midnight, at one in the morning, and so on. In this way, he covers them all, reaching the last village at four thirty or five in the morning. If you ask him, 'Why did you start the night before?' he will reply, ' My job is to blow the conch and I blow it. The dawn will come when it comes.' Because of this practice, 'blowing the conch' is a common expression in some South Indian districts. The practice itself is a kind of prayer considered to be very important for keeping away all undesirable events such as drought, disease, and so on, so that the village will have plenty and prosperity.

Similarly, a teacher of Vedanta blows the conch! The dawn of knowledge will come when it comes. In some cases, the conch may have been blown a little earlier than necessary, perhaps. However, when a conflict arises in the teacher's mind, he or she has only to say, 'Just blow the conch!' Otherwise, a person who has this knowledge has to sit quietly in one place and talk only to those who come and ask to be taught. Really speaking, this is the thing to be done rather than giving this knowledge to anyone and everyone irrespective of the fact whether the person is ready or not. It is because this knowledge is not like any other knowledge. It is *uttama-rahasya*, and is best given to those who ask for it.

'Therefore, Arjuna,' Kṛṣṇa might have said, 'I did keep this knowledge away from you. However, do not blame me. I kept it away from you only because you did not ask for it.' Then Arjuna's next question would have been, 'Alright, but why did you choose to teach me today?' In anticipation of such a question, Kṛṣṇa says here, 'Because you said you were my student and you asked me to teach you.'

Once Kṛṣṇa recognised Arjuna as a student, as a devotee, Arjuna may have felt that he had lost a friend, although he had gained a teacher. This often happens in self arranged and mutually consented marriages. A husband or wife is gained and a friend is lost. Until marriage, the other person is a good friend, but as soon as the marriage takes place, the friendship goes. It is the most unfortunate situation because friendship between husband and wife is to be maintained.

To reassure Arjuna that their friendship is not lost, Kṛṣṇa tells him, 'Not only are you my devotee, *bhakta*, you are also my friend, *sakhā*.' Thus, Arjuna was doubly blessed. He not only gained a teacher, but he could continue to talk to Kṛṣṇa as a friend. When Kṛṣṇa says, 'You are my friend, *me sakhā asi*' he does so as Mr. Kṛṣṇa, not as Īśvara, the Lord. After all, their friendship was not an age-old one; it could be counted in years.

But, when Kṛṣṇa says, 'You are my devotee, *bhakto'si me,*' he is talking as Īśvara as well as a *guru.*

On this point, Arjuna asks a question to clear up a doubt, one that is in the minds of many people. Arjuna had heard that Kṛṣṇa was Bhagavān Viṣṇu himself. He certainly knew that Kṛṣṇa possessed great powers because he had seen Kṛṣṇa demonstrate them. Perhaps Arjuna, having been told that Kṛṣṇa was Viṣṇu, wanted to hear it straight from Kṛṣṇa himself. In his commentary, Śaṅkara says that Arjuna's question was simply to remove the doubts in the minds of those who do not recognise Kṛṣṇa as the Lord.

Verse 4

Arjuna's question

अर्जुन उवाच ।
अपरं भवतो जन्म परं जन्म विवस्वतः ।
कथमेतद्विजानीयां त्वमादौ प्रोक्तवानिति ॥ ४ ॥

arjuna uvāca
aparaṁ bhavato janma paraṁ janma vivasvataḥ
katham etad vijānīyāṁ tvamādau proktavān iti (4)

arjunaḥ – Arjuna; *uvāca* – said;
bhavataḥ – your; *janma* – birth; *aparam* – not so long ago; *vivasvataḥ* – of Vivasvān; *janma* – birth; *param* – long time ago; *tvam* – you; *ādau* – in the beginning; *proktavān* – told; *iti* – thus; *etat* – this; *katham* – how; *vijānīyām* – am I to know

Arjuna said:

Your birth was not so long ago; (whereas) Vivasvān's birth was long time ago. How am I to know that you told this (to Vivasvān) in the beginning?

In the first verse of the fourth chapter, Kṛṣṇa had said that he gave this knowledge to Vivasvān, which seems to be a contradiction since Kṛṣṇa lived at a much later time than Vivasvān. Therefore, Arjuna says, '*aparaṁ bhavataḥ janma*, your birth was later.' Arjuna knew the exact date of Kṛṣṇa's birth. They were contemporaries. There was no doubt in Arjuna's mind that Kṛṣṇa had been born at a given time and place, in the prison where his father, Vasudeva, and his mother, Devakī, were being held. All of this Arjuna knew very well. Vivasvān, on the other hand, was born long, long ago, at the time of the creation itself. Thus Arjuna said, '*paraṁ janma vivasvataḥ*, Vivasvān's birth was long before (your birth). How then, Kṛṣṇa, can you say that you taught Vivasvān?' This is Arjuna's question.

What a question! It is like Arjuna saying, 'You could not have taught Vivasvān, Kṛṣṇa! You were not even there.' By asking this question, Arjuna seemed not to know that Kṛṣṇa was Īśvara, the Lord. Therefore, Śaṅkara in his commentary explains that when Kṛṣṇa says he taught Vivasvān, he is not talking as Mr. Kṛṣṇa, the person Arjuna knew as his contemporary. Rather, Kṛṣṇa is talking as the one who had initiated this knowledge, who can only be Īśvara.

Whether Kṛṣṇa is Īśvara or is only presented as Īśvara by Vyāsa does not really matter to us. All we need to know is that the entire dialogue that is the *Gītā* is between Kṛṣṇa as Īśvara and Arjuna, a *jīva*, an individual. Because the dialogue is between Īśvara and *jīva*, the *Gītā* is called as *īśvara-jīva-saṁvāda*. If Kṛṣṇa is an *avatāra*, an incarnation of the Lord himself, then Kṛṣṇa as Īśvara is literally true and the dialogue can be taken to be between Kṛṣṇa the *avatāra* and Arjuna the *jīva*. Otherwise, the *Gītā* can simply be taken as a story, *ākhyāyikā*, with the understanding that, what Vyāsa was presenting was the knowledge of the Veda in the form of a dialogue between the Lord and an individual.

Here, Arjuna wants to know how Mr. Kṛṣṇa, a person who was born at a given time, could say that he was the one who taught Vivasvān. Śaṅkara believes that Arjuna knew that Kṛṣṇa was Īśvara; otherwise, before the battle, when he was given the choice of having Kṛṣṇa's army or Kṛṣṇa himself on his side, he would not have chosen Kṛṣṇa. 'Either you take me as one who is unarmed, as one who is not going to fight, or you take my entire army' was the choice Kṛṣṇa had given Arjuna. If Arjuna had known Kṛṣṇa only as Mr. Kṛṣṇa, he would not have chosen him, thinking that Kṛṣṇa would have been just one more mouth to feed in wartime.

However, Arjuna did choose Kṛṣṇa and, because of this, Śaṅkara says that Arjuna knew all about Kṛṣṇa, but wanted to hear it from Kṛṣṇa himself, for his own satisfaction and for the sake of those who do not know. Thus, Arjuna asks the question that necessitated the commencement of the fourth chapter. Otherwise, the *Gītā* would have been over, the knowledge having already been given and the teaching concluded by Kṛṣṇa with a praise of this knowledge at the end of the third chapter.

Kṛṣṇa had completed the teaching once before, in the second chapter, but seems to have expected a question from Arjuna. If Arjuna had not asked his question, then Kṛṣṇa, being the excellent teacher he was, would have recognised the last verse of the second chapter as a good exit point.

However, Arjuna did ask a question. He asked, 'If knowledge is superior to action, why are you asking me to do this terrible action?'[4] And in response, Kṛṣṇa begins to teach again. Having concluded the teaching once again in the third chapter, Kṛṣṇa praises the knowledge as ancient. Then Arjuna asks this question and Kṛṣṇa begins to answer.

Verse 5

Kṛṣṇa answers

श्रीभगवानुवाच ।
बहूनि मे व्यतीतानि जन्मानि तव चार्जुन ।
तान्यहं वेद सर्वाणि न त्वं वेत्थ परन्तप ॥ ५ ॥

śrībhagavān uvāca
bahūni me vyatītāni janmāni tava cārjuna
tānyahaṁ veda sarvāṇi na tvaṁ vettha parantapa (5)

śrībhagavān – Śrī Bhagavān; *uvāca* – said;
me – for me; *tava ca* – and for you; *bahūni* – many; *janmāni* – births; *vyatītāni* – have passed; *aham* – I; *tāni* – them; *sarvāṇi* – all; *veda* – know; *tvam* – you; *na vettha* – do not know; *parantapa* – (Arjuna) scorcher of foes!

---

[4] *Gītā* 3.1

Śrī Bhagavān said:

Many births have passed for me and for you too, I know them all (whereas) you, (Arjuna) the scorcher of foes! do not know.

In the previous verse, Arjuna questioned how Kṛṣṇa could have taught Vivasvān in the beginning when Kṛṣṇa himself was not yet born. This verse is Kṛṣṇa's response to Arjuna's question. Kṛṣṇa says that both he and Arjuna had many births before their present ones, the only difference being that Kṛṣṇa could remember all of his births and Arjuna could not. Here, Bhagavān Kṛṣṇa is talking as Īśvara alone. He says, 'As Īśvara, I have had many births and I can remember them all. And as a *jīva*, Arjuna, you also have had many births, but you do not remember them.'

Arjuna did not know his previous births because, being a *jīva*, he was naturally conditioned by an *antaḥ-karaṇa*, a mind, which itself was born out of past actions – *dharma-adharma, puṇya-pāpa*. His own *karma* brought his body into being along with a limited mind and senses. Naturally, then, Arjuna's power to know, *jñāna-śakti*, was limited and, because of this, he could not understand what Kṛṣṇa means by saying that he had taught Vivasvān. Thus Kṛṣṇa explains, the only difference between them was that Arjuna was born of *karma* and he was not. Moreover, Kṛṣṇa was aware of this fact, while Arjuna was not.

What Kṛṣṇa says amounts to, 'I am ever enlightened, *nitya-buddha*, and therefore, I am never bound at any time in any way whatsoever, even when I assume a body. You are also *nitya-buddha*, Arjuna, but you do not know it because you have ignorance, *āvaraṇa*. I am always free from bondage – *karma*, the body, birth, and so on, whereas you are a *jīva* for the time being; therefore, you do not know this fact about yourself. My power to know is not covered by ignorance, whereas yours is. All this you must know, and it is for the sake of gaining this knowledge that you have been given an *antaḥ-karaṇa*.'

So, Kṛṣṇa tells Arjuna that he knew everything he had done before taking this particular birth, which is why he could say that he had given the knowledge to Vivasvān. Then the question of Kṛṣṇa's birth itself came up, even though the event called birth generally is for the *jīva* alone.

The cause of birth for the jīva

The nature of the *jīva* is to be born repeatedly. In other words, birth is continuous for the *jīva*. Because the *jīva* looks upon himself as a doer, a *kartā*, he is subject to *karma* and therefore, rebirth. The *jīva* does not recognise his true nature, his *svarūpa, ātmā*. This non recognition is the very basis for his status as a *jīva, jīvatva*. Thus, the status of *jīva* is superimposed upon the *ātmā*, the self.

The *jīva* is the doer, *kartā* and the enjoyer, *bhoktā*. Now you are a doer, now you are an enjoyer. It goes on and on. *Jīvatva* implies a sense of limitation and, therefore, there is a desire to overcome the sense of limitation. Wherever there is desire or want, there is *karma* and its result, *karma-phala*. *Karma-phala* is two-fold, the seen result, *dṛṣṭa-phala*, and the unseen result, *adṛṣṭa-phala*.

The *adṛṣṭa-phala* can fructify either in this life or later. Because of the *adṛṣṭa-karma-phala* that is accrued to the doer, the person is reborn. The person performs *karma*, for which there will be unseen results, and again, the person will be born. This is what is meant by *saṁsāra* and it is only for the *jīva*.

Īśvara, on the other hand, has no doership, no *kartṛtva*. Although Īśvara creates, sustains, and dissolves the creation, he has no doership because he has no ignorance. For him, the capacity to create is only a power, and wielding this power, he creates everything. Knowing that he is not a doer, and therefore, being free from doership, Īśvara does not have enjoyership, *phala-bhoktṛtva*, either. Nor does he receive the results of action that cause him to be born again. In fact, since *dharma-adharma*, *puṇya-pāpa* and *karma-phala* are not there for Īśvara, he cannot be born at all.

Kṛṣṇa's response to Arjuna's question could only have added to his confusion. If they both had previous births and Kṛṣṇa knew about his, then, he must be Īśvara. But, if he was Īśvara, how could he have been born since Īśvara can never be born? Kṛṣṇa explains this to Arjuna in the next few verses.

Verse 6

Wielding māyā I come into being 'as though' by my own creative power

अजोऽपि सन्नव्ययात्मा भूतानामीश्वरोऽपि सन् ।
प्रकृतिं स्वामधिष्ठाय सम्भवाम्यात्ममायया ॥ ६ ॥

ajo'pi sannavyayātmā bhūtānām īśvaro'pi san
prakṛtiṁ svām adhiṣṭhāya sambhavāmyātmamāyayā (6)

ajaḥ api san – even though being one who is unborn; *avyaya-ātmā* (*san*) – (being) one whose knowledge does not wane; *bhūtānām* – of all living beings; *īśvaraḥ api san* – also being the Lord; *svām* – my own; *prakṛtim* – *prakṛti* (the material cause for the creation); *adhiṣṭhāya* – wielding; *ātma māyayā* – by my own creative power; *sambhavāmi* – I come into being

> Even though, being one who is unborn, one whose knowledge does not wane, and also being the Lord of all living beings, still, wielding my own *prakṛti*, I, 'as though' come into being by my own creative power.

We see from this verse that Kṛṣṇa's birth is a very peculiar birth indeed. Being one who is never born, he 'as though' comes into being. Also, Kṛṣṇa describes himself here as one whose power to know does not wane or decline, as *avyayātmā*, meaning one for whom there is no state of ignorance or delusion. We can also say that, being one who is never born, he is not subject to death either.

Furthermore, he is the Lord of all beings, the one who made the entire creation for the enjoyment of all, and the one who introduced and wields all the laws and who is therefore not bound by them. He is also the *karma-phala-dātā*, the giver of the fruits of actions.

Īśvara is the cause for the entire creation–both the subtle world, *sūkṣma-prapañca* and the physical world, *sthūla-prapañca. Māyā, prakṛti,* which is non-separate from Īśvara becomes the material cause for this creation. And wielding this *māyā*, his *śakti*, he 'as though' comes into being in the form of this creation. Since Kṛṣṇa, as Īśvara, is on one side of *māyā* and Arjuna was on the other side, Arjuna could not see him as he was. This is like a magician who always keeps the audience in front, so that they see only the magic, not the *māyā*, the trick. And of course, the magician never comes under the spell of his or her own magic. Otherwise, there would be no magician.

Because you, a *jīva*, are within *māyā* itself, you do not wield it, whereas Īśvara does. Therefore, the difference between *jīva* and Īśvara is based solely on which side of *māyā* they are on. Kṛṣṇa wields the *māyā* because of which the entire world and its beings exist. Being deluded and ignorant under the spell of this *māyā*, people do not see the *ātmā* that is Kṛṣṇa, Īśvara. While the *jīva* does not see the *paramātmā*, Īśvara has no such problem because he has the *māyā* under his control. So, the world itself, which is born of *māyā* is under his control.

The idea being conveyed here is that the *jīva* does not know his real nature, *svarūpa*. Not knowing one's *svarūpa* is called *avidyā*, ignorance. Whereas, as Īśvara, Kṛṣṇa can say, as he did here 'Keeping my *māyā* under my control, I become one who 'as though' has a body.' This is the definition of an *avatāra*.

When it is said that an *avatāra* is one who comes down, what is meant is that he 'as though' assumes a body. 'As though' because he is not lost in the body. In other words, he does not take himself to be the body. A *jīvan-mukta*, one who is liberated, can also say, 'I 'as though' have a body,' because this person knows the real nature of 'I,' the *ātmā*. To say this one requires knowledge and to acquire this knowledge one has to be living. And a person who has such knowledge is a *jīvan-mukta*, living, he is liberated.

Before this knowledge takes place, the *jīva* comes into this world as a result of the past *karma* alone. By the force of *karma*, meaning one's past actions and their results, a physical body is born in time and place, with a parentage along with a mind and senses. We call this person a *jīva*. Only by acquiring the knowledge that he or she is *paraṁ-brahma* can the *jīva* be free from the cycle of birth and death and all that goes with it. Knowing thus, the person is free, but the body continues to exist, because it is the creation of Īśvara, *īśvara-sṛṣṭi*.

Thus, Kṛṣṇa tells Arjuna here that, as Īśvara he keeps the *māyā* under his control. His powers, *jñāna-śakti*, the power to know, *kriyā-śakti*, the power to do, and *icchā-śakti*, the power to desire, are all under his control and are not limited in any way. Since his power to know is without limitation, he does not require an *antaḥ-karaṇa*, a mind, to know. Without the mind, he has all-knowledge. All-knowledge, omniscience, cannot depend upon a given mind because any mind will have some limitation. Furthermore, the mind itself is a creation and, before creating it, the Lord must have knowledge. Therefore, Īśvara requires no mind. The very *māyā* makes him omniscient. He is called Parameśvara who alone becomes the world. This is the *māyā*, the trick of it all.

An understanding of avatāra

In order to understand the Vedic and Puranic literature, one needs to have some understanding of the concept of *avatāra*. In the *Bhāgavata*, *Rāmāyaṇa*, and the *Mahābhārata*, Rāma, Kṛṣṇa and others are presented as *avatāras*. '*Avatāra*' means

'God incarnate.' Because of its significance here, this concept will be analysed briefly in terms of orders of reality.

In general, we can divide the orders of reality into three. One is the absolute reality, *pāramārthika,* that which is *satya-jñāna-ananta-brahma* free from all attributes, and upon which the entire world depends. Then there is the empirical reality, *vyāvahārika,* which accounts for the world and all that is in it– space, air, fire, water, earth, the sun, moon, and stars, the natural laws, and so on. Included in this order of reality are the various situations that cause joy and sorrow, as well as your physical body, mind, and senses. All means and ends, *sādhana* and *sādhya,* also have an empirical reality. While some of them are already known to you, others are revealed by the Veda. For instance, there are Vedic rituals that are prescribed for having a child or for going to heaven. The heaven mentioned by the *śāstra* is considered to be as empirically real as a material object here in this world. Thirdly, there is a subjective order of reality, *prātibhāsika,* such as that we experience in a dream.

Empirical reality

A pot, for instance, is not something that you imagine; it actually holds water. But it cannot be considered to be independently real, absolutely real, because it is dependent on something else for its existence, the material out of which it is made. Therefore, you cannot say it is *pāramārthika-satya.* Nor can you dismiss it as non-existent because it holds water! If you say the pot is absolutely real or that it is absolutely non-existent, your very statement does not hold water. Only an existent pot can hold water, a non-existent pot cannot.

The existent pot is something that has a history. It was born at a given time and has lived in various homes. It has gone through certain process of growth and old age, holes and repair work. It has seen ages and has passed through many hands. Now, having had its day, this old useless pot is parked in a corner somewhere. So, the pot definitely enjoys a degree of reality, that has a name and form, *nāma-rūpa,* and behaves within certain laws. This is what is meant by empirical reality, *vyāvahārika-satya*. And, for understanding the empirical reality, we have sense perception and other *pramāṇa*s such as inference and presumption.

When the Veda talks about ends like heaven and the means for attaining them, it is talking only about empirical reality. If heaven is a place, it is something within the creation and, therefore, is included in this order of reality. The various rituals enjoined by the Veda imply a doer, *kartā*, who performs certain *karma*s in order to achieve the desired ends. Since the means and ends are interconnected, the means also have an empiricality, whether they involve worldly action, *laukika-karma*, or scriptural injunction, *vaidika karma*. Because means and ends are dependent upon something else, they are not absolutely real. Therefore, they are not *pāramārthika*, but *vyāvahārika,* being totally within the empirical sphere.

The word 'empirical' is the closest English translation there is for *vyāvahārika*, which covers everything known and unknown within the sphere of the creation that is not created by a given mind. It includes everything that is understood at a given time. It also includes what is not understood now but which may be understood later. This kind of world and the mind itself – the mind stuff, brain cells, and so on – belong to the empirical world. The physical body and its organs, the senses and their constituents, the capacity to remember, to love, to think, and to know, are all *vyāvahārika*, meaning that they have an empirical reality.

Subjective reality

The third order of reality is purely subjective and is called *prātibhāsika* in Sanskrit. The dream is an example of this order of reality. Something exists because you see it. Any form of projection, mistaken notion, and unknown fears, are also *prātibhāsika*. For instance, you take a post for a man, *sthānau puruṣa darśana*, or imagine that some one does not like you, it is a projection, purely subjective, *prātibhāsika*. What you see is not there, but still you see it. The very seeing gives your projection certain reality.

Everyone projects; everyone commits mistakes. *Prātibhāsika* reality is possible because the mind is limited; it is not omniscient. Also, the mind has a particular background that creates for itself prejudices, fears, anxieties, disappointments, sorrows and perceptions. This is why everyone, at one time or the other sees what is not really there and does not see what is there. Even though a person has some love for you, you may not recognise it, seeing instead some dislike, simply because you happen to notice the person frowning and you know not why! Projections, mistakes are possible because you have a mind. You think so, and therefore it is. Since this reality that exists only for you has no empiricality, it is called *prātibhāsika*.

Wherever there is *prātibhāsika* reality, there is error and, wherever there is error, the correction of error must be possible, that is, knowledge must be there. Suppose, while making pastry you mistake the salt for sugar; what you want is pastry, but what you get is something quite different. Both sugar and salt have an empirical reality because the senses are able to differentiate between them. At the same time, there is a mistake because sugar produces pastry and salt produces something else. If you use salt thinking it will make pastry, you are committing a mistake. Given this particular fact, this law, error is always possible.

This is all within our experience. *Ātmā* is the self-evident experience. Consciousness is experience. All experiences are strung into this consciousness, by this consciousness, like even a string that holds the beads together. Consciousness is there in all the three forms of experience – sleep, dream and waking. These three experiences, severally and totally, are held in one experience called consciousness, which is all-evident.

It is evident that we create our own subjective realities and it is also evident that we are dealing with a world, which conforms to an order, which behaves in an orderly way. So, we have a cosmos, which is empirical, a chaos which is subjective, and that which is constant, *sat-cit-ānanda-ātmā*. This *sat-cit-ānanda-ātmā* seems to exist in the form of a three fold reality. For lack of a better term, we use this term, namely, the three-fold reality. In fact, there is only one reality, *satya-jñāna-ananta-brahma*.

The relationship among the three orders of reality

Between the empirical reality and the subjective reality, there is a difference. The entire creation, empirical reality, is called *īśvara-sṛṣṭi,* the Lord's creation, and the projection of one's own mind is called *jīva-sṛṣṭi,* the individual's subjective creation. At all times, we are confronting these two orders of reality, the empirical and the subjective, on the basis of the one absolute reality, *satya-jñāna-ananta-brahma.*

With this understanding of the orders of reality, let us return to the verse. Kṛṣṇa says, 'I am born wielding the *māyā,* the *prakṛti,* in my hands. In this way, I assume a body.' Because the Lord can create the whole world and also assume a body, there is no problem in seeing that Kṛṣṇa's birth is referred to here as an incarnation of Īśvara based on the concept of *avatāra, avatāra-vāda.* But the next question would be, 'To which order of reality does the physical body that the Lord assumes belong?'

When Kṛṣṇa points out that he is unborn, never born, he is pointing out the absolute reality, *pāramārthika-satya.* In fact, from the standpoint of absolute reality, no one is born. Thus, from this standpoint, Kṛṣṇa is not born and Mr. Kṛṣṇa, who is standing before Arjuna, cannot be that *pāramārthika-satya.* It must be kept in mind here that we are not talking about Kṛṣṇa who is *paramātmā,* but we are talking about Mr. Kṛṣṇa who was born in prison, who had a body, who wore a yellow piece of cloth, who played a flute, and who was seated in Arjuna's chariot, holding the reins of the horses in his hands. Is this Kṛṣṇa, who was teaching Arjuna, *pāramārthika*? No, he is not, because his body is not *pāramārthika.*

Surely, then, we can say that Kṛṣṇa's body is empirically real, *vyāvahārika*. But if it were to be taken as empirically real, would Kṛṣṇa not have been born of his own *karma* and therefore, would he not also be a *saṁsārī* like Arjuna? If he were born of his own *karma*, would there not be *puṇya* and *pāpa* along with *dharma* and *adharma*, doership and enjoyership for him? If he were bound by *karma*, where would be the possibility of his wielding the *māyā*? In order for his birth to be considered empirical, Kṛṣṇa had to have been under the spell of *karma*, meaning that without his volition, his birth would have been determined by the very laws. Only then his birth can be considered to be empirical like that of Arjuna.

The empirical reality of a jīva's birth

Arjuna, being a *jīva*, was born of *karma*. Even though he was born a prince, he had to go to the forest for twelve years and then live incognito for one year, all of which could be attributed to his past *karma*. The destiny of Arjuna's eldest brother, Dharmaputra, was also controlled by his own *puṇya* and *pāpa*. Because of his *pāpa*, he lost the kingdom; otherwise, the dice would have rolled out differently or he would not have thrown them at all! Some *prārabdha-karma* was there for him. The *śāstra* itself talks about this kind of *karma*.

Arjuna was a person, a *jīva*, born of *karma*. So his birth, *janma*, was empirically real. He had a parentage and a physical body, mind and senses, all of which have an empirical reality, as we have seen. Kṛṣṇa, on the other hand, said that, as Īśvara, keeping the *māyā* under his control, he was born. We will see why he was born.

The reality of Kṛṣṇa's birth

The body that is born is available for our perception. But what is available for our perception is not always totally true – the blue sky, for example, or a magician's tricks. Therefore, perception itself cannot establish the empirical reality of Kṛṣṇa's birth.

If, as Īśvara, Kṛṣṇa is born, keeping the *māyā* under his control, his birth is definitely not subject to any *puṇya* or *pāpa*. Therefore, being not bound by *karma*, it has no empirical status. Birth itself, being what it is, cannot be *pāramārthika* either. Nor can Kṛṣṇa's birth be totally non-existent, *atyanta-asat*, since he was not a *vandhyā-putra*, the son of a barren woman! He was born of Devakī and Vasudeva. Thus, it was not a totally non-existent Kṛṣṇa who was talking to Arjuna.

Then, how are we to explain Kṛṣṇa's birth in terms of reality? With reference to his birth, Kṛṣṇa is *prātibhāsika*, you see him, therefore, he is. His birth is not due to *karma*; it is only apparent. *Prātibhāsika* means that there was a Kṛṣṇa whom everyone saw, but his birth and his body were purely *māyā*. Like everything else, they were born of *māyā* but without the force of the law of *karma*. This kind of birth means Īśvara does not have the state of *jīvatva*. He merely assumes a particular body due to a necessity alone.

Why does Īśvara assume a physical body?

What is it that makes it necessary for the Lord to assume a physical body? In the *purāṇas* it is said that before every incarnation there is a collective petition to the Lord in the form of prayers on the part of the good people and even the *devas* – 'O Lord, please do something! Please come and remedy this situation. It is time. Time is up, in fact! Why haven't you come? The tyranny of these people is too much for us to bear,' and so on. These prayers themselves become the material cause, the *upādāna-kāraṇa*, for the Lord to introduce himself in a particular form, meaning that he assumes a body.

The prayers of the *jīvas* become the *puṇya* because of which a particular body is born for a given purpose. This incarnation of the Lord is what is meant by *avatāra*. The purpose of the *avatāra*'s coming may be just to do one job, like *Narasiṁha-avatāra* or *Vāmana-avatāra*, or to do many, as was the case with Rāma and Kṛṣṇa. In addition to the many jobs they came to do, Rāma and Kṛṣṇa also served as examples with reference to how people should live their lives. Rāma exemplified how one can live a life of *dharma* in the face of all adversities and Kṛṣṇa was an embodiment of joy and wisdom.

It should be clearly understood that the concept of *avatāra* is not required at all in order to worship Kṛṣṇa as the Lord. A picture of Kṛṣṇa as Īśvara is all that is needed for invoking the Lord. In fact, we can invoke the Lord in anything, even a rock. Invoking the Lord in a particular form and the concept of *avatāra* are entirely different. We discuss it here only because the verse is referring to Kṛṣṇa as *avatāra*. Kṛṣṇa himself says, "By my own powers of *māyā*, I 'as though' assume a body." Śaṅkara says in his commentary to this verse, while explaining how Īśvara assumes a body, '*dehavān iva, jātaḥ iva*, as though with a body, as though born.' The word, '*iva*, as though' in Śaṅkara's commentary indicates that there can be no empiricality here because Kṛṣṇa's birth was not out of *puṇya* and *pāpa*.

If there were *puṇya* and *pāpa* for Īśvara, then he would not be Īśvara at all! Therefore, when Īśvara assumes a body, he is only 'as though' born. He has a body, but his body has no empiricality because it was not born out of *puṇya* and *pāpa*. If there were *puṇya* and *pāpa* for Īśvara, we would have the problem of an Īśvara with limitations with reference to the *antaḥ-karaṇa*, which is not acceptable. And, as we have seen, that is not possible, because Īśvara is all-knowledge. Therefore, Kṛṣṇa tells Arjuna here, 'Without *puṇya* and *pāpa*, I am born,' which is the very concept of *avatāra*.

Verse 7

Īśvara assumes a physical body when
there is decline in right living

यदा यदा हि धर्मस्य ग्लानिर्भवति भारत ।
अभ्युत्थानमधर्मस्य तदात्मानं सृजाम्यहम् ॥ ७ ॥

yadā yadā hi dharmasya glānirbhavati bhārata
abhyutthānam adharmasya tadātmānaṁ sṛjāmyaham (7)

bhārata – O descendent of Bharatas (Arjuna)!; *yadā yadā* – whenever; *hi* – indeed; *dharmasya* – of right living; *glāniḥ* – decline; *adharmasya* – of wrong living; *abhyutthānam* – increase everywhere; *bhavati* – is; *tadā* – then; *aham* – I; *ātmānam* – myself; *sṛjāmi* – bring into being (assume a physical body)

Bhārata (Arjuna)! Whenever there is a decline in right

living and an increase in wrong living (everywhere), I bring myself into being (assume a physical body).

We saw in the previous verse that Kṛṣṇa's birth represented the concept of *avatāra*. Even though he is unborn and therefore, not subject to death, there being no birth or death for *ātmā*, and even though he is Īśvara, the Lord of the entire creation, still, by the powers of his *māyā* alone Kṛṣṇa was 'as though' born. Without being subject to his own *dharma* and *adharma*, *puṇya* and *pāpa*, he was 'as though' born in this particular form.

The creation is Īśvara's form and, in that creation, *jīva*s are born. From the standpoint of consciousness, *caitanya*, there is only one, *paramātmā*. Thus, consciousness being one, each *jīva* is *paramātmā*, Brahman. From the standpoint of someone who is looking at the world, however, the one becomes the many and there is difference between the *jīva* and Īśvara, the Lord.

The *jīva* is a person who looks upon himself or herself as the physical body, mind and senses, *kārya-karaṇa-saṅghāta*, due to ignorance, *avidyā*. And because of this ignorance, the *jīva* continues to be born as a *jīva*. Out of ignorance, the person continues to perform actions that produce *puṇya* and *pāpa* resulting in yet another birth. This, of course, is from a particular point of view. As a *jīva*, you look at the world and yourself, seeing differences where there is none. This is the standpoint from which all these discussions and arguments take place – the standpoint of *vyavahāra*, empirical reality, not *pāramārthika*, absolute reality.

A *jīva* is born of his own *karma*, whereas an *avatāra* is not born because of *karma*. Otherwise, the *avatāra* would be a *kartā*, a doer and, being a doer, would have *avidyā*. If this were the case, the *avatāra* would be a *jīva*, not Īśvara. This is the difference between a *jīva*'s birth and Īśvara's birth.

The whole creation is Īśvara. When Īśvara assumes a particular form for a given purpose at a given time, we call that form an *avatāra*. The concept of *avatāra* is not mentioned in the Veda, although *deva*s or gods are referred to. Rāma and Kṛṣṇa, for instance, are presented as *avatāra*s in the *purāṇa*s. But, for our purposes here, it does not matter whether Vyāsa put the wisdom into Kṛṣṇa's mouth when he wrote the *Mahābhārata* or if a historical Kṛṣṇa actually did the talking.

If we look upon *Mahābhārata* as historical, as is generally the case, then Kṛṣṇa himself talked. The word '*itihāsa*' meaning, *iti ha āsa*, this is how it was, gives the epic a certain historicity. However, it is also recognised that many of the stories found in the *Mahābhārata* have been spun around actual historical events.

The *Mahābhārata* is also considered to be poetry, just as the *Rāmāyaṇa* is both historical and poetic. This means that the poet has the poetic license to create the *rasa*s, the aesthetic values, and different kinds of situations at will. Like in *Rāmāyaṇa*, we find Rāvaṇa with ten heads and Hanumān, who talks in the form of a monkey, along with many other situations not generally accepted as having happened or even imagined. Even so, the *Rāmāyaṇa*, like the *Mahābhārata*, is a story considered to have been based upon certain historical facts.

Kṛṣṇa, then, is presented as an *avatāra,* which is something like an actor who appears on a stage. The actor knows very well that he is not the role. Since Kṛṣṇa knew, he was playing a role, his birth can be considered neither *pāramārthika,* absolutely real, nor *vyāvahārika,* empirically real. Thus, in terms of orders of reality, there is only one possibility remaining to account for an *avatāra, prātibhāsika,* albeit a different type of *prātibhāsika* because the *avatāra* knows he is playing a role that it is not real, just play.

Similarly, a *jñānī* performing an action does not look upon himself or herself as a *kartā.* This means there is no real *vyavahāra* for a *jñānī.* From his or her standpoint, that is *ātmā,* everything is *prātibhāsika.*

Īśvara appears as though he is a person with a given physical body. What he does, of course, is in the realm of *vyāvahārika,* but from his standpoint, from the vision of Īśvara, an *avatāra* is purely *prātibhāsika,* purely *māyā.* This is like a magician who makes things appear by his or her own powers. For those who are watching what the magician is doing, everything is real, but for the magician it is all *māyā,* magic.

Because this is the kind of birth being discussed, the questions about when and why, naturally arise – When is Īśvara born? How often is he born? Is he born daily? Is he born every century? Or is he born every other day in different places? How is he born? For what reason is he born? These are addressed in this verse and the next.

Because human beings enjoy free will, there may be abuse, which can lead to the destruction of law and order, *dharma.*

When this destruction occurs, a person can no longer follow legitimate means for achieving legitimate ends. Nor can the person follow the means for gaining *mokṣa* because the society is not at all conducive to such a pursuit. So, for the majority of people to pursue prosperity legitimately, there must be an order, an infrastructure, a structure of law and order.

We can see this in a simple game of football. If no one follows the rules of the game, there is no game. Suppose the players dispose off the referees and blow their own whistles whenever they are not winning. How can there be any game? There is no football played; there is only a free for all. Similarly, the game of life cannot be played and enjoyed if there are no rules.

In a home, certain rules are required so that daily life can proceed in an orderly way. If these rules are not followed, there will be no home, only a mess. Society is the same. It is true that there will always be some foul play, as there is in any game. But if the majority of players refuse to follow the rules, the problem becomes enormous and cannot be ignored. This kind of a problem is called *dharmasya glāniḥ*, the decline in right living.

The infrastructure for human behaviour is based upon one's free will. When this free will is abused at every turn, something drastic needs to be done. To put things in order requires a drastic action, and this drastic action is done by Īśvara, although Īśvara himself does not really decide to do anything. Like all actions, this drastic action is a result, a *karma-phala*, of another action, a total action – everyone's prayers, a total prayer. When people who want to follow *dharma* suffer at the hands of others, they find it impossible to follow *dharma*. As a result, *mokṣa* is not possible. When such a situation occurs, everyone prays because they want something to be done.

Adharma is the real cause for the destruction of dharma

Strictly speaking, *dharma* is not something that can be destroyed. It is not something that can be burnt up, for example. *Dharma* is not a thing; it is a value that people follow. Only in these terms, then, can *dharma* be destroyed. If people do not follow *dharma*, then *dharma* is said to be destroyed, *dharmasya glāniḥ bhavati*

Also, the cause for the destruction of *dharma* is not merely the failure of people to follow it. All that really happens if people do not follow their *dharma* is that they do not get certain results. The real problem here is that when there is a decline in *dharma*, there is always a corresponding increase in *adharma*. If a person is not following *dharma* and cannot remain quiet, what will that person do? Such a person has to do something and that something will be *adharma* since the person does not follow *dharma*. This is what really brings about the destruction of *dharma*.

If the law and order are not followed and if values are not respected, an increase in *adharma*, *adharmasya abhyutthānam*,[5]

---

[5] *abhi-abhitaḥ* – everywhere; *utthānam* – rise

will be the natural result. There will be rampant, flagrant *adharma* everywhere. It means that people will be following *adharma*, not *dharma*. What can be done when such a situation occurs?

As a result of the prayers of all those who want to follow *dharma* but are not able to because they are suffering at the hands of those who follow *adharma*, Īśvara assumes a particular form and that assumed form is called *avatāra*. This concept is not important in the understanding of Vedanta. However, with reference to this particular verse, one does need to know that there is such a thing as *avatāra*, just as one needs to know that *karma* can be in the form of rituals, prayers, and so on. What they are, how they are connected, are to be understood. Vedanta itself is nothing more than '*tat tvam asi*.' The reality of the self being the whole is Vedanta, and everything else is brought in to support one's understanding of this fact.

Kṛṣṇa himself presents the concept of *avatāra* here by saying, 'Then, I bring myself into being in a particular form, *tadā ātmānam aham sṛjāmi*.' This is where immaculate conception comes in. Even though it was known that Kṛṣṇa was born of Devakī, his statement indicates that he wilfully entered into this particular body. We find in the literature that Kṛṣṇa who was essentially none other than Viṣṇu was also born out of a pillar on another occasion – *Narasiṁha-avatāra*. Therefore, his births are definitely not the result of *prakṛti*. They are not the product of chromosomes inherited from the parents. Kṛṣṇa clearly states here that he brought this particular physical body into being by himself.

Having said that he assumes a body when there is decline in *dharma* and a rise in *adharma*, Kṛṣṇa then goes on to explain why he does this.

Verse 8

I come into being to protect those who are committed to dharma

परित्राणाय साधूनां विनाशाय च दुष्कृताम् ।
धर्मसंस्थापनार्थाय सम्भवामि युगे युगे ॥ ८ ॥

paritrāṇāya sādhūnāṁ vināśāya ca duṣkṛtām
dharmasaṁsthāpanārthāya sambhavāmi yuge yuge (8)

sādhūnām – of the people committed to *dharma*; *paritrāṇāya* – for the protection; *ca* – and; *duṣkṛtām* – of those who follow *adharma*; *vināśāya* – for the destruction (conversion); *dharma-saṁsthāpanārthāya* – for the establishment of *dharma*; *yuge yuge* – in every *yuga*; *sambhavāmi* – I come into being

For the protection of those who are committed to *dharma* and the destruction (conversion) of those who follow *adharma*, and for the establishment of *dharma*, I come into being in every *yuga*.

Why does an *avatāra* come? It is not to enjoy *puṇya-pāpa*, because these do not apply to an *avatāra*. Nor does an *avatāra* come to suffer the life of a *saṁsārī*. An *avatāra* comes for a three fold purpose. First, he protects the people who are committed to a life of *dharma* – *paritrāṇāya sādhūnām*. If they are protected, then *dharma* is protected.

This protection is carried out in many ways, one of which is chastising those who do things that are not in keeping with *dharma*, *vināśāya duṣkṛtām*. *Vināśāya* means, for the sake of destruction of those who follow *adharma*. Here the word destruction is more in the sense of conversion of those who follow *adharma* to the path of *dharma*. This is the second reason for the *avatāra* to come. In either case, his real task is to establish, or perhaps more appropriately to re-establish *dharma* – *dharma-saṁsthāpanārthāya*. This is the third but real reason for the advent of an *avatāra*.

Protection of dharma implies protection of culture and religion

How can the order, *dharma*, be re established? By making the people live in accordance with it. This is all that can be done. There is no other way of establishing *dharma*. Because it is not properly understood, people establish institutions of *dharma*, huge organisations, large buildings, and so on. But even if you create a building for *dharma* that is bigger than the largest building on earth, those who do not follow *dharma* will destroy the very building itself, and make sure that all efforts to restore it are also destroyed!

Religious organisations begin with the intention of establishing *dharma*, but eventually many of them become *adhārmika*. Institutions do not establish *dharma*; people do. How? Only by living a life of *dharma* can *dharma* be established and protected. How can *dharma* be protected any other way? To understand this better, let us look at scholarship and how it is protected.

Can protecting libraries protect scholarship? Libraries are protected only when there are scholars to use them. They are meant for scholars. Only when the scholars are encouraged, is scholarship protected. Scholars can be encouraged by creating an atmosphere conducive for scholarship. Then there is an infrastructure, a value for scholarship.

For instance, if teachers are the lowest paid people in society, as they frequently are, they will naturally be attracted to other vocations. Why should a professor who earns thirty thousand dollars a year stay at a university when he or she can make twice as much elsewhere and even more on the side? California's Silicon Valley has attracted many university professors this way.

If incomes in the universities were comparable to that elsewhere, those who have a value for study and teaching would stay in the universities. But this does not happen when the gap in earnings is too large. It is true that the people, who have a real love for study, and the leisure to do so, will stay, but it must also be recognised that many of those who remain may be doing so for little more than the extended holidays that the academic year permits! When the atmosphere encourages scholars, everyone will become a scholar, or at least make the attempt, and scholarship will be protected.

Similarly, *dharma* is protected when there is an infrastructure conducive to following it, meaning that the *dharmīs*, those who follow *dharma*, are protected. To protect *dharma* nothing else can be done.

The protection of *dharma* comes through various forms – through music and the other performing arts, through the fine arts and various other human expressions. Therefore, you encourage only those institutions, meaning customs, culture and so on, that are rooted in *dharma*. Cultural institutions have a bearing on *dharma* and therefore, are to be supported. All of these become the means for protecting *dharma*.

It is only when the people who follow *dharma* are not protected that you find everything goes punk, not just the music! Because all aspects of living are so intricately connected, *dharma* just goes if the people who follow it are not protected.

There is no culture and religion apart from people

Therefore, protection of *dharma* implies the protection of culture, religion and so on. But there is no culture or religion apart from people. The people alone are religion. No institution is independent of people, especially those institutions connected to *dharma*. And if, within a given structure, there are those who do what is not to be done and do not do what is to be done, such people have to be taught, converted.

There was a time in Rishikesh when only *sādhus* lived there. They spent all their time studying the *śāstra*. When other people came because they had become disenchanted with the world, they too would begin studying. A man may have decided to become a *sādhu* because he had lost his wife, his business, or whatever. The choice of becoming a *sādhu* has always been available in Indian society. And although this man had become a *sādhu*, he might not have been interested in studying. But, finding that everyone else was studying, he too would begin to study.

Today, the reverse happens all too often. A *sādhu* may go to Rishikesh and those he meets may not be studying. If he starts doing whatever everyone else is doing, he can end up running an ashram or studying the *vīṇā*! There is nothing wrong with learning music. Music can be used as a kind of *sādhana* sometimes; it can create devotion. But one should not become a *sannyāsī* to do this. To become a *sannyāsī* and then learn music is not right, but this is what is happening.

Other *sannyāsī*s learn a few *yoga-āsana*s and then go to America and open an ashram. Being able to stand on your head for five minutes is not a great accomplishment. There is a *sādhu* in Rishikesh who stands on his head for two hours on a rock! What happens to him by performing this *āsana* is not clear, except for the fact that he gets very hungry and eats an enormous number of rotis. This is not to say that *āsana*s are useless; they definitely have a purpose. But the point being made here is that we have heads and we do not use them for the purpose they were intended!

Is it time for Īśvara to come again?

Someone may well ask, 'Is it time for the Lord to come again in the form of an incarnation?' No, the time is not right because this teaching still attracts people. If, however, a teacher of *Gītā* was being constantly stoned and people were being prevented from coming to the classes, then Kṛṣṇa, as Īśvara, would come. But as long as people are still able to listen to classes on the *Gītā*, he need not come. If, in a place of one hundred people, eighty people are given to a life of *adharma*, the other twenty cannot follow *dharma*, they can only pray. Only then does Īśvara come.

Dharma only needs to be protected when the *adharma* is rampant, when there is no law and order whatsoever, when there are no ethics, when no one cares about anyone else, when everyone is totally selfish. Under such circumstances, everyone goes for the convenient and does not bother about following *dharma* properly.

Only when there is rank selfishness, *adharma,* does the protection of *dharma* become a necessity. When more *dharmī*s, people who follow *dharma,* are created, the *duṣkṛta*s, the people who do wrong deeds, change; and *adharma* is destroyed. Whenever an *avatāra* comes, people are converted. They do change. They give up their life of *adharma*. This is what is meant by the destruction of *adharma, vināśāya ca duṣkṛtām*. The *adharmī*s themselves do not have to be destroyed; only the *adharma* has to be given up and *dharma* re-established.

Therefore, Kṛṣṇa says, 'In every age, I am born, *sambhavāmi yuge yuge*.' It is not to suggest that there is a rule whereby one incarnation occurs in every *yuga*. The only rule here is that, whenever *dharma* declines and *adharma* increases, whenever *adharma* is rampant everywhere, when there is no way that *dharma* can survive, only then Īśvara assumes a particular form with the purpose of upholding *dharma*. This form is called an *avatāra*.

Verse 9

Kṛṣṇa talks about his birth and the truth

जन्म कर्म च मे दिव्यमेवं यो वेत्ति तत्त्वतः ।
त्यक्त्वा देहं पुनर्जन्म नैति मामेति सोऽर्जुन ॥ ९ ॥

janma karma ca me divyam evaṁ yo vetti tattvataḥ
tyaktvā dehaṁ punarjanma naiti mām eti so'rjuna (9)

arjuna – O Arjuna!; *me* – my; *divyam* – divine; *janma* – birth; *ca* – and; *karma* – action; *yaḥ* – the one who; *evam* – in this way; *tattvataḥ* – in reality; *vetti* – knows; *saḥ* – that person; *deham* – body; *tyaktvā* – giving up; *punaḥ* – again; *janma* – birth; *na eti* – does not gain; *mām eti* – attains me

The one who knows in reality my divine birth and action in this way, Arjuna! Giving up the body, that person is not born again. He attains me.

Divya means heavenly in the sense of not worldly. Kṛṣṇa's birth is referred to as *divyaṁ janma* in order to convey the idea that it is unlike any other birth, but extraordinary. By adding the word '*aiśvaram*' here, Śaṅkara makes it clear in his commentary that Kṛṣṇa's birth is the kind of birth that belongs to Īśvara and is not the same as the birth of a *jīva*.

Also, we are told here that Kṛṣṇa's actions are not like any other *karma*. All other *karma*s are born out of personal want and produce *puṇya* and *pāpa*. Because this is not the case here, Kṛṣṇa's actions are of a different type and are called *divyaṁ karma, aiśvaraṁ karma*.

The subject of the verse is the one who knows, *yaḥ vetti,* the truth about Kṛṣṇa's peculiar birth and *karma*. This person knows them as they are in reality, *tattvataḥ vetti*. One who knows this truth very clearly does not look upon Kṛṣṇa as just another person, one who is born, who is different from the world, or who comes and goes. This person sees Kṛṣṇa's birth and actions as they are, in reality.

In the second chapter, Kṛṣṇa had said that what is real, *sat,* is not going to change at any time and that which is not real, *asat, mithyā,* is not going to be there all the time. So, whether Kṛṣṇa's body is *vyāvahārika,* empirically real, or *prātibhāsika,* a projection, either way, it is still *mithyā,* not absolutely real. The one who knows the body to be *mithyā* and *ātmā* to be *satya* is the one who knows clearly, *tattvataḥ vetti*. Such a person knows that there is no real birth happening and no real *karma* being done.

The one who knows in reality that Kṛṣṇa, Īśvara, is not other than oneself, and that 'I am that Parameśvara,' is a *jñānī*. Such a person, knowing this, having given up the physical body, that is, when the person dies, does not gain another birth. To know Īśvara is to know the *satya,* the reality, that which always is. *Sat* is *ātmā* and, therefore, to know Parameśvara is to know oneself. In fact, to know oneself is the only way to know Parameśvara, Brahman.

This is how a person is liberated. While living, the person gains self-knowledge, which is *mokṣa* after which there is no future birth for the person. The *jīvatva* is gone and the person is called *jīvan-mukta,* meaning, liberated while living. Knowing that one is not a *kartā,* the *jīvan-mukta,* who is a *jñānī* has no *karma*, and therefore, no *puṇya* or *pāpa* to initiate another birth. Only when one takes oneself to be a doer can there be action that leads to future births.

What happens to the jñānī after death?

If the *jīvan-mukta* does not take another birth, where does he or she go then? Does a *jñānī* become permanently lodged somewhere? This question is based, of course, on the assumption that if the *jīvan-mukta* is not subject to rebirth, he or she must be somewhere else. Therefore, is there eternal imprisonment or internment of some kind after death? If not, what is it that happens to the *jñānī*?

In response to this question, Kṛṣṇa says, 'That person becomes myself, *saḥ mām eti*.' The *jīva* is gone. Īśvara as everything remains. When there is no *jīva*, there is only Īśvara. Only when the *jīva* cannot gain identity with Īśvara, in terms of knowing they are one and the same, are there two seemingly different entities, Īśvara and *jīva*.

Here, the use of the word '*eti*, gains' must be clearly understood. If it were used in its usual sense, gaining identity with Īśvara would mean that the *jīva* is like an amoeba ingested by Īśvara. But in reality if the *jīva* is a false entity and one understands the nature of oneself, then there is no *jīva* at all, no individual separate from Īśvara for all that is there is Īśvara.

The problem is one of separation. There is no separation in fact! All that is there is Īśvara. It is not that Īśvara is someone who is located somewhere and the *jīvan-mukta* joins him there. Gaining Brahman is strictly in terms of knowledge.

Kṛṣṇa makes use of Arjuna's question, 'How could you have given this knowledge to Vivasvān in the beginning?' To reveal the nature of *ātmā*. The cause for grief and how one can cross over it is the subject matter of the *Gītā*. Although Kṛṣṇa discusses many topics, he unfolds the subject matter in one continuous flow. Here, having answered Arjuna's most recent question, Kṛṣṇa once again picks up the thread, 'You grieve for those who should not be grieved for, *aśocyān anvaśocastvam*[6] and continues:

Verse 10

Purified by the discipline of knowledge
many have come back to my nature

वीतरागभयक्रोधा मन्मया मामुपाश्रिताः ।
बहवो ज्ञानतपसा पूता मद्भावमागताः ॥ १० ॥

vītarāgabhayakrodhā manmayā mām upāśritāḥ
bahavo jñānatapasā pūtā madbhāvam āgatāḥ (10)

vīta-rāga-bhaya-krodhaḥ – free from craving, fear and anger; *manmayāḥ* – totally resolved in me; *mām upāśritāḥ* – taking refuge in me; *jñānatapasā* – by the discipline of knowledge; *pūtāḥ* – purified; *bahavaḥ* – many; *madbhāvam* – my nature; *āgatāḥ* – have come back

Free from craving, fear and anger, totally resolved in me, taking refuge in me, purified by the discipline of knowledge, many have come back to my nature.

---

[6] *Gītā* 2.11

We have seen that the one who knows Kṛṣṇa in reality knows that there is no real birth, *janma*, or action, *karma*, for the person. If there is no real *janma* or *karma*, then who is that person? Here, the person cannot be Mr. Kṛṣṇa who was born at a given time and place. So, too, for everyone, he or she can only be *paramātmā*. Thus, Kṛṣṇa says, 'The one who knows this reaches me.'

To know Kṛṣṇa in this way is to know oneself. One who is a *jīva*, an individual, who does not know the identity between oneself and Īśvara, cannot understand Īśvara. The limited individual is not going to know that which is all-knowledge, omniscient. Even to spell the word 'omniscient' is a problem. Therefore, the most that can be said is that Īśvara's knowledge is not limited.

All knowingness, *sarvajñatva*, can never be understood by an *alpajña*, one with limited knowledge. But *sarvajñatva* is only in relation to *alpajñatva*. Both limited knowledge and all-knowledge are adjuncts, *upādhi*s with reference to each other, the division between them being due to *upādhi* alone. Kṛṣṇa's statement, 'Only the one who knows the *paramātmā* reaches me,' is to be understood in terms of the *paramātmā* not being separate from oneself. Kṛṣṇa had said this before and is merely confirming it here, before picking up the topic of sorrow.

Kṛṣṇa tells Arjuna that this knowledge had been around since the beginning, and people had always been reaching him in this manner, by knowing. There was nothing new about it. Here, again, Kṛṣṇa says that any number of people have reached him, *bahavaḥ madbhāvam āgatāḥ*. And why is it that everyone does not reach him? There is no difficulty involved in reaching him, but first one needs to recognise that he must be reached. Having recognised this, how is one going to reach him if one's craving, fears and anger drive one?

In fact, there is nothing to reach because one is already *paramātmā*. The question, therefore, is how far one's discerning power extends and what is it that one is choosing. In this verse, the people for whom the craving, fears and anger have gone away, *vīta-rāga-bhaya-krodhaḥ*, are described as those who have reached him in terms of knowledge.

Raga-dveṣas are fraught with fear and anger

We have seen that *rāga* is the craving for objects and once *rāga* comes, *dveṣa* in the form of dislike and avoidance is also there. These two always go together and, being powerful, are binding in nature. Fear, *bhaya*, then becomes inevitable because there is always some apprehension with reference to one's *rāga*s and *dveṣa*s. Every *rāga* is fraught with fear of the undesirable unknown. This is all that a binding desire or like is about.

When there is a binding *rāga-dveṣa*, such as 'this must happen for me (*rāga*),' 'this must not happen for me (*dveṣa*),' how can there be absence of fear? There is always the fear of things not happening according to our expectations because *rāga* implies expectation. And whenever there is expectation, there is a possibility of it not being fulfilled and, when this happens, there is a sense of failure. Fear of failure will always be there because we are not omniscient. That things do not always go our way is very clear to us. What we need to understand is that fear of the undesirable unknown will be there as long as we are driven by our *rāga*s and *dveṣa*s.

*Rāga-dveṣa*s are not only fraught with fear, they are also fraught with anger, *krodha*. If a *rāga* is not fulfilled, your desire, *kāma*, turns into anger against whatever is preventing the desire from being fulfilled. If the obstacle is another person, someone who is standing between you and what you want to accomplish, then your *kāma* turns into *krodha*. If a binding *kāma* is not there, there is no *krodha*. But if you think a certain thing must happen and your life will be incomplete if it does not, you cannot avoid anger because your *rāga* is binding.

When there is obstruction that is preventing you from fulfilling your *rāga*, there cannot but be anger when your *rāga* is binding. The *kāma* itself turns into anger. Thus, *krodha* is also there when your life is controlled by *rāga-dveṣa*s. Whereas, when you live a life of *karma-yoga*, the *rāga-dveṣa*s are neutralised. By paying attention to your *rāga-dveṣa*s, with the right attitude, you become *vīta-rāga-bhaya-krodhaḥ*, meaning you are relatively free from desire, fear and anger. These are the people Kṛṣṇa is discussing here when he says, 'They become one with me, *manmayāḥ bhavanti*.' Such people have the vision of Īśvara as essentially non-separate from the *jīva*.

The vision of non-difference between Īśvara and jīva

In reality there is no difference between the *jīva* and Īśvara. Any seeming difference being brought about by *upādhi* alone and is, therefore, *mithyā*. Since the difference is *mithyā*, non-difference is *satya*, which is all that counts. This vision of *abheda-*

buddhi, non-difference, the identity of *jīveśvara* reflected in the statement, 'You are that, *tat tvam asi*' is made clear by further analysis, *manana,* and contemplation, *nididhyāsana.* Those people in whom this vision is clear are referred to in this verse as *māmupāśritāḥ,* those who have totally resolved into Parameśvara alone. For them, there is no longer the mistaken notion that the *jīva* is separate from Parameśvara.

The self is *paramātmā.* The one who has no doubt whatsoever with reference to this particular vision is called *pūta,* meaning *śuddha,* absolutely pure. In such people there is not even a dash of impurity because the self, being *paramātmā* is always pure. The self is not rendered pure; it is pure. If the self were something that had to be rendered pure, some impurity would always be there.

And how do these people become pure? By the purifying fire of knowledge, *jñāna-tapasā.* Knowledge is the means, the *sādhana.* Here, *tapasā* means 'by the fire of knowledge.' By the discipline of knowledge, these people become pure. How does one become pure by knowledge? The knowledge that the self has never performed any action and, therefore, it is not guilty of any action. Nor is it subject to any hurt because it is not and never was an object of anyone else's action. Since the self, *ātmā* is neither the doer of action nor the object of action, it is always *nitya-śuddha,* eternally pure.

The people being discussed in this verse were already *vīta-rāga-bhaya-krodhas;* they already have the necessary preparedness of mind, the *antaḥ-karaṇa-śuddhi* through *karma-yoga.* However, it should be noted that *antaḥ-karaṇa-śuddhi* can never be absolute; there is always some *aśuddhi* in the form of *rāga-dveṣa*s. This is to say, whatever *antaḥ-karaṇa-śuddhi* that one gains through *karma-yoga* is always relative. Absolute *śuddhi* is never achieved but can only be understood, because *ātmā* is ever *śuddha*. Whereas relative *śuddhi*, *antaḥ-karaṇa-śuddhi*, is something that is accomplished in the mind.

Relative and absolute śuddhi

Relative *śuddhi* is a process of growth, a process of maturity, wherein a life of alertness, discipline, commitment, and prayer is involved. It is a life of purification and, being a process, it takes certain length of time. Absolute *śuddhi* cannot be a process of purification because the impure can never become pure by any amount of purifying, no matter what the process is. The self, who is absolutely *śuddha*, is already pure.

Purity means freedom from *rāga-dveṣa*s, *puṇya-pāpa*s; freedom from everything, in fact. This purity is the nature of *ātmā* which is *nirguṇa*, free of all attributes, *akartā*, free from doership and so on. And those who know this are also pure, *pūta*s, meaning that they have understood the fact that as *ātmā*, they are eternally pure. They are, *madbhāvam-āgatāḥ*, as Kṛṣṇa puts it, meaning, 'they have come back to be me.'

This 'coming back' of *bahavaḥ*, so many, *jīva*s is to be understood in terms of the identity between *jīva* and Īśvara. It is not that all these *jīva*s have come to Īśvara and are sitting upon him! Nor has he collected them all to him so that they have become an integral part of his heart or his being. This particular knowledge reveals the fact that the *jīva* is Īśvara.

Those who know this fact are called *jñāna-niṣṭhās* because not only have they gained the knowledge, but they are well-established in it. Reaching Bhagavān is not dependent upon any *tapas* other than knowledge. Thus, to say, 'purified by discipline, *tapasā pūtāḥ*,' is not enough. The word '*jñāna*' has to be added because there are other forms of *tapas*.

The pursuit of knowledge is the primary tapas

The word '*tapas*' refers to any spiritual or religious discipline. For example, a person who chants the *gāyatrī-mantra* for six hours is said to be doing religious *tapas*. A person who observes silence for a length of time is also doing *tapas* provided, of course, he or she is doing it for religious purposes, as a mental prayer. However, to keep quiet purely out of consideration for others is entirely different; it is not *tapas*.

When a person is performing a spiritual discipline like contemplation or studying the *śāstra*, it is *tapas*. *Svādhyāya*, study of the *śāstra*, is considered to be a great *tapas*. Therefore, those who are committed to listening to the *śāstra*, *śravaṇa* and to self enquiry, *vicāra*, are doing *tapas*.

Although there are many forms of *tapas*, to become established in this knowledge requires only *jñāna-tapas*. The pursuit of knowledge is the *tapas*. The word, *jñāna* is prefixed to *tapas* to show that *jñāna-niṣṭhā* does not depend upon any other *tapas*. It is because *mokṣa* is not any thing other than being established in this knowledge. There is no other *mokṣa*. For *mokṣa* you require knowledge and for knowledge you do not require anything else except *vicāra*, enquiry. Thus, the pursuit of knowledge itself is the means.

Then what about all the other disciplines? They are meant for preparing the mind so that this knowledge can take place. This is what is meant by purification of the mind, *antaḥ-karaṇa-śuddhi*. The other disciplines are secondary means, whereas knowledge is the primary means.

To say that the other disciplines are secondary is not to say that they have no place. The distinction to be understood is that the other disciplines are indirect means for *mokṣa* in that they prepare or purify the *antaḥ-karaṇa*, while the pursuit of knowledge is the direct means for the knowledge that is *mokṣa*.

Does everyone come back to Īśvara?

Because Kṛṣṇa uses the word '*bahavaḥ*, many' here, Arjuna could assume that only some people come back to Īśvara and others do not. *Bahavaḥ*, being plural, can refer to any number of *jīva*s, starting with three.[7] The point here is that, even if it is just three, a million or more, a finite number is implied. Arjuna may therefore have asked Kṛṣṇa why does he not allow everyone to come to him. To such a question, Kṛṣṇa could have only answered, 'I can only take them to me if I am separate from them. But I am them! If we were separate, perhaps there might be something I could do about it. But since they are non-separate

[7] In Sanskrit, there are three numbers, singular, dual and plural, and therefore, the plural indicates three and anything more than three.

from me, what can I do? It is not a case of my having to bring them to me because I am already identical with them. There is nothing here that I have to do. As Īśvara, they can invoke me and, in whatever form they invoke me, I bless them. Whatever they desire, they get. Therefore, I am not to blame in this particular situation. I do not have any *rāga-dveṣa*s to fulfil in this matter. Nor do I take names out of a hat every day to see that some people suffer and some remain happy and so on. I do not follow any such rule.'

Kṛṣṇa paves the way for the next section in which he explains how Īśvara is free from any kind of blame with reference to what happens in one's life. Otherwise, we would be left asking why Īśvara blesses one person and not another, and why he is so partial.

Verse 11

In whatever way people invoke me – I bless them in the same form

ये यथा मां प्रपद्यन्ते तांस्तथैव भजाम्यहम् ।
मम वर्त्मानुवर्तन्ते मनुष्याः पार्थ सर्वशः ॥ ११ ॥

ye yathā māṁ prapadyante tāṁstathaiva bhajāmyaham
mama vartmānuvartante manuṣyāḥ pārtha sarvaśaḥ (11)

ye – those who; *yathā* – in whatever way; *mām* – me; *prapadyante* – worship; *tathā eva* – indeed in the same way; *aham* – I; *tān* – them; *bhajāmi* – bless; *pārtha* – O Arjuna!; *manuṣyāḥ* – people; *sarvaśaḥ* – in all ways; *mama* – my; *vartmā* – path; *anuvartante* – follow

> Those who worship me in whatever way, I bless them in the same way. Pārtha (Arjuna)! People follow my path in all ways.

Again, Kṛṣṇa is talking as Īśvara here. This is an important verse because it answers the question about how the Lord is to be worshipped. With what degree of devotion, with what inner commitment, with what purpose and in what form are the people to worship him?

According to Kṛṣṇa, it is simple: 'I bless them in whatever form they invoke me, according to their *karma*, according to their prayer. For instance, those who want wealth and steal to get it are blessed with a prison sentence. It is as simple as that; so do not blame me.'

If a devotee worships the Lord in the form of Kṛṣṇa, it is the form in which the devotee will see the Lord. In other words, seeing the Lord as Kṛṣṇa is purely subjective, even though this vision is very real to the devotee. Devotees will sometimes say, 'I saw Kṛṣṇa yesterday.' For a devotee who has been worshipping the Lord in the form of Kṛṣṇa for a long time, it is possible to visualise the Lord in that form. But this kind of a Lord comes and goes, which means that the vision is bound by time, whereas the person who saw Kṛṣṇa remains. Does this not mean that the devotee is greater than the Lord who comes and goes? If so, what kind of a Lord is this!

And what if the Lord appears in some other form? What if he appears as a western Lord with suit and boots? The devotee will become confused. Thus, Kṛṣṇa says, 'In whatever form I am worshipped, in that form alone I appear.'

This statement can apply to the purpose as well as to the form: 'For whatever purpose I am worshipped, that purpose I serve.' People usually want only limited results. For instance, they want relief when they are in distress. Although this particular verse is with reference to Vedic rituals and prayers, it can also be considered beyond its religious scope when Kṛṣṇa says, 'I am available to you as the various resources in the world, the various laws, powers, and possibilities. In whichever form you invoke me, in that form I am going to appear.'

A person who does weight lifting in the gym daily because he or she wants to develop biceps, is invoking the Lord in the form of biceps and will be blessed with biceps. In other words, the Lord will appear in the form of biceps alone! And if the person develops only the left arm, the Lord will bulge out only there! This, then, is the Lord.

The *śruti* says that in whatever form people invoke, in that form the result will come. Therefore, if biceps are the goal you have dedicated yourself and your life to, then biceps will be what you invoke and biceps will be what you get. The goal, the end, is always Bhagavān, the Lord, even though the person who has no other goal than biceps may not recognise Bhagavān in the form of biceps. Thus, you will find that in whatever form you invoke the Lord, in the same form the Lord, the result,will come.

Simple understanding of what prayer is

Although different religions have their own forms of prayer, no one form is more efficacious than another. Regardless of the language used to invoke the Lord, the Lord is invoked. When tribal people perform a rain dance, for instance, the rain comes. Similarly, when a person performs a very elaborate, sophisticated Vedic ritual, the rains do come.

When these rituals, be they Vedic or tribal, are performed with *śraddhā*, with faith and sincerity, there will be rain. Without *śraddhā*, the rains will not come. The mode can be different, but the result, the *phala*, is the same. Any form of prayer is as efficacious as any other prayer. This must be understood well, not as tolerance for or accommodation of forms of worship other than one's own, but in terms of simple understanding alone. There is no pagan's prayer; there is only prayer.

When tribal people repeat a prayer in a dialect that does not have a structure, script or grammar, we may not understand it, but Bhagavān understands it. Language is there; the people think they have said something and they have. Thus, there is communication between themselves and the Lord, which is all that matters. Even in religions where the believers repeat words in a language unknown to them, it is understood that the Lord understands the language being used. Nothing more is required. Just as when you send telegram, the other person should be able to read it, so too, when you talk to the Lord, he should be able to understand you. A prayer is a feeling expressed in a particular form, language, the meaning of which you may not even know. But the feeling, the intention, is definitely there, and this is what is conveyed to the Lord in prayer. As for the words of the prayer themselves, the Lord knows all languages. All you have to do is express what you have to.

This is not religious accommodation; it is simple understanding of what prayer is, what Īśvara is. No expansiveness of heart is required here. Nor do you need to be a great *sādhu* or saint.

Understanding the nature of prayer is not to be confused with how each religion defines God, which is where all kinds of problems arise. When it comes to real issues, concepts and so on, there are problems, but these have nothing to do with prayer. The real issues are – 'What is freedom?' 'Why exactly am I praying?' 'Is it for a limited result or for some other reason?' If *mokṣa* is what I want, then there is something to be understood. That I am the whole is a fact, not a belief, and is entirely different from what is being said by the various religions of the world. Because it is a fact, it is to be understood quietly, which has nothing to do with my commitment to religion as such or to one religion in particular.

What Bhagavān says here is not only with reference to prayer, but also applies beyond prayer, that is, even a person who has no connection to religion is blessed. It includes people who claim not to be religious and those who are critical of religion. For some people, religion is nothing more than money and power, for a communist religion is statism.[8] Whatever is the religion for them, in that form alone they are blessed, meaning, they are not condemned.

In this verse, Kṛṣṇa tells Arjuna, 'All human beings follow me alone, *mama vartmā anuvartante manuṣyāḥ pārtha sarvaśaḥ*.'

---

[8] Statism – The practice or doctrine of giving a centralised government control over economic planning and policy.

In other words, 'Whether they know I am the one that is sought after or not, they are on my track alone. At the end of the track, I am always there. They may think a particular destination is their destination, but that is only a lap in their journey. If money or power is their destination, they are still on the road to me because power and money are also me. Remember, Lakṣmī, the Goddess of wealth, is with me. Power also is with me alone.'

There are different types of wealth, Lakṣmī. Those who dedicate their entire lives to health, for example, may enjoy Lakṣmī in the form of health. And those who dedicate their lives to acquiring power may gain the power they seek, if everything goes well. If their prayers are appropriate and their previous *karma, prārabdha-karma,* is not totally against it, they will have power. Thus, Kṛṣṇa says, 'When people ask for small ends or big ends, they are all on my track, whether they know it.'

Everyone wants to be free from feeling small

In reality everyone is seeking identity with *paramātmā,* whether they know it. They want to be free from being small, which is why they are seekers. Everyone is a seeker of this freedom. Seeking fullness is no different from seeking freedom from being small. They are one and the same. Furthermore, to say you are seeking fullness is not really true because you do not really know what fullness is, whereas you definitely know what smallness is. And you want to be free from this smallness. Freedom from being small is what is meant by fullness, *pūrṇatva*. Everyone wants to be full, to be happy, even those who drink. If drinking did not give a person some happiness, some *sukha*, no one would do it.

Fullness and happiness is the Lord's very nature; he is *pūrṇa-svarūpa* and *ānanda-svarūpa*. Because all people seek this fullness, happiness, they are on the Lord's track alone, although they may not know it. A person who does not know exactly what he or she is seeking keeps on seeking. Thus Kṛṣṇa might have said, 'They do not know they are seeking me. Therefore, they spend their time seeking small thing that is of me.' It is like wanting to marry someone but marrying his or her little fingernail or piece of hair! What kind of marriage is it? People do not know they are doing the same thing when they seek power, name and fame, quietude, or whatever. They do not know that these ends are nothing more than the nails and hairs of Bhagavān, Kṛṣṇa the infinite. Thinking themselves to be separate from him, they seek one aspect alone and exclude everything else.

Everything is Bhagavān and what is excluded, by pursuing one aspect alone, is also Bhagavān. When you seek power to the exclusion of everything else, you are not seeking Bhagavān. Kṛṣṇa says, 'They are on my track alone. But they do not seek me because they do not know they are on my track. If they knew, then the small things would not hold them up along the way.'

The path of self-knowledge is not an arduous one

While travelling to a particular destination, people may enjoy a few things along the way, but they do not lose sight of their destination. Self-knowledge need be no different.

The beauty of its pursuit is that, not only is the ultimate destination beautiful, but the means to it is also beautiful. It is like driving through the Rockies or going on a pilgrimage in the Himalayas. There are four centres of pilgrimage in the Himalayas, namely, Badrinath, Kedaranath, Gangotri and Yamunotri, where a lot of devotees go, this being one of the things to be done in a Hindu's life. Badrinath, to take but one, is situated in a valley of great beauty, and the way to Badrinath is also beautiful.

It is often said that the spiritual path is extremely arduous. But, if you really understand what 'spiritual' is, you will find there is nothing arduous about it. What is arduous about constantly hearing that you are fullness, *ānanda*?

The spiritual path has also been likened to a razor's edge, 'stop not; be very cautious! One wrong step and the fall is great. The higher you go, the farther you fall!' If you go to the pinnacle and lose your footing, not even a single bone will remain there to be picked up, it seems. Then how can the last rites be done for you? Such talk is based on an assumption that there is something to be achieved. In fact, there is something to be understood.

If the goal is *ānanda*, fullness, happiness, how can the way to the goal be unpleasant? To the extent that you understand, the way is *ānanda*. The path is *ānanda* and both sides are *ānanda*. There is never a dull moment, just as when you go on a pilgrimage to a mountain. As you proceed along the steep paths, every one of their many turns opens up a new vista, a new valley, a new scene. At one moment, the Ganges will be travelling alongside of you and at another she will have left you far behind. Further along, you will again find her right beside you. Sometimes she is down below. Sometimes she is playing. Sometimes she is roaring. The mountains themselves present new vistas – sometimes barren, sometimes green, sometimes wearing snowy white caps.

Similarly, the path to self-knowledge is not an arduous one. The path itself is pleasant and the end is pleasantness itself. Nor, as one often hears, can the path be described as difficult in the beginning and pleasant later on or pleasant in the beginning and bitter later on. It is often said that spiritual path is bitter in the beginning and pleasant later on, while the material path is pleasant in the beginning and bitter later on. But is this really the case? Is not the material path always a problem, in the beginning, later and in between?

The material path does enable me to pick up some joy along the way. It is only because Bhagavān is everywhere. He is not just in one place. In fact, upon analysis, we find that there is no such thing as material; all matter, all material, is nothing but Bhagavān. There is nothing separate from Bhagavān. How then can I say this is material and this is Bhagavān?

All these divisions are made by our *buddhi*, which is a dividing *buddhi*, a dualistic *buddhi*. Wherever it goes, the *buddhi* creates division – spiritual and temporal, profound and profane. Because it is basically a dualistic *buddhi*, it continuously attempts to create dualism. In fact, this divisive *buddhi* is the very nature of the *jīva*.

Kṛṣṇa says, 'Whether people know it, whenever they pick up a moment of joy, it is me alone.' The only problem is that they rest content scraping some small joys out of him when, in fact, he is the joy that is their very own nature. Not knowing themselves as Īśvara, the very column of joy, they settle for a small crumb that has somehow escaped from out of themselves. 'This,' Kṛṣṇa says, 'is a tragedy.' The tragedy is not that Īśvara denies the people anything but because they do not see their identity with him. 'Still,' Kṛṣṇa says, 'they are on my track. There is nothing to worry about. They will come to me eventually because until they become full, they will not stop seeking. No one is going to settle for anything less than fullness. No one is away from me.'

Verse 12

People do not seek Īśvara because of their fascination with quick results

काङ्क्षन्तः कर्मणां सिद्धिं यजन्त इह देवताः ।
क्षिप्रं हि मानुषे लोके सिद्धिर्भवति कर्मजा ॥ १२ ॥

kāṅkṣantaḥ karmaṇāṁ siddhiṁ yajanta iha devatāḥ
kṣipraṁ hi mānuṣe loke siddhirbhavati karmajā (12)

karmaṇām – of actions; *siddhim* – the result; *kāṅkṣantaḥ* – desiring; *iha* – here (in this world); *devatāḥ* – deities; *yajante* – they worship; *hi* – because; *mānuṣe loke* – in the human world; *karmajā* – born of action; *siddhiḥ* – result; *kṣipram* – very quickly; *bhavati* – comes

> Desiring the result of actions here (in this world), they worship (different) deities. For, in the human world, result born of action comes very quickly.

Kṛṣṇa had said earlier that many people had come to him, meaning that they had discovered their identity with him. But why do not all people come to him? Does he prefer only some people and leave the others out? Does the Lord have such *rāgas* and *dveṣas*? If he does, then he is no different than anyone else.

Kṛṣṇa responds to this question by saying that he denies nothing to anyone. If, as a *jīva*, a person chooses to have only so much within Īśvara's creation, only that much he or she will get. He blesses even his greatest devotees in the form in which they invoke him, the Lord being impartial in every way.

This means that the form in which you invoke the Lord becomes the Lord for you. If you invoke the Lord as a deity, Indra for example, then the Lord is Indra. If you invoke him as the giver of a particular result of action, then he becomes that *devatā*, deity. He can even be invoked as Jupiter, Saturn, Mars, or any planet, which is done in relation to a person's horoscope. Some of the planets in particular locations have been found to indicate certain problems or situations for the person. Here Īśvara is invoked as the planet itself, the *prārabdha-karma-adhiṣṭhāna-devatā*, the presiding deity of the *prārabdha-karma*. Such invocations are possible only because the Lord is available in whatever purpose he is invoked, the purpose being served by the invocation itself.

Even people who have nothing to do with the Vedas get results. Rank materialists, for example, interested only in money and power, definitely get results. We also find that, without religion, Russia and China are surviving. Previously they survived with religion and, now, without religion, they are surviving, perhaps even better! Rituals and prayers have no meaning whatsoever to them. An ideal has become their religion. They are devotees of the state. For them, the state is God.

Communism is nothing but statism, that is, the state is more important than the individual. Everything belongs to the state and nothing belongs to the person. Whatever is there is to be shared by all. The idea itself is good, no doubt. However, to enforce it, individual freedom is destroyed. Anyone who raises his or her voice against the system is either prevented from speaking altogether or is sent where other human beings cannot hear him or her. Thus, individuals do not count at all. For those who hold this particular ideology, the state becomes God. Of course, such people will not call it God, but it is what God is for them.

Why do people misplace God like this? Why do they not become *mumukṣu*s and go after liberation, freedom? Because they are unable to see beyond the immediate results that they see here in the world. And to gain those results, they worship different deities, *devatāḥ yajante*, which can be anything such as money, power, biceps and so on.

Desiring the results of various forms of action, *kāṅkṣantaḥ karmaṇāṁ siddhim*, people invoke these various deities. They do not invoke Parameśvara, the total as such, 'They do not seek me. They do not go after me. They do not want to know me.

They want only to have these small results that they can see. They are *bhakta*s, alright, but they worship me as small deities alone,' says Kṛṣṇa.

Why do they do this? Because, having doership, *kartṛtva,* they think, 'I am an independent person, capable of doing what is necessary to get certain results.' Only human beings have this capacity to choose action based on this *kartṛtva,* the sense of doership. Animals do not have this sense, nor do the *deva*s; they have only enjoyership, *bhoktṛtva.*

The idea here is that people want immediate results. They do not want to wait. They see in this world the result or accomplishment born out of any *karma* takes place immediately. Many young people do not complete college because of the desire for a more immediate result even though they are encouraged by their parents and older members of the society to struggle for a few years so that they can enjoy a better life later.

A young man who plays a guitar, may think he is a musician. Seeing others who have become very popular and are making a lot of money, he wants to do the same. Therefore, going to college does not interest him. He even draws his father's attention to those people who became successful and made a lot of money with very little or no formal schooling whatsoever. Of course, he fails to mention those who did not educate themselves and are rotting in the streets. Instead, he will point to a particular uncle who did not go to school, but who happened to be at the right place at the right time and made some money. He then married a woman who also had some money and bought a piece of property, which escalated in value merely because someone decided to build a shopping mall in that very location.

Young people do not want to study because they want quick results. Or, they may only pretend to be interested in music or electronics; in fact, they are not interested in anything. Still other young people may want to do nothing more than travel to faraway places with a pack on their back. Those people who have interrupted their studies for quick results find it very difficult to resume studying later because they lack the necessary discipline.

In every university campus, there are people in their forties and fifties struggling to complete college degrees. Since these people obviously have gained a value for education, why do young people not want to study? Like the older people before them, they too go for quick results, immediate success, without really knowing what they want in life.

This is what is meant by people invoking small deities whether they are devotees, the deities of money, power and so on. The desire for quick money is what makes a person deal in drugs and buy lottery tickets. If at all one prays, one does so at the time of buying a lottery ticket, 'O Lord! Please let this be the winning number!'

If Īśvara is to be established, the concept should be a rational one

Therefore, Kṛṣṇa is saying here, 'Do not blame Me. Do not say that I am partial and that because of my likes and dislikes, all these things happen, to people.' But his statement can still be questioned based on the seemingly unjust differences we see among different types of people. If, as Kṛṣṇa says, he is the author of the world, *sṛṣṭi-kartā*, the one from whom everything has come, then ultimately he is the author of all the people in the world. Why, then, has he placed some people in elevated positions and others in lowly positions? Why, in the Vedic context, is one person called a *brāhmaṇa*, another a *kṣatriya*, yet another a *vaiśya*, and still another a *śūdra*? How is it that there are such differences in the world? The *brāhmaṇa*s have their own position in society, as do each of the others. It looks that there is an order, a hierarchy, wherein one group of people seems to be superior to another while the others have no place in the system at all.

As the author of this world, is Īśvara not responsible for all these differences? And if he is responsible, he must certainly have a problem, the blemish of partiality. Why else would he put a silver spoon in the mouth of one person, a gold spoon in the mouth of another, a platinum spoon in the mouth of yet another, and no spoon at all, not even a plastic one, in the mouth of many others? And there are people born with no mouths at all! Why does Īśvara do these kinds of things?

If this question cannot be asked and answered, why bother about God at all? It is not enough to say, 'This simply means that God does whatever he does and, because he is God, no one can question him?' Well, he may be God, but I am the sufferer. First you say he made me and then you say he knows my problems better than I do. How? I am the one who was born crippled, who cannot see and muchless hear. God does not seem to know that being crippled, blind and deaf is not a pleasant life since he made me this way. But I know better! If God knew what I know, he would definitely have made me differently. And since he did not, isn't he just another defective manufacturer?

If you buy a car in which even the slightest flaw is detected, there is such a furore made about it that the manufacturer calls back all the cars of that particular design, if only to change one bolt in the brake system. But Īśvara as a manufacturer, cannot be questioned, it seems. Nor does he call back anything. He does not say, 'I am so sorry. That was a hurried job. Please send it back to me and I will give you new legs or whatever.' Instead, the person has to suffer through life without legs, eyes, ears and so on.

What kind of God is this, who sits above us somewhere, having a wonderful life, while some unfortunate person has to inch along the ground because he or she is lame? And if God must make a crippled person, the least he could do is to put the person in America where motorised wheelchairs are readily available. Even this much he does not do for the person! How can we look at such differences and say that God is justified in all that he does. What kind of justification is this?

You find some people born with parents while others who do not even know who or where their parents are. A child may be born of parents in South Korea and brought up in Vancouver by foster parents. One thinks one is doing very well, but, in fact, he is not because he is painfully aware that he is noticeably different from his parents, his brothers and sisters. If his original parents had raised him in Korea, he would look the same as everyone else and would not have the problems he has growing up in Vancouver.

Adoption, even as a baby, really does not work. Even the adopted animals have problems adapting to a new habitat. Why would a baby have to be adopted in the first place? Whether in this country or elsewhere, why should the child not be with his or her own parents? Because we do not know where the father and mother are, we say the child is an orphan. If God creates everyone, can we say people create an orphan? No. Again, God seems to be some kind of a sadist.

Further, I am told that, not only has God made me, but he has also said that I must follow him. And how do I know this? Someone else tells me. The least God could do is to come and tell me himself. It would mean something to me. In fact, God should tell everyone. Instead, someone else tells me that God told him and asked him to tell me. If God wants me to know this, why does he not tell me himself? Then there is another person who comes along and says, 'God told me to tell you that the earlier person is no longer current and what you are now going to hear from me is the latest word from God!' In fact, we would all be better off without this kind of God.

If God is someone who is to be established, the concept should be a rational one, at least. What is unreasonable cannot be accepted. Thus, the issue being addressed here is valid–If God made all these divisions among people, *brāhmaṇa*s, *kṣatriya*s, *vaiśya*s and *śūdra*s, to use the Vedic context, then he must definitely be partial because the *brāhmaṇa*s seem to be better off.

Verse 13

The four-fold group of people based on duties and qualities

चातुर्वर्ण्यं मया सृष्टं गुणकर्मविभागशः ।
तस्य कर्तारमपि मां विद्ध्यकर्तारमव्ययम् ॥ १३ ॥

cāturvarṇyaṁ mayā sṛṣṭaṁ guṇakarmavibhāgaśaḥ
tasya kartāram api māṁ viddhyakartāram avyayam (13)

mayā – by me; *guṇakarmavibhāgaśaḥ* – a division based on duties and qualities; *cāturvarṇyam* – four-fold grouping (of people); *sṛṣṭam* – was created; *tasya* – its; *kartāram* – author; *api* – even though; *mām* – me; *avyayam* – ever changeless; *akartāram* – a non-doer; *viddhi* – know

The four-fold grouping (of people), a division based on duties and qualities, was created by me. Even though I am its author, know me to be a non-doer, ever changeless.

Here, Kṛṣṇa is referring to the Vedic system that divided people into four groups, saying that he has created both the people and the groups. As the creator of everything, *sṛṣṭi-kartā*, the Lord cannot deny his authorship, nor does he here, while talking to Arjuna.

Although this classification into four groups refers to the Indian context, what Kṛṣṇa says here is universally applicable. In other contexts, we see people divided in terms of royalty, nobility, wealth and poverty. Still others refer to groups of people as the upper class, upper middle class, middle class, lower middle class and so on. Wherever there are people, such classifications or groups are always to be found.

In the Vedic context, people are divided into four groups on the basis of their qualities, *guṇataḥ vibhāgaḥ*, and on the basis of what they have to do, *karmataḥ vibhāgaḥ*. Bhagavān created this division. About this, Kṛṣṇa says, 'Understand Me to be the maker, the *kartā* of this four fold division.' At the same time, he also says, 'Understand that I am not the *kartā*. I am the non doer, *akartā*, because I am changeless, *avyaya*. I do not undergo any change whatsoever. I do not undergo the change to become the *kartā*.'

How can Kṛṣṇa say he has created all this and also say he is not the doer? In order to resolve this apparent contradiction, we will first look at the division of people based on *guṇa* and *karma*. Then, we will look at how Īśvara can be their *kartā* and, at the same time, be a non-doer.

The division of people according to guṇa

The division of people according to qualities, *guṇa-vibhāgaḥ*, is found not just in India, but all over the world. The qualities upon which this division is based are psychological, that is, that they refer to the composition and disposition of the mind. The division based upon the quality of the mind, *manoguṇa* is four fold, as we shall see a little later.

The *guṇa*s, qualities, are three in number – *sattva*, *rajas* and *tamas*, the meanings of which we shall also see. Everyone has these three qualities and, from certain combinations of these three qualities, four groups are derived.

One possible composition of the three *guṇa*s is *sattva-rajas-tamas*, wherein *sattva* is predominant, *rajas* is less predominant, and *tamas* is the least predominant. A second composition in the order of predominance is *rajas-sattva-tamas*. Similarly, the third composition is *rajas-tamas-sattva* and the fourth is *tamas-rajas-sattva*. These are the only four compositions possible. There can be shades of each of these four, but a fifth composition is not possible.

One may ask, why not *tamas-sattva-rajas* or *sattva-tamas-rajas* be a fifth and sixth composition? By looking at each of the three *guṇa*s involved, we shall see why only four *varṇa*s, groups of people are possible when the division is based on their *guṇa*s.

Sattva stands for any type of thinking, *rajas* stands for activity and *tamas* for dullness, inactivity. Contemplativeness, enquiry, silence (*śānti)*, and the disciplines, *śama* and *dama*, are *sattva*. Discipline is also found in a person in whom *rajas* is predominant, but there will also be a lot of ambition, energy, and enthusiasm along with it; a go getter, for example. *Tamas* is dullness, lethargy and laziness.

Everyone is a combination of these three and, as we have seen, the combinations can vary. Babies, for example, are *tamas-rajas-sattva*. *Tamas* being predominant, they sleep most of the time. As they get older, *rajas* predominates, and they become very active. Finally, when they are grown, we expect them to be *sāttvika*s.

The *sattva-rajas-tamas* composition is a very beautiful description of a person's inner disposition. A person can be predominantly contemplative, a thinking person, because of which certain things are very evident to him or her. An emotionally mature person, an enquirer, philosopher, anyone who thinks predominantly about fundamental values, the ends in life and so on, is naturally a combination of *sattva-rajas-tamas* respectively. In such a person, *sattva* is predominant backed by *rajas* in second place and *tamas* taking the third place. This is one type of person.

The second type will naturally have *rajas* as predominant with either *sattva* or *tamas* as the second. When *rajas* is predominant, the person is very active, fired by certain ambition. When this ambition is directed to the welfare of others and to certain ideals, there is a lot of thinking involved. Therefore, *sattva* is in second place; the person's enthusiasm and actions are backed up by thinking. Such people generally become good leaders. The world needs such leaders.

The third group of people are those who are always active, having *rajas* predominant, but who have *tamas* rather than *sattva* in second place. It means there is ambition rather than thinking behind their actions. An example of ambition without thinking is when someone goes after money, power, and so on, without any consideration for others. Because such a person also has certain *sattva*, some thinking capacity, he or she will not only be very active but may also be very clever and intelligent. But, because *tamas* is predominant over *sattva*, there will be a lot of scheming, manipulation and exploitation of others.

If, on the other hand, *sattva* is backing up the *rajas*, there will be consideration for other people. There will be respect for life, for wealth and for the freedom of others. Whereas, when *tamas* backs up *rajas*, there is only disrespect for *dharma*, meaning there will be no regard for others. For such a person, individual ambition is most important and he or she becomes a despot. *Rajas* being predominant, such people also become world leaders. If they do not become leaders, only their families and perhaps their neighbours suffer. However, if such people assume world leadership roles, the results can be devastating.

The fourth type of person, wherein *tamas* predominates, presents no such problem. At worst, these people are small time criminals and, at best, simple employees, not out of any real contentment or anything but simply because of dullness. Such people have no ambition whatsoever, not even to make money. In fact, they have already decided that they cannot make money. 'If I could make money, I would have made it long ago,' they will say. And then, to justify their laziness, they add, 'Who needs money anyway?' If such a person has a little ambition for something, he or she will not work to make it happen and will compromise at every turn. This is meant by dullness, *tamas*.

If a *tamas-rajas-sattva* person wants to become *sattva-rajas-tamas,* he or she has to become *rajas-tamas-sattva* first, then *rajas-sattva-tamas,* and only then, *sattva-rajas-tamas*. There is no jumping possible here. It is a process involving growth and it is what maturity is about. It is also what we mean by *karma-yoga* whereby one becomes mature by doing *karma* with a *karma-yoga* attitude.

Up to *rajas-tamas-sattva,* growth is simply a matter of performing *karma,* pursuing one's own ends according to *dharma.*

Only when one performs *karma* with the attitude of *karma-yoga* does the person become *sattva-rajas-tamas*. This is the person who can become a *sannyāsī*.

Shades of difference exist within each of these four groups. For instance, *rajas-tamas-sattva* can be a criminal or just an ambitious sales person. When the latter invites you into his or her place of business with a smile, you may end up paying for the smile too! There is rank selfishness in this type of person that makes him or her convert every action into dollars and cents. *Rajas-tamas-sattva* people can follow *dharma* or *adharma*, shades of difference being there. When one reaches *rajas-sattva-tamas*, one automatically follows *dharma*.

These are the three qualities that cause the differences in groups of people, not only in India but the world over. *Sattva*, *rajas* and *tamas* belong to *prakṛti*, nature, which belongs to Bhagavān. On the basis of this *prakṛti*, the division of people according to qualities, *guṇa-vibhāga*, is done. People come under the four groups formed by the possible combinations of the three *guṇa*s, since everyone has to work his or her way through the four compositions in order to mature.

In the Vedic context, people having the first combination, *sattva-rajas-tamas*, are called *brāhmaṇa*s, those having the second combination, *rajas-sattva-tamas*, are called *kṣatriya*s, those having the third, *rajas-tamas-sattva*, are called *vaiśya*s and those having the fourth combination, *tamas-rajas-sattva*, are called *śūdra*s. This, then, is the *guṇa-vibhāga*, the four-fold division based on qualities, referred to in this verse.

The division of people according to duties

There is another kind of division inherent in this system, also four fold, the people of each division being called by the same names. This division is based on duty, *karma-vibhāga*. The duty of a *brāhmaṇa*, for example, is to teach and to officiate at rituals. His life is one of prayer for the welfare of the society and he lives a simple life with no more than the barest essentials. He must practise *śama* and gain *dama*. He studies the Veda, teaches and serves as an officiating priest, undertaking all the liturgical activities that are the duties of a priest. The society requires that certain religious activities be conducted and the *brāhmaṇa* is responsible for them. He is a priestly person.

So, there is a *guṇa* wise *brāhmaṇa* and a duty-wise *brāhmaṇa*. Similarly, there is a *guṇa* wise *kṣatriya* and a duty-wise *kṣatriya*, whose duty is to protect *dharma*, be committed to knowledge and protect the Vedas. As a *kṣatriya*, Arjuna's duty was to rule and protect the people, in terms of administration, judiciary, law enforcement and defence. All these functions fall under *kṣatriya dharma* and are duties to be done in every society.

A *vaiśya* is a person who deals in commerce, wealth, farms, agriculture and so on. Commerce involves bringing things from the place where they are produced and selling them in other places where they are needed. Thus, a *vaiśya* is the one whose duty is to make things available to people.

The people in the fourth division, *śūdra*, provide the hands and legs, eyes and ears, for the others. Their duty is to serve and, without such people, nothing could be accomplished.

The activities they perform are found in all societies in the world and must be done if the society is to function.

In the Vedic religion, the activities of each of the four groups of people are converted into duties and are enjoined according to family. We do not know when it started, but whoever was doing the duties of a *śūdra*, a *vaiśya*, a *kṣatriya* or a *brāhmaṇa* kept passing the same duties down to his or her children.

Strictly speaking, anyone who does the work of a particular group should be known by the name of that group regardless of which group he or she is born into. A person who is born in a *brāhmaṇa* family, but does *vaiśya-karma*, is a *vaiśya*. A true *brāhmaṇa*, on the other hand, is one who, having been born into a *brāhmaṇa* family, lives a simple life so as not to exploit the society, studies and teaches the Veda, and performs the obligatory rituals for the welfare of the people, just as his father, grandfather and great grandfather did before him.

Duties being there, we have these four groups of people. Of course, duties can be transgressed, but it is not the point here. The duties, the *karma* themselves, are the basis for the division of people, each group having its respective duties. So, there are *brāhmaṇa* duties, *kṣatriya* duties, *vaiśya* duties and *śūdra* duties.

A man who is a *brāhmaṇa* in terms of *karma*, duty, may chant the Veda, officiate at rituals, and so on, but *guṇa* wise, he may be ambitious and may want recognition. Such a person is not *sattva-rajas-tamas*. If, however, he carries out his duties with the attitude of *karma-yoga*, he is *sattva-rajas-tamas*.

Then his attitude is, 'This is my *karma*, my duty. These duties are to be done by me. They are my offering to the Lord.'

Karma-yoga and a duty-based society

Karma-yoga is relatively easy for a person who is born into a structure where the concept of duty is clearly defined. When the spirit behind the structure is understood, all the person has to do is what has to be done. The person need not choose a vocation in life. He or she knows exactly what is to be done based on which family he or she is born into. One's duty is written over one's forehead at birth, so to speak.

For a person who believes in the law of *karma*, there is no other reason for him or her to have been born into a particular family. Some *karma* is the governing factor and what is now to be done is clear. For example, a man who is born into a *brāhmaṇa* family knows that he has to study, perform *yajña*s and so on, and he does so, happily. While performing his duties, he does not mutter, 'If only I were an administrator, I would have earned a lot of money by now. Instead, I have nothing!'

If earning money is the main criterion, a system based on duty cannot work. Everyone will look to see which vocation produces the most money and go for that. If medicine produces money, one will become a doctor. And when a glut develops in the field of medicine, one will turn to another field where there is more opportunity, more money. If money and power are the main criteria, there will be no structure, really speaking. Money and power will set up the structure for one's education, profession, marriage and so on.

In the Vedic vision, *mokṣa*, liberation, is the main aim. The Veda says that you are perfect and you have to gain this knowledge, which is *mokṣa*. For this, you must have a mature mind, and such a mind can be gained only by living a life of *karma-yoga*. *Karma-yoga* necessarily implies clarity with regard to your duty, what you are to do. When you are clear about what your duty is, then you can perform any *karma*, activity, as duty.

We have seen how the duties of a *brāhmaṇa* are very evident to the person. Similarly, the duties of a *kṣatriya* are very clear to him and he performs his *karma* as a duty, cheerfully. A *vaiśya* also knows exactly what is to be done by him. His father is engaged in either commerce or cultivation, or he may have a cattle farm. The son chooses one of the three or involves himself in all of them. Whatever he chooses to do is done as his duty and for a reasonable profit. A *vaiśya* too is not supposed to exploit the society in any way. For example, he must not create a scarcity by buying all available stock, storing it somewhere, and then releasing it in small amounts at large profits when the people begin clamouring for it. Such practices are definitely not in conformity with *dharma* nor are they *vaiśya-dharma*. Thus, when a *vaiśya* performs his duties happily, according to his own *dharma*, it can be *yoga* for him. The duties of a *śūdra*, *śūdra-karma*, are the same. They are not lowly or demeaning *karma*; they are simply duties to be done.

Superiority is determined by one's maturity – not duty

No duty is superior to another. Each duty is as good, as necessary, as every other duty. Therefore, one group of people is not superior or inferior to another group of people. All are but Parameśvara, irrespective of which group they belong to. In every society, there are certain activities to be performed and these activities or duties fall into four general groups. Thus, the groups that people belong to differ from each other only in terms of the duties attached to them.

When a person belonging to any group performs his or her duty with an attitude of *karma-yoga*, that person becomes, *guṇa* wise, *sattva-rajas-tamas*. A *brāhmaṇa* who chants the Veda for the sake of personal glory becomes *rajas-sattva-tamas*. If he does it for money alone, with no other ambition, he becomes *rajas-tamas-sattva*. And if he performs a ritual in the temple with an attitude of dullness, for no other reason than to feed himself, he is *tamas-rajas-sattva*.

There is another kind of *brāhmaṇa* who enjoys what he does and does it well but, at the same time, wants everyone to listen to him. He is always looking around to see who is coming! There are also those who, seeing someone who has a lot of money coming, will stop right in the middle of performing a *pūjā* and fawn all over the person. God has to wait, it seems! Thus, there are several varieties of *brāhmaṇas*–*brāhmaṇa-brāhmaṇas*, meaning *brāhmaṇas*, both duty-wise and *guṇa*-wise; *kṣatriya-brāhmaṇas*, those who are *brāhmaṇa* duty-wise and *kṣatriyas* *guṇa*-wise; *vaiśya-brāhmaṇas*, those who are *brāhmaṇas* duty-wise and *vaiśyas* *guṇa*-wise; and *śūdra-brāhmaṇas*, those who are *brāhmaṇas* duty-wise and *śūdras*, *guṇa*-wise.

In the same way, there are *brāhmaṇa-kṣatriyas*, *kṣatriya-kṣatriyas*, *vaiśya-kṣatriyas*, *śūdra-kṣatriyas*; *brāhmaṇa-vaiśyas*, *kṣatriya-vaiśyas, vaiśya-vaiśyas, śūdra-vaiśyas; brāhmaṇa-śūdras, kṣatriya-śūdras, vaiśya-śūdras, and śūdra-śūdras*. Who is superior in all of this? A *brāhmaṇa-brāhmaṇa, brāhmaṇa-kṣatriya, brāhmaṇa-vaiśya,* and *brāhmaṇa-śūdra* are all equal. So the *brāhmaṇa* is superior. This statement must not be misunderstood. When we refer to a *brāhmaṇa* as superior, we are not talking about a person who performs the duties of a *brāhmaṇa*. We are talking about the quality, the maturity, of the person's mind. There is a lot of confusion around this very point that has given rise to the prevalence of caste related problems.

If a man who performs *brāhmaṇa* duties says that he is superior, he is definitely demonstrating a lack of the qualities of a *brāhmaṇa* and is therefore, not a *brāhmaṇa-brāhmaṇa*. You will find many great historical saints who were not *brāhmaṇa*s by birth being worshipped in temples in India. Some were *śūdra*s and others were *harijans*, meaning those who do not belong to any of the four groups. Most of these saints were duty wise *śūdra*s, but they have places in the temple because they were *brāhmaṇa-śūdra*s. Therefore, *guṇa*-wise, people can be *brāhmaṇa*s while belonging to any of the four duty based divisions.

Duties may change but qualities do not

This classification of duties and people can apply anywhere, not just in India. Here, the only difference in the four fold division is that it was reflected within the family structure itself, each family belonging to one of the four groups. Probably less than one percent of the people still follow this system, but amongst those who do, the son of a *brāhmaṇa* still studies and teaches the Veda, performs the prescribed rituals, prays for the society, and lives a simple life. The system is almost gone because it requires certain protection that it no longer enjoys.

No system can survive unless it is protected. Prior to the Mogul invasions, the royal families protected the four fold classification structure in India. However, during the eight hundred years of Muslim rule, it was destroyed. Later, in the interests of survival, people concerned themselves only with doing what had to be done to look after themselves and their families. Because a man no longer bothered about what his father's *karma* was, the whole structure changed in terms of duty.

However, in terms of quality, *guṇa-vibhāga,* the division of people does not change. This is where *karma-yoga* as an attitude becomes clearer. A *karma-yogī* is one who does what has to be done with the proper attitude. Such a person is also a *brāhmaṇa, sattva-rajas-tamas,* with reference to the quality of his or her mind. Only this *brāhmaṇa* can be a *sannyāsī*. The mandate that only a *brāhmaṇa* can be a *sannyāsī* is based on quality of the mind alone and has nothing to do with which group a person is born into in terms of duty.

The Vedic culture, then, divides people into four groups, *catvāraḥ varṇāḥ,* according to their duty, *karma* – the system itself being possible because of the three *guṇas, sattva, rajas and tamas,* found in everyone. And Kṛṣṇa, as Īśvara, could say, 'I created them all, but do not blame me. I am not the doer. Because of their own *karma,* they are born differently.' To blame Īśvara is like putting your finger in the fire and, when the fire burns it, asking the fire:

'Did you burn my finger?'

The fire replies, 'Yes, I burnt your finger.'

'Why did you burn my finger?'

'I did not burn your finger.'

'But, you told me you were the *kartā*. You were the one who burnt. You said you did it.'

'Yes, I said it.'

'But you also said you are not the *kartā*. You said you are *akartā*. Why?'

'That is because I did not burn,' the fire says.

'But you burnt!'

'Yes, I burnt.'

'But you said you did not burn.'

'Yes, I agree because I did not burn.'

What is all this? The fire says it is the *kartā* and also the *akartā*. Then the fire explains, 'I did it because I burnt the finger. Nobody else burnt the finger. It was me. But I did not do it because I did not go after your finger, did I? You stuck your finger into me. You asked for it and you got it. After all, I am fire, Lord Agni. In whichever form you invoke me, in that form I will bless you. You can try again. I can boil water for you. I can warm up your room or your hands. And I can burn your fingers, too. What do you want from me? Tell me, and I will give it to you. But do not blame me. From my own standpoint, I am not the *kartā*. From the standpoint of what you receive from me, I am the *kartā* because you get whatever your *karma* deserves. I am the law and I cannot transgress the law that I am.'

Similarly, as Īśvara, Kṛṣṇa says that he had created the particular structure reflected by the four groups of people as a part of this creation. Therefore, we are to know Īśvara as the *kartā*, the maker or creator of this four-fold division. At the same time, he is also to be understood as *akartā* because he says, 'I have not done this at all. I am a non doer.' How can this be?

Only from the standpoint of the world and the four groups of people in it can we take Kṛṣṇa to be the doer, the *kartā*, whereas, in reality, from his own standpoint as Parameśvara, he is not the *kartā* of anything. Therefore, he is not subject to blame. A person has a particular *karma* that determines whether he is a *brāhmaṇa*, *kṣatriya*, *vaiśya* or *śūdra*. Which group a *jīva* is born into is the *jīva*'s own doing and has nothing to do with Īśvara.

This four fold division is in the creation. Those who have *sattva* as a predominant quality become *brāhmaṇa*s. Those who have *rajas* as predominant become *kṣatriya*s or *vaiśya*s. It all depends on one's composition. Everyone has the capacity to change his or her composition because everyone has a free will. One's composition has nothing to do with Īśvara; he is only the giver of the results of actions, *karma-phala-dātā*, and is completely impartial in this regard.

Īśvara is *kartā* from the standpoint of what is created and *akartā* from the standpoint of his knowledge about himself, meaning for him, there is no notion of 'I am the doer.' Īśvara has no *kartṛtva-buddhi*. Kṛṣṇa said earlier that this was not only true for him but for everyone too. Anyone who looks upon Īśvara as oneself, *ātmā*, as the *akartā*, is also *akartā*.

Verse 14

The one who has clear knowledge of Īśvara is not bound by actions

न मां कर्माणि लिम्पन्ति न मे कर्मफले स्पृहा ।
इति मां योऽभिजानाति कर्मभिर्न स बध्यते ॥ १४ ॥

na māṁ karmāṇi limpanti na me karmaphale spṛhā
iti māṁ yo'bhijānāti karmabhirna sa badhyate (14)

karmāṇi – actions; *mām* – me; *na limpanti* – do not affect; *karmaphale* – with reference to the result of action; *me* – for me; *na spṛhā* – there is no longing; *iti* – in this way; *yaḥ* – the one who; *mām* – me; *abhijānāti* – knows clearly; *saḥ* – that person; *karmabhiḥ* – by actions; *na badhyate* – is not bound

> Actions do not affect me. There is no longing with reference to the result of action for me. The one who knows me clearly in this way is not bound by actions.

In this verse, Kṛṣṇa reveals a fact about himself as Bhagavān and also extends it to the individual. Even though Bhagavān has created the world and everything in it and performs actions to keep it going, these actions, whatever be their nature, do not affect him. Hence he says, '*na māṁ karmāṇi limpanti*, the actions do not touch me.' They do not bind him, meaning, they do not create *sukha* and *duḥkha* for him because they do not create *puṇya-pāpa* for him as they do for a *jīva*. And why do his actions not affect him? Because, the notion, 'I am the doer,' is not there for him.

The *jīva*, on the other hand, superimposes the notion of doership upon the *ātmā* and then thinks that the self is doing all the actions. And once you have doership, *kartṛtva*, you also have enjoyership, *bhoktṛtva*. A person who looks upon himself or herself as a doer has to answer for the actions he or she does. But, in fact, the self is not a *kartā*. When one knows this particular fact, one no longer looks upon oneself as a *kartā* and is, therefore, unaffected by *karma*.

Now the question here is, if Kṛṣṇa knew he was not a doer, why did he do *karma*? Was it because of a desire to accomplish something? 'No,' he says. With reference to the result of action, there was no longing, no craving, no want, whatsoever in him, *na me karma phale spṛhā*. Therefore, when he performed *karma*, it was not for gaining a result for himself. He did not look upon himself as one who was going to be better by performing an action.

You may ask, 'While this may be true for Īśvara, what about me, the individual, the *jīva* who is affected by my actions and who also longs for the results? This verse tells us that this state of affairs is only for the ignorant. The one who knows him clearly, *yaḥ māṁ abhijānāti*, Kṛṣṇa says, can also say, 'Actions do not affect me. I do not long for their results, *na māṁ karmāṇi limpanti na me karma phale spṛhā.*' Actions do not bind such people. Nor do they crave for the results of action to make themselves better.

The word, *jānāti* means 'knows' and *abhijānāti* means 'knows clearly.' The one who knows Īśvara clearly as oneself is being talked about here. There is no other way of knowing the non-doer *paramātmā*. The *ātmā* that is common here is the one who does not do, the one who is free from attributes. This is the *ātmā* that Kṛṣṇa is talking about. For *ātmā* there is no doership, no enjoyership.

As long as the notion of doership is there, there is a distinct entity. When this notion of doership is gone, the enjoyership also goes, leaving only the *ātmā* that has no distinguishing features whatsoever–the *ātmā* that is non-doer, non-enjoyer, performs no action whatsoever.

If *ātmā* has no distinguishing feature of its own, how many *ātmā*s can there be? Absence of distinguishing features means that there is only one *ātmā*. There is no *īśvara-ātmā* and *jīva-ātmā*. No difference, *bheda*, exists between the two. There is only one *ātmā* who is Īśvara, who is *jīva*. Why then the seeming difference? It is all due to *upādhi* alone. One *upādhi* is total, *samaṣṭi-upādhi*, which is Īśvara, and the other is individual, *vyaṣṭi-upādhi*, called *jīva*.

A person who knows *ātmā* as neither a doer nor an enjoyer knows Īśvara as oneself. Like Kṛṣṇa, this person is not bound by the various *karma*s that he or she may do – *sa karmabhiḥ na bhadyate* – whether these actions be scripturally enjoined or worldly, *vaidika-karma* or *laukika-karma*.

This particular verse is said to be a *mahā-vākya* because *jīva* and Īśvara are equated. Kṛṣṇa's words, 'I am not bound and anyone who knows me is also not bound,' reveal the identity between Īśvara and *jīva*, an identity that must be understood. This understanding is liberation, *mokṣa*.

Verse 15

Kṛṣṇa tells Arjuna how to gain this knowledge

एवं ज्ञात्वा कृतं कर्म पूर्वैरपि मुमुक्षुभिः ।
कुरु कर्मैव तस्मात्त्वं पूर्वैः पूर्वतरं कृतम् ॥ १५ ॥

evaṁ jñātvā kṛtaṁ karma pūrvairapi mumukṣubhiḥ
kuru karmaiva tasmāttvaṁ pūrvaiḥ pūrvataraṁ kṛtam (15)

evam – in this manner; *jñātvā* – knowing; *pūrvaiḥ mumukṣubhiḥ* – by seekers of ancient times; *api* – even; *karma* – action; *kṛtam* – was performed; *tasmāt* – therefore; *tvam* – you; *pūrvaiḥ* – by those who came before; *pūrvataram* – in the ancient past; *kṛtam* – was done; *karma* – action; *eva* – indeed; *kuru* – perform

> Knowing (me) in this manner, even seekers of ancient times performed action. Therefore, perform action indeed as even it was done by those who came before in the ancient past.

Knowing Kṛṣṇa, the Lord, 'in this manner, *evam*,' refers back to what was said in the previous verse, 'Actions do not affect me, *na māṁ karmāṇi limpanti*.' There, Kṛṣṇa said that he had no craving for the results of any action because *ātmā* is *pūrṇa*, complete, and therefore, *asaṅga*, free of all attachment. *Ātmā* is free from all actions; it has no doership whatsoever.

Ātmā's nature is pure consciousness, free from any kind of volition. Volition is dependent upon the *ātmā* but *ātmā* is independent of all volition, all doership. Therefore, with reference to the result of action, *karma-phala,* there is no *tṛṣṇa,* longing, in *ātmā*. Because there is no doership for the *ātmā,* actions do not affect Kṛṣṇa and also the person who knows that the self, *ātmā,* and Īśvara are one.

Who gains this knowledge? Kṛṣṇa pointed out earlier in the tenth verse of this chapter, that many people had already reached him in this way. He did not mean everyone, but only those who were seekers, *mumukṣus*, who wanted liberation. And once they had the knowledge, what did they get? Actions no longer affected them and they no longer yearned for the results. In fact, this is what *mokṣa* is; there is no other *mokṣa*.

Having the knowledge does not preclude action

And what did the seekers, who had gone before, do once they had the knowledge? They performed action, *pūrvaiḥ karma kṛtam*. Therefore, Kṛṣṇa tells Arjuna that he should do the same, *tasmāt tvaṁ karmaiva kuru,* which meant that Arjuna should not take to *sannyāsa*. He should do what was to be done by him. Śaṅkara makes it very clear in his commentary of this verse that Arjuna was not to sit quietly nor was he to take *sannyāsa, na tūṣṇīm āsanaṁ nāpi sannyāsaḥ kartavyaḥ*. He was to do the *karma* that was his to do, just as earlier seekers had done, even those who already had this knowledge.

Kṛṣṇa is telling Arjuna that if he is a *mumukṣu*, then he should perform action because, previously, those people who were *mumukṣus* did *karma* and reached him. Arjuna should do what other seekers before him had done, *pūrvaiḥ pūrvataraṁ kṛtam*, not what people in general had done.

The use of the word *mumukṣu* is very relevant here, a *mumukṣu* being a person who wants to gain liberation. Those who are still ignorant and want liberation need to gain the knowledge that will liberate them. Having said that others acquired the knowledge in this way, Kṛṣṇa says, 'Therefore, with *śraddhā*, faith, that you too will gain liberation, please do *karma* and gain this knowledge.' Śaṅkara adds here that a *mumukṣu* who is not yet a *jñānī*, and therefore, not totally clear about this knowledge, should perform action in order to cleanse the mind of all its *rāga-dveṣa*s.

Even if one knows the *ātmā* completely, one should also perform action, not for *antaḥ-karaṇa-śuddhi* but for the sake of others, *loka-saṅgrahārtham*. Because of the *jñānī*'s *prārabdha*, there is something to be done, meaning, whatever presents itself for him or her to do is to be done for the good of the people. This action does not affect the *jñānī* in any way because the person does not take himself or herself to be the doer.

The word *mumukṣu* can indicate either a seeker or one who is already liberated, *jīvan-mukta*. 'In either case, *karma* is to be done,' Kṛṣṇa says. Arjuna himself could decide whether he was an *ajñānī* or a *jñānī*, but still he was to perform action. Either way, he would not lose anything by doing what was to be done.

Inaction never leads to liberation

Kṛṣṇa wants to make sure that Arjuna did not think he would be liberated by not doing *karma*. But, at the same time, it must be clearly understood that doing *karma* is not going to liberate a person either. It can only bring about *antaḥ-karaṇa-śuddhi*, as we have already seen. Doing *karma* is not a direct means of liberation, but it is an indirect means because it helps prepare your mind so that the knowledge can take place. The point here is that not doing *karma* will not help in any way.

An undone *karma* never helps you because something that is not done cannot produce a result of any kind. On the other hand, a *karma* that is done, *kṛtam-karma*, always produces some result, either an ordinary *karma-phala* or *antaḥ-karaṇa-śuddhi*, or both.

Naiṣkarmya, the state of actionlessness that is *mokṣa*, is not gained by not doing *karma*. Not doing action does not amount to total actionlessness because you will always be doing one thing or the other. Non-doership is to be understood as the very nature, *svarūpa*, of oneself. Therefore, Kṛṣṇa says to Arjuna here, 'All these *karma*s you see me doing do not affect me in any way. I am totally unaffected by all of them.'

Because he is totally unaffected by action and their results, Kṛṣṇa as Īśvara has no partiality either. If Kṛṣṇa wanted certain results, that is, if he had *phala-spṛhā*, he would be doing one thing for one person and another for another, based on what he wanted from these people. There would also be those for whom he would do nothing because there was nothing to be gained from them. He would help only those people who, day after day, flatter him with the same words, 'O Bhagavān! You are so wonderful, so great. You are everything.' And about the others he would say, 'Since they do not care for me, I am not going to care for them.' This would mean that Bhagavān also wants to be cared for and loved, and not just by one person but by everyone!

God does not have such problems because he has no longing for the result of any action, *na me karma phale spṛhā*. He does not get anything out of people loving him. He is completely detached from all of this – and so are you just by knowing Īśvara. Hence, Kṛṣṇa says, 'The one who knows me clearly, *yaḥ mām abhijānāti*, is also out from this *karma* and is not bound by it at all.' By telling Arjuna that a number of people since ancient times had achieved him by doing *karma*, Kṛṣṇa is saying that Arjuna should also do *karma*. He did not want Arjuna to become confused, thinking that by not doing *karma* he would gain *mokṣa*, actionlessness. Since there can be so much confusion around the concept of actionlessness, Kṛṣṇa begins a new section here.

Verse 16

The true meaning of action and inaction

किं कर्म किमकर्मेति कवयोऽप्यत्र मोहिताः ।
तत्ते कर्म प्रवक्ष्यामि यज्ज्ञात्वा मोक्ष्यसेऽशुभात् ॥ १६ ॥

kiṁ karma kim akarmaeti kavayo'pyatra mohitāḥ
tatte karma pravakṣyāmi yajjñātvā mokṣyase'śubhāt (16)

kim – what; *karma* – action; *kim* – what; *akarma* – actionlessness; *iti* – thus; *atra* – here (with reference to this subject matter); *kavayaḥ* – seers (scholars); *api* – even; *mohitāḥ* – confused; *yat* – which; *jñātvā* – knowing; *aśubhāt* – from that which is inauspicious (*saṁsāra*); *mokṣyase* – you will be released; *tat* – that; *te* – to you; *karma* – action; *pravakṣyāmi* – I shall tell

> Even the seers (scholars) are confused with reference to what is action (and) what is actionlessness. I shall tell you about action, knowing which you will be released from what is inauspicious (*saṁsāra*).

The subject matter under discussion is *karma*, action. *Kavayaḥ* is the plural of *kavi*, which can mean a poet, a seer, or the Lord. *Kavi* can also refer to an informed person, one who is intellectually highly accomplished, a *medhāvī*. A person who simply stores information in his or her memory and blurts it out on command, just like a floppy disk does, is not a *medhāvī*. A *medhāvī* is one who understands a subject thoroughly and retains it, complete with all the details.

There are still others who can understand a subject matter and not retain the details. Such a person is also blessed. In this verse, *kavayaḥ* refers to those who are able to understand the subject matter and can also retain the details. Even such people, Kṛṣṇa says, are confused, *mohita*, about *karma* and *akarma*, action and actionlessness.

What is action, *kiṁ karma*? What is actionlessness, *kiṁ akarma*? Since even informed people are not very clear about this subject matter, it cannot be assumed that *karma* refers only to action done and *akarma* to action not done. Obviously, such an approach is too simplistic. Therefore, Kṛṣṇa says to Arjuna, 'I will tell you what *karma* is, *te karma pravakṣyāmi,' karma* meaning both *karma* and *akarma*.

Śaṅkara confirms, in his commentary on this verse, that *karma* here stands for both *karma* and *akarma* (*karma ca akarma ca*). To understand *karma, akarma* must also be understood, knowing which you will be liberated, *yajjñātvā mokṣyase,* from the inauspicious, *aśubhāt,* meaning from *saṁsāra*. *Śubha* is a very beautiful word to refer to something that ends well. It is often found at the end of books, in the same way that we find the word, 'finis.' While 'finis' merely means the book has ended, *śubha* means that it has ended well.

Anything auspicious and good is *śubha*. *Aśubha* means the opposite, that which is inauspicious or not very good. Here, we can take it, as Śaṅkara does, to mean *saṁsāra*. *Saṁsāra* is *aśubha* and it ends in *mokṣa*. Therefore, *mokṣa* alone is *śubha*. When *saṁsāra* ends, there is *mokṣa,* which is called *śubha*. Until then, it is *aśubha, saṁsāra*. The grand finale of *saṁsāra,* the auspicious end, is called *śubha*. From this inauspicious *saṁsāra,* you will be relieved, liberated, freed. This is one way to take the word *aśubha* in this verse.

There is another way of looking at *aśubha* here. As long as you have any doubts in your head, they gnaw you and create problems. They are like bugs with many wings and legs bustling around in your ears and creating a disturbance. Doubts, therefore, are called *aśubha*. They have to come to an end and they do so only when everything is understood clearly. What has to be understood here is the nature of *karma* and *akarma*.

We shall see that the understanding of *karma* itself is the understanding of *ātmā* and *anātmā*. In fact, a thorough understanding of any topic will always end up in *ātmā*. If you take any one thing – *śānti, sukha, duḥkha, jagat,* name, form, mind, its nature and so on – and analyse it, it will resolve into *ātmā*, which is why we can begin anywhere. Everything is connected; nothing is unconnected.

If you remove the doubts with reference to *karma*, you will remove *saṁsāra* for good. You are released from the doubts themselves and this release is the gain of *mokṣa*. When ignorance, the knot of the heart, is resolved, doubts fall apart. All the *karma*s standing in one's account are destroyed when Brahman, the *paramātmā*, that is Īśvara and *jīva*, is understood. And this happens in one stroke! 'In one stroke' should not be misunderstood to imply action. It all happens in terms of knowledge alone, the stroke of knowledge.

Verses 17&18

Kṛṣṇa explains why karma and akarma have to be known

कर्मणो ह्यपि बोद्धव्यं बोद्धव्यं च विकर्मणः ।
अकर्मणश्च बोद्धव्यं गहना कर्मणो गतिः ॥ १७ ॥

karmaṇo hyapi boddhavyaṁ boddhavyaṁ ca vikarmaṇaḥ
akarmaṇaśca boddhavyaṁ gahanā karmaṇo gatiḥ (17)

karmaṇaḥ – of actions; *api* – also; *boddhavyam* – is to be known; *vikarmaṇaḥ* – of the forbidden action; *ca* – and; *boddhavyam* – is to be known; *akarmaṇaḥ* – actionlessness; *ca* – and; *boddhavyam* – is to be known; *hi* – because; *karmaṇaḥ* – of *karma*; *gatiḥ* – nature; *gahanā* – (is) difficult (to understand)

Action (enjoined by the scriptures) is to be known. Forbidden action and actionlessness must also be known. (This is) because the nature of *karma* is difficult (to understand).

Here, Kṛṣṇa first divides *karma*, that is action in general, into two types – *karma*, action that is to be done, and *vikarma*, action that is not to be done. What is to be done must of course be known and what is not to be done must also be known. Furthermore, if you think that actionlessness, *akarma* is not doing *karma*, then *akarma* also has to be known. You must know what is meant by not doing *karma*. Is it the non-performance of action or is it the absence of doership? This you have to know. If *akarma* is the absence of doership, then the non-performance of a given action does not amount to *akarma*, as Kṛṣṇa himself would clarify later.

Why is this analysis needed? Because one should not take *karma* in a simplistic way. Nor is it easy to understand. People sometimes tell me, 'Swamiji, I have heard enough about *karma*. I want *jñāna*.' If *karma* were known by these people, they would have the knowledge, *jñāna*, too! *Karma* has to be known, but it is difficult to know, *gahanā*. The simple do's and don'ts are not what is to be known. What must be known is the very nature of *karma* itself.

Gahanā means that the subject matter of *karma* and *akarma* is shrouded in confusion. Because you do not see it clearly, you need to clear away the mist. And to do this, you have to bring in light. *Karma* is not as simple as you think. If you understand the nature of *karma*, you will understand reality,

Brahman, everything being connected as it is. To say that *karma* is to be known is to say that everything else connected with it has to be known also.

Thus, Kṛṣṇa introduces the subject matter of *karma* and *akarma* in this verse and the preceding one. The answer to the question, what is *karma* and what is *akarma*, is given in the next verse, along with some words in praise of the person who clearly understands action and actionlessness.

कर्मण्यकर्म यः पश्येदकर्मणि च कर्म यः ।
स बुद्धिमान् मनुष्येषु स युक्तः कृत्स्नकर्मकृत् ॥ १८ ॥

karmaṇyakarma yaḥ paśyed akarmaṇi ca karma yaḥ
sa buddhimān manuṣyeṣu sa yuktaḥ kṛtsnakarmakṛt (18)

yaḥ – the one who; *karmaṇi* – in action; *akarma* – actionlessness; *paśyet* – would see; *ca* – and; *yaḥ* – the one who; *akarmaṇi* – in actionlessness; *karma* – action; *paśyet* – would see; *saḥ* – that person; *manuṣyeṣu* – among human beings; *buddhimān* – wise; *saḥ* – that person; *yuktaḥ* – (is a) *yogī*; *kṛtsnakarmakṛt* – who has done everything that is to be done

The one who sees actionlessness in action and action in actionlessness is wise among human beings. That person is a *yogī*, who has done everything that is to be done.

Śaṅkara writes an extensive commentary, *bhāṣya*, on this verse, setting out the various arguments that are relevant to this important topic. In order to gain a clear understanding of *karma* and *akarma*, we will look into this particular *bhāṣya* in some detail.

It was said that even the informed are deluded with reference to the nature of action and inaction. *Karma* here means action in general and is not restricted to scripturally enjoined rituals, as it is elsewhere in the *Gītā*. Because even the learned are confused, Kṛṣṇa says he would reveal to Arjuna the nature of *karma*, which implies *akarma* also, knowing which he would be liberated from doubt, from *saṁsāra*.

What is to be done and what is not to be done are both considered to be *karma*, action. Killing, for example, and helping someone are two different actions. Killing is a prohibited action, *niṣiddha-karma* and helping another person is an enjoined action, *vihita-karma*.

A command, *vidhi*, is always with reference to an action, either to do it or not to do it. Because we may hurt another, the *śruti* enjoins us not to hurt anyone. 'May one not drink alcohol' and 'May one not eat meat' are also scriptural injunctions, the 'don'ts' with reference to the actions we perform. Similarly, there are a number of commands concerning the do's, the actions that are to be done. Thus, there is a list of do's and don'ts for people to follow, all of which are *karma*.

Akarma is also to be understood in terms of *karma*. Is *akarma* simply not doing action or is it something more? The very nature of action, its *svarūpa*, is what we are trying to understand here. Only when action is properly understood can we understand what non-action or the absence of action is.

People generally understand the absence of action as not doing action. If you do not do something, non-performance is the absence of action. When a man who is walking stops walking, the action of walking has stopped. There is a standstill, no action. But standing still is also an action. Try standing still and you will understand how difficult an action it is! Similarly, sitting still is an action, which is why you cannot do it for very long. To think that you are going to gain inaction by sitting still is to be deluded. There is no such inaction in fact.

To think that not performing action is inaction is no different than thinking that printing more currency will resolve a country's tight money situation. Such a simplistic approach cannot solve the problem and will create additional problems because it is not that easy. Similarly, to understand inaction is not as easy as it seems. What Kṛṣṇa says in this verse is in keeping with what he had said earlier in the second, third and fourth chapters. Although the present verse is very cryptic, it can be understood by keeping in mind what has gone before.

Here, Kṛṣṇa describes a person who could see inaction in action and action in inaction. What kind of a person is this? If he or she sees a man walking, does the person see him as standing still? And if he is standing still, does the person see him as walking? This is like watching someone eating and having the person tell you he or she is not eating at all. Usually, we would think that such a person was mentally deranged in some way. But here Kṛṣṇa says that one who sees action in inaction and inaction in action is a wise person, *buddhimān*.

Then, to top off the confusion, Kṛṣṇa goes on to say that such a person is a *kṛtsnakarmakṛt*, someone who has done everything that is to be done. It means that there is nothing more for this person to do. He or she is free, whereas for others there remains a long list of 'to be done' and 'not to be done.'

This list, as long as it exists, is unending because the items to be done and not to be done are difficult to fulfil. What you ought to do is not always possible to do. Nor can you always avoid doing or saying what is not to be done or said. Also, the to be done and not to be done goes on increasing. With reference to the food you eat or personal ambitions, for example, there are a number of things to be done and not to be done. So, everyone has a long list and even if some of the items are fulfilled, many others pop up in their place. Some items on the list are very clear to you, while others may be vague. Yet, they are there below the surface and will become clearer in time, like a Polaroid film. This is the situation for everyone.

Here, Kṛṣṇa describes the person who has managed to fulfil all the items on the list as being one who is able to see action in inaction and inaction in action. He praises such a person and refers to him or her as being wise, *buddhimān*! If seeing is all that one has to do to be wise, the seeing itself must be very difficult. The words themselves reveal the difficulty. How can you see action in inaction and inaction in action?

Inaction in action

In the expressions, 'inaction in action' and 'action in inaction,' the usual locative case meaning for the word 'in' does not apply here. When we say, 'Where is he sitting?' the response, 'on the ground,' denotes a location where the action of sitting is taking place. Similarly is the case with the statement, 'The book is in my hand.' However here, Śaṅkara dismisses any sense of location with reference to action and inaction, saying that action cannot become the location or the basis for inaction. Inaction being the absence of action, it is not there to be located upon action.

Inaction does not exist. We cannot say that a non-existent inaction sits upon action, just as we cannot talk about the horns that sit on our heads. Horns do not exist for us and what does not exist cannot be said to be sitting anywhere. Similarly, we cannot say that the *vandhyā-putra*, son of a woman who never gave birth to a child, is sitting on the ground because there is no such person.

In the same way, inaction being the absence of action does not exist for it to have any location. Therefore, action cannot be the basis for inaction. Nor inaction, which does not exist, be the basis for action. Therefore, the use of the locative case here is not to be taken in its usual sense. Rather, it means, 'with reference to.' With reference to action, this person is able to see inaction and with reference to inaction, he or she can see action.

In the absence of action, *karma abhāva*, the wise see action and in the so called action they see no action at all. When you perform an action, there is the notion, 'I perform an action, *ahaṁ karomi*.' What is involved in 'I perform an action'? What is this action that you are doing? When you say, 'I am talking' or 'I am walking,' the talking and the walking are actions centred on what? This is the question.

When you say, 'I walk,' your legs and feet are involved in the action of walking. The mind is also involved, since there has been a decision, a *saṅkalpa*, to perform the action of walking. Without a *saṅkalpa,* you do not perform a deliberate action. There is a thought, a desire, involved. So, in the action of walking, the mind is involved, the legs and feet are involved, and even the eyes are involved. And, when you say, 'I perform an action, *ahaṁ karomi,*' I, *aham,* is also involved.

In this process, the mind, senses and the physical body are all involved. The physical body is called *kārya* in Sanskrit, meaning 'product,' and the mind and senses are called *karaṇa,* meaning 'instrument.' This assemblage of *kārya* and *karaṇa* is involved in the action that belongs to you. That is why you say, 'I perform this action.' The 'I' is also implied in action, 'I' meaning *ātmā*.

The results of action belong to the doer

Why do I perform action? For a certain result. And when the result comes, to whom does it go? Whom does it affect? It comes to me, the one who is the *kartā*, the doer. Therefore, as the doer, I am the enjoyer. I perform this action for the sake of getting the desired result, *karma-phala-bhogāya aham idaṁ karomi*. In this way we see that action involves the *kārya-karaṇa-saṅghāta*, the physical body-mind-sense complex, and also *aham*, I, the *ātmā*.

When I say, 'I am the doer,' 'I am the enjoyer,' etc., on whom is the doership and enjoyership centred? It is centred on myself. Then a question arises, 'Is the I, the *ātmā*, a *kartā*, doer, or *akartā* a non-doer?' If *ātmā* is *kartā*, then I definitely perform action, *karma*, which produces a result for me. This is real *karma*, binding *karma*.

No action is possible without there being an agent, doer, of the action, a *kartā*. For example, when we say, 'Rāma goes, *rāmaḥ gacchati*,' the going is done by Rāma, the agent of the action of going. Although action is dependent on its agent, the agent is not dependent on action. It means that the agent, the doer, has a choice in terms of action – he or she can perform an action, need not perform the action, or can perform the action differently. This independent doer, the *kartā* who enjoys such freedom in terms of action, is what is reflected by the first or nominative case in Sanskrit, *prathama-kāraka*.

There are a number of factors, other than agency, that are also connected to action. Whatever is connected to an action, because of which the action is made possible, is called *kāraka*. There are six kinds of *kāraka*s, the agent of the action being the first, the *prathama-kāraka*, as we saw above. Then there is the object of an action. When Rāma goes, *rāmaḥ gacchati*, where does he go? He goes to the forest, *vanaṁ gacchati*, forest being the object of the action of Rāma's going. Thus, we have a doer and an object of doing, *kartā* and *karma*, referred to grammatically as the nominative and accusative, first and second cases. Then, how does Rāma go to the forest? Does he go on foot or does he go in a chariot? What is the means of his going? The means by which he goes, on foot, is the third *kāraka*, instrumental case. And why does he go? What is the purpose of his going? Rāma went to the forest to fulfil the words of his father, *pitṛ-vākya-*

paripālanāya, giving us the fourth *kāraka*, dative case. From where does he go, from which place? From the city of Ayodhyā, *ayodhyā-nagarāt*, he went to the forest. This gives us the fifth *kāraka*, ablative case, since it is also connected to the verb, the action of going. The final *kāraka* is the locative case, as in 'Rāma lived in the forest, *rāmaḥ vane avasat*.' Here forest is in the seventh case expressing location.

Not doing karma also requires a doer

Returning to the first *kāraka*, the *kartā*, Śaṅkara says that whether you say, 'I did this action' or 'I did not do this action,' the I, the *ahaṅkāra*, is involved. Both, *pravṛtti*, the doing, and *nivṛtti*, the not doing, are centred on *ahaṅkāra*, the *kartā*. Therefore, if I am the *kartā*, I am the *kartā* in both action as well as inaction.

However, if I am not the *kartā*, then there is no action at all for me because all action depends upon the *kartā*. If I am someone who is not an actor, then I perform no action, *na kiñcit karma karomi*. The 'I' is always free from action; it does not do any action. *Ātmā* neither does action nor impels or prompts anything to act, *na karoti na kārayati*.

Mistaking action for inaction and inaction for action

If *ātmā* is neither a simple *kartā* nor a *kārayitā*, one who causes action to be done, how can there be any *karma*? And if there is no *karma*, why does Kṛṣṇa simply not say so? Why does he talk about seeing inaction in action, *karmaṇi akarma yaḥ paśyet*? Śaṅkara says, the problem is that we superimpose *kartṛtva* on the *ātmā,* which is really *akartā* and say, 'I do this action or that action,' when really the action belongs to the *kārya-karaṇa-saṅghāta*. To illustrate this problem, Śaṅkara gives an example that everyone can relate to.

When you are in a boat moving in a river, you see the trees on the river's bank moving in the opposite direction. Even though you are moving in one direction, the trees seem to be moving in the other and you seem to be constant. What does this mean? The trees are not really moving at all. They are not performing any action. But, in these trees that are really standing still, you see an action, *akarmaṇi karma-darśanam*. This kind of seeing is called *viparīta-darśana,* erroneous sight.

As long as 'I am the *kartā*' notion is there, not doing any action does not make you an *akartā*. Therefore, whenever you say, 'I am sitting quietly, I am not doing any action, *ahaṁ tūṣṇīm āsam na kiñcit karomi*' you consider yourself to be a *kartā*. Therefore, you are doing the action of 'not doing any action.' To illustrate this, Śaṅkara gives the following example. Suppose you are standing on the riverbank and looking at the boat that is moving away from you. Having reached a distance, the boat seems not to be moving at all. To you it appears stationary. Thus an object can also appear to be constant when it is actually moving very fast. An example of this, one not available to Śaṅkara in his time, is a movie on a screen. Although it is a movie, a succession of rapidly moving frames, things like trees, mountains and so on appear to you to be stationary. Here you see inaction in action, *karmaṇi akarma-darśanam*.

So, in the world, we see *karma* in *akarma* and *akarma* in *karma*. Similarly, with reference to *karma* and *akarma* themselves, there is *viparīta darśana*, seeing what is not there. *Darśana* means sight, seeing, and *viparīta* means other than what is. The self does not perform any action and therefore, there is no action. The action you see is really inaction. In other words, there is no action in action because *ātmā* is *akartā*.

Knowing this, the wise person performs action but, at the same time, knows he does not perform it at all. Doing, the person does not do, *kurvan na karoti*. Seeing, the person does not see, *paśyan na paśyati*. Hearing, the person does not hear, *śṛṇvan na śṛṇoti*. Similarly, smelling, one does not smell; tasting, one does not taste; walking, one does not walk; talking, one does not talk; thinking, one does not think.

Even being confused, the person is not confused. A wise person can be confused in that his or her mind can become confused with reference to a particular thing. For instance, there may be confusion about the direction to be taken in order to reach a place. So, 'Being confused, the person is not confused,' does not mean that the wise do not get confused. What does it mean? For the wise, the 'I,' the *ātmā*, in the statement, 'I am confused,' remains untouched by any action because it does not perform any action.

If a man is acting, we say he is acting and if he is not, we say he is keeping quiet. But is there really a time when he is not doing action? Keeping quiet simply means the person does not have a job. And he may not even keep quiet. He may talk a lot, eat as much, hang around, and, at the same time, he says he is keeping quiet!

Therefore, not doing anything is definitely an action and for that action there is an agent, a doer, a *kartā*. Because people think they do action, they also think they do not do action. It is because both action, *pravṛtti,* and non-action, *nivṛtti,* are attributed to *ātmā* instead of the *kartā,* which is superimposed, *āropita,* upon the *ātmā.* So, *ātmā* is taken to be the *kartā,* and the doing or not doing of an action, centred on that *kartā,* is mistakenly attributed to *ātmā.*

At the same time, no action is totally independent of *ātmā.* In *ātmā,* there is no action whatsoever. Because people do not know this, they are under the spell of delusion, ignorance, seeing action in inaction and inaction in action.

One who is able to see *ātmā* as *akartā* never performs any action, even when he does an action, *karma.* Such a person will see *akarma* in *karma* because he knows that *ātmā* does not perform any action whatsoever.

The nature of ātmā

The nature of *ātmā,* the self, is in the form of pure consciousness. The very word 'self' implies that it does not need to be revealed to you by anything else. You require no means of knowledge, *pramāṇa,* to prove your existence. That which requires no *pramāṇa,* which is self-evident, is the self, *ātmā.* And what is its nature? It is in the form of pure consciousness, knowledge as such. Because *ātmā* is unqualified knowledge, there can be particular knowledge, which is nothing but consciousness plus some qualification that appears in the form of the particular object of knowledge.

Knowledge as such must be there before it can be qualified. For example, for there to be pot-knowledge, *ghaṭa-jñāna*, cloth-knowledge, *paṭa-jñāna*, man-knowledge, *puruṣa-jñāna* or woman-knowledge, *strī-jñāna*, there must be knowledge as such, unqualified by anything. This unqualified knowledge is the nature of the *ātmā*. Knowledge as such gets seemingly qualified in the form of thought, *vṛtti*. With *vṛtti*, knowledge seems to be qualified and without *vṛtti*, it is unqualified. This unqualified knowledge is consciousness, the nature of *ātmā* that performs no action.

Why do we say that *ātmā* performs no action? One reason is that action implies motion or some change. Try to think of an action without motion or change. Any motion or change from one condition to another, from one form to another, is action. Even a chemical reaction is an action. But can we say that *ātmā*, whose nature is consciousness, is subject to action?

Consciousness is not subject to motion because being all pervasive, it is not located at one point for it to move to another point. Consciousness does not move within itself either. Nor does it have any part to undergo any change, consciousness not being an assemblage of things. Only that which is put together can undergo change. Things that are put together will naturally fall apart without anything being done. It is their nature to fall apart, which is also an action. A car that is kept unused for twenty five years will undergo some change; even a Rolls Royce is no exception. Whether the car is running or not, it is subject to change simply because it was put together, *saṁhatatvāt*. There is always entropy for things that are put together.

A good way to understand entropy is to leave your room as it is for some time without doing anything about it. Just live in it; do not sweep the floor, do not clean, do not put anything back in its own place. What will you have? Entropy.[9] Anything that is put together tends to dissipate, to fall into disorder. This movement from order to disorder is entropy, which is also action. Only the self is not subject any entropy.

Consciousness, the nature of 'I,' the self, does not tend towards disorder because there is no order, *ātmā* not being made up of parts. Only when there is creation, is there an order and therefore, disorder. *Ātmā* is one whole, limitless in nature. *Ātmā* being not limited in any way, what can it do? It cannot go anywhere because it is not limited place wise. It cannot change or modify itself into anything. It cannot grow into something or dissolve into something. No action is possible for *ātmā*.

There is not even *saṅkalpa*, decision, in *ātmā*. Nor is there any kind of thought, which is also action. To say, 'I remain quiet,' means there are other times when one is not quiet. Consciousness does not say this because consciousness is always quiet, *nirvikalpa*. It undergoes no modification, *vikalpa*, whatsoever. Because there is nothing that is separate from consciousness, *vikalpa* is not possible. There is no such thing as the self going into something or reaching out to the world. It has already reached out to the infinite. It is one whole, free from all limitation, in the form of pure, simple consciousness.

---

[9] Inevitable and steady deterioration of a system or society

Ātmā performs no action nor does it prompt something else to perform action, and in its presence alone, all activities take place.

When there is an action in the mind, senses or the body, there is the presence of *ātmā*, the *kartā* being nothing but *ātmā*. *Ātmā* is not the *kartā*, but when the *kartā* is there, *ātmā* is there. 'I am not the *kartā* is a fact that is not known. I know myself only as the *kartā* – I am the seer, hearer, thinker, doubter and so on. I know that I am the doer of all these actions. But I do not know that I am *akartā*, non-doer. Not knowing I am *akartā*, the *kartā* naturally becomes 'I' for me and 'I' becomes the *kartā*. In fact, the *kartā* is, 'I,' but 'I' is not the *kartā*. The problem occurs when the *kartā* is 'I' and 'I' also is the *kartā*. This happens when the 'I' is not known.

A person who knows the self sees inaction in action and action in inaction, which is other than that what we generally understand by *akarma*, and *karma*. Because doership, *kartṛtva*, is there, *akarma* is reduced to *karma*, there being a *kartā*, an agent, for *akarma* also. The person who says, 'I do not do any action,' is doing action because there is doership and the person takes himself or herself to be a doer of 'no action.' As long as the *kartā* is there, *karma* is also there for the person, be it *pravṛtti* or *nivṛtti* action or inaction. Both belong to the *kartā* alone.

The one who sees things as they are has wisdom

If the person knows I am not the *kartā*, he sees *akarma* in both *karma* and the so called *akarma*. Kṛṣṇa says that the one who sees *ātmā*, the self, as one that is free from *kartṛtva*, doership is a *buddhimān*.

The literal meaning of *buddhimān* is one who has an intellect, *buddhi*, just as *dehavān* refers to one who has a physical body, *deha*. But everyone has a *buddhi*. Why, then, does Kṛṣṇa call this person a *buddhimān*? *Buddhi* has to be understood here as wisdom in the form of self-knowledge. Thus, the one who has *buddhi* has the knowledge of the self and is therefore, wise, *buddhimān*.

Wisdom is seeing things as they are. One who sees things as they are, in terms of reality, has wisdom and is therefore wise. Wisdom does not mean that the person has generated a new line of thinking. Here, Kṛṣṇa refers to a person who is able to see *karma* and *akarma* as they really are as a *buddhimān*, a wise person among human beings, *saḥ buddhimān manuṣyeṣu*.

Kṛṣṇa also calls this person a *yogī* – *saḥ yuktaḥ*, meaning that he or she has lived a life of *yoga*, which has paid off in terms of wisdom. *Yoga* being meant for gaining this knowledge, and such a person living a life of *karma-yoga*, has gained what it had to offer him. He is a real *karma-yogī*, an accomplished *yogī*. Understanding what is to be understood, he or she is a person of fulfilment, *kṛtsna karmakṛt*.

Saṁsāra – the orbit of action and result

To know oneself as *akartā* is to know oneself as *abhoktā*, one who is not an enjoyer. If you are not the enjoyer of the results of any action, then there is no *puṇya* or *pāpa* for you. And when there is no *puṇya* or *pāpa*, there is no *sukha* or *duḥkha*, meaning that you are above *sukha* and *duḥkha*. *Sukha* and *duḥkha*, being the net result of *karma*, are also *karma-phala*, the result of action. You may have performed certain *karma* and received some money. Because of that money you have a big house, you are very comfortable and happy. Being comfortable, being happy, is a *karma-phala* for you.

Duḥkha is also a *karma-phala*. The house you bought turned out to be in a bad neighbourhood. You were happy with the house until it was broken into and you were robbed. No matter how many new alarm systems you install, the results are the same, frequent robberies and vandalism. So the same house that made you *sukhī* for some time has now made you *duḥkhī*, unhappy. Either way it is all *karma-phala*, *puṇya* and *pāpa*. You asked for it and you got it!

Because all unseen results, *puṇya* and *pāpa*, fructify in the form of *sukha* and *duḥkha,* all *karma*s are capable of producing *sukha* and *duḥkha* for the *kartā*. As long as you take yourself to be the *kartā*, you are subject to *sukha* and *duḥkha*. To be subject to *sukha* and *duḥkha* is *saṁsāra*. *Sukha* and *duḥkha* themselves are not *saṁsāra*. The notion that you are subject to them is *saṁsāra* and makes you a *saṁsārī*.

That the physical body is subject to pain is a fact. But if you say, 'I am subject to pain' there is *saṁsāra*. 'I am subject to pain' is different from 'the physical body is subject to pain.' If you say the body is subject to pain, it is a simple truth because it states a fact about the empirical world; the creation is like that. The body is endowed with the sensation of pain as a means of protection. Otherwise, you would not pay attention to it. Pain indicates that something is wrong and needs attending to. Therefore, physical pain is an important part of the creation.

That the body is subject to pain is true. 'I am subject to pain' is a notion which is *saṁsāra*. It is not true because *ātmā* is not the enjoyer of the results of action, *karma-phala-bhoktā*. *Ātmā* is not the enjoyer because it is not the *kartā*, the doer. One who knows that he or she is not the enjoyer is called *kṛtsna-karmakṛt* here. When one is able to recognise oneself as free from doership, he or she also becomes free from enjoyership.

Being free from enjoyership means the *puṇya* and *pāpa* standing in one's account are taken care of. Such a person who is free from a sense of doership and enjoyership is called a *kṛtsna-karmakṛt*. For him, everything that has to be done now or later has been done. No new incarnation has to be taken by the person. No *karma* remains to prompt another birth. In this life too, whatever the person thought he or she would do is gone because the person is *ānanda, pūrṇa*, fullness. He or she is above *sukha* and *duḥkha*, liberated from the subjugation of *karma*, and therefore, *kṛtsna-karmakṛt*.

One who is *kṛtsna-karmakṛt* sees very clearly that there is no action whatsoever in action, *karmaṇi akarma-darśanam*, and that there is action in inaction, *akarmaṇi karma-darśanam*. In his understanding, inaction, *akarma*, the so called absence of action, is converted into action because of the presence of the *kartā*. The one who says, 'I perform this action,' is also the one who says, 'I do not perform this action.' To say, 'I do not perform this action,' does not mean there is no action because this particular inactivity is dependent upon or is centred on the *kartā*, the doer.

Kartṛtva is a notion – 'I am the doer, *ahaṁ kartā*.' Because this notion is there, the person says, 'I do not perform this action now,' which does not mean that he or she does not perform any action at all. While the person may not perform certain actions, he or she continues to perform some action or the other. No one can remain, even for a second, performing no action whatsoever, as we saw in verse five in the third chapter.[10] Therefore, it is impossible for anyone to say, 'I am not doing any action.'

Even making such a statement is acting because speaking is an action. A person who says, 'I perform no action at all. I am keeping quiet,' is performing the action of speaking. There is no such thing as inaction in the sense of a total absence of activity. When Kṛṣṇa says that the wise person is able to see action in inaction, he means that the person does not see inaction as an absence of action. What the person is able to see in action is freedom from action, not the absence of action. In the absence of action, there is action and even in that action, the wise person, *buddhimān*, is able to see a freedom from action.

The *buddhimān* has the wisdom, the *buddhi*, that enables him or her to see inaction in action because the person sees *ātmā* as *akartā*. Thus, there is the recognition of the fact that the self is not an actor in any way whatsoever. The self does not perform any action, and in its presence all activities take place.

The problem here is that all actions are centred on the *kartā*, the actor. Only when the *kartā* is there, there is the possibility of action. Therefore, all actions emanate from the *kartā*, which

---

[10] न हि कश्चित् क्षणमपि जातु तिष्ठत्यकर्मकृत्।

is not separate from *aham*, I, the *ātmā*. The problem comes because the person thinks that he or she is the *kartā*. This thinking, this particular notion, is the only evil there is. If at all there is such a thing as original sin, it is only in the notion, 'I am the *kartā*,' because from this all problems arise.

'I am the *kartā*' is a notion and it is this notion that binds a person to *karma*. Why? Because the one who is the enjoyer of the result of action is the one who performed the action, *kartā eva bhoktā bhavati*. When I perform an action, a result accrues. And this result accrues to me, the *kartā* alone. In this way, I am bound by the results of my actions and thus by the actions themselves. Even a person who makes money and distributes it to others, leaving none for himself or herself accrues the result of a good action. People rightly exalt such a person, which is a *karma-phala* that belongs only to the person who distributed the money. But the person is still a *kartā* to whom *karma-phala* accrues because of which he or she is also an enjoyer.

Karma and its results, *karma-phala*, are the cause for *saṁsāra*. They account for all of one's problems. The results of *karma*, in the form of *puṇya* and *pāpa* according to this particular model, account for one's incarnation also. We have seen that *karma* is born out of desire, *kāma*, and is therefore, nothing but an expression of desire in the form of likes and dislikes, *rāga-dveṣas*. Although *saṁsāra* is accounted for by *karma-phala*, *karma-phala* itself is only possible because there is *karma*, which in turn is possible because there is *kāma*, desire. And for whom is the *kāma*? The *kartā*. Therefore, *kartā* is the cause for all the *karmas* and *karma-phalas*. And because of ignorance, one takes oneself to be the *kartā*.

The problem here is that if you are really a *kartā*, you have no way of getting out of *saṁsāra*. You are in its orbit, the orbit of action and its results, *karma-cakra*. Because of *karma-phala*, there is birth, *janma*, and because of birth there is *karma* to perform, if you are able to gain a human body or its equivalent. Then you perform new *karma*s and gather more *karma-phala*s, thereby perpetuating the cycle. Because of *karma* there is *karma-phala*, because of *karma-phala* there is *janma*, because of *janma* there is *karma*, and because of *karma* there is *karma-phala* – an orbit you will continue to be in as long as you take yourself to be the *kartā*.

There is no way of getting out of this *saṁsāra-cakra*, wheel of *saṁsāra*, this unless you get out of the orbit of *karma* – *karma-phala* – *janma* – *karma*. And how do you get out? The only way is to nullify the *kartṛtva*, doership. If the doership is real, you will not be able to nullify it because anything real cannot be nullified. By the same reasoning, if doership can be nullified, it is not real.

How to get out of the orbit of *saṁsāra*?

There is an argument that suggests that by performing only good *karma*s, a person will be liberated from *saṁsāra*. It cannot be true. To perform only good *karma*s means that all the actions done by a person have to be good. There would be no wrong actions at all. This is not possible at all as we shall see later. A person doing only good actions will gain only *puṇya*. But gaining any amount of *puṇya* will not release the person from this cycle. *Puṇya* being *karma-phala*, the person with a lot of *puṇya* will have lot of births and maybe with a lot of comforts. And the tendency of a person who has more and more comforts, in the form of money and power, for example, is eventually towards wrong actions.

More the money a person gathers, more the power he or she may have, and power tends to corrupt the person who has it. If by having gathered so much *puṇya*, a person could conceivably gain absolute power, then he or she may become absolutely corrupt. Absolute corruption will then result in the accrual of *pāpa*, for which more births are gained.

Furthermore, it is impossible for a person to perform only good actions, *puṇya-karma*. No one can avoid doing *pāpa-karma* at some time or the other. All it takes is one unconscious swatting of a mosquito! Unknowingly, you are destroying millions of bacteria everyday. Nor are all the varieties of *pāpa-karma* known to you; some are unknown too. Therefore, you cannot avoid doing *pāpa-karma* altogether.

Even if you could do nothing but *puṇya-karma*, you would not get out of the orbit of *saṁsāra*. *Karma* itself keeps the *saṁsāra* going. Only when the *kartā* is not there, will there be the absence of *karma* for you. And, if the *kartā* is a reality, *karma* will definitely be there.

However, the *kartā* is not absolutely real; it is only a superimposition upon the *ātmā*, which is absolutely real. It means that while the *kartā*, the doer, is *ātmā*, 'I,' 'I,' *ātmā* is not the doer. This being so, *kartṛtva*, doership, becomes *mithyā* having no independent existence, because it depends upon 'I' whereas, 'I,' the *ātmā*, does not depend on doership. It is *satya*.

The definition of mithyā and satya

Anything that does not exist on its own, that depends for its existence upon something else, that draws flesh and blood from something else for it to exist, is called *mithyā*. That which does not depend upon anything else in order to exist, is *satya*.

In terms of reality, then, a shirt becomes *mithyā* and the cloth it is made of becomes *satya*. The cloth itself becomes *mithyā* and the yarn that makes up the cloth becomes *satya*. The yarn becomes *mithyā* and its fibres become *satya*. The fibres become *mithyā* and the particles that make up the fibres become *satya*. The particles become *mithyā* and the concept becomes *satya*. The concept becomes *mithyā* and *ātmā* becomes *satya*. At this point, a question may arise, if *ātmā* becomes *mithyā*? This question is not valid because the entire enquiry is possible only because there is an *ātmā*, which is *satya*, that which is not negatable.

I am neither the doer nor the enjoyer

Consciousness that is self-evident *ātmā* does not need to be revealed by anything else. The self alone is self-evident and everything else is evident to the self, *ātmā*, that is not the *kartā*. The *kartā* is something that comes and goes. For instance, there is no *kartṛtva*, doership, in deep sleep. Since I am always there, self-evident, if I am the *kartā*, then the *kartā* should not come and go. I should always be the *kartā*. If I am an enjoyer, *bhoktā*, I should always be *bhoktā*. But, this is not so. Sometimes I am *kartā* and sometimes I am *bhoktā*. It means that I am neither *kartā* nor *bhoktā*.

Kartā appears when the mind, *antaḥ-karaṇa*, is there. Doership, *kartṛtva*, means the status of being the subject with reference to any type of activity, whether it is mental activity like perception, inference and thinking, or physical activity. For any activity, a subject is always necessary and this subject is called the ego, *ahaṅkāra* or *kartā*. The word 'ego' must be understood well because there are a number of problems associated with its general use.

Ego is that which owns up to any type of activity. For instance, when I see, I say 'This is my sight.' The one who owns up to the activity of seeing, the one who is the subject behind the seeing or behind hearing, tasting, smelling, thinking, or doing anything, is what is meant by the ego, *kartā* or *ahaṅkāra*.

Surrender is an attitude

To say that one should surrender one's ego to the Lord is a very common statement that is too simplistic in terms of understanding what is meant by surrender. First of all, I do not know who or what the Lord is. So why should I surrender the only ego that I have to this Lord? As it is, I have only a few things and these things are owned by this ego. If I surrender it to the Lord, what will I get in return? 'Everything,' I am told.

The question that would arise would be, 'If the ego is already surrendered, who will get everything?' Once I have surrendered my ego, I become totally decimated. Then who is there to get anything out of that surrender? Nobody. Therefore, that type of surrender is useless. Also, the next question is, 'Who is surrendering the ego?' Somebody has to do the surrendering. It is the ego that has to surrender itself. And that is not possible. Again, if I am wearing a coat, I can surrender the coat. I can hang it somewhere or put it on someone's shoulders. Also, when I am the owner of the coat, it is easy to surrender it. If I am not the owner of the coat, I can ask you to take it, but I cannot surrender it because it does not belong to me.

Similarly, I am told that the *ahaṅkāra*, the ego, belongs to the Lord and that I must surrender it. How can I surrender what does not belong to me? I can only surrender what belongs to me. And if it belongs to the Lord, how is it that I do not know this? In fact, I think that everything belongs to me, including the Lord. Why else would I address him as 'My Lord'? To address the Lord, I must be there; because I am here, he is the Lord. If I am not here, where is the Lord? He is the Lord because I call him 'Lord'!

And if there is a Lord, and this Lord includes everything, then I have nothing to surrender. I have only to know. Furthermore, if I have to surrender to a Lord who is separate from me, then I am the ego. Who is to surrender this ego? The ego alone has to surrender. How can the ego surrender? The one who surrenders is the ego. And being the one who surrenders, the ego can only surrender what it owns. The owner cannot be surrendered. If the ego has to surrender to the Lord, something else must be there to surrender it, which can only be another ego because whoever owns up to the act of surrender is the ego. The ego requires an ego which requires yet another ego! Thus, we find ourselves in infinite regression. How, then, are we going to surrender our ego to the Lord?

Surrender is an attitude, a mature attitude. There is no other surrender than this. Surrender as such is not possible for the ego because it cannot surrender itself. But, with an attitude of surrender, I can deflate the ego. I can appreciate that there is nothing in this creation that is authored by me, that everything is given to me, including my physical body, mind, and senses. What is given to me is not mine. When I say, 'I am just a trustee, O Lord, and you are the giver,' the ego is what tells me all this. Thus, surrender can be only in terms of attitude.

Then how does one get rid of *saṁsāra*? Only by getting rid of the ego, the *kartā*. And, if surrender is not possible, how does one get rid of the ego? In the name of getting rid of everything else, the ego remains in one form or the other because it cannot get rid of itself. It remains to say things like, 'I am the most charitable person around.' Even a person who does not talk about his or her good actions, may think of himself or herself as a humble person and say, 'I never mention all of the charities I have done. I do not boast about them. Ask anyone and they will tell you that it is so.' The ego knows very well how to sustain and perpetuate itself in so many ways.

Because the ego, the *kartā*, is always there in one form or the other, it cannot be defeated, except by the one who undertakes an enquiry into 'Who am I.' A person can study every philosophy there is and the ego will remain, saying, 'I am a philosopher.' Only when the question, 'Who am I,' is asked, is the ego in trouble. Why? Because the ego, the *kartā*, is really an impostor, a superimposition. There is no *kartṛtva*, doership, in fact, because it is *mithyā* dependent on *ātmā*.

The destruction of self-ignorance through knowledge

When the truth of oneself is recognised, the ego does not go, strictly speaking. Rather, this recognition is what makes one see the ego as *mithyā*. The 'going' of the ego, then, is purely in terms of negation, *bādhā*, or destruction, *nāśa*, by knowledge. The word 'destruction' is generally used in a physical sense where an object no longer exists in that form. Here, destruction of the ego is purely in terms of negation, *bādhā*.

Negation by knowledge occurs when an object is there, but its reality is taken away. For instance, you can enjoy the blue sky and, at the same time, knowing that the sky is not really blue, dismiss its blueness. Or, enjoying a movie, you can dismiss its reality. A child, on the other hand, cannot dismiss the movie as unreal because, for the child, the elephants, tigers and everything in the movie are real. The child may even cry, not knowing that the objects and situations in the movie are only appearances and therefore, *mithyā*. Until the child knows the movie is *mithyā*, the movie will remain real. This knowing comes by negation, *bādhā*, understanding an object or situation and removing the reality of it.

Similarly, the ego is not removed, but the fact that it has no independent existence is understood. And what does the ego that everyone has, depend upon? What is it that exists independently without depending on the ego upon which everything else depends? The ego depends for its existence on the self, which is not the ego. Therefore, the truth of every ego and everything that is done by the ego, is *satya*, *ātmā* or the self. The self is the very content of the ego, without which there is no ego. This *satya, ātmā,* is not the ego and is *akartā*. Then who is the *kartā*? The ego alone is the *kartā*.

To be a *kartā*, you must have thought and this thought has its being in 'I,' consciousness. Therefore, you say, 'I am the doer.' Doership itself is a thought centred on 'I.' What is to be understood here is that while thought is centred on 'I,' 'I' itself is not centred on thought. Recognition of this fact is not the elimination or removal of thought. It is understanding – understanding the truth of 'I.'

You may ask, 'How does the ego know the *ātmā*? The ego generally knows everything else, but how can it know *ātmā*, *ātmā* not being an object of the ego?' In response to this question, there are those who will say, 'The *ātmā* will transcend the ego and you will know.' But what does transcending the ego mean? Does the ego go away? Does it come back?

If the ego goes away, there is no one there. And, if having transcended the ego, the ego does not come back, who will be there to know the *ātmā*? If such were the case, gaining this knowledge would amount to becoming a vegetable! If the ego is transcended in order to know *ātmā*, it is definitely not going to come back. Therefore, this explanation is not acceptable.

If you transcend the ego, understand the *ātmā*, and the ego comes back, who is it that who understood the *ātmā*? It is the ego that has to understand the *ātmā*. These kind of statements about surrendering the ego and transcending the ego in order to understand the *ātmā* are very confusing to people. Unfortunately, they are too often to be found in the modern books on Vedanta and must, therefore, be seen for what they are.

In fact, the ego, *ahaṅkāra*, alone uses the *pramāṇa*, the means of knowledge available – perception, inference and so on. The ego uses perception and, analysing the data gathered by perception, gains inferential understanding also. Thus, perception and inference are in the hands of *ahaṅkāra*, the *kartā*, the subject who, wielding these two instruments of knowledge, perceives and infers.

The *kartā*, subject is the one who employs a means of knowledge. Therefore, in the employment of any means of knowledge there is a subject, *kartā*; an instrument, *karaṇa*; action, *kriyā*; and the result of action, *karma-phala*. Whether a piece of knowledge or an action produces a result, there is always a *kartā* behind it.

Perception and inference, wielded by the ego, are not going to help you know *ātmā* because *ātmā* is the very essence of the ego. *Ātmā* is that which is behind the ego, meaning it is the truth of the ego. How, then, is the *ātmā* to be known?

This is where *āgama-pramāṇa*, revelation in the form of words, *śabda*, comes in. When *śabda* is the *pramāṇa*, the means of knowledge, the ego does not do anything. What happens is that *śabda* creates a thought, a *vṛtti*, showing you that you are the *ātmā* that is Brahman, and not the ego. The consciousness that is *ātmā*, which is limitless, is you. This is the teaching, the *upadeśa*, and it removes your ignorance of yourself.

A person who takes himself or herself to be the ego thinks, 'I am only this much.' Nothing more is known about oneself than this. This ignorance, because of which the ego is there, is destroyed by the *vṛtti*, 'I am Brahman,' born of the teaching.

With the destruction of this ignorance, the notion that 'I am the ego,' disappears. Nothing more is necessary.

What happens to the ego in the wake of self-knowledge? Even though the ego comes and goes, you are no longer the ego because ignorance about the *ātmā* has already been destroyed. You know that the ego is *ātmā,* whereas *ātmā* is not the ego. Knowing this, you do not get lost in or caught up by the ego and its activities.

The knowledge of *ātmā,* once gained, is never lost because you have no more ignorance about *ātmā.* Even if the ego comes, *ātmā* cannot be mistaken as the ego anymore. Ego is *ātmā,* but *ātmā* does not become the ego just because the ego is, or because there is a perception or an inference is made, an action is done or a result is gained; just because something happens, *ātmā* does not become the ego. Everything is *ātmā* – *ātmā eva idaṁ sarvam,* while *ātmā* is not any of them.

When any action is done, the ego is there, but *ātmā* is free from all action because it is not the ego. Similarly, the means of doing an action or its result is also *ātmā,* whereas *ātmā* is neither the means, the doing, nor the result. This truth being known, the person sees actionlessness in action, *karmaṇi akarma darśanam.*

Knowledge is the only way to destroy ignorance about *ātmā. Āgama* alone, knowledge in the form of words alone, destroys the ego because you are not really wielding a *pramāṇa* here. Rather, you are exposing yourself to the *pramāṇa,* to the words revealing Brahman, like *Brahmāstra.* In the *Rāmāyaṇa,* Rāma used the *Brahmāstra* to kill Rāvaṇa. *Astra* means a weapon that leaves your hand and *śastra* is that which remains in your hand. So too, the various forms of practice such as prayers, rituals, and so on, are the *śāstras*, whereas the statement, '*tat tvam asi*, you are that,' is the *astra*. It comes from a teacher and hits you. It is intended to hit you, in fact. The statement comes out like a bullet and hits the exposed ego, causing it to die.

When the ego gets exposed to the teaching, '*tat tvam asi*,' it naturally dies like even the many headed demon, Rāvaṇa when he was shot by the *Brahmāstra*. '*Tat tvam asi*,' the *Brahmāstra*, destroys the ego called Rāvaṇa once and for all. Rāma tried various methods to destroy his enemy Rāvaṇa; but nothing happened. He would remove one head, but by the time he destroyed the second head, the first one was back again. This is like trying to remove all our desires. Just when we think one is gone, we find that another one has popped up in its place. Finally, Rāma was told to use the *Brahmāstra*. Only then did Rāvaṇa die, and only then did Rāma get back his joy, Sītā.

When the weapon '*tat tvam asi*' is used against the exposed ego, it is destroyed. Thus, you need not do anything except expose yourself to the teaching. The difference between employing perception and inference and exposing yourself to the teaching is what distinguishes this particular means of knowledge from all others. Exposing yourself to the teaching is lending yourself to an entirely different type of *pramāṇa* operation. It comes from outside and destroys the ego by saying that you are Brahman. For this, no action is performed. You need to just expose yourself to the *pramāṇa* with *śraddhā*, faith, that the *pramāṇa* will give you self-knowledge. *Śraddhā* is not doing anything and, at the same time, being totally alive to the *pramāṇa,* having abandoned prejudices about you, the world and God; in fact, it is *śraddhā* that grants you this type of exposure. It is the attitude behind the exposure that brings you the knowledge. And against this knowledge, the ego is helpless because it is an error that has been corrected by knowledge.

Knowledge and error cannot co-exist

No error is capable of standing as a co-existent partner to knowledge because knowledge and error cannot co-exist. Nor can the error come back once knowledge has taken place. The object of error cannot return to the same locus where knowledge already is.

You may question this statement using the rope snake example. You may mistake a piece of rope for a snake and remove the error by seeing that the snake is actually a rope. But the very next day, you may again make the same error. This is possible because the existence of both the rope and the snake depends on a means of knowledge, your perception. And because the defect in your perception can occur again, the error can also occur again. Whereas, the existence of *ātmā* does not depend on any *pramāṇa*. It is not that the self is first seen by you and then recognised, like in the rope snake. The self always is. Once the ignorance about the nature of the self is removed, there is no question of ignorance coming back.

With reference to objects, out of sight can be out of mind. But *ātmā* is never out of sight or out of mind. You may be out of mind, but you can never be out of *ātmā*, the self. This self is not what is meant when people talk about the psychological self, biological self, anatomical self, familial self, or genetic self. These are subject to defects of every kind such as genetic, pathological, physiological, and mental. Therefore, such a self is always unacceptable to you. Even anatomically you cannot accept yourself. Your nose is not of the right shape, your hair is not of the right colour and so on. But this is not what we are discussing here. The self is different from all of this.

Everything is the self and, therefore, there is no way of being out of yourself. When the ignorance goes, the ego also goes, in terms of knowing 'I am not the ego.' The ego that comes after this knowledge has taken place is not the same ego that was there before. It is an enlightened ego. Because there is knowledge that there is no real, self-existent ego, you refer to it as enlightened, *jīvan-mukta*, one who is liberated while living. This is the person that Kṛṣṇa refers to as a *buddhimān* in this verse.

A buddhimān is one who has understood the realities

Buddhimān, the wise person, is one who sees that even the so called *akarma*, inaction, is nothing but *karma* – *yaḥ akarmaṇi karma paśyet saḥ buddhimān*. *Ātmā* being *akartā*, and because one understands this fact about *ātmā*, one sees *akarma* in *karma* itself; and because of that, he is a *buddhimān* – *yaḥ karmaṇi akarma paśyet saḥ buddhimān*. The person recognises the fact of *ātmā* being actionless and that recognition, if it is true, is not altered whether *karma* is done or not done. This recognition has nothing to do with *karma*; it is the recognition of the *svarūpa*, the nature, of *ātmā*.

When we talk about the *svarūpa* of *ātmā*, we say that *ātmā* is essentially *akartā*. This statement is made with reference to *kartṛtva*, doership, which is superimposed on the *ātmā* due to ignorance. Generally one has the mistaken notion, 'I am a doer, *ahaṁ kartā*.' And the correction of this mistake makes you =see that you are *akartā*. That you are *akartā* is a fact to be recognised. Therefore, you cannot ask, 'When will I become an *akartā*?' Nowhere is it said that you have to become an *akartā*, a non-doer. You only need to see *akarma* in *karma* itself.

There is no question of your becoming *akartā*. You are *akartā*. *Ātmā* is *akartā* and, to be *akartā*, you only have to see the fact. Then you are a *buddhimān*, a wise person, among the people who have *buddhi*s but do not use them.

The meaning of *buddhimān* is something like that of *dhanavān*, a rich person, as we said before. To have money does not mean that you are a rich person. Only if you have money to give are you a rich person. A man who has money to spend on himself, and on others when necessary, is a rich man. Whereas, a man with money who does not think he has enough to spend on himself or for a cause is just a moneyed man, not a rich man.

It is important to understand the difference between a moneyed person and a rich person. The rich person is one who feels rich. A man who has only a rupee in his pocket and gives it to someone who has not eaten for two days is a rich man because, although he had so little, he had money to spare. He has no money, but he is rich; he is ready to spend. Whereas, another man may have millions of rupees but cannot spend it on himself or on others. Such a person is moneyed but not rich, in other words, a miser, *kṛpaṇa*.

In the *Bṛhadāraṇyakopaniṣad*, Yājñavalkya tells Gārgī,[11] 'The one who dies not knowing Brahman is a miser.' Why is he or she considered a miser? Because the person had an intellect that he or she never used. Just as money is of no use to a person who will not spend it, what is the use of having an intellect if one cannot or will not use it?

One who has a *buddhi* and does not spend it is also a miser. Such a person uses the intellect as little as possible, keeping it as it is. A man may exercise his intellect just a little to learn something in order to please his parents. He may even get a job. But that is the maximum he is willing to use his intellect for. He does not read anything, not even the newspaper. He sits staring at the TV, without using his intellect at all. Why should he use it? For this kind of life, he need not use it at all. No real thinking is ever done by such a person.

Real thinking is thinking about realities. Because you are dealing with reality, there must be thinking; otherwise, you are dealing only with shadows. If the realities are not known, you may be fighting in areas where no fighting is required. One who thinks about the fundamental reality of himself, the world and God, who knows what it is all about, is a *buddhimān*. This person is rich – he or she has an intellect to use and to spare. The *buddhimān* has used the *buddhi* for himself or herself and shares the knowledge gained with others.

---

[11] Refer to Volume 2 – page 25

Thus, in this verse, Kṛṣṇa is saying that among the people who have *buddhi*s, this person is the only one who is wise – *saḥ buddhimān manuṣyeṣu*. Just as some people have money without being rich, some people have *buddhi*s without being wise. A *buddhimān*, however, is a *yogī*, a *kṛtsna-karmakṛt*, one who has done all that is to be done.

By discovering the *ātmā* to be *akartā*, the wise person has completely destroyed all the *karma*s. The self being full, *pūrṇa*, there is nothing more for this person to do at any time. The self as *akartā* is not a sometime affair. Once the self is known to be *akartā*, it will never become *kartā* again.

When we say *ātmā* is *asaṅga*, we mean that it is free from being a *kartā* and *bhoktā* which means it is free from *sukha* and *duḥkha*, *saṁsāra*. When it is said that *ātmā* is always *ānanda*, it means that *ātmā* is *pūrṇa*, full, limitless. This knowledge makes a person a *kṛtsna-karmakṛt*. Everything that is to be done has been done in one stroke. Nothing needs to be done for the person to be happy. Whatever *karma*s the person had to fulfil by taking many births have been fulfilled; the *karma*s are completely taken care of. Any activity he or she undertakes later is born of joy, not for gaining some security and happiness. The person may continue to do the same thing he or she did before. What one does, does not alter the fact that one is *akartā*.

As long as there is a doer, a *kartā*, there is action even in so called inaction. A wise person, *buddhimān*, is able to see this. Because 'I am not doing anything' also implies a *kartā*, both *karma* and *akarma* become *karma* in the vision of the wise.

Wherever there is doership, there is always some action or the other. Therefore, everything becomes action, be it action or inaction.

The *buddhimān* is also able to see *akarma* in both *karma* and *akarma* because, for such a person, there is no doership in the self, *ātmani kartṛtva-abhāva*. He or she knows that while *kartā*, the doer, is non-separate from the self, the self is not the doer. Because the person has this knowledge, he or she is said to be wise among human beings and is described as one who has done everything that is to be done, without exception, *saḥ buddhimān manuṣyeṣu saḥ kṛtsna karmakṛt*.

When there is no *kartṛtva* in the *ātmā*, what *karma* is there for me to do? If I am not the *kartā*, how can I perform action even if all four Vedas enjoin me? If they say, 'O *kartā*, please do this ritual,' I can only respond if I am the *kartā*. When someone says, 'John, please come here,' only John will come, no one else. Just as an individual is being addressed here, so too the Vedas also address the individual, 'O person, please do these *karma*s – *karma kuru*.'

Who is the person the Vedas are addressing? Is it the *sat-cit-ānanda-ātmā* or the *kartā*? They are definitely addressing the *kartā*. And what happens if there is no *kartā*? There is no response. A wise person does not respond because he is not a *kartā*. Only when there is a *kartā*, a doer, does the addressing of the Vedas have an effect. Otherwise, it is useless. The enjoined *karma*s are also useless because they are all 'as well done' for the *kṛtsna-karmakṛt*. Even *karma-yoga* no longer applies to the wise person.

There is no karma-yoga for the jñānī

A *karma-yogī* is one who takes care of his or her *rāga-dveṣas*, likes and dislikes, by doing what is to be done with a proper attitude towards the actions and their results. The Vedas address both the *karma-yogī* and the person who performs action strictly to accomplish certain desirable ends because both of them have *kartṛtva*, doership. Only the *jñānī*, the one who sees inaction, is not addressed by the Vedas because such a person sees *ātmā* as *akartā*, the non-performer of action.

If I am the non performer of action, any enjoining done by the Vedas or anything else does not come to me at all. Therefore, whatever was to be done before is all over; I am a *kṛtsna- karmakṛt*. There is nothing more for me to do. And anything that is to be done later is also taken care of.

Before knowledge, all actions are meant for me, for my *sukha*, happiness. I want some cheerfulness, tranquillity, *antaḥ-karaṇa-śuddhi*. Then, with such a mind, I can achieve self-knowledge, which is seeing non-action in action, *karmaṇi akarma-darśanam*. To see non-action in action is to understand that I am *akartā*, a non-doer. Thus, for the sake of self-knowledge alone, I perform all the *karma*s that are to be done by me.

Even a *kāmī*, one who is not interested in self-knowledge but just wants to fulfil certain desires, has to perform actions which are meant for the *kāmī*, the one who has desires. Because the person feels inadequate, he or she has desires that necessitate the performance of action. Suppose one understands that the self is not inadequate, it is adequate or more than adequate, then there is no desire for action. In fact, because the self is full, words like adequate and inadequate do not even come into the picture. Therefore, for the person who knows this, there is nothing to be done, *kāryaṁ karma na vidyate.*

When the mind, meaning the *ahaṅkāra*, ego, is resolved in the *ātmā*, there is nothing for the person to do. In the wake of knowledge, *ahaṅkāra*, the I-notion, the *kartā*, is resolved in the *ātmā* and there is no longer any question of *ātmā* being the *kartā*. When there is no *kartā*, there is nothing to be done, which is why the person is called *kṛtsna-karmakṛt*. One has done everything that is to be done, in the past as well as in the future.

The person for whom there is nothing to be done is a *jñānī*, a wise person. Because there is nothing to be done for such a person, he or she is free to do a lot of things. When there is nothing to be done, what is there that is not to be done? There is no mandate for a *jñānī* enjoining him to do any particular action or prohibiting him from doing any particular action. His or her job is over. Hereafter, the person's will has no place at all. Whatever will the person had before knowledge, has been successfully used up, having served its purpose. This is why *sannyāsī*s do not leave wills when they die. They have no will to leave a will. Only when will is there can there be a will! Sometimes, if the *sannyāsī* has many disciples, not leaving a will can cause problems as to who is to succeed him or her and so on. Whereas, if he or she is a traditional, *paramparā-sannyāsī*, and the disciples have been taught well, there will be no problem. There will be no vying for the *sannyāsī*'s seat because there is no seat. There is no organisation for a seat to be there. Each disciple is the seat, in fact.

In the Hindu tradition, *vaidika-dharma*, there is no organisation or hierarchical structure – no papacy, diocese, parish, or congregation. *Dharma*, of course, has no organisation and in that *dharma*, there is a person, a *sannyāsī*, who also has no organisation. The word *sannyāsī* means that the person just lives with only the sky above him or her. The person is the only organisation that is there. There is no organisational head or organisation. And if he has any disciples, every disciple there may be, is an organisation. The *sannyāsī* does not even need the text of the *Upaniṣads* or the *Gītā*. Everything is in the form of understanding within the person's head. This is how the *paramparā*, tradition, is.

Once self-knowledge is gained, the job of the wise person is over and there is no will left. It has been used up. The will is useful only until *mokṣa*, just as one's chequebook is useful as long as one's account is not closed. Once the account is closed, what is the use of the cheques that you still have? They are useless. You can fill them out and give them to people, but they have no meaning. Similarly, when *mokṣa* is gained, the will is useless. The account is closed. The accountant has struck out the person's name with a red pen and has removed the file. One more *jīva* is gone, finished, and with this *jīva* goes everything else, meaning that all the *karma* term deposits simply evaporate. There is no longer anyone to claim them. Just as when a person dies, his or her file is marked, 'Deceased,' so too the *jīva*'s file is closed and dispensed with because there will be no further transactions or complications. No one else is going to claim the *jīva*'s *karma*; it is all over. The file is shredded and burnt with no trace left behind. Therefore, the person is *kṛtsna-karmakṛt*. Having gained *mokṣa,* the person has nothing more to do.

Objections presented in Vedanta

Here, there is one small but highly technical objection raised by Śaṅkara. The objection is based on a different interpretation that is sometimes given to this verse.

Objections are raised in various ways in Vedanta. Certain philosophies are presented as sparring partners for us, like the *Sāṅkhya* and *Vaiśeṣika* schools of thought. There is also a person referred to as *Pūrva-mīmāṁsaka* who is a little more than a sparring partner. *Mīmāṁsā* is the analysis of the sentences of the Vedas. The analysis of the sentences in the earlier portion, *pūrva-bhāga* or *karma-kāṇḍa* is called *pūrva-mīmāṁsā* while the analysis of the sentences of the *uttara-bhāga,* the later portion which is Vedanta is called *uttara-mīmāṁsā.*

Then, there are those who are not really sparring partners at all; they are opponents, like the *bauddha*s and *jaina*s who have their own philosophies and have to be answered. To understand what Vedanta is saying, we use all of these as sparring partners by analysing their particular arguments. Some are permanent sparring partners, others are by invitation only, and with still others we do shadow fighting.

The philosophy of the *Pūrva-mīmāṁsaka* is very simple. The Veda is eternal and is the final word in everything. According to the *Pūrva-mīmāṁsaka,* the Veda enjoins you to do *karma* alone. For this person, knowledge is not *mokṣa;* performing *karma* is the only way to gain *mokṣa*. Because the *Pūrva-mīmāṁsaka* analyses the *pramāṇa* so well, we make use of his method of analysis in Vedanta.

The *Pūrva-mīmāṁsaka*'s argument:

According to the *Pūrva-mīmāṁsaka*, all sentences of the Veda deal primarily with action and therefore, do not really convey anything that is already there. It should be clearly understood that the sentences throughout the Veda can be taken as commands in terms of what is to be done, *vidhi-vākya* or what is not to be done, *niṣedha-vākya*. Any sentence that reveals the nature of an object is connected to or subserves either a *vidhi-vākya* or a *niṣedha-vākya*.

This analysis of *karma*, *karma-mīmāṁsā* is very important because the orientation of any human mind, even the minds of those who are lazy, is towards *karma*, action. A person who is lazy is bothered because of the action that he or she does not perform. Thus, both the active and the lazy are oriented towards *karma* alone. That there is something to be done is the truth about everyone. For the *Pūrva-mīmāṁsaka*, then, *mokṣa* can only be gained by performing *nitya-naimittika-karma*.

*Nitya-karma*s are daily rituals that one has to perform daily and regularly on certain days. *Naimittika-karma*s are those *karma*s that have to be done on certain occasions, as at the time of an eclipse. And these *nitya-naimittika-karma*s are to be done by everyone.

Mokṣa, according to the *Pūrva-mīmāṁsaka*, also involves not doing any *kāmya-karma*, the actions done for a specific desirable result. One must do only those actions which are duties.

The idea here is to avoid both *puṇya* and *pāpa*. By not planning or performing any *kāmya-karmas*, *puṇya* is avoided and by not doing what is not to be done, *pāpa* is avoided. In this way, the *prārabdha-karma* that brought this body into being will exhaust itself without your needing to do anything about it. The capital will be lost and the body will die. Having avoided all *puṇya* and *pāpa*, there will be no new *karmas* for you and therefore, no cause for a new birth. All you have to do is keep eating daily and do your *nitya-naimittika-karma*. This is one argument for gaining *mokṣa*, through *karma* – the simple argument of the *Pūrva-mīmāṁsaka*.

The two sets of *karma, nitya-karma* and *naimittika-karma*, are called duties. The *Pūrva-mīmāṁsaka* argues that because they are duties, there is no result for you when you do them. In other words, they do not produce *puṇya*. And when you do not do these *karmas*, the omission attracts *pāpa* to you. This is the crux of the *Pūrva-mīmāṁsaka*'s argument.

How can one attract *pāpa* by not doing an action? An example is given. When a person bathes, no one notices. Because it is a common activity, no one says, 'O! you seem to have taken a bath today.' But suppose the person does not bathe? This omission is definitely noticed, if not by all, definitely by some! Thus, the *Pūrva-mīmāṁsaka*'s argument is that there are actions to be done and if these are not done there is a result. *Nitya-naimittika-karmas* do not attract any result when they are done. Only when they are not done, do they attract results, *pāpa*. This verse can, therefore, be seen from this standpoint. For the *Pūrva-mīmāṁsaka*, the word *karmaṇi* in the expression, '*karmaṇi akarma yaḥ paśyet*' means *nitya-naimittika- karmaṇi* – in the actions that are to be done daily or occasionally. And *akarma* refers to the absence of any result, *phala-abhāva*. Thus, the expression is taken to mean that one who sees *akarma*, the absence of result, in *nitya-naimittika-karma* is wise.

However, if there is no result to be gained, *nitya-naimittika-karma* cannot be called a *karma* at all because there is no doer. To this, the *Pūrva-mīmāṁsaka* says, 'No, there is a doer. *Ātmā* is the *kartā*; therefore, you cannot nullify the doer. The result alone is not there. And because there is no result, the *karma* becomes as good as *akarma*.'

If there is no result, why perform action?

At this point in the argument, any practical person is going to ask, 'If there is no result, why should I perform the action? After all, is it not more pleasant to do nothing? To do all these *nitya-naimittika-karma*s takes a lot of time. If there is no result, surely I need not do them. 'No!' comes the reply, because if you do not do them, you will bring trouble upon yourself. There are many people who choose to go to heaven only because they are mortally afraid of hell, not because they are interested in heaven. Hell has been painted so vividly in their minds that naturally they cannot stand to think of having to go there. Even to hear about it makes their blood pressure go up. Therefore, they want to avoid hell by going to heaven. This kind of heaven hell discussion is what pushes people into religion, in fact. If the heaven and hell aspects were removed, these religions would topple. No one would even look into them.

When the *karma* that is to be done by you is not done, you attract *pāpa* and, therefore, it is to be done, according to how some people interpret the '*karmaṇi akarma*' portion of this verse. And the expression, '*akarmaṇi karma*' is interpreted as not doing an action that is to be done. According to this argument, if the to be done action is not done, a result, *phala*, is produced, and it becomes *karma*. Therefore, *karma* is *akarma* and *akarma* is *karma*. *Akarma* produces *phala* and *karma* does not. The one who sees it in this way is wise among human beings and has done all that is to be done, *saḥ buddhimān manuṣyeṣu saḥ yuktaḥ kṛtsna-karmakṛt*. This is the *Pūrva-mīmāṁsaka*'s argument to which, Śaṅkara responds as follows.

Śaṅkara's response:

If what you do does not produce a result, and what you do not do, produces a result, why do any *karma* at all? Thus, Śaṅkara argues that, what is not done does not produce unseen result, *adṛṣṭa-phala*, in the form of *puṇya* and *pāpa*, although there can be *dṛṣṭa-phala*, seen results.

The omission of to be done action can produce conflict or worry, which is a *dṛṣṭa-phala*. For example, when you have to write a letter and you do not do it, there may be some conflict. In this way, there can be *dṛṣṭa-phala*, but no *adṛṣṭa-phala*, which is *puṇya* and *pāpa*, the invisible results that accrue to the person who performs the action.

We are talking only about *puṇya* and *pāpa* here. For a *karma* that is not done, there can be no *pāpa* or *puṇya* and for a *karma* that is done, results cannot be avoided. *Karma-phala* will always be there as long as the *karma* is there. Even *nitya-naimittika-karma* produces results in the form of *puṇya*. Any to be done action, when it is performed, produces a result and not doing it produces only *dṛṣṭa-phala*, seen results and not *pāpa*.

When what is to be done is not done, there is always an inner irritation, some sense that you have missed out. Daily meditation, for instance, definitely produces *puṇya*, if you do it, of course. If, however, out of laziness or for some other reason, you do not perform this action, your omission will not produce *pāpa*, although it may produce some irritation. You may feel bad that you did not do it and, if you did not do it the day before either, you may become sadder, but this is *dṛṣṭa-phala*, not *adṛṣṭa-phala*.

For an action that is not done, no result can accrue. Only for action that is done can there be *adṛṣṭa-phala*, either *puṇya* or *pāpa*. If the action is proper, it will attract *puṇya* and if it is improper, it will attract *pāpa*.

Śaṅkara argues that if an action that is not done can produce results, then that which does not exist, *asat*, can produce *sat* which exists. To say that a non-existent thing can produce an existent thing is like saying that a non existent mother can bear a son. It contradicts all means of knowledge, *sarva-pramāṇa-virodha*. It is equally contradictory to say that *karma*s that are done do not produce results. You cannot throw a stone and expect that there will be no result. There will be a result, especially if it hits someone! Something must take place; some kind of reaction will be there. Therefore, action without reaction makes no sense at all.

Again, how can one become a *kṛtsna-karmakṛt* by the mere knowledge that performing *nitya-naimittika-karma* is equivalent to *akarma* and non-performance of the *nitya-naimittika-karma* is equivalent to *karma*? Śaṅkara raises yet another objection to the *Pūrva-mīmāṁsaka* 's argument.

Jñāna is being talked about here, knowledge of *karma* and *akarma*. Mere knowledge does not produce results; doing something produces results. How then can you say that the person is *kṛtsna-karmakṛt*? You cannot; you can only say he or she is the one who knows all the *karma*s that are to be done and not to be done – *kṛtsna-karmavit bhavati na tu kṛtsna-karmakṛt bhavati*.

Kṛtsna-karmakṛt refers to a person of fulfilment, one who has achieved everything, a liberated person, *mukta-puruṣa*. Kṛṣṇa makes this point clear not only here, but before also, when he said that he would tell Arjuna about action and inaction, knowing which one is liberated – *tat te karma pravakṣyāmi yajjñātvā mokṣyase śubhāt*.[12] Had there been anything to be done, Kṛṣṇa would have used the expression '*yat kṛtvā*, doing which,' and not '*yat jñātvā*, knowing which.'

In analysis, *mīmāṁsā*, what has been said before must always be kept in mind. Otherwise, there would be no analysis. When Kṛṣṇa says, 'knowing which,' he meant knowing what *karma* is and what *akarma* is, which is not as easy as you may think. *Karma* is not to be taken as merely performing action; nor is *akarma* to be taken as not doing action. The real nature of *karma* and *akarma* is something that has to be understood by

---

[12] *Gītā* 4.16

you, knowing which you will be released from all *puṇya* and *pāpa* that is inauspicious.

The *Pūrva-mīmāṁsaka* says that you have to do *karma*, but what is said here is that by knowing the nature of *karma* and *akarma*, you are released from all *puṇya* and *pāpa*. This is what is meant by *vākyārtha-vicāra,* enquiry into the sentence. The enquiry is done to find out what the sentence means and whether it has any other meaning. If there is another meaning possible, it will reveal a philosophy, a stand. Here, a particular stand is analysed by Śaṅkara and then dismissed as not being what was intended, as not being the meaning of the sentence.

Verse 19

Karma for a wise person is burnt by the fire of knowledge

In this verse, Kṛṣṇa is referring to knowledge alone. His description of one who has this knowledge continues in the next verse.

यस्य सर्वे समारम्भाः कामसङ्कल्पवर्जिताः ।
ज्ञानाग्निदग्धकर्माणं तमाहुः पण्डितं बुधाः ॥ १९ ॥

yasya sarve samārambhāḥ kāmasaṅkalpavarjitāḥ
jñānāgnidagdhakarmāṇaṁ tamāhuḥ paṇḍitaṁ budhāḥ (19)

yasya – for whom; *sarve* – all; *samārambhāḥ* – undertakings; *kāma-saṅkalpa-varjitāḥ* – free from desire (for results) and will; *jñāna-agni-dagdha-karmāṇam* – whose actions are burnt up by the fire of knowledge; *tam* – him; *budhāḥ* – the sages; *paṇḍitam* – wise; *āhuḥ* – call

The one for whom all undertakings are free from (binding) desire and will, whose actions are burnt by the fire of knowledge, the sages call him as wise.

The person who was earlier described as being able to see inaction in action and action in inaction is again praised here. This person understands the nature of *karma* and *akarma*. He or she knows that *akarma* does not mean not doing an action; rather, it is seeing oneself, in the very action itself, as *akartā*, a non-doer. This is self-knowledge, the knowledge that makes you free, that makes you a *sarva-karmakṛt*, one who has done everything that is to be done.

There is a difference between action and activities that is to be noted here. An activity is an undertaking that implies a number of actions, various steps that you take. Behind each activity there is a plan and, based on this plan, the activity is undertaken for achieving a given purpose. Any given activity meant to produce a given result has a beginning, whether the activity is building a house, cooking, or doing business. All such undertakings are called *samārambhāḥ*.

When a wise person undertakes any activity, he or she does so without *kāma*, desire, and *saṅkalpa*, will. *Kāma*, desire, is wanting to achieve something, for which there is a will, *saṅkalpa*. A *saṅkalpa* is saying, 'By doing this, I will achieve that.' What happens and for whom does it happen when a wise person undertakes activities free of *kāma* and *saṅkalpa*?

It has already been said that a wise person is *kṛtsna-karmakṛt*. Since *kṛtsna-karmakṛt* means the one for whom everything that has to be done has been done, there is nothing to be done by the person.

The person has the vision of *ātmā*, the self, as *sat-cit-ānanda* and knows that he or she is *akartā*. This vision being there, the person is limitless, full, *pūrṇa*. How, then, can there be any activity for a person who has this knowledge? How can he or she talk, walk, see, hear, or think? For such a person, everything is over. The will has been used up; it has been fulfilled. And if the will is not there, desire is not there. How then, is activity possible for the person?

Further, if activity is not possible for the wise person, then anyone who talks does not know the *ātmā*. In fact, this is another contention. Some people think that as long as a person talks about *ātmā*, he or she does not know. And once the person knows, he or she does not talk about it. It means before knowing *ātmā*, you can talk about it and after knowing *ātmā* you cannot talk at all! A very common contention, prevalent in certain circles, is that one who sees does not talk and one who talks does not see. This is why in India there are so many *maunī bābā*s, *sādhus* who do not talk.

According to this contention, if you become a *jñānī*, you perform no activity whatsoever; you do not even breathe. Since not breathing means dying, who would want knowledge, *jñāna*, under such circumstances? If I tell you I am going to give you *jñāna*, but the moment you get it, you will die, you will naturally ask when you will be getting this *jñāna*. I can only tell you that you may get it tomorrow or today, or even at this very moment. After all, being knowledge, it can happen at any time. It also means that at any time you can die – today, tomorrow, or right now! If having heard my response, you ask,

'Swamiji, where will you be in twelve years?' I will know that you have decided to live twelve more years. The period of time will vary depending on how old you are now and how much you still want to do. But, definitely, you will postpone gaining this knowledge. In fact, no one will ever be interested in a *mokṣa* that amounts to death because no one wants to be mortal. Everyone is interested only in being immortal. Even if I say, 'You will die and become immortal,' no one will go for it. Everyone wants to live and be immortal at the same time.

In fact, if this contention were correct, there would be no teacher. We would have a situation where only those who do not know can perform the activity of teaching and those who know cannot because they are *kṛtsna-karmakṛt*. Since the person who does not know cannot teach and the *kṛtsna-karmakṛt* also cannot teach because teaching is an activity, who would teach? Therefore, the meaning of *kṛtsna-karmakṛt* is not what is being conveyed here.

Although *kṛtsna-karmakṛt* means there is nothing for the person to do, it does not mean that he or she does nothing. Kṛṣṇa drove the chariot and was teaching Arjuna. Śaṅkara wrote a number of commentaries and Vyāsa wrote any number of books. Assuming they knew what they were teaching, they were definitely engaged in activities. Even in terms of talking alone, they were very active. So how can you say a teacher is *kṛtsna-karmakṛt*?

For the teacher also, there is something to do. He or she has to teach. And why does the teacher teach? Does the person teach because he or she is going to get something out of it?

If so, then the person does not know. Only when a teacher teaches, knowing, 'The teacher is me, but 'I,' the *ātmā*, is not the teacher,' does the person really know what he or she is teaching. And if this is clear, why should a person not teach?

If you ask why the person should teach, I will ask why should he or she not teach? By teaching, the person does not come out of himself or herself. In *karma*, he or she sees *akarma*. Whatever you may know about yourself, that self is always there. No one ever comes out of this self. In fact, you are whatever you know about yourself. Therefore, if a person knows, 'I am *sat-cit ānanda* and I perform no action,' there is no question of any mistake being made. The person always sees *akarma* in any *karma*. Why, then, should he or she not teach or do anything else? Such a person teaches because there is no reason why he or she should not teach. This is the only reason, in fact. If there is someone who wants to listen, to learn, why should the person not teach? There should be no other reason for teaching. Someone wants to learn and, therefore, someone teaches. There should be nothing more to it than this.

If a person thinks action is bondage, then action becomes *satya* for that person. To think certain actions are bondage and other actions are not bondage is confusion. And to remove such confusion, *karma* must be understood. Because people do not understand *karma* and *akarma*, they say *vedānta-śāstra* is a theory and it is *karma* alone that produces *mokṣa*. Kṛṣṇa, himself, said that even sages are confused about *karma* and *akarma*.[13]

---

[13] *Gītā* 4.16

Karma is not an ordinary topic and is not easy to understand. Many people, even those who are very serious, have lost themselves in it because they do not understand. Organisations and many social services have been born out of the non- understanding of this topic. Therefore, *karma* is to be understood.

For the one who understands *karma* and *akarma*, teaching is not an action, even though there is action, because the person sees inaction in action, knowing himself or herself to be *akartā*. For such a person, there is no *karma*, *akarma*, or anything else, no desire or will. There is not even the desire to teach. If a teacher who knows what it is all about does not have an opportunity to teach, he or she does not lose anything. The person will not become lonely or be at a loss for something to do. Nor is anything lost if the person teaches.

Anyone who thinks that he or she teaches in order to save the world is under the spell of a great delusion. In fact, the person is in need of being saved and, in the meantime, the world should be saved from such a person. Self-appointed saviours definitely create problems. If the person thinks that God appointed him or her to save the world, the question can be asked, 'Why should God have appointed you to do this? He can save the world himself. What God is he who would appoint someone to save the world when he himself is almighty? Why should an almighty God want an intermediary?'

That you are going to save the world is the greatest delusion. How can you save the world when you yourself need an entire society to keep you going? Your food, clothing, and shelter, all come to you because so many people work to grow the food, sew the clothes, and build the houses. Who are you to save anyone? You are as helpless as anyone else. And what is it or who is the one that you can save?

On the other hand, if you have something that you can spare and still survive, and there is someone who needs it and can be helped by it, there is no problem. It is human. There is no question of anyone saving the world. Such thinking is nothing but delusion, *ahaṅkāra*, ego.

The world has survived for so many years without you. Even now, in spite of you, it continues to survive. So, how many people are you going to save? Whereas, if you say that you have something and can share it with another who needs it, you are a mature human being. What everyone has is to be shared. Whether you have enough to give one person or to one thousand people makes no difference. If you do not have money to share, you may have some time to share and you share it. Or you have some good words to share with those who need them and you do so.

Good words are not words that place one's hopes somewhere. Nor are they good news. Good words are the words that speak of your accepting the person as he or she is totally without judging. Such words boost the morale of the person, and are not promises in terms of the future, after death, and so on. Who wants or needs such things? They only postpone resolving the problem. No practical person wants to hear that there is no hope here, but only later in heaven, and that they should ensure that they go to heaven and not to damnation. What kind of philosophy is this? Who wants these kinds of words? What a person needs are simple words that makes one feel acceptable.

Words that tell me that there is one person who understands me as I am and that I am acceptable to that person, are very beautiful words indeed. They create an atmosphere wherein I am accepted. This is all anyone wants. No one saves anyone. I do not learn Vedanta to save people, much less the world. To think that if I enlighten the majority of people, society will be transformed is the greatest delusion. To save me from condemning myself is enough. By doing so, there will be one problem less for the world to deal with.

Also, by being a cheerful person, I am not radiating my sorrow to others. Sorrow is a very contagious disease. Doors and windows cannot stop it. Even though I keep my doors and windows locked, somehow the sorrow of others manages to creep in. It has its own ways of travelling and does not even need keyholes. So, if there is one person on earth who is happy with himself or herself, that person is doing a great service to the world because he or she has no sadness to radiate to others.

You may say that you keep your sadness to yourself so that it does not radiate to others. Doing this just creates additional problems because eventually the build-up will result in outbursts of anger and frustration. Therefore, you better not keep your sadness to yourself. Talking about your sorrow to someone is definitely better than holding on to it.

All that you can do, then, is save yourself from your own persecutions. The world does not persecute you. You persecute yourself with your own self condemnation, which is why it is said that you are both your own best friend and your own worst enemy. You can be cruel to yourself and you can be kind to yourself. To save yourself from your own persecutions is freedom. And when that freedom is there, any discerning pair of eyes with a mind that has some leisure will recognise it. People will ask you how you became so free. 'You seem to have something, what is it that you have? Please tell me.'

Wisdom has no name – it is just knowledge

Vedanta is a name, but wisdom, *jñāna*, has no name. It is just knowledge. Others will see that you seem to be free and will naturally want to know what you know. Your word may ring true to them and they will want to know more provided, of course, they know you as someone they can trust, someone they can meet without being judged. If there is such a person in the world, people would naturally go to that person and become his or her student.

This is how the wise become teachers, not because they want to teach but because there are people who want to learn. Such a person has no *kāma* or *saṅkalpa* even though he or she performs certain activities.

In this verse, the person is further described as *jñāna-agni-dagdha-karma*, one whose actions are burnt up by the fire of knowledge. For the one who has this knowledge, all the *karma*s standing in his or her account are totally wiped out. This is the person the sages call as wise.

Only the wise can call another person wise. If one who is not wise calls someone wise, there is a problem because the person is doing so based on his or her own concept of wisdom. Here, it is said that the sages, *budhāḥ*, call the same person wise who was described earlier as *kṛtsna-karmakṛt*. Such a person is able to see the actionlessness as the nature of *ātmā*. Because he or she sees actionlessness as the nature of the self, the person recognises himself or herself as *akartā*, a non-doer, action being impossible for *ātmā*.

Even when activities take place, the *kartā*, the doer, is *ātmā*. The activities themselves are also *ātmā*, along with the *karaṇas*, instruments of action. Because everything is *ātmā*, there are no differences such as *kartā*, *karma* and *karaṇa*. If the self is *akartā*, all three are the same. In fact, the subject-object distinction is not there. Only when the self is mistaken for a *kartā*, a doer, does everything else naturally become different from the doer.

Who is the *kartā* then? The self as the doer has to be recognised as the physical body-mind-sense complex. That alone will be the self for one who sees the self as a doer. If this is the conclusion, then, there are differences – in the form of *kriyā*, the action coming from the *kartā*, the person; *karma*, an object of action; and *karma-phala*, the result of action that accrues to the person. This is exactly what is meant by the expression '*saṁsāra-cakra*,' the wheel of *karma*.

If a person who looks upon himself or herself as a *kartā* is able to recognise that the nature of the self is always actionlessness, that 'I am that actionlessness, free from any *karma,*' then action becomes purely apparent, *mithyā,* for the person. And when action is *mithyā,* the actor also becomes *mithyā,* as does the result of action and everything else. Because the person sees the self in this way, there is no real action on his or her part at any time. This is what is meant by the statement in the previous verse, *karmaṇi akarma yaḥ paśyet.* The wise person is one who, even when performing an action, is able to see the actionlessness in it.

There is no particular state involved here. It is recognition, knowledge of the self, free from doership, which is why the person was described as *kṛtsna-karmakṛt.* Seeing oneself free from doership, the person has done all the actions that are to be done. The *kṛtsna-karmakṛt* is also free of desire and will, *kāma-saṅkalpa-varjita,* as we have seen. Being free of *kāma* and *saṅkalpa* means the person is not controlled in any way by whatever desire or will, he or she may have. Therefore, the desire is not a binding desire and whatever *saṅkalpa* that may be there is also non-binding.

Karma never returns for the wise person

The desire and will of a wise person is like a seed that has been roasted, *dagdha-bījavat,* and therefore, cannot germinate and bear fruit. *Dagdha-bīja,* a roasted seed, is a particular expression used here for the purpose of analysis. If seeds are sown, they are capable of producing results, whereas if they are roasted, they are good only for the enjoyment of those who eat them. They cannot be used for cultivation because they are no longer capable of germinating.

Similarly, all the *karma*s of a wise person are only for enjoyment, *bhogārtha*, in the sense of *karma-phala-bhoga*, enjoying the results of action. The *prārabdha-karma*, the person came with, has to run its course. Therefore, any *karma* one does, knowing the *ātmā* is *akartā*, is only *bhoga*, experience, the exhaustion of *prārabdha-karma* alone. The person's actions cannot produce anything because he or she is *akartā*. Such a person is called a *paṇḍita*, wise, and a *jñāna-agni-dagdha-karma*. *Jñāna-agni-dagdha-karma* is, therefore, another compound describing the wise person. *Jñāna*, knowledge, is referred to as fire, *agni* and this fire of knowledge, *jñāna-agni*, burns up all the person's *karma*s. Therefore, the person is called *jñāna-agni-dagdha-karma*, one whose *karma*s have been destroyed by knowledge.

One may ask, 'Will the *karma*s return?' The destruction of *karma* referred to here is not like what happens when a tree is cut down and grows back again from the roots. The *karma*s are destroyed totally. They have no more existence whatsoever; they are burnt to ashes as it were.

As long as a person has not understood that *ātmā* is *akartā*, then there is a *jīva* who is a *kartā*. And, ignorance being its cause, the *jīva* has no beginning. In other words, because ignorance is not something that was created, the *jīva* is also not created at a given time. Anything that is not created cannot have a beginning. All creation is only in terms of one's body-mind-sense complex and the world in which one lives.

Consciousness is also not something that is created. Therefore, consciousness being *ātmā*, the Lord did not create *ātmā*, the self. He created only those objects that we call bodies, along with various other forms, and this he did according to laws. What we call creation is for the *jīva*, whereas the *jīva*, who in reality is *ātmā*, is not created. In the creation, there is one thing that is not created, the consciousness that is *ātmā*. Everything else, which we call creation, has been created due to the *jīva*'s *karma* alone.

And why is this *karma*? Because, the *jīva* is a *kartā*. Why is the *jīva* a *kartā*? Because *ajñāna*, ignorance is. When did this ignorance begin? Ignorance is *anādi*, it has no beginning whatsoever. From the standpoint of *jīva*, there is an account, a *karma-phala* or *puṇya-pāpa* account.

This *karma-phala* has been gathered by the *jīva* over countless number of births whose beginning cannot be established. Therefore, these births can also be considered to be infinite in number. In this infinite number of births, in different periods of time, an infinite number of *karma*s have been collected. Being so numerous, these *karma*s cannot fulfil themselves in one physical body at a given time and place. Only one set of *karma*s can be exhausted in a given incarnation. Thus, in this particular incarnation, I can exhaust a certain set of *karma*s and the rest remain in my account for future incarnations. Some of the *karma*s in this set can be exhausted only when you are born in India and others can be exhausted only when you happen to be in the United States.

Three types of karma

Even though this particular set of *karma*s is being exhausted in a given incarnation, there are still infinite *karma*s in your account waiting to be exhausted. These 'term deposit' *karma*s are called *sañcita-karma*s, *karma*s that cannot be exhausted in this particular body. Also, while exhausting *karma*s in this incarnation, you gather new *karma*s as long as you enjoy the status of doership, *kartṛtva*. These are called *kriyamāṇa-karma* or *āgāmi-karma*, *karma* that is being gathered now, in this lifetime. *Āgāmi karma* means futuristic *karma*. You gather new *puṇya* and *pāpa* because you enjoy a free will and these new *karma*s join the others that have accumulated in your account.

Because all the *puṇya-pāpa* that you have gathered is lodged in one general account, you cannot say that this life is due to your immediate past. The most you can say is that it is due to the past. The *puṇya-pāpa* is credited to this general account from which certain *karma*s precipitate and from there again another set of *karma*s precipitate. Therefore, a particular incarnation can be the result of *karma*s collected in the previous birth plus those you collected from a thousand births previously. Since all types of *karma*s can join together and create a new birth, the choices are plenty. In this way, any of them can join together, giving you another lease.

The set of *karma*s that began to fructify from the moment this physical body was conceived is called *prārabdha-karma*, *karma* that has already begun, *ārabdha*. These are the three types of *karma* – *sañcita*, *āgāmi* and *prārabdha* generally referred to as *karma*.

Knowledge destroys all karmas

For the person who is able to recognise the self as *akartā*, there is no longer any doership, *kartṛtva*. And, since there is no *kartṛtva* all the *karmas* standing in his or her name are burnt up, *dagdha*, by the fire of knowledge, *jñāna-agni*. Whereas, without this knowledge there is no end to the number of births and the gathering of *karmas*. This is why *saṁsāra* is said to be endless.

So, there is only one way out – by the fire of knowledge that destroys all the *karmas*. They are destroyed because there is no *kartā*. All the *sañcita-karmas* standing in the general account, any *āgāmi-karmas* that one reaps in this life are totally destroyed. *Puṇya* and *pāpa* will no longer come to the person because there is no *kartṛtva* in terms of knowledge. Therefore, the person is called *jñāna-agni-dagdha-karma* here.

From the standpoint of *ātmā* one is also free of *prārabdha-karma*. *Prārabdha* is only from the point of view of the physical body, mind and senses. Because the person is still here, still seen, we say there is *prārabdha-karma*, but we cannot say that *ātmā* is suffering due to *prārabdha*. The person has destroyed all *karmas* by the fire of knowledge and is therefore, wise, *paṇḍita*. He or she is now a free person, a *jīvan-mukta*. The word *jīvan* means 'while living' and the word *mukta* means 'liberated.' This person is liberated right now while living and not later after death. So, he or she is called a *jīvan-mukta*.

Given this understanding, then, can a *jñānī* be defined in terms of whether or not he or she performs *karma*? It all depends on the person's *prārabdha*. Based on his or her *prārabdha*, the *jñānī* has to undergo certain experiences, which is why you will find varieties of *jñānīs*. They may be *gṛhasthas*, married people with children. They may also be doing business or ruling a country, like King Janaka. A *jñānī* can be doing anything or give up everything and take to the lifestyle of *sannyāsa*.

As long as a *jñānī* is a *gṛhastha* there are *karma*s to be done. He cannot simply say, 'I am a *jñānī*,' and avoid what he has to do. He has to continue to do the rituals that *gṛhastha*s are enjoined to do. But even though the *jñānī* performs these rituals, it is not *karma* because the person knows the *ātmā* to be *akartā*. At the same time, a *jñānī* does not want to set a wrong example for the people and so, as a *gṛhastha*, he or she will perform *karma*. Nor does the person lose anything by doing it. Thus, a *jñānī* performing action is not a problem.

For the *jñānī*, there is no *kāma* or *saṅkalpa* in action. He or she does not say, 'I am going to accomplish this so that I can be that.' Therefore, the person may do anything. He or she may act out the drama, play the role, and play it well. Or the person may see the drama and its roles as useless, naturally so because there is uselessness there, and take to *sannyāsa*.

Even as a *sannyāsī* the person may or may not do *karma*. He or she may or may not teach. The *sannyāsī* may be a *maunī bābā* and not teach or he or she may teach. If a *sannyāsī* teaches, the teaching may be done in a simple manner or in a highly organised manner. It all depends upon the *prārabdha* of the *sannyāsī*. Those *sannyāsī*s who have taken *sannyāsa* as a lifestyle for the sake of gaining knowledge, have only one role to play. They are completely freed from all obligations except those attached to their role as a student. When they gain *jñāna*, they will continue to live a life of *sannyāsa*.

Ātmā is the same, but because of *prārabdha*, there are many kinds of *jñānīs*, more of which we shall see in the next few verses.

Verse 20

All that is given up is one's attachment to the results of action

त्यक्त्वा कर्मफलासङ्गं नित्यतृप्तो निराश्रयः ।
कर्मण्यभिप्रवृत्तोऽपि नैव किञ्चित्करोति सः ॥ २० ॥

tyaktvā karmaphalāsaṅgaṁ nityatṛpto nirāśrayaḥ
karmaṇyabhipravṛtto'pi naiva kiñcit karoti saḥ (20)

saḥ – he; *karmaphala-āsaṅgam* – deep attachments to the results of actions; *tyaktvā* – giving up; *nityatṛptaḥ* – always contented; *nirāśrayaḥ* – being not dependent on anything; *karmaṇi* – in action; *abhipravṛttaḥ* – fully engaged; *api* – even though; *kiñcit* – anything; *eva* – indeed; *na karoti* – does not do

Giving up the deep attachment to the results of action, always contented, being not dependent on anything, he (or she) does not do anything even though fully engaged in action.

Saṅga is attachment and *āsaṅga* is deep, fast attachment towards the results of action, *karma-phala*. The wise person has no fast attachment towards the *karma-phala*, the result. Because no one performs action without expecting results, the word *āsaṅga* is used in this verse. The point to be understood here is that a *jñānī* does not get anything out of a result. The person's welfare is not bettered or his or her happiness increased, no matter what the action or its result is. It is because the wise person has given up all dependence on and attachment to the results of action.

It is not the *karma* or the *karma-phala* that is given up by the *jñānī*, only the deep attachment that one has to the results of action. This is made very clear here because the possibility of giving up *karma-phala* is often questioned. The only reason a person performs action is because one has an eye on the result of action. Even while walking, the place you want to reach is kept in view. You turn here and go straight there because that is what you have to do to arrive at where you are going.

Without keeping the end in view, you cannot undertake any type of action. How, then, can this attachment be given up? If you are not able to reach your destination, why should you not become upset? In fact, this is exactly what happens to people and is what we call *āsakti* or *āsaṅga*. If you are unable to accomplish something and it affects you, then you have *karma-phala-āsakti, karma-phala-āsaṅga*.

Suppose, there is someone who is always contented, *nitya-tṛptaḥ*. For such a person, there is nothing to accomplish, the self being what it is and also known to the person. There is no dependence whatsoever upon any particular *karma-phala* for his or her contentment. From this description of a wise person, we understand that other people do things for satisfaction, *tṛpti*, for achieving something out of the action done. If you are dissatisfied with yourself, you undertake something or other in order to get some kind of satisfaction, some self approval.

Because there is some satisfaction in self approval, you want to prove yourself to be somebody, either in your own eyes or in the eyes of another. The problem here is that you do not accept yourself as you are. This is the only reason someone else's opinion can be so important to you and is, in fact, the problem of any *saṁsārī*. Only when the self is clear, when there is self-knowledge, can one be happy by oneself with oneself, as we saw in the third chapter. This happiness does not depend on anything else; it is in oneself alone. For such a person, there is nothing to be done and even when he or she does something, it does not affect the person's happiness in any manner. This always contented person is one who has given up all attachment to the results of action.

Such a person is also described as *nirāśrayaḥ*, free from all dependence. He or she does not depend upon anything for security or happiness, knowing that there is nothing more secure than the self. In fact, everything exists because of this self. In the self everything has its being. Even the mind has its being in the self alone, as does everything that is reported to the mind by the thoughts.

Existence itself is the nature, *svarūpa*, of *ātmā*. Therefore, everything has its *āśraya*, dependence or basis, in *ātmā*, just as the pot depends upon the clay for its existence. A better example would be the situation of seeing a snake on a rope. When you take the rope to be a snake, the snake has its existence, *sattā*, in the rope. The rope snake has no existence except the existence of the rope. Similarly, the world, *jagat*, has no existence except the existence of the self.

The person who is aware of this fact is *nirāśraya*, one who depends on nothing for his or her fullness or satisfaction, because the self as the whole is already full. The person knows, 'I am the whole. I am the *āśraya* of everything. In fact, everything is me.' This person has given up all attachments to the fruits of action, not as an attitude, not by *karma-yoga*, but by knowledge.

A *karma-yogī* also gives up attachment to *karma-phala*, but by attitude, accepting Īśvara as the giver of the results, *karma-phala-dātā*. This person takes everything as *prasāda*, without reacting; but it is *yoga*, not *jñāna*, which is entirely different. *Yoga* is relative and, therefore, the person's tranquillity is also relative. While this kind of mind is definitely useful for gaining the knowledge, the distinction between *yoga*, which is an attitude implying an understanding of Īśvara, and *vidyā*, knowledge, must be very clear.

Because the *karma-yogī* accepts Īśvara as the *karma-phala-dātā*, he or she has an attitude of taking things as they come and leaving them as they go. It means the person has a mind that does not react and, is, therefore, not under the spell of *rāga-dveṣa*s. Here, in these verses, the same *karma-yogī* has the knowledge of the self as *akartā*. So, even though this wise person may be engaged in an enormous number of activities, the self is not taken to be the doer.

King Janaka was said to be such a person. Even though he was a *jñānī*, he ruled a kingdom and he ruled it well. He had a handle on everything and always knew what was going on. The kingdom was prosperous and everyone was happy. Thus, a *jñānī* can enthusiastically engage himself or herself in a number of activities and still perform no action, *naiva kiñcit karoti saḥ*, in terms of knowing that he or she is not the doer.

An actor who plays the role of a killer does not take himself to be a killer, even before he removes the makeup! He sees himself as not doing anything. And if, while playing a role, he kicks someone, he knows he does not kick. When he goes backstage later, he does not say to the person, 'I am sorry I kicked you.' Nor does he need to excuse himself in this way. He may however, ask whether it was a good kick, to which the other person may reply, 'Yes, it was a good kick. It did not hurt me at all. You kicked very well.' Because they know they are playing roles, they can talk only about the nature of the action. But they cannot talk about it as though one person did something to the other and needs to apologise. The actor who kicked is not to blame. Nor is there any action involved because there is no doership, there is *kartṛtva-abhāva*. And there is no *kartā* either.

Karma and jñāna are two different topics

Kartṛtva, doership, is the whole problem. In fact, *saṁsāra* is centred on doership alone. *Ātma-jñāna* the subject matter of Vedanta is opposed to *karma* in that *jñāna* and *karma* are entirely distinct. Most of the Veda is *karma-kāṇḍa*. *Jñāna*, Vedanta, comes at the end. The end of the Veda, the last chapter, is Vedanta. Even though it is the last chapter, Vedanta is mentioned separately because there are two different topics involved, *karma* and *jñāna*. One being entirely different from the other, the two are in opposition.

Karma means *saṁsāra*, *jñāna* is *mokṣa*. *Karma* implies *kartā*, *jñāna* destroys the *kartā*. *Karma* implies ignorance, *Jñāna* destroys ignorance. Therefore, *Jñāna* implies *akartṛtva* and *karma* implies *kartṛtva*. Keeping the *kartā*, that is already there, in view, the Veda tells you to do *karma*. This is where *karma* can be converted into *yoga*. The *kartā* is retained and the *karma* is converted into *yoga* to gain the maturity that prepares the mind for *jñāna*, the discovery that you are *akartā*.

There is no shortcut to maturity and one does have to be mature for gaining knowledge. Maturity takes its own time. Therefore, it is not a question of doing it in five years, ten years, or twenty years. When one may have had numerous births before, twenty years or ten years or five years mean nothing. A man may have been studying Vedanta for eighty years before he begins seeing clearly. When he is 99 he may say, 'Now I have understood.' What does it matter that he has only one more year to live? Even if a person does not start until he is eighty years old and understands when he is 98, what does it matter? After knowledge, all that remains is *prārabdha*. Whether he lives another year or more means nothing whatsoever.

That it takes a person so many years to understand does not mean anything. The maturity required for the knowledge to take place, *antaḥ-karaṇa-śuddhi*, has to be gained and there is no hurry. Hurrying it does not work, in fact it is like waiting for a banana to ripen. You cannot sit beside the banana tree and say to a green banana, 'Come on, hurry up and mature. Ripen, so that I can eat you!' You have to let it ripen; only then will it be soft and tasty. It takes its own time and there is nothing you can do about it.

All processes of ripening and growth are the same, including the maturity of the mind. *Yoga* is meant for this purpose, *antaḥ-karaṇa-śuddhi*. In this sense, then, *karma* is useful. Once the mind is ready, *jñāna* takes place. Therefore, while *jñāna* is opposed to *karma*, *karma* contributes to *jñāna*, which is why *karma* comes first in the Veda and *jñāna* comes afterwards. *Karma* has to come first because it is due to *ajñāna*, ignorance. If a person takes himself or herself to be a *kartā*, a doer, the person is ignorant. Therefore, as *kartā*, retaining the *kartṛtva*, the person has to mature. Only then can *jñāna* come.

Maturity implies two levels, the subjective and the empirical. Subjectively, we gather a lot of problems, all of which have to be accounted for and taken care of. Then, empirically, there are wrong conclusions in terms of values, relationships and so on, which also have to be taken care of. It is with reference to these levels of maturity that *karma-yoga* comes in. *Karma-yoga* leads to *jñāna*, the knowledge, that 'I am a non-doer, *aham-akartā*.' Once this knowledge is gained, the person performs no action.

Thus, the Veda has two entirely different subject matters, *karma* and *jñāna*. The first portion of the Veda that deals with *karma* is called *karma-kāṇḍa*. The second portion that deals with *jñāna* is called *jñāna-kāṇḍa*, Vedanta. An analysis of the *karma-kāṇḍa* in terms of what *karma* is to be done, how it is to be done and so on is called *karma-mīmāṁsā*[14] or *pūrva-mīmāṁsā*. This is in the form of *karma-mīmāṁsā-sūtra*s written by Jaimini a disciple of Vyāsa. Similarly an analysis of *jñāna-kāṇḍa* is called

---

[14] *Mīmāṁsā* – analysis

uttara-mīmāṁsā. This is in the form of *Brahma-sūtra*s written by Vyāsa himself. In the *Brahma-sūtra*s the sentences of the *Upaniṣad*s are fully analysed. The subject matter is further analysed in the light of various schools of thoughts. This analysis is called *manana*. Finally what Vedanta itself says is established.

Vedanta is separate because *karma* and *jñāna* are two different topics, neither of which is ordinary. This is the entire subject matter of Kṛṣṇa's teaching in the *Gītā*. When you understand *karma* and *jñāna* properly, you are free. This knowledge implies understanding the nature of *ātmā* as being *akartā*. Given the importance of continuing in the same vein, Kṛṣṇa continues.

Verse 21

The one who knows the self is free from expectation

निराशीर्यतचित्तात्मा त्यक्तसर्वपरिग्रहः ।
शारीरं केवलं कर्म कुर्वन्नाप्नोति किल्बिषम् ॥ २१ ॥

nirāśīryatacittātmā tyaktasarvaparigrahaḥ
śārīraṁ kevalaṁ karma kurvannāpnoti kilbiṣam (21)

nirāśiḥ – free of expectations; *yata-citta-ātmā* – one whose body, mind and senses have been mastered; *tyakta-sarva-parigrahaḥ* – one who has given up all possessions; *kevalam* – mere; *śārīram* – for the sustenance of the body; *karma* – action; *kurvan* – doing; *kilbiṣam* – sin; *na āpnoti* – does not incur

The person who is free of expectations, whose body, mind and senses have been mastered, who has given up all possessions, doing only action that sustains the body, does not incur sin.

While describing a wise person, a *jñānī*, Kṛṣṇa presents different kinds of people in terms of *karma*. We saw the *jñānī* who engages in numerous activities knowing he or she is not doing anything, *karmaṇi abhipravṛtto'pi naiva kiñcit karoti saḥ*. In this verse, while still describing the *jñānī*, Kṛṣṇa introduces a different type of person who knows that *ātmā* is *akartā*.

As in the previous verse, here also the first line describes the *jñāna* and the second line describes the lifestyle of the person. In this verse, the one who knows the self is said to be *nirāśiḥ*, one who is free from expectations, *āśis*. *Āśis* also means hope but here, the negative prefix '*ni*' in *nirāśiḥ* does not mean that the person is hopeless. It means he or she is free from hope, free from expectations. Thus, *jñānī* is one from whom all expectations have dropped away. And how does this happen?

The hopeless person has expectations – expectations that are hopeless for him or her, in that there is no way of fulfilling them. Because the person has given up hopes of fulfilling his or her expectations, he or she is desperate. It means that the person has not grown out of them. Such a person is frustrated and is different from the *jñānī*, one from whom all expectations have dropped away because of discovering the self to be free from everything.

A person who lives maturely before gaining knowledge is almost free. Because of *yoga*, the person is not under the spell of likes and dislikes and is, therefore, already relatively free.

Once such a person discovers the self, he or she is totally free and does not have to fulfil desires in order to be full and happy. Thus, the person is described as *nirāśiḥ*, free from expectation.

This freedom is in part due to prior accomplishment in terms of mastery over the body-mind-sense complex. Thus, the *jñānī* is also described in this verse as *yatacittātmā*, one who has mastery over the physical body, mind and senses. *Citta* stands for the entire mind – memory, knowledge and all forms of thinking. *Ātmā*, in this particular compound, *yatacittātmā*, refers to the physical body, which, along with the mind, is mastered. Mastery here means that the body, mind and senses are with the person. They are in their proper places; they are as they are. The one whose body, mind and senses are mastered, is called *yatacittātmā*. Before knowledge, the person had this qualification relatively, and now, with knowledge, he or she has it absolutely.

Kṛṣṇa also says here that this particular *jñānī* is *tyakta-sarva-parigraha*, one who has given up his or her possessions, meaning that the person being described is a *sannyāsī*. Either the person had already taken to the lifestyle of a *sannyāsī* before gaining knowledge or was a *gṛhastha* who, having gained the knowledge, decided to give up everything.

Having a variety of possessions can be a problem. For example, a person may have a large house and find that it takes up too much time and money to maintain it properly. He or she may, therefore, consider selling the house, investing the money, and moving into a comfortable apartment. But then there is the problem of what to do with all the furniture and other things collected over a period of time. All of them will definitely not fit in an apartment. Look at this – first you buy a house and then embellish it with a lot of things. Now, because you have a lot of things, you want a house! It is all confusion. Why don't you sell the things when you sell the house? 'No, no,' you may say, 'All these are valuable pieces.' It means that you are attached to the pieces and, to hang on to them, you require a house! It is a very typical problem.

The wise person discussed in this verse does not have the problem of attachment to possessions. He or she has given up all possessions. The *tyakta-sarva-parigraha* has nothing – no house, no furniture, no job. This person is a *sannyāsī*, one who can walk out at any time from any place, not an ordinary person, a holy hobo. One has nothing else to do except to sustain the body, *śārīraṁ kevalam karma*. Such a person eats, bathes and does whatever else is necessary to maintain a reasonable degree of health in the body.

For the wise there is no identification with the body

The orientation of a *jñānī* towards the body is important to note here. Whatever the person has to do to maintain a fairly healthy condition, he or she does. It is quite a different orientation from that which overemphasises the body and uses *yoga* to give the body a certain form or an inordinate amount of energy. This is focusing only on the body and its health and can become an obsession. It must be kept in mind that even a healthy body dies one day. Also, an apparently unhealthy body has been known to drag on until it is 92! Either way, healthy or unhealthy, the body will suddenly pop off. It is something we see happening in the world all the time. Therefore, maintaining one's health should not become a hang up or the main focus of attention. In terms of maintaining the body alone, health is something to be kept in view, nothing more. If one's attention is on the body and what it eats or does not eat, for example, it will not be on *ātmā*. Overemphasising on such things is just a waste of time.

For the wise person, there is no identification with the body. Such an orientation is not there as Śaṅkara makes it very clear here in his commentary. The *jñānī* is not particular of how the body should be. He or she maintains a sense of proportion with reference to diet, exercise and lifestyle. If the body pops off sooner or later, what does it matter? If you have not gained the knowledge in forty years and the body goes, you can come back, perhaps with a better one. You either have the knowledge or you do not. To think that you have something to complete before the body goes is silly. There is no question of completion here. You are already complete and need only understand this fact. If the body goes before this understanding takes place, then you simply pick up the thread and continue. Therefore, why should you care unnecessarily about this particular body? This should be the attitude.

What happens to the *jñānī* when, being free of expectation and having relinquished all possessions, he or she performs only those actions that maintain the physical body? The person gains no *puṇya* and *pāpa*. In other words, he or she does not gain any *karma-phala*.

Good actions also bind a person

From the standpoint of *mokṣa, puṇya* is also a cause of bondage, *saṁsāra*. Whether a shackle is made of iron or gold, it is still a shackle. A prince who has committed a felony may be bound with a golden shackle and an ordinary person with an iron shackle. While the material of which the shackle is made can be different, there is no difference whatsoever in terms of being bound. Neither can remove their hands from the shackle that binds them. If the penalty for the felony is death, both will be executed. Here again, the prince may be executed with a golden sword and the ordinary person with a steel sword, but what satisfaction is this to the prince? He will be as dead as the ordinary person!

Similarly, with reference to *karma, puṇya* is the golden shackle. But, as long as *puṇya* is helpful in gaining what I want, I need *puṇya*. If I want *puṇya* to take me to this knowledge, to give me the circumstances that are conducive for my gaining this knowledge, then until I gain this knowledge, *puṇya* will be helpful to me. Afterwards, I no longer need *puṇya*. Therefore, from the ultimate standpoint, *puṇya* and *pāpa* are considered bondage.

Once the knowledge has been gained, the person no longer gains either *puṇya* or *pāpa* because there is no doership. The person has achieved all that can be achieved by *karma*. Knowing that he or she is not the doer, is what makes the wise person a *kṛtsna-karmakṛt*, one who has done everything that is to be done.

All that *karma* can achieve is *karma-phala*, nothing else, and this *karma-phala* is for my own sake, not for the sake of *karma* or for the sake of result. Nor is *karma-phala* for the sake of desire; it is for the one who has the desire for *karma-phala*. And if all the *karma-phala*s are for my sake, should they not add something to me? This conclusion is valid only if such addition is possible and it is only possible if I am inadequate. If *ātmā* is inadequate, then I definitely require some addition so that I can feel better.

On the other hand, if the self is already full, *pūrṇa-ātmā*, and everything is *ātmā* alone, then there is nothing other than *ātmā*. Where is the question of my doing anything that is going to enhance my security and happiness? The person who knows *ātmā* to be fullness becomes *sarva-karmakṛt* or *kṛtsna-karmakṛt* in one stroke, as we have seen. Such a person does nothing even though he or she performs action – *karmaṇi abhipravṛtto'pi naiva kiñcit karoti saḥ*.

Śaṅkara raises a doubt here regarding the possibility of an alternate meaning for the expression, *śārīraṁ kevalaṁ karma*, action performed only to sustain the body. It should be noted that the *sannyāsī* alone is being discussed here, the *tyakta-sarva-parigraha*, one who has given up all possessions.

Anything that is done with the body, physical action, is called *śārīraṁ karma*. If we take this to be the meaning here, then the expression, *śārīraṁ kevalaṁ karma*, will mean 'only the *karma* that is done physically,' because the word *kevala* means 'only.' Thus, the only *karma* that will not attract *puṇya* or *pāpa* will be that which is done with the physical body. If this is indeed the meaning, then whatever is done by word or by the mind will attract these results. Since the *śāstra* talks about physical, verbal and mental *karmas*, this interpretation cannot work and, on these grounds, Śaṅkara dismisses it.

Verse 22

Unaffected by the opposites, a sannyāsī accepts whatever comes by chance

To understand this verse correctly, you need to understand the spirit of *sannyāsa* and how a *sannyāsī* lives his or her life. A person who lives according to this lifestyle does only that which is necessary to maintain the physical body, without any identification with it. The *sannyāsī* does not grow his or her own food or work to earn money to buy it. Instead, he or she lives on alms, *bhikṣā*, which is not the same as begging. To live on *bhikṣā* means that the person eats whatever comes along without any planning or scheming about how to acquire the food. Whatever chance brings is food enough for the *sannyāsī*, an attitude described further by Kṛṣṇa in the next verse.

यदृच्छालाभसन्तुष्टो द्वन्द्वातीतो विमत्सरः ।
समः सिद्धावसिद्धौ च कृत्वापि न निबध्यते ॥ २२ ॥

yadṛcchālābhasantuṣṭo dvandvātīto vimatsaraḥ
samaḥ siddhāvasiddhau ca kṛtvāpi na nibadhyate (22)

yadṛcchā-lābha-santuṣṭaḥ – one who is happy with whatever comes by chance; *dvandvātītaḥ* – one who is unaffected by the opposites; *vimatsaraḥ* – one who is free from jealousy; *siddhau* – with reference to success; *asiddhau* – and with reference to failure; *samaḥ* – one who is even minded; *kṛtvā api* – even though performing action; *na nibadhyate* – is not bound

> The one who is happy with whatever comes by chance,
> who is unaffected by the opposites, free from jealousy,
> and even-minded with reference to success and failure,
> is not bound even though performing action.

In the compound, *'yadṛcchā-lābha-santuṣṭa,' lābha* refers to something that you gain *yadṛcchayā*, by chance, without any planning or scheming. In other words, whatever chance brings is *yadṛcchā-lābha*. A wise person is called a *yadṛcchā-lābha-santuṣṭa* in this verse because he or she is totally happy with whatever comes by chance, even in terms of basic necessities.

This same person is also called *dvandva-atīta*, one who is above all the opposites, who is not caught on either side of these opposites or in between. People tend to swing from one extreme to the other and can therefore, get caught at either end or in between. And what are these opposites, *dvandva*s?

Cold and hot, *śīta* and *uṣṇa*, are one set of opposites, either of which can make a person unhappy. In the winter, the person complains of cold and in the summer he or she finds it too hot. And the two months in between, one month of spring and one month of autumn, are spent saying, 'Oh! summer is coming soon and it will be so hot,' and then, 'Oh! the winter is coming soon and it will be so cold.' In this way, the entire year is spent complaining about either the heat or the cold; and every year is the same!

Thus, for those who get caught in the extremes or in between, everything is a matter for complaint. It is in fact, the lot of all *saṁsārī*s. When there is some *sukha*, something comfortable, the person is up, and when there is anything uncomfortable, *duḥkha,* the person is down. The *dvandva-atīta* is one who is *sama,* who has an inner composure with respect to all the opposites. Such composure is natural in one who can see *akarma* in *karma* because the person who knows *ātmā* is not a doer. And because this composure, *ānanda,* is the person's nature, it never goes away.

Success and failure, victory and defeat and so on, are varieties of opposites upon which the *dvandvātīta* does not depend for his or her security and happiness. Whereas these opposites constantly catch others; one makes them happy, the other, its opposite, makes them unhappy. The wise person, however, is above these opposites; he or she can be objective towards them and do whatever is to be done without coming under their spell. This person is therefore, called *dvandvātīta.*

To be above the opposites is different from the middle path, which is only a *sādhana,* a means. A person who lives according to the middle path, sometimes called the 'Middle Way' or the 'Golden Way,' is between the opposites and not at either extreme. Extremes are always a problem because they become fads. To avoid faddism, which is not a very happy situation, some people do not veer to either side, but remain in the middle in everything.

As a *sādhana,* a means, the middle path is considered to be the golden path. Then afterwards, you find that you are above the opposites; they are in your hands, in the sense, they do not upset you at all. A person who is above the opposites no longer needs to take care about being in the middle; he or she is a *dvandvātīta,* one who is naturally above the opposites.

Kṛṣṇa further explains a *dvandvātīta* in the verse as *siddhau asiddhau ca samaḥ*, one whose attitude towards success, *siddhi*, and failure, *asiddhi*, is the same. Because the person is *dvandvātīta*, he or she is not affected by any of the opposites, including success and failure. We must remember that the person being discussed in this verse is a *sannyāsī* for whom success may mean nothing more than receiving some food or being able to go to a quiet place. To be unsuccessful, then, simply means that the person does not receive any food or is not able to go to a quiet place. Thus, there are successes and failures even for a *sannyāsī*, but in either case, the person is always the same.

The six-fold afflictions

The *jñānī* is also described here as *vimatsara*, *matsara* meaning jealousy. To say that a person who is content with whatever comes by chance and who is free from the opposites is also free from jealousy seems to be somewhat out of place. Why then would Kṛṣṇa have said this?

Matsara, jealousy, and it is one of the six-fold problems.[15] Here, Kṛṣṇa takes jealousy to represent all six. *Matsara*, jealousy, is an *upalakṣaṇa* for all of them. '*Upalakṣaṇa*' means using one member of a group to represent all the members of a group. Therefore, here, the person who is described as *vimatsara* is free of all these six-fold problems. If this practice

---

[15] The six-fold problms are: *kāma*, desire; *krodha*, anger; *lobha*, greed; *moha*, delusion or false values; *mada*, vanity; and finally *matsara*, jealousy.

of taking one to cover all items in the group is not understood, the mention of *vimatsara*, one who is free from jealousy here, will disturb the even flow of thought.

We have seen the meaning of *matsara* before. When someone is happy or seems to be happy, you become sad. You may think the person is happy because he or she has what you want, but the person may not be happy at all. Perhaps this person bought the house you wanted to buy, married the person you wanted to marry, or got the promotion you were after. If another person has anything that you value, it can create jealousy, *matsara*, in you. Seeing someone's achievement, someone's success, you can be afflicted with a particular type of thinking, *matsara*, an emotion that makes you sad.

Kṛṣṇa singles out jealousy here because it is the worst affliction among the six cited above. All six, in fact, are common to everyone. Because a person feels incomplete, he or she has likes and dislikes, called *kāma*, that have to be fulfilled in order to be happy and secure.

Wherever there is *kāma*, *krodha*, anger, is possible. When someone or something stands between you and what you want, this obstruction turns your *kāma* back to yourself. This reflected beam of desire is *krodha*, anger. *Kāma* itself turns into *krodha*. When your desire, your expectation, is not fulfilled, there is anguish that turns into anger and the obstruction becomes the target of your anger even if the obstruction is yourself. Or, not knowing who is responsible, you take your anger out on anyone or anything, even God!

Then, there is greed, *lobha*. *Lobha* is a problem for those who are so insecure that, even if they have more than enough money, they cannot spend it on themselves or on others, and they think that they have to accumulate more. Like *kāma* and *krodha*, *lobha* is to be expected in one who is insecure and immature.

Having false values is also a problem, it is *moha*. A person has false values because the society in which he or she grows up has false values. To think that the colour of one's hair determines how much fun you will have, exemplified by the well known expression, 'Blondes have more fun,' is a false value. In the same way, a man may think he has made it only when he has a big boat, an apartment in Manhattan, and a cabin at Lake Tahoe! Since the society itself has these false values, *moha* is also to be expected.

Every society has false values and these false values are taught; they grow upon you. When, for instance, the society thinks that to be single means to be lonely, this particular thinking seeps into everyone's psyche. In fact, being single has nothing whatsoever to do with being lonely. A person is lonely when another person does not understand him or her. Thus, if you want to be understood, you will be lonely. You can be lonely in the midst of million people. You can live in a house with twenty people and still be lonely, especially if you sit in a corner thinking that no one likes or understands you.

When you grow up in a society that has such values, naturally you are going to imbibe these values. This imbibing is natural and whatever is imbibed can remain with you throughout your life. False values are very difficult to remove by *vicāra*, enquiry, because they have rooted themselves so firmly. To shake them loose requires a lot of understanding. To think that money, power, or anything else will save you or make you somebody is *moha*, delusion. However, given the false values of the society the person is brought up in, *moha* is understandable.

Vanity, *mada*, occurs when you do not believe in your own capacity. Most people have an underlying sense that they are useless based on the humiliation they have experienced from the time when they were three years old. In the second year of life, you think you are the only ego around; you are an absolute ego, in fact! And then you discover your mother's ego, your father's ego, your sister's ego and your brother's ego. You also discover that all these other egos are different from yours and that yours is only one among the many. This discovery is the first humiliation, followed by many more – not being first in the class, not winning the race, not coming even close and so on. In the face of all this, how will the child look at himself or herself? And who is going to escape such humiliation? You will definitely look at yourself as incompetent in some ways, if not in all.

That 'I am incompetent' is the original problem of everyone. No one need even tell me so. And if someone compliments me, I am very happy, taking it to be some grace I have received, because I think of myself as incompetent. Even if I am competent in some ways, this conclusion 'I am incompetent' is unavoidable. And when a person who thinks this way happens to accomplish something, vanity, *mada*, may be the result, which is nothing but another form of inferiority complex. Because I cannot stand my incompetence, I have to pump myself up with a kind of thinking or boasting, 'Oh! I am so wonderful' and so on. This vanity, *mada*, is also understandable given that people take themselves to be generally incompetent.

Jealousy – the least legitimate affliction of all

Kāma, krodha, lobha, moha and *mada* are all legitimate problems in that they are understandable. But, why does a person become unhappy when someone else is happy? When someone is happy, can I not at least be happy that someone, thank God, is happy? This kind of happiness is surely a very simple thing. To see someone happy because he or she has got something and to be happy for the person costs me nothing. I can work for the same thing and also get it. Instead, however, there can be unhappiness, called jealousy, which is the most illegitimate of the six fold problems.

Therefore, of the six, Kṛṣṇa singles out jealousy by saying that the wise person is free from jealousy, he is called a *vimatsara*. To be free from jealousy, *matsara*, is also to be free from desire, anger, greed, false values, and vanity. Together, these are the six fold afflictions or enemies, the *ṣaḍripus*.

The verse goes on to say that even though this wise person performs action, he or she is not bound, *kṛtvā api na nibadyate*, by the results of the action. Why? For the same reason given earlier – there being no doership, *kartṛtva-abhāvāt* in terms of knowledge. The person knows that he or she is not the doer and therefore, is not bound by action or its results.

Verse 23

The action of a jñānī who is not a sannyāsī in terms of lifestyle

Now, Kṛṣṇa returns to the other person, the one who is not a *sannyāsī,* in terms of lifestyle, but who is a *jñānī.* The *jñānī* who is engaged in activity, who has duties to do because he or she does not happen to be a *sannyāsī,* continues to play the roles. With each role there is a script and this person fulfils the script. In the next verse, Kṛṣṇa describes what happens when this type of *jñānī* performs action.

गतसङ्गस्य मुक्तस्य ज्ञानावस्थितचेतसः ।
यज्ञायाचरतः कर्म समग्रं प्रविलीयते ॥ २३ ॥

gatasaṅgasya muktasya jñānāvasthitacetasaḥ
yajñāyācarataḥ karma samagraṁ pravilīyate (23)

gatasaṅgasya – of the one who is free form attachment; *muktasya* – of one who is liberated; *jñāna-avasthita-cetasaḥ* – of one whose mind is rooted in self-knowledge; *yajñāya* – for the sake of daily *yajña; ācarataḥ* – of the one who performs; *samagram* – totally; *karma* – action; *pravilīyate* – resolves

> The *karma* of one who is free from attachment, who is liberated, whose mind is rooted in self-knowledge, who performs for the sake of daily *yajña,* resolves totally.

Although the *jñānī* may be in the midst of various activities, he or she is not attached to anything. All attachment, *saṅga,* has gone, *gata,* for the person because of self-knowledge. Thus, the *jñānī* is described here as *gata-saṅga.*

This person is also *mukta*, one who is liberated from ignorance, *ajñāna*, doership, *kartṛtva*, and therefore, from *dharma* and *adharma*, right and wrong, *puṇya* and *pāpa*. To be free from right and wrong means there is no longer any good *karma* or bad *karma* for the person because there is no doer; doership is not there. Therefore, whatever *karma* the *jñānī* does is naturally good because he or she is freed from both right and wrong.

Why is the person free? Because the mind, *cetas* of such a person is rooted in knowledge, *jñāne avasthita*. It is rooted in the sense that for this person the knowledge is clear; there is no vagueness or doubt. It is much more than simple insight. The *jñānī*'s knowledge is well-rooted and, therefore, he or she is described as *jñāna avasthita cetas*, one whose mind is rooted in knowledge of the self as a non-doer.

Any *karma* to be done by such a person, any daily duty or ritual, *yajña*, is done without any result whatsoever being accrued to the person. The *karma* done may be a prayer or an elaborate ritual; it may be a duty attached to his role as a member of a particular family or society, as an employee or an employer, or the variety of roles that he or she plays.

Samagraṁ karma means all action, action in its entirety, meaning, action along with its result. 'All' can also be taken to mean all *karma*. For the *jñānī*, then, all *karma* and its results are resolved totally, *pravilīyate*, because there is no doership for the person.

It should be noted here that it is the *jñānī* who is being described, not the *karma-yogī*, for whom there is still doership. Thus, there are two levels involved, one level being an attitude and the other being well-ascertained knowledge.

The cheerfulness that a *karma-yogī* gains by proper attitude towards what is to be done is what turns into *pūrṇatva*, fullness, by knowledge, thereby giving the person freedom from any sense of limitation. Because doership is removed by knowledge, everything else that was imposed upon *ātmā* is also removed and the person is free.

The connection between *karma-yoga* and *jñāna* is to be clearly understood. The *Gītā* teaches both *yoga-śāstra* and *brahma-vidyā*. *Karma-yoga* is right attitude and includes values, disciplines, right living, prayer and so on. Whatever is gained relatively by all these, is gained in full measure, absolute measure, through knowledge. There is tranquillity in *yoga* and tranquillity in knowledge. There is cheerfulness in *yoga* and cheerfulness in knowledge. In *karma-yoga*, the tranquillity and cheerfulness are in varying degrees, whereas in *jñāna* they are abiding and natural.

You often hear that a *karma-yogī* also is not bound by *karma*. This means that he or she is not affected by *karma-phala* in the sense that the person is not depressed by failure and elated by success because of a mature attitude towards these opposites. A *jñānī*, on the other hand, is not touched by *karma-phala* at all. To say that a *jñānī* is not bound by *karma* means that he or she is completely untouched by *karma-phala* because the self is not a doer. For such a person, everything is Brahman.

Brahman and the self are identical for a jñānī

To understand that I am *akartā* means 'I am Brahman.' The mind is also Brahman. The mind is 'I,' but I am not the mind. The *buddhi* is 'I,' but I am not the *buddhi*. The body is 'I,' but I am not the body. The world is 'I,' but I am not the world. Thus, everything is Brahman, but Brahman is not any one thing. The self and Brahman are identical. Knowing this is self-knowledge.

Whatever *karma* you do, you will find it is all the same. What is done is Brahman, the one who does it is Brahman, where it is done is Brahman, by what it is done is Brahman, and what is to be achieved is also Brahman. It means there is nothing to achieve.

When a fire ritual is performed, there is a person who performs the ritual, an altar of fire where the fire has been kindled in a particular way, and something that is offered into the fire. There is also a ladle with which the oblation is offered, a particular *mantra* or chant, and a purpose for which the ritual is being done. The person performing the ritual may want a son or the *puṇya* necessary to go to heaven or may be doing the *karma* for *antaḥ-karaṇa-śuddhi*. For this person, who wants any of the above rituals, all these factors are distinct and separate from himself and are separate amongst themselves. But for a *jñānī* they are all nothing but Brahman that is himself.

Verde 24

Kṛṣṇa uses a Vedic ritual to unfold knowledge

ब्रह्मार्पणं ब्रह्म हविर्ब्रह्माग्नौ ब्रह्मणा हुतम् ।
ब्रह्मैव तेन गन्तव्यं ब्रह्मकर्मसमाधिना ॥ २४ ॥

brahmārpaṇaṁ brahma havirbrahmāgnau brahmaṇā hutam
brahmaiva tena gantavyaṁ brahmakarmasamādhinā (24)

brahma – Brahman; *arpaṇam* – (is) the means of offering; *brahma* – Brahman; *haviḥ* – (is) the oblation; *brahma-agnau* – into the fire which is Brahman; *brahmaṇā* – by Brahman; *hutam* – is offered; *brahma-karma-samādhinā* – by the one who sees everything as Brahman; *tena* – by him; *brahma* – Brahman; *eva* – indeed; *gantavyam* – is to be reached

> The means of offering is Brahman. The oblation is Brahman, offered by Brahman into the fire, which is Brahman. Brahman indeed is to be reached by him who sees everything as Brahman.

In the preceding section, the nature of *ātmā* was described as *akartā*, meaning that the self performs no action. Action takes place based on desire and will, types of thoughts that belong to the *buddhi*. The physical body, *kāya*, organ of speech, *vāk*, and the mind, *manas* are the three means of action, *karaṇa*s. Here, the physical body refers to the hands and legs, the limbs that are used to perform action. Any action that is done can be grouped under any or all these three. For example, when you offer a prayer, it can be either a mental or a verbal action or a ritual involving physical limbs. All three involve the mind.

If *ātmā* is the body-mind-sense assemblage, which is the basis for all actions to take place, then I become the actor. Whereas, if this assemblage is not *ātmā*, then *ātmā* is free from the body, mind and senses. It is in the form of pure consciousness, *śuddha-caitanya-svarūpa*, and performs no action whatsoever. Thus, it was said that even while performing action, the wise person does no action whatsoever because doership is not there for the person.[16]

Also, if the *jñānī* performs only those actions that are necessary to sustain the physical body, no results will accrue because, again, there is no doership.[17] In this way, two types of *jñānī*s were pointed out. One type is in the thick and thin of various activities, totally engaged in action, and the second type is not. But, even for the *jñānī* who performs activities, it was said that no action is performed. Why? Because, the person sees *akarma* in all *karma*s, meaning that he sees *ātmā* as actionless in the very activity itself. How much or how little activity one does means nothing. What is important is whether one sees *ātmā* as *akartā*.

There is no rule how a wise person should be. One person may be very active and another may be a *sannyāsī*. A *sannyāsī* can also be active or not that active. He may perform only those activities necessary to sustain the body or may be involved in the world because of his *prārabdha*. Either way, there is no *karma* for the person and no results accrue to him because there is no doership.

Here, in this verse, we see that for the wise person, *karma* and everything connected to *karma* is Brahman. In fact, this is what self-knowledge is all about. There is nothing separate from *ātmā*, which is Brahman. This is the knowledge that

---

[16] *Gītā* 4.20

[17] *Gītā* 4.21

makes the person wise. *Ātmā* is equated to Brahman. Brahman is *jñāna*, pure consciousness, and therefore, not subject to time, space, or any attributes. It is *satya*, pure existence, and *ananta*, limitless, which is the basis, the truth of everything. In terms of time, *ātmā* is limitless, and in terms of space also, it is limitless. There is nothing that is independent of this *satya*, *ātmā*. Being dependent on *satya* which is *paraṁ-brahma*, everything else is nothing but *paraṁ-brahma*, which is *ātmā*, oneself.

One who sees *ātmā* as free from action sees *ātmā* as Brahman, and this is *jñāna*. Therefore, we have to understand *ātmā* as a non-doer, as *paraṁ-brahma*. With this knowledge, all actions and everything connected to them, including the results, are nullified, negated.

The statement made earlier, *karmaṇi akarma yaḥ paśyet*, was made clearer when it was said, in the last verse, that all the *karma*s of the wise person are totally resolved, *samagraṁ karma pravilīyate*. To say that a wise person sees *akarma* in *karma* implies that there are actions being done. For example, speaking is an action done for which there is someone who speaks, a subject matter, a way of speaking, a reason for speaking and so on, all of which the *jñānī* understands as being non-separate from *paraṁ-brahma*.

The *kartā*, agent of action is Brahman. The *karma*, object of action is Brahman. The *karaṇa*, instrument of action, is Brahman and the place where the action is done is Brahman. This vision that everything is Brahman is unfolded in the present verse by using a Vedic ritual as an example. Kṛṣṇa is not pointing out the ritual itself here; he is pointing out the wisdom, the vision that is Vedanta.

A Vedic ritual is as good as a prayer. It is an action in which a purpose and a result are involved. There is a person who wants a particular result and there is a method of offering a particular oblation. All the *kāraka*s, the factors involved in an action, are presented in this verse – an agent of action, an object, a means, a purpose, a place from where the action is coming, and a place into which the action is going.

What Kṛṣṇa is conveying here is that every *kāraka* is Brahman. The means of offering is Brahman, *brahma arpaṇam*. Here *arpaṇa* means that by which something is offered, *arpyate anena iti arpaṇam*.[18] What is the oblation? *Havis*, the oblation that is offered, is also Brahman, *brahma haviḥ*. Where is the offering made? *Brahma-agnau,* into the fire of Brahman, the fire that is Brahman. By whom is the offering made? The offering is made by Brahman, *brahmaṇā hutam*. The *kartā*, the doer, is Brahman. For what purpose is the offering made? The offering is made for the purpose of gaining Brahman alone, *brahma eva tena gantavyam*. By whom is this Brahman to be gained? By one who sees everything as Brahman, *brahma-karma-samādhinā*.

Arpaṇa is that by which something is offered like a wooden ladle or a *mantra* with which an offering is made. And while

[18] *anena,* by means of this; *arpyate,* is offered; *arpaṇam* – the means, the instrument with which the oblation is offered into the fire during a ritual and this could mean both the wooden laddle and the *mantra* with which the offering is made

offering, a particular *mantra* is chanted to indicate exactly to which *devatā*, deity the oblation is being offered. For instance, the words, '*indrāya svāhā, indrāya idaṁ na mama*' are to invoke the *devatā* called Indra and they mean, 'This is being offered to Indra; (this) does not belong to me any more.' Similarly, '*agnaye svāhā agnaye idam na mama*' means, 'This is for Agni; (this) is no longer mine.' In this way, you are not making the *devatā* indebted to you. You offer the oblation to the chosen *devatā*, saying, 'This is for you alone. I am giving it to you. It is no longer mine.' This is the meaning of *arpaṇa*.

Whether a ladle or a *mantra*, how is this *arpaṇa* separate from Brahman? Nothing is separate from Brahman. Therefore, sound is Brahman, word is Brahman, knowledge is Brahman, Indra is Brahman. Everything is non-separate from Brahman. Because of the wise person's *brahma-buddhi*, he or she performs the ritual seeing Brahman in everything, just as when you see a clay pot, the clay is not missed, or when you see a golden ornament, the gold is not missed, or when you see a shirt, the cloth is not missed.

The satya and mithyā of the ritual

Similarly, when a *jñānī* sees anything, Brahman is not missed, Brahman being the cause of everything. Brahman being the truth, the *satya* of everything, everything is dependent upon *satya brahma* and is therefore *mithyā*. It means that *arpaṇa*, the ladle, the *mantra*, and so on, are *mithyā*. Thus, *arpaṇa* is Brahman, *brahma arpaṇam*.

The object offered is *havis*, clarified butter or any other thing that is offered as the oblation. This is also Brahman.

And it is offered by Brahman, *brahmaṇā hutam*. That is, the person who offers the oblation is also Brahman, a fact known to the wise person. *Hutam* means, 'is offered.' This word refers to the act of offering, the *kriyā*. The oblation, *havis*, is offered unto the fire, *agni*, the location in which the act of offering takes place. Here, too, *agni* is nothing but Brahman, born of Brahman, and therefore non-separate from Brahman.

We see that all the *kāraka*s are covered here. The first *kāraka*, the *kartā*, the one who offers is Brahman; the second *kāraka*, the *karma*, object is Brahman; the third *kāraka*, the *karaṇa*, instrument is Brahman; the purpose that takes the fourth case is Brahman; and the fifth *kāraka*, from where the action comes, is Brahman. Because the sixth *kāraka*, the possessive or genitive case, generally does not relate to an action, it does not represent one of the six. The seventh, which takes the locative case is also here in the verse. Here, it is said, 'in the fire of Brahman, *brahmāgnau*.' Therefore, the fire into which the offering is made is also Brahman.

If I perform a ritual for the sake of heaven, I am a *kartā*. Because I am a *kartā*, I want to go to heaven and this heaven is separate from me. Therefore, if I do this particular *karma*, the *karma-phala* will be *puṇya* and I can encash this *puṇya* later for a ticket to heaven. This is the meaning of a ritual if I am a *kartā*, whereas if I know that I am Brahman, it is altogether different.

Brahman is everything, including heaven. This being the case, what is to be gained by the person of knowledge? Brahman alone is to be gained by the wise person, *brahmaiva tena gantavyam*. This is to say that nothing is to be gained because the *jñānī* is Brahman.

Gantavyam means, 'that which is to be reached' or 'that which is to be accomplished.' Because the person is already Brahman, there is nothing to be gained. Everything being Brahman, there is nothing away from Brahman and, therefore, nothing to be gained that is not Brahman. While this may be a fact, one has to know the fact. Otherwise, the person is a *kartā*. Then, looking at everything in a ritual as Brahman becomes a form of meditation, *upāsanā*. Wherever you deliberately superimpose something exalted on the ordinary, there is *upāsanā*. Like you deliberately superimpose the United States on a piece of cloth with so many stars and stripes.

Superimposition need not be deliberate always; it can happen when you mistake an object for something else. For instance, you may superimpose a snake on a piece of rope, without any deliberation. This is a mistake. But, to take a wooden or stone statue of Viṣṇu for the Lord is not a mistake, unless of course, you take the given form alone as Viṣṇu. This is *upāsanā*.

Knowledge alone is involved here

Whereas, when a person realises the fact, 'I am Brahman,' it is knowledge, not *upāsanā*. Here, in this verse, knowledge alone is involved, the ritual being performed by one who sees Brahman in all actions, *brahma-karma-samādhi*. Seeing Brahman everywhere is called *brahma-karma-samādhi*.

How can one see Brahman everywhere? If one goes around with eyes wide open will Brahman be seen in everything? When a chair is seen, do you go beyond the chair and see Brahman? Seeing Brahman is not like looking at a shirt and seeing the cloth. When you see a shirt, you see only the shirt. Obviously, then, you do not see Brahman in this way. In fact, you will not see Brahman because you are Brahman! The thought that objectifies the chair is Brahman. The space in which the chair is sitting is also Brahman. And the chair itself, every particle of it, is nothing but Brahman.

The object of any thought is non-separate from the consciousness that is Brahman and the knowledge of the object, the thought itself, is also non-separate from this consciousness. The one who knows, who has the knowledge of the object, is also nothing but consciousness. Therefore, the knower, the knowledge, and the object of knowledge are Brahman, consciousness, which is *satya*.

So the statement, 'I am Brahman,' means *ātmā* is Brahman which is *nirvikalpa*, that which does not have the knower-knowledge-known distinction, *jñātṛ-jñāna-jñeya-bheda*. *Nirvikalpa* does not mean the absence of thought but points to the non-difference between the knower, knowledge and known. Because knowledge is myself, the knower is myself, and the object of knowledge is myself, these three are only apparently different. To say, 'I am *nirvikalpa*,' is to refer to the fact that there is no real difference between the knower, knowledge, and known. This knowledge is always *nirvikalpa*, there being no second thing. Whether I know it or not, this knowledge is always there. Similarly, when I see, the seer, the sight, and the seen are Brahman. And when I hear, the hearer, the hearing, and the heard are also Brahman.

Being in any situation is seeing Brahman everywhere, *sarvatrabrahma-darśanam*. It is not a matter of opening one's eyes and trying to see Brahman. Brahman is not an object to be seen with the eyes. To see Brahman everywhere is to recognise the fact that the knower, *jñāta*, is Brahman, the knowledge, *jñāna*, is Brahman, and what is known, *jñeya*, is Brahman. All three are Brahman, but Brahman is independent of all of them.

Seeing Brahman everywhere is knowledge

In fact, all three, knower-knowledge-known, can be shaken off; they can be removed. And they can return to be removed again. You have them, you remove them, you have them, you remove them, and all the while Brahman always is. The one who has this knowledge, who sees Brahman everywhere, is called *brahma-karma-samādhi*.

Brahma-karma-samādhi here refers to a person who has a *buddhi* that appreciates that everything is Brahman, *brahma eva karma, brahma-karma, brahma-karmaṇi samādhiḥ* (*samāhitā buddhiḥ*) *yasya*.[19] And what is to be gained by the *brahmakarma-samādhi*, one who sees Brahman in all action? What is to be gained when everything is Brahman? Nothing, except Brahman, *brahmaiva gantavyam*. If everything is Brahman, what result can there be? If the doer is Brahman, the done is Brahman, the doing is Brahman, and the reason for doing it is Brahman, where is the result? For whom is the result? And for what purpose is the result?

Knowing that everything is Brahman, the *jñānī* who is engaged in activity performs action for the sake of the people,

---

19 ब्रह्मैव कर्म ब्रह्मकर्म तस्मिन् समाधिः यस्य, सः ब्रह्मकर्मसमाधिः। (शङ्कर भाष्यम्)

loka-saṅgrahārtham. Even though there is nothing for the wise person to accomplish, his time is available for helping people. The *jñānī* requires nothing to be secure or happy and therefore, his time is no longer required for himself. Whatever time is left in the person's life can therefore be given to the people for them to make use of as best as they can.

Even if the *jñānī* does not talk, people can go and sit with him, as they did with Ramana Maharshi. He did not talk much and would speak only a few words, now and then. This also is a type of teaching, a quiet teaching. When you sit with someone who sits quietly, happily, you also become quiet. Your mind becomes quiet because you have to come back to yourself. What else can you do when the person you are sitting with does not talk?

When there is no interaction, you come back to yourself. And what kind of self, do you come back to? Not the historical self, because the person you are sitting with is all silence; he does not even blink! The situation naturally takes you back to yourself. This is not enlightenment; it is only experiential.

There is some *śānti*, peace and contentment. People like this experience and therefore, they seek it out. But afterwards, the *śānti* is gone. It is only something they can remember and talk about, just like when they come out of a movie and talk about how enjoyable it was. The 'was' aspect of experience is there because there is no enlightenment. The experience itself is something you can only recall and interpret in your own way. Still, the person who gives some *śānti* to people is helping them and it is certainly better than giving them excitement!

The rock musician gives people excitement for which they pay money. You sit with the *jñānī* and you are happy. At least, here, the *śānti* is free. Excitement may provide some release for pent up emotions, but coming back to yourself is even better. And it is beautiful, as well. Thus, the *jñānī* who can give you some *śānti* is performing action for the sake of the people by not talking.

This is exactly what Ramana did. Hundreds of people used to go and sit with him. A few, of course, were disappointed when they realised that he would not talk, but a lot of other people enjoyed the peace and silence. Therefore, a *jñānī* may be performing a variety of activities for the sake of the people or he may just sit quietly, an activity that also helps people. In reality, however, whatever is done or not done is still *akarma*. It is not an action or an activity because actions, *karma*s, have been nullified by the knowledge of Brahman.

Whatever an actor does on stage, he knows that he is not the role and that the role is himself. He sees this very clearly because of his knowledge that the action he performs is *mithyā*. So, too, the wise person knows, 'I am not the role. I am *satya* and the role is *mithyā*.' While actions come only from the person, he knows that his nature is *satya*. This being understood, he performs no action in reality.

In this verse, which is unfolding this vision through a ritual, *karma* is converted into *akarma*, all the *kāraka*s being nothing but Brahman. In this way, the *kāraka*s are nullified, *bādhita*.

They no longer exist. When one knows that everything is Brahman, doership is gone. When the doership is gone, there is no real *karma* anymore. Therefore, in answer to the question, how can one see *akarma* in *karma, karma* is completely negated here and only Brahman remains.

For *karma* to be there, there must be a *kartā*, a doer, who is different from the *kriyā*, the action, one who performs the *kriyā* through the *karaṇa*, the means of action, for a given purpose. There will also be a *karma-phala*, a result, and the person is bound by that *karma*. However, when the *ahaṅkāra* itself, the one who performs the action, is resolved, the *ahaṅkāra* becomes identical with Brahman. But Brahman is free from the *ahaṅkāra*.

Here one could get confused in the following manner and think that if the *ahaṅkāra* is Brahman and Brahman is not *ahaṅkāra*, all that has happened is that the *ahaṅkāra* has gained a new name. *Ahaṅkāra* becomes a synonym for Brahman. I thought of myself as an ego, *ahaṅkāra*, the doer. Now I have come to know the doer is also called Brahman. Since the doer is Brahman and Brahman is not the doer, the doer gains a new name. There is nothing more to it than that. But it is not so.

Here, the doer is Brahman, doing is Brahman, everything is Brahman, whereas Brahman is free from all of them. From this we understand that there is *akarma* in the *karma* itself and *karma* itself is *bādhita*, negated. Thus, this verse unfolds the vision of *ātmā*. Giving up *karma* by knowledge, negating it, is called *jñāna-karma-sannyāsa*. It is also the title of this chapter.

This verse unfolds the vision and as such cannot be a form of meditation

Here, Śaṅkara raises an objection and answers it. Why not interpret the verse as a kind of meditation by looking upon the *arpaṇa*, offering, as Brahman, just as the Lord is invoked in an idol? But if it were intended to be a meditation, why was it said that the person would gain Brahman, *brahmaiva tena gantavyam*? To take the verse in this way would also be ignoring the knowledge previously stated that, one sees *akarma* in *karma*.

The vision of *ātmā* as *akartā* is the knowledge. Because everyone takes himself or herself to be a *kartā*, there is *saṁsāra*. *Kartṛtva* is indeed *saṁsāritva* and nothing else. When you look upon yourself as a *kartā*, you are taking yourself to be the physical body-mind-sense complex, *kārya-karaṇa-saṅghāta*. The body, mind and senses become the 'I,' the *ātmā*, for you. This is the only way you become a *kartā*. And, if you take the body, mind, and senses as *ātmā*, then you are a *saṁsāri*. This is why *kartṛtva* means *saṁsāritva*. When the *kartṛtva*, doership, is there, *saṁsāritva* is there, meaning that there is an enjoyer of the results of action, *karma-phala-bhoktā*. Where there is *kartṛtva*, doership, there is *bhoktṛtva*, enjoyership and this is what we call *saṁsāra*.

The main problem of *saṁsāra*, *kartṛtva*, is negated in this verse by unfolding the vision of *ātmā* as *akartā*. Therefore, to take it as meditation, for which there can be only a limited result, is not correct. Moreover, the verse also says that Brahman is to be gained, *brahmaiva tena gantavyam*. Brahman, being limitless, is not a limited result. Besides, because the person is non-different from Brahman, there is nothing to be accomplished for one who can appreciate this vision. Thus, the verse is an unfoldment of this vision and, as such, cannot be a meditation.

By presenting a *karma*, a ritual, Kṛṣṇa unfolds the knowledge of *ātmā* as Brahman, free from any doership and enjoyership. It is how *akarma* can be seen in *karma*. You do the *karma* and, at the same time, you see the *akarma*. You see the *karma* and you negate it, just as you see a movie and then negate the reality of it by knowing that the scenes you see are projected on a plain surface by means of light and shadows. *Ātmā* itself is always detached, *asaṅga*. It remains clean, just like the screen upon which a movie is seen. This is the nature of a *jñānī*. *Ātmā* performs no action, *naiva kiñcit karma karoti*, and does not enjoy the fruit of action, *na karma-phalam bhuṅkte*.

Because the verse presents the clear vision of *ātmā* as Brahman and *karma* as *akarma*, no other meaning is possible here. To show that *karma* is *akarma*, the vision had to be presented in the form of a *karma* and here it is presented in the form of a *yajña*. The vision is that all *karma*s are Brahman and, to praise this vision, Kṛṣṇa presents other *yajña*s in subsequent verses.

In order to praise or understand something, a background is always necessary. For example, to bring out colour or shape of a precious stone, a particular background is provided. A frame for a painting is also selected in keeping with the colours on the canvas and those of the surroundings in which it will hang. Here, too, the Vedic background of various rituals and disciplines are provided for the knowledge of Brahman unfolded by the Vedas.

In the following section, a discipline is called a *yajña*. It refers to anything that is to be done or offered by someone for the purpose of self purification and steadiness of mind. The Lord presents the pursuit of knowledge itself as *yajña, jñāna-yajña*, against the background of various other *yajña*s that are helpful for preparing the mind to gain the knowledge.

Verse 25

Yajñas include various forms of discipline

दैवमेवापरे यज्ञं योगिनः पर्युपासते ।
ब्रह्माग्नावपरे यज्ञं यज्ञेनैवोपजुह्वति ॥ २५ ॥

daivam evāpare yajñaṁ yoginaḥ paryupāsate
brahmāgnāvapare yajñaṁ yajñenaivopajuhvati (25)

apare yoginaḥ – some *yogins* (*karma-yogīs*); *daivaṁ yajñam* – ritual invoking deities; *eva* – alone; *paryupāsate* – perform; *apare* – others (*sannyāsīs*); *brahmagnau* – unto the fire (knowledge) of Brahman; *yajñam* – the self (*ahaṅkāra*); *yajñena eva* – by the self (*ahaṅkāra*) itself; *upajuhvati* – offer

> *Karma-yogīs* perform only those rituals that invoke the deities, while others (*sannyāsīs*) offer themselves by themselves unto the fire (knowledge) of Brahman.

At the beginning of the third chapter, Kṛṣṇa told Arjuna that he had given the world two committed lifestyles.[20]

[20] *Gītā* 3.3

One lifestyle is *sannyāsa* wherein the commitment, *niṣṭha,* is pursuit of knowledge alone. The other lifestyle is *karma-yoga,* a life of activity wherein the pursuit of knowledge is coupled with *karma*. Kṛṣṇa also made it clear that both lifestyles are for the sake of *mokṣa,* liberation.

Here, in the verse under discussion, both the *karma-yogī* and the *sannyāsī* are discussed. For *karma-yogī*s, *apare yoginaḥ,* the enjoined *karma* is only for *antah-karaṇa-śuddhi,* not for any other end. It is for preparing their minds for the knowledge that is *mokṣa,* all of which we have seen in the previous discussions on *karma-yoga.*

When the *karma-yogī*s perform rituals, *yajñaṁ-paryupāsate,* the Lord or the Lord in the form of a deity is always kept in view. Anything that is done with the Lord or a deity, a *deva,* in view is called *daiva*. Indra is a *deva,* so is Agni, fire, and Āditya, the sun. Thus, any action done invoking their grace is *daivaṁ karma*. *Karma-yogī*s worship in this way and do not see everything as Brahman as the *sannyāsī* does. They are simply performing rituals invoking the *devatā*s, invoking the Lord's grace for gaining *antah-karaṇa-śuddhi*.

We know the verse is not referring to those who perform rituals for ends other than *antaḥ-karaṇa-śuddhi,* like heaven etc., *svargādi loka,* because the people performing the action here are called *yogī*s. Those who are not *yogī*s may perform rituals for the sake of gaining children, wealth, heaven, and so on. There are many rituals in the Vedas that can produce these types of results and the people who perform them are called *kāmya karmī*s. Because the word *yoginaḥ* is used in this verse, we know that the people under discussion perform rituals for *antah-karaṇa-śuddhi* alone.

These rituals are performed meticulously, meaning that they are performed with *śraddhā*, with faith, alertness, and in careful adherence to the rules. The prefix '*pari*' with the verb '*upāsate*' conveys the sense of the meticulousness with which the *yajña*s are performed to invoke the grace of the *devatā*s.

Apare, which usually means 'others,' is used here to distinguish between the *karma-yogī*s and the *sannyāsī*s discussed in this verse.

Offering oneself to the fire of knowledge

In the expression *brahmāgnau*, fire of Brahman, fire stands for knowledge, the knowledge of Brahman. The word *yajña*, besides meaning ritual and discipline, means *ātmā*, the self. Because there is a sacrifice involved for one who pursues knowledge, knowledge also can be looked upon as *yajña* and is therefore, called *jñāna-yajña*.

In any *yajña* there must be a performer of the *yajña*. Here, the performer of this *jñāna-yajña* is the seeker, a *mumukṣu*, a *jijñāsu*, one who wants to know. The verse points out that the seeker offers himself or herself. Since the seeker alone is offered, who is it that does the offering? If someone else offered the seeker unto the fire, it would be a simple case of homicide, but here, because the seeker offers himself or herself, it seems to be suicide, not homicide, and a willing suicide at that! One offers oneself, *yajñaṁ yajñena upajuhvati*. Here, *yajña* means the self.

Unto the fire of Brahman is offered the *ahaṅkāra*. The ignorant person looks upon himself or herself as one who has doership and enjoyership because he or she takes the body, mind and senses to be the self. It is this small person, the seeker, who is offered unto the fire of Brahman, the knowledge of Brahman.

To offer the *ahaṅkāra* unto the knowledge of Brahman is the best form of 'hara-kiri'[21] there is. The seekers, the *sannyāsī*s, offer themselves by themselves into the fire (knowledge) of Brahman. This means they are both the *kartā* and the *karma*, the performer of the action of offering and the object offered. The doer of the *jñāna-yajña*, is myself, the one who knows is myself, what is known is myself, and what is offered unto the fire of Brahman is also myself. It means that I am Brahman.

This knowledge that I am Brahman is called *samyag-darśana*, clear vision, and, being clear vision, it is opposed to the *deva- yajña* performed by *karma-yogī*. As Kṛṣṇa told Arjuna in the third chapter, when *sannyāsī*s follow pure *jñāna*, it is *jñāna-yoga*, which is the *jñāna-yajña* mentioned in this verse. The two types of people are not being compared here but the two types of *yajña*, *deva-yajña* and *jñāna-yajña*, are being compared.

Having said this much, Kṛṣṇa goes on to describe other *yajña*s, after which he would again praise *jñāna-yajña*. The *yajña*s, mentioned in the next few verses are not rituals at all,

[21] hara-kiri, means belly-cutting, a traditional Japanese form of suicide, performed in cases of disloyalty to the emperor. Obligatory hara-kiri was abolished in 1868 but voluntary forms have persisted.

but because they are disciplines whose purpose is to accomplish *mokṣa* by *antaḥ-karaṇa-śuddhi*, they are considered to be *yajña*s. Such disciplines can accomplish two ends. One is, certain composure, tranquillity and steadiness of mind. The second end that can be accomplished is maturity, a freedom from the thraldom of one's *rāga-dveṣa*s, likes and dislikes, that hold one hostage. You can release yourself from their hands by prayers and rituals, which help you gain certain attitudes. These disciplines can also help you gain alertness and are performed by *sannyāsī*s and *karma-yogī*s, alike. They may be practised in order to gain *mokṣa* or for lesser results, such as a degree of composure or discipline in your life so that the other disciplines may be practised.

There is no rule governing which disciplines are to be performed by whom. You may choose one or another, depending upon what you need. Thus, Kṛṣṇa mentions a few disciplines performed as *yajña*s.

Verses 26&27

The offering of one's sensory activities

श्रोत्रादीनीन्द्रियाण्यन्ये संयमाग्निषु जुह्वति ।
शब्दादीन्विषयानन्य इन्द्रियाग्निषु जुह्वति ॥ २६ ॥

śrotrādīnīndriyāṇyanye saṁyamāgniṣu juhvati
śabdādīn viṣayān anya indriyāgniṣu juhvati (26)

anye – others; *saṁyamāgniṣu* – into the fire of self-mastery; *śrotrādīni* – organs of hearing ; *indriyāṇi* – senses; *juhvati* – offer; *anye* – others; *śabdādīn* – sound, etc., *viṣayān* – sense objects; *indriyāgniṣu* – into the fire of the senses; *juhvati* – offer

Others offer (their) organs of hearing and other senses into the fire of self-mastery, (while still) others offer sound and other sense objects into the fire of the senses.

The first *yajña* described in this verse relates to the sense organs, the ears and so on, *śrotrādīni indriyāṇi. Śrotra* means ear and the suffix *ādi,* meaning 'etc.' refers to the eyes, nose, tongue, and skin, sense of touch. These five are the organs through which sense perceptions such as, hearing, seeing, smelling, tasting, and touching, respectively, take place. Here, the organs of sense perception and the organs of action are offered unto the fire of self-mastery.

Does this mean that the organs themselves are offered? Does one pluck off the ears and nose or pull out the eyes and tongue to offer them unto the fire? Of course not. In fact, the person does not do anything. The discipline described here is control of the senses or inner mastery, *saṁyama.* People who follow this discipline are practising *saṁyama,* meaning that they do not go by their fancies. In other words, they practise alertness with reference to the senses.

A discipline is not an end in itself

We see this alertness or deliberateness in Buddhistic meditation. Those who practise this discipline remain aware of everything that they do, even the opening and closing of their eyes. This practice definitely has its benefits, but it can also create tension and should be followed up with enquiry. Enquiry should be the main emphasis, whereas the practice itself is a discipline, meaning that it is not an end in itself. This discipline is a means for gaining certain composure.

Thus, the first *yajña* mentioned in this verse is a discipline wherein the sensory activities, dictated by fancies, are offered unto the fires of self-mastery *saṁyama-agniṣu.* The sense organs being many, fire appears in its plural form here. It should be noted that it is the activities that are offered, not the senses. All fanciful and mechanical activities are offered unto the fire of deliberation, meaning that all one's activities are conscious and deliberate. This is what is meant by control.

The other *yajña* described here is the offering of the sense objects, sound and so on, *śabdādi viṣayān,* which include touch, form, taste and smell. These sense objects are offered unto the fires of the sense organs, *indriya-agniṣu.* But then, this seems to be no different than what is happening everywhere in the world today. People are lining up to see all kinds of movies and are listening to all kinds of music, feeding their sense organs with whatever sense objects they want. This, of course, is not what is being said here.

Śaṅkara explains the compound *indriya-agniṣu* as, *indriyāṇi eva agnayaḥ,* meaning that the senses alone are the fires. Unto the fires of sense organs the sense objects are offered. Taken literally, it would seem that sounds are offered unto the ears, forms are offered unto the eyes, smells are offered unto the nose, tastes are offered unto the tongue, and touch is offered unto the sense of touch. This is what we commonly do throughout our entire lifetime. Where, then, is the discipline here? We are talking about *yajña,* which means discipline.

Discipline in activity

To clarify this point, Śaṅkara says that for the people discussed in this verse, there is a discipline in all this. Just as a mother decides what her child should eat, how much and when, which becomes a discipline for the child until he can decide these things for himself, so too, *yogīs* follow certain disciplines. Some follow *śama,* which is mentioned in the first line of this verse, and others follow *dama,* mentioned in the second line.

The senses are offered with a certain discipline – how much to see, how much to hear, how much to talk, how much to walk, and so on. Knowing how much to eat, for example, the person eats no more, even though there may be a desire for another helping. These are disciplines which are the practice of *dama.* Initially, *yogīs* practise mainly *dama* so that they can come to *śama* later. In this way they live their lives with discipline.

With reference to every sense organ, there is a sense object. The *yogī* offers the sense objects to the sense organs, but he or she holds the trump card as it were. The sense objects do not carry the person away. Even though one lets the sense organs go out into the world, the person practises restraint, *dama,* by ensuring that only *dharma* is followed, not *adharma.* The *yogī* feeds the sense organs with whatever is proper, *dharma aviruddha. Aviruddha* means that which is unopposed to one's pursuit or conducive to one's welfare. This point is crucial in understanding the meaning of *yajña* here. Without harming his pursuit, without hurting the *dharma,* the *yogī* perceives and enjoys the sense objects, feeding the sense organs in a manner that is conducive to his pursuit of knowledge.

The word '*juhvati,*' in this verse, is also important. It does not simply mean to feed the sense organs or to sacrifice something. It means that you are doing the offering, you hold the trump card and are not letting the senses feed themselves. The senses want more; your fancies always demand more, but you say, 'No!' This is like a child wanting the chocolates that he had collected on Halloween, but the mother says, 'No!' 'Why not,' the child says, 'they are my chocolates. I went around and collected all of them. Why should I not eat all of them?' 'Yes,' the mother explains, 'they are your chocolates all right, but I will keep them for you. You may have one today and another one tomorrow.' Even though the child may cry, the mother remains firm. Here, you do the same for yourself. You mother yourself by disciplining the demands of your fancies, which is the practice of *dama*.

Further Kṛṣṇa says:

सर्वाणीन्द्रियकर्माणि प्राणकर्माणि चापरे ।
आत्मसंयमयोगाग्नौ जुह्वति ज्ञानदीपिते ॥ २७ ॥

sarvāṇīndriyakarmāṇi prāṇakarmāṇi cāpare
ātmasaṁyamayogāgnau juhvati jñānadīpite (27)

apare – others; *jñāna-dīpite* – lighted by knowledge; *ātma-saṁyama-yoga-agnau* – in the fire of self-mastery; *sarvāṇi* – all; *indriyakarmāṇi* – activities of the senses; *prāṇakarmāṇi* – activities of the organs of action; *ca* – and; *juhvati* – offer

> Others offer all the activities of the senses and the organs of action unto the fire of self-mastery lighted by knowledge.

The seekers discussed in this verse are *sannyāsī*s but not *jñānī*s. Because they are *sannyāsī*s with no obligatory duties to perform, they offer their activities, except those required to maintain the body, unto the fire of self mastery, *ātma-saṁyama-*

yoga-agnau juhvati. Such people live a life of meditation and contemplation, called *ātma-saṁyama-yoga*. Unto this fire of meditation that is helpful in self-knowledge, those who are given to meditation offer all sensory and other activities.

For the people discussed here, the usual activities of life resolve into one life of meditation. Thus, they do nothing but meditation and whatever that is necessary to maintain the body so that the knowledge can be gained. The previous verse talked about seekers who live in the world, but the seekers in this verse are renunciates. They remain where they have to remain, live a life of meditation, and pursue knowledge. Here, then, meditation is being emphasised. These seekers are *sannyāsī*s as well as *yogī*s. For them there is *viveka,* their discipline being lighted by knowledge, *jñāna-dīpita*. In other words, they know exactly that they want the knowledge that is *mokṣa*.

Here, *jñāna-dīpite* means lighted by knowledge, a knowledge of what is right and wrong, what is *nitya* and *anitya*, real and unreal. Thus, both *vairāgya* and *viveka* are there, but *dama* and *śama* are yet to be gained. In order to gain this self-mastery, these seekers have given up activities and have taken to a life of meditation. Such *sannyāsī*s are many.

Verse 28

Kṛṣṇa describes more yajñas

द्रव्ययज्ञास्तपोयज्ञा योगयज्ञास्तथापरे ।
स्वाध्यायज्ञानयज्ञाश्च यतयः संशितव्रताः ॥ २८ ॥

dravyayajñāstapoyajñā yogayajñāstathāpare
svādhyāyajñānayajñāśca yatayaḥ saṁśitavratāḥ (28)

tathā – so too; *apare* – (are the) others; *dravya-yajñāḥ* – those who share (their) wealth; *tapo-yajñāḥ* – those who follow prayerful disciplines; *yoga-yajñāḥ* – those who practise *yoga*; *ca* – and; *svādhyāya-jñāna-yajñaḥ* – those who pursue recitation of their own Veda and self-knowledge; *saṁśita-vratāḥ* – those of firm vows; *yatayaḥ* – those who make efforts

> So too, there are those who share (their) wealth, those who follow prayerful disciplines, those who practise *yoga*, and those of firm vows and efforts who pursue recitation of their own Veda and self-knowledge.

Here, Kṛṣṇa points out various other disciplines, *yajña*s that different types of seekers are engaged in. Those who distribute wealth in the form of money or whatever else that may be given as charity are called *dravya-yajña*s. To distribute one's wealth, *dravya* can be purely charity or it can be given as a *yajña*, as an offering, to the Lord, as a means of invoking the Lord in the form of this sacrifice. A person who does this is called a *dravya-yajña*[22] here in this verse.

For example, in India, a good part of the wealth, in the form of cows, land, gold, clothing, vessels, or grain, that a man leaves behind when he dies is distributed to the people. In fact, this distribution is the main part of the ritual

[22] तीर्थेषु द्रव्य-विनियोगं यज्ञ-बुद्ध्या ये, ते द्रव्य-यज्ञाः । (शङ्कर भाष्यम्)

tīrtheṣu dravya viniyogaṁ yajña buddhyā ye te dravya yajñāḥ (*Śaṅkara-bhāṣyam*)

Those who perform *dravya-yajña*s, that is, distribute money as *yajña* are called *dravya-yajña*s performed after death. Before the cremation, the distribution takes place. To distribute one's wealth as a *yajña,* while living, helps one gain *antaḥ-karaṇa-śuddhi* because there is giving involved.

Another set of seekers described in this verse are the *tapo-yajñas*. Those who practise various types of *tapas* are called as *tapo-yajñas*.[23] *Tapas* refers to any kind of prayerful discipline undertaken for the sake of atonement or discipline. The vows that one takes are also *tapas*. Some people, for example, take a vow of not eating on *ekādaśī,* the eleventh day of the moon, each month and spend the day in prayer. Such people are called *tapo-yajñas*. *Tapas* is not just any discipline; it is prayerful discipline. Otherwise, even jogging and aerobics would become *yajñas*! Here, the attitude is religious and therefore, is again for *antaḥ-karaṇa-śuddhi*.

Seekers who follow *aṣṭāṅga-yoga*, eight limbed *yoga,* are called *yoga-yajñas. Aṣṭāṅga-yoga* is a prayerful discipline wherein the Lord is worshipped. *Īśvara-praṇidhānam* is one of its prescribed observances, *niyamas*. Still others who are *yatayaḥ saṁśitavratāḥ*, people of effort and whose vows are very clear, are *svādhyāya-jñāna-yajñas*, those who follow the discipline of study and knowledge.

Svādhyāya-yajña refers to those who learn to chant or recite their own Veda. There are some people who, having learned

---

23 तपः यज्ञः येषां ते – तपोयज्ञाः । बहुव्रीहि-समासः ॥

tapaḥ yajñaḥ yeṣāṁ te – tapoyajñāḥ (*bahuvrīhi-samāsaḥ*)

Those who practise the various types of disciplines as *yājña* are called as *tapoyājñas*.

the Veda in this way, do nothing but recite a portion of it daily. Such people are called *svādhyāya-yajña*s, those who perform the *yajña* of *svādhyāya*. And those who study Vedanta, who enquire into the *vedanta-śāstra* are called *jñāna-yajña*s, those who perform the *yajña* of pursuing knowledge, *jñāna*. Here, the *svādhyāya-jñāna-yajña*s are the people of great effort, *yatayaḥ*, whose commitment to knowledge is complete, *saṁśitavratāḥ*. And these people do both these *yajña*s and are therefore, referred to as *svādhyāya-jñāna-yajña*s in this verse.

Verse 29

Prāṇāyāma is also looked upon as yajña

Other seekers follow the discipline of *prāṇāyāma* or breath control, one of the eight limbs of *aṣṭāṅga-yoga*, which is also looked upon as a *yajña*, as we shall see in the next verse.

अपाने जुह्वति प्राणं प्राणेऽपानं तथाऽपरे ।
प्राणापानगती रुद्ध्वा प्राणायामपरायणाः ॥ २९ ॥

apāne juhvati prāṇaṁ prāṇe'pānaṁ tathā'pare
prāṇāpānagatī ruddhvā prāṇāyāmaparāyaṇāḥ (29)

tathā – so too; *apare* – others; *prāṇāyāma-parāyaṇāḥ* – those who are committed to the practice of *prāṇāyāma* (breath control); *prāṇa-apāna-gatī ruddhvā* – stopping the flow of inhalation and exhalation; *apāne* – into the incoming breath; *prāṇam* – the outgoing breath; *prāṇe* – into the outgoing breath; *apānam* – the incoming breath; *juhvati* – offer

So too, others who are committed to the practice of *prāṇāyāma* (breath control), stopping the flow of inhalation and exhalation, offer the outgoing breath into the incoming breath (and) the incoming breath into the outgoing breath.

Those who practise breath control as a *yajña* are called *prāṇāyāma-parāyaṇās*. These are people for whom *prāṇāyāma* is the *param ayanam*, the ultimate end. The primary end for such people is the practice of *prāṇāyāma*. In other words, they are committed to this practice for the time being. In the word *prāṇāyāma*, *prāṇa* means breath and *āyāma* means discipline. Thus, the discipline of breath control is called *prāṇāyāma*.

Prāṇa has several meanings, all of which imply living or breathing in one sense or another. Life itself is called *prāṇa*. Sometimes, *prāṇa* is used to refer to metabolic activity or to the entire physiological activity. Digestion, circulation and so on, are each referred to as different *prāṇa*s.

In addition to these general meanings, *prāṇa* also has a more specific meaning. The outgoing breath or exhalation is called *prāṇa* and the incoming breath or inhalation is called *apāna*.[24] *Apāna* also has a more general meaning, referring to the system responsible for elimination of anything that is thrown out of the body. In this verse, the more specific meaning of *prāṇa* and *apāna*, exhalation and inhalation, is implied wherein the act of respiration is presented as a discipline which is performed as a *yajña*.

---

24 प्राक् गमनवान् वायुः प्राणः। अधोगमनवान् वायुः अपानः।
prāk gamanavān vāyuḥ prāṇaḥ, adhogamanavān vāyuḥ apānaḥ
The air that goes out, that goes out in front of the person, is called *prāṇa*. The air that goes down, that goes in, is called *apāna*.

Inhalation and exhalation as a discipline

Filling the lungs by inhaling the breath is called *pūraka* and emptying the lungs by exhaling is called *recaka*. One can pause between inhalation and exhalation and again between the exhalation and the next inhalation. During these pauses, the air is retained inside the lungs and this is called *kumbhaka*. Each of these activities is a discipline can be followed deliberately and consciously. When followed, varying the duration of each according to the type of *prāṇāyāma*, the *prāṇāyāma* itself becomes a *yajña*.

In this verse Kṛṣṇa mentions three types of *prāṇāyāma*s, the very practice of which become *yajña*s. The first is the one in which the *prāṇa,* exhalation is offered unto inhalation, *apāna*. This is a kind of *pūraka-prāṇāyāma* in which the inhalation is given predominance over exhalation, *apāne juhvati prāṇam*. The second is the one in which *apāna,* inhalation is offered unto *prāṇa,* exhalation. This is a kind of *recaka-prāṇāyāma* in which the *prāṇa,* exhalation, is given predominance over *apāna,* inhalation, *prāṇe juhvati apānam*. The third is the one in which the flow of both exhalation and inhalation are stopped, and the air is retained either inside the lungs or outside the lungs. This is the *kumbhaka-prāṇāyāma*. Here, the inhalation and exhalation are offered unto the retention, *prāṇa-apāna-gati-ruddhvā*.

Breath retention – kumbhaka

The exhaling flow of breath is called *prāṇa-gati,* and the inhaling flow is called *apāna-gati*. Both the *prāṇa-gati* and the *apāna-gati,* are stopped by the person, meaning that the breath is retained in the lungs for a length of time. This retention is called *kumbhaka, kumbha,* meaning a 'pot.' Just as water is retained in a pot, so too, breath is retained in the lungs.

During *kumbhaka*, the person does neither *prāṇa* nor *apāna*. Stopping both the flow of *prāṇa* and the flow of *apāna, prāṇa-apāna-gati-ruddhvā,* the person offers one into the other. The exhaling breath, *prāṇa,* and the inhaling breath *apāna* are each offered in breath retention called *kumbhaka-prāṇāyāma*.

Kumbhaka is two-fold – the retention that takes place after inhalation, called inside retention, *antaḥkumbhaka,* and the retention that takes place after exhalation, called outside retention, *bahiṣkumbhaka.* The duration of each of these *kumbhaka*s depends on the relative duration of inhalation and exhalation.

Because the person practising *prāṇāyāma* is carefully measuring the breath, he or she does not cut short any of the three disciplines involved – inhalation, retention or exhalation. Any impulse to do so is not followed by the person. He or she maintains the stipulated time. Therefore, there is *yajña* in the discipline. Into the outgoing breath, the incoming breath is offered and into the incoming breath, the outgoing breath is offered. This, then, is what we call the practice of breath control, *prāṇāyāma-abhyāsa*, performed as a *yajña, prāṇāyāma yajña* for gaining certain tranquillity, alertness and steadiness of the mind.

Prāṇāyāma and a steady mind

The logic here is very simple. By converting the involuntary action of breathing into a voluntary action, you come back to yourself. All you do is breathe, but by breathing deliberately, there is a discipline involved that helps you gain a steady mind. When this is the end in view, the discipline becomes a *yajña* and, because there is a prayer involved, there is *antaḥ-karaṇa-śuddhi* as well. Nothing purifies the mind like prayer. Thus, the seekers here gain *antaḥ-karaṇa-śuddhi* and also steadiness of mind because of the discipline.

Verse 30

Disciplined eating as a yajña

अपरे नियताहाराः प्राणान्प्राणेषु जुह्वति ।
सर्वेऽप्येते यज्ञविदो यज्ञक्षपितकल्मषाः ॥ ३० ॥

apare niyatāhārāḥ prāṇān prāṇeṣu juhvati
sarve'pyete yajñavido yajñakṣapitakalmaṣāḥ (30)

apare – others; *niyata-āhārāḥ* – who regulate their food intake; *prāṇān* – their desire to eat more; *prāṇeṣu* – unto the digestive fires; *juhvati* – offer; *sarve* – all; *api* – without exception; *ete* – these; *yajña-vidaḥ* – who observe religious disciplines; *yajña-kṣapita-kalmaṣāḥ* – (become) those for whom the impurities of the mind have been destroyed by the *yajña*

> Others, who regulate their food intake, offer their desire to eat (more) unto the digestive fires. All these (people) who observe religious disciplines (become), without exception, those for whom the impurities of the mind have been destroyed by the *yajña*.

Those who regulate or measure their food are called *niyata-āhāras*. 'Only this much will I eat and no more,' they say.

While *āhārā* refers to anything that goes inside oneself, *āhriyate iti āhārāḥ*, including the sense objects enjoyed by the senses, generally it means food, drink, and whatever else that goes into one's stomach. There is a rule governing the quantities to be taken in, which says half of the stomach is to be filled with solids, one quarter with liquids, and one quarter is to be left empty for the movement of air. In other words, the fourth quarter is to be left alone! Nothing is to be put into it. This, then, is how the quantity of food is to be measured by those who practise this form of discipline.[25]

In disciplined eating, there is *yajña* because there is the desire to eat more or not to eat at all if the food that is available is not very tasty. Therefore, not responding to the desire to eat or not to eat becomes a *yajña* by observing measured eating, which is why such people are called *niyata-āhāra*s. They offer their desires with reference to eating unto the digestive system, which creates the hunger and thirst, *prāṇān-prāṇeṣu-juhvati*. Even though the person may still feel hungry, he or she stops after the appropriate quantities have been consumed. And, if eating between meals is what is to be avoided, then the person does not take even the smallest snack, regardless of his or her hunger. Such desires for eating are offered unto the *prāṇa* of digestion, unto the fires of digestion, unto the fire of hunger that causes digestion.

---

[25] पूरयेदशनेनार्धं तृतीयमुदकेन तु ।
वायोः सञ्चरणार्थं तु चतुर्थमवशेषयेत् ॥
pūrayedaśanenārdhaṁ tṛtīyamudakena tu,vāyoḥ sañcaraṇārthaṁ tu caturthamavaśeṣayet

Those who follow this discipline as a *yajña* also live a life of prayer, in common with the other types of seekers mentioned in these verses. A life of prayer enables the seekers to gain control and self mastery over themselves. Here, those who offer their desires for food into the fires of digestion also offer their prayers, thereby making this particular discipline another kind of *yajña*.

There are various *yajña*s practised in terms of food, none being superior or inferior to another. Everyone practises his or her own discipline and such people are called *yajña-vid*s in this verse, meaning those who follow various *yajña* or disciplines in terms of eating – what to eat, when to eat, how much to eat and so on. Such practices may be based on religious or cultural traditions or may be purely individual.

Any type of discipline is considered a *yajña* if it is a religious discipline. If a discipline is practised for the sake of health alone, for example, it is not considered a *yajña*. A diet is also a discipline with reference to eating, but it is not a *yajña* because there is no prayer involved in it. Only when there is prayer involved is a discipline considered to be religious and therefore, a *yajña*.

The results of performing yajña

The word *kalmaṣa*s in this verse means 'impurities' and can refer to any type of defect, including any impurity in the mind, *antaḥ-karaṇa-aśuddhi*. One's *rāga-dveṣa*s, likes and dislikes, and unsteadiness that may be in the mind because of the pressures of the *rāga-dveṣa*s, are all *kalmaṣa*s. These *kalmaṣa*s are destroyed, *kṣapita* for those who practise *yajña*.

From the standpoint of the result gained and the means employed, a name is given to these people, *yajña-kṣapita-kalmaṣāḥ*, those whose impurities of the mind have been destroyed by *yajña*.

All religious disciplines are efficacious for achieving this purpose. Certain integration, *antaḥ-karaṇa-śuddhi*, is gained whatever be the discipline followed. No one discipline is superior to another. Which one to practise depends on what one wants, what one needs. This alone must be kept in view when practising any religious discipline.

The difference between a religious discipline and any other discipline has to be properly understood. Religious disciplines are not mere disciplines, which is why we do not call aerobics or following a special diet a *yajña*. For any discipline to be considered a *yajña*, it must be religious.

Verse 31

By performing these religious disciplines the mumukṣus gain eternal Brahman

यज्ञशिष्टामृतभुजो यान्ति ब्रह्म सनातनम् ।
नायं लोकोऽस्त्ययज्ञस्य कुतोऽन्यः कुरुसत्तम ॥ ३१ ॥

yajñaśiṣṭāmṛtabhujo yānti brahma sanātanam
nāyaṁ loko'styayajñasya kuto'nyaḥ kurusattama (31)

kuru-sattama – O best among the *Kurus* (Arjuna)!; *yajña-śiṣṭa-amṛta-bhujaḥ* – those who partake of the nectar (the result) that is left over after the *yajña; sanātanam brahma* – eternal Brahman; *yānti* – reach; *ayajñasya* – for the one who does not perform *yajña; ayam* – this; *lokaḥ* – world; *na asti* – is not; *anyaḥ* – another; *kutaḥ* – how?

> Arjuna, the best among the Kurus! Those who partake of the nectar (the result) that is left over after the *yajña*, reach the eternal Brahman. For the one, who does not perform *yajña*, nothing (is gained) in this world. How, then, (can anything be gained) in any other (world)?

Any *yajña* that is performed has a result. *Amṛta*, nectar, here means the *prasāda*, the result, whatever is *śiṣṭa*, left over, after the offering is made in the *yajña*. And those who enjoy or partake of the results of these various *yajña*s are called *yajña-śiṣṭa-amṛta-bhuja*s in this verse.

What do they gain by performing these religious disciplines? They gain steadiness and purity of mind which enables them to enjoy certain composure and tranquillity. And, if they are seekers, *mumukṣus*, this kind of mind will help them gain the self-knowledge they are pursuing. Whether or not the person is a *mumukṣu*, there is always a result in the form of *puṇya* when a *yajña* is performed. And the *puṇya* will give them whatever it can give, either in this life or future ones. But *mokṣa* can only be gained if the person is a *mumukṣu*, a seeker.

Since we are talking about *karma-yogī*s here, the word *yoginaḥ* having been used previously, the people referred to in this verse will naturally be *mumukṣus*. Being desirous of *mokṣa*, such people will gain the kind of mind that can enquire productively; in other words, their enquiry will bear fruit. They will gain eternal Brahman, *yānti brahma sanātanam*.

Here *yānti* means they go to or they reach Brahman, both going and reaching indicating time, *kāla*. Even though Brahman is the very nature of oneself, to say that Brahman will be reached implies that an enquiry must be conducted, for which some time is required. Enjoying the result of the *yajña*, a purified or steady mind, they enquire and gain the knowledge of Brahman. It is the only way people can 'go to' or 'reach' Brahman. The knower of Brahman being non-separate from Brahman, *ātmā* already being Brahman, knowledge of this fact alone makes seekers gain Brahman.

The knower of a thing does not usually become that thing. For example, the knower of micro-biology does not become the microbes that he or she knows. Nor does the knower of history become history. In such instances, the knower is always different from what he or she knows. Whereas, in the famous story of the tenth man, the knower of the tenth man is the tenth man. If I am the tenth man and I am also seeking the tenth man, then as the knower of the tenth man I become the tenth man. I am the tenth man and, because I left myself out while counting, I found the tenth man missing. When someone tells me, 'Hey, you are the tenth man,' I gain the knowledge of the tenth man as myself alone. Thus, the knower of the tenth man is indeed the tenth man.

So, where the knower and the object known are identical, the knower of the object is the very object known. Whereas, where the object is separate, the knower of the object is different from the object. Here, Brahman is myself, *ātmā.* Therefore, the knower of Brahman becomes Brahman, which is the peculiarity of this particular knowledge.

The word '*yajña*' is used because knowing has to take place. The seekers have to know Brahman. *Mokṣa* cannot be gained simply by performing *yajña*; knowledge of Brahman has to be gained, the gaining of which is *mokṣa*. Śaṅkara makes it very clear in his commentary that the verb 'gains' is used here to indicate that an enquiry has to be conducted, which involves time, and that through this enquiry, those who are *mumukṣus* will gain eternal Brahman, *sanātanam brahma yānti*.

The use of praise and criticism in the Gītā

A common method of presenting the teaching, found throughout the *Gītā*, is demonstrated in this verse, the use of *stuti*, praise, followed by the use of *nindā*, criticism. Praise is of the knowledge or the *śāstra*. The teacher and the student are also praised. Even the result is praised. To praise the *jñānī* is, in fact, to praise the result, *mokṣa*.

Nindā, criticism is done for no other reason than to create *vairāgya* in the student to what is inimical to the vision and to create a proper interest in this vision and therefore, a stronger commitment to it. People may come to the study with lukewarm enthusiasm. To stoke this mild enthusiasm into a burning desire to know, the *Gītā* employs criticism and praise, *nindā* and *stuti* – *stuti* always coming first. Thus, wherever you find *stuti*, you will find *nindā* later.

Here, in this verse, the result, the *phala*, is stated first – they gain eternal Brahman. It means that the performance of such disciplines, sacrifices and prayers is productive in that it will indirectly help you gain the knowledge of Brahman.

Presenting them against the background of what your lot will be if you do not perform them further increases whatever taste you already have for them, whatever degree of commitment you have towards performing them. This is done in the second line of this verse.

Only when contrasted against *stuti,* praise, can *nindā,* criticism, be properly understood. A child, for example, should be praised or congratulated when he or she deserves it and judiciously chided when necessary. When you tell a child first what he or she has done is right, then when you point out what is wrong, the child will understand. This psychology is seen uniformly throughout the *Gītā*. First, there is praise and then, immediately afterwards, comes *nindā*.

In this verse, the importance of the *yajña* is easily understood because of this method of *stuti* and *nindā*. Those who perform various *yajña*s already presented, and a few others found in the Veda and other *śāstra*s that back up the Veda, gain Brahman. And those who perform none of these prayerful disciplines do not gain anything. Such a person is called *ayajña,* one who performs no *yajña*.

The importance of proper attitude and discipline

This world that is commonly shared by everyone has certain things to give, from simple pleasure to the joy of maturity. But, if there is no discipline, the world has nothing for you, *ayaṁ lokaḥ nāsti*. If you do not have a prayerful attitude and discipline, the world can give you only bumps and potholes, nothing else. When your back is in trouble, even a small bump becomes excruciatingly painful.

Without having certain attitude, there are a lot of bumps in life, lot of situations and events that you find you cannot swallow and that are not very pleasant. Without a proper attitude, how are you going to face them? And what are you going to accomplish without discipline? Even material success is not possible. Thus, it is said here that even this world, *ayaṁ lokaḥ,* which holds out certain joys to everyone, cannot be had by the *ayajña*. Even small joys are not available for such a person. Where, then, is the possibility of any other world, *anyaḥ lokaḥ* for you? No other world is possible. And where is the guarantee that you will be born again as a human being? All you can do is wait for another set of *karma*s to give you a human body and another chance to make better use of it.

If you cannot gain what this world has to offer, how can you hope to gain another world, *kutaḥ anyaḥ*? Any other world, a better life, a better world of experience like heaven and so on requires *puṇya* and therefore, *sādhana*, meaning rituals and prayer, special meditations, and good acts all of which are possible only when you have discipline. Therefore, there is no other *loka* available for you without prayerful discipline in some form or the other.

Eternal Brahman, *sanātanaṁ brahma* is what is to be gained in life and for the person without discipline, it is very far away indeed. Thus, if even this world is not there for him, then what to talk of eternal Brahman?

One may make money but, to enjoy what one has, there must be an attitude, for which some education is required. The person who does not have a proper attitude always postpones the enjoyment of what he or she has, thinking, 'When I get such and such, it will be wonderful. Then I will enjoy.' But when such and such is gained, the person does not feel wonderful at all, and the postponement begins all over again. Something else has to be gained, over and over again!

If the discipline is not there, if the prayerful attitude is not there, if the values are not there, you cannot really get anything. Whereas, if you have discipline, even if you have no money, you can gain a lot. It costs nothing to enjoy the stars, for instance. Like this, there are a lot of things to be enjoyed that do not require money. There are different books available in public libraries. In fact, you need not even buy a book. Without money, you can always borrow a book, read on any topic, and enjoy.

Whereas with money, but without the proper mind, what can you enjoy? All enjoyments require a mind, after all. If the mind is always concerned with the future and has no glad acceptance of what is, where is the question of any enjoyment for the person? All go getters are futuristic people who do not enjoy what they have. This futuristic attitude motivates them to do all kinds of things and then they rationalise their behaviour by saying they are success oriented people. But what value does such success have when they cannot enjoy what they have?

Success should necessarily be viewed from two standpoints. What one gets out of this life is one type of success, and what one accomplishes is another. The first one, that is, what one gets out of life is the one that really counts. For one who has no discipline, life will not even yield small gains and, as for eternal Brahman, it will be very far away indeed. From this verse we understand that *yajña* is definitely to be done. Kṛṣṇa then concludes this section.

Verse 32

Knowing these yajñas to be born of karmas (and therefore anātmā) you will be liberated

एवं बहुविधा यज्ञा वितता ब्रह्मणो मुखे ।
कर्मजान्विद्धि तान्सर्वानेवं ज्ञात्वा विमोक्ष्यसे ॥ ३२ ॥

evaṁ bahuvidhā yajñā vitatā brahmaṇo mukhe
karmajān viddhi tānsarvān evaṁ jñātvā vimokṣyase (32)

brahmaṇaḥ – of the Veda; *mukhe* – in the mouth (words); *evam* – in this manner; *bahuvidhāḥ* – many and varied; *yajñaḥ* – religious disciplines; *vitatāḥ* – are very elaborately mentioned; *tān* – them; *sarvān* – all; *karmajān* – born of *karma*; *viddhi* – understand; *evam* – thus; *jñātvā* – knowing; *vimokṣyase* – you will be liberated

> In this manner, many and varied religious disciplines are very elaborately mentioned in the words of the Veda. Understand them all to be born of *karma* (and therefore, *anātmā*). Knowing thus, you will be liberated.

Here, Kṛṣṇa sums up this section on the various religious disciplines, all of which are *karma*. In *karma*, he had said, the wise person sees only *akarma*. Then he talked about rituals and other forms of *yajña* in order to present the knowledge that *ātmā*, the self, is *akartā*, non-doer.

Kṛṣṇa also mentioned these disciplines because they are useful in the form of disciplines themselves in addition to bringing about *antaḥ-karaṇa-śuddhi*. At the same time, what is ultimately to be gained through all of them is the knowledge of *ātmā* as *akartā*, as Brahman. The word '*brahma*' in the present verse refers to the Veda in whose pages or words the various types of religious practices already discussed are very elaborately detailed.

Now Kṛṣṇa says, 'Understand all these religious disciplines to be born of *karma – tān sarvān karmajān viddhi*.' Whether they are physical actions, *kāyika-karma*s, oral, *vācika-karma*s, or mental, *mānasa-karma*s, they are born of certain activity on the part of the doer, *kartā*. For this reason, they are called *karmaja*s. Born of this three fold *karma*, they are *anitya* and therefore, are only *anātmā*.

Who is the doer, the *kartā*, here? The disciplines are *karmaja*s, born of *karma*, not *ātmaja*s, that is, not born of *ātmā*. It means they are born out of the instruments, *karaṇa*s, alone, born of the *antaḥ-karaṇa*, the mind, the *vāgindriya*, the organ of speech and the *karmendriya*s, the organs of action. They are either born purely of the mind or of the mind with the help of the senses and organs of action. Therefore, the *kartā* can only be the body-mind-sense complex, the *kārya-karaṇa-saṅghāta*.

This is a very interesting verse. It has confused a lot of people, as we see by some of the interpretations, English translations, and commentaries that have been written on it. Having said that the religious disciplines are presented in the Veda and that they are all born of action, Kṛṣṇa then says that knowing this, you will be liberated. How can this be?

How can you be liberated by understanding that these *karmas* are born of various activities performed by the physical limbs, organ of speech or the mind?

The point to be clearly understood here is that these disciplines are not born of *ātmā*. One has to go back to the statement, '*karmani akarma yaḥ paśyet,*'[26] and remember that Kṛṣṇa is summing up here. To make this point clear, Śaṅkara glosses the word *karmajān* as *anātmajān* and says that, 'Understand that all of these are born of *anātmā – tān sarvān anātmajān viddhi.*' The physical body, *deha*, is *anātma* as are the mind and all the *indriyas*, the organs of perception and the organs of action, which include the organ of speech. This is why Śaṅkara uses the word *anātmajān*. *Karmajān* means *anātmajān*, born of *anātmā* alone. They are *anātmā* because they are *karmas*,[27] objects, for you, the *ātmā*.

The physical body is not the *kartā*; it is only *karma*, itself being an object. The *karma* is an object for the subject, the *ātmā*. And the subject, *ātmā*, is not subject to objectification. Being a *karma*, the physical body is *anātmā*; it is not *ātmā*. It is an object, not the subject. The disciplines are born out of the physical body, the organ of speech, and the mind, all of which are objects, *anātmā*, for you, *ātmā*, the subject. Therefore, *karmajān* means *anātmajān* Śaṅkara makes it very clear that this fact is to be well understood.

---

[26] *Gītā* 4.18

[27] Here in this statement and the following paragraph, Swamiji uses the word *karma* to mean the *karma-kāraka*, the object of a transitive verb as used in grammar and does not mean action as it has been used all along.

Once you understand that these disciplines are born out of *anātmā* and not out of *ātmā*, you know that *ātmā*, the self, is *akartā*, free of any type of activity, *nirvyāpāra*, free from any action. We need only to see that the disciplines are born of *anātmā* for it to become evident that they are not born of *ātmā*.

All the *karma*s elaborately detailed in the pages of the Veda, some of which are mentioned here, are *anātmaja*s, born of *anātmā* alone. They are born out of *kārya-karaṇa-saṅghāta*, the body-mind-sense complex. Since they are *anātmaja*s, we understand that *ātmā* is not the *kartā*. This vision is called *karmaṇi-akarma-darśanam*, seeing *akarma* even when *karma* is performed.

We have seen earlier in this chapter how, even as one performs *karma*, the *kartā* is negated, everything being Brahman – *brahmārpaṇaṁ brahmahaviḥ brahmāgnau brahmaṇā hutam.*[28] The other *kāraka*s, the object of action, the means of action, the purpose of action, from whence the action comes, and the location in which the action takes place, are all nullified along with the *kartā*. Even though the *kāraka*s are seemingly there, their reality is nullified by negating the contention that there are divisions between them and Brahman. This negation is called sublation, sublating the reality of division as such, seeing that there is no division whatsoever.

Knowing *ātmā* as *akartā*, knowing the *kārya-karaṇa-saṅghāta* to be the doer, knowing that the doer is *ātmā* but *ātmā* is not the

---

[28] *Gītā* 4.24

doer, one is liberated from *karmas* and *karma-phalas* (*aśubha*). *Aśubha* means that which is not auspicious, that which is not good for you. Thus, as Śaṅkara says in his commentary on this verse, you are liberated from inauspicious *karma-phala*, which includes both *puṇya* and *pāpa* – *aśubhākyāt karma-phalāt vimokṣyase*

Liberation from bondage through knowledge

Liberation can also be expressed in terms of release from *saṁsāra*. You are released from the bondage of *saṁsāra*, which is due to ignorance about *ātmā* being *akartā*. The moment you take *ātmā*, the self, as *kartā*, *saṁsāra*, is born and you become a *saṁsārī*. Knowledge of *ātmā* as *akartā* is the clear vision, *samyag-darśana* of *ātmā* as it is. Knowing this, you will be freed from all *karmas* and *karma-phalas*, which is what *saṁsāra* is all about.

Karma-phala is what accounts for a given birth, *janma*, during which there is again *karma* and therefore, more *karma-phala* accrued to you, which results in yet another birth. This cycle continues until you come out of its orbit by knowing that you are not the doer. As Śaṅkara puts it in the last line of his commentary, you know that all the activities that you perform are not your activities. You know that you are *nirvyāpāra*, free from all activities, and that you perform no action whatsoever.

Knowing that I am *nirvyāpāra* does not mean that I am indifferent to everything or that I do not exert myself, which is sometimes how the word *nirvyāpāra* is understood. That I am devoid of activities is a fact, whereas to not exert myself is a condition of laziness.

Śaṅkara defines *nirvyāpāra* as *udāsīna*, meaning here that *ātmā* is always the *sākṣī*, a witness who never gets involved in activity. Thus, without me, no activity can take place but, at the same time, I am indifferent to all activities, meaning that I am independent of all activities.

When you say, 'I am indifferent,' there is definitely a *kartā* involved, an attitude of doership. But, here, *ātmā* is purely the *sākṣī*, the witness. It does not perform any action. When this is your vision of yourself, *ātmā*, you will be *mukta*, free, from the bondage of *saṁsāra – saṁsāra-bandhanāt vimokṣyase*. Seeing doership in the self, *ātmani kartṛtva-darśana*, is the only cause for bondage; there is no other.

If you see doership in the *ātmā*, meaning that you take yourself to be a doer, then there will be *saṁsāra* for you. And if you take yourself to be a non-doer, you are free, released from the bondage of *saṁsāra*. This is the only difference there is between bondage and liberation, as this verse makes clear.

Verse 33

Kṛṣṇa praises the knowledge that is liberation

श्रेयान्द्रव्यमयाद्यज्ञाज्ज्ञानयज्ञः परन्तप ।
सर्वं कर्माखिलं पार्थ ज्ञाने परिसमाप्यते ॥ ३३ ॥

śreyān dravyamayād yajñājjñānayajñaḥ parantapa
sarvaṁ karmākhilaṁ pārtha jñāne parisamāpyate (33)

parantapa – O scorcher of foes (Arjuna)!; *dravyamayāt yajñāt* – as compared to the religious disciplines performed with materials; *jñānayajñaḥ* – the discipline of knowledge; *śreyān* –

is superior; *pārtha* – O son of Pṛthā (Arjuna)!; *sarvam* – all; *karma* – action; *akhilam* – in its entirety; *jñāne* – in knowledge; *parisamāpyate* – is resolved

> Arjuna, the scorcher of foes! This discipline of knowledge is superior to religious disciplines performed with materials. Pārtha (Arjuna)! All actions in its entirety get resolved in knowledge.

In verse 24, the clear vision of *ātmā, samyag-darśana* of the nature of the *ātmā*, was given the status of a *yajña*, that is, it was explained in the form of a *yajña*. It was done in order to present *ātmā* as a non-doer by converting all the *kārakas*[29] into Brahman, which means that everything is Brahman.

To unfold this knowledge, many kinds of *yajña*s were mentioned, each of which can help a seeker gain a purified mind so that the knowledge can take place. Because of their usefulness in gaining *antaḥ-karaṇa-śuddhi*, these *yajña*s were pointed out. However, one must avoid being carried away by the disciplines themselves because they have a limited end; they can only prepare the mind for the knowledge. The ultimate end, *mokṣa*, can only be gained by knowledge, not by the performance of religious disciplines.

Disciplines are only a means – not an end

Therefore, the discipline itself is not an end. Any discipline is but a means for a given end, one of which is *antaḥ-karaṇa-*

---

[29] The factors related to the action such as the *kartā*, the doer of the action, *karma*, the object of the transitive verb, *karaṇa*, the instrument and so on.

śuddhi, purification of the mind, and another is *antaḥ-karaṇa-naiścalya*, steadiness of the mind. With such a mind you will surely gain the *samyag-darśana*, the clear vision of the nature of the self, being totally free from action.

This *samyag-darśana* is praised in this verse by contrasting it with the various *karma*s mentioned previously. Clear vision means the clear knowledge of oneself. And how do you gain this clear vision? Not by any of these disciplines, Kṛṣṇa points out here. The *samyag-darśana* needs to be understood, for which there is also a *yajña* to be done, *jñāna-yajña*. This *yajña* is being praised here.

Kṛṣṇa addresses Arjuna as *parantapa* in this verse, meaning one who scorches enemies. We have seen that the word 'enemy' can stand for one's afflictions such as *kāma*, *krodha*, *rāga*s, *dveṣa*s and so on. Since Arjuna was a *kṣatriya*, a warrior, the word can apply to enemies in the usual sense of the word as well.

We are told here that *jñāna-yajña* is *śreyān*, something superior, meaning that it is definitely the thing to be done. Wherever the word 'superior' appears, the question always arises, superior to what? But, there is no real comparison here. Instead, Kṛṣṇa is pointing out what *jñāna-yajña* is. It is superior, *śreyān*, because it gives you *mokṣa*. Therefore, there is not the usual sense of better and best here. Here the word '*śreyān*' means 'the best.'

Dravya-yajña refers to a *yajña* that is performed using oblations, which implies the use of certain materials or objects. All rituals fall into this category. Because *dravya-yajña*s can only give you limited results, in the form of *puṇya* and a certain satisfaction, *jñāna-yajña* is described here as being superior to them. For instance, when you offer a prayer, there is an immediate satisfaction, which is *dṛṣṭa-phala*, a seen result. That you are able to pray is an end in itself and, as a result of prayer, you will also have some relative contentment. This too is *dṛṣṭa-phala*. There will also be *adṛṣṭa-phala*, an unseen result, in the form of *puṇya*.

Knowledge swallows the doer

Thus, there are two types of *phala* for prayer. One is the immediate result that you gain and the other is the invisible result that is accrued to you. Any ritual implies a *kartā*, a doer, as well as various materials, and it is therefore, an initiator of results, whereas *jñāna-yajña* is a swallower of all results. The pursuit of knowledge itself is the *yajña* – *jñānam eva yajñaḥ*.

Because *jñāna-yajña* swallows the *kartā*, the doer, it does not further perpetuate the *saṁsāra*; it swallows the *saṁsāra*. *Jñāna-yajña* does not initiate any result, *na phala-ārambhakaḥ*, because it devours the very doer. The moment you begin to ask what is *jñāna*, what is *ātmā*, and so on, the *kartā* is very much in question. As long as you are questioning with your inference and perception, however, the *kartā*, the one who enquires, infers and perceives, will remain. If, on the other hand, the *kartā* is exposed to the teaching of Vedanta, the *kartā* will be swallowed.

Vedanta will tell the *kartā*, 'You are *akartā* but you think you are *kartā* because you do not understand what *ātmā* is. Doership is just a thought that comes and goes. When that thought is not there, like in sleep, where is the *kartā*?

Or, between two thoughts, where is the *kartā*? There is no *kartā*; you are *akartā* only. You perform no action at any time. You are not the thought; you are the one behind every thought. The thought is you, no doubt, but you are free from the thought. When thought goes, you are and when thought is, you are.' Like this, Vedanta teaches the *kartā* that he or she is *akartā*, thereby knocking off the *kartā*.

Knowledge is beyond the range of comparison

To say that this verse is comparing *jñāna-yajña* to the religious disciplines mentioned earlier is not appropriate because *jñāna-yajña* destroys all *karma*. To say that something is better than something else, implies that the something else is still there. Here, the *karma* that *jñāna-yajña* is supposedly being compared to is gone, destroyed by *jñāna-yajña*. How, then, can it be said that *jñāna-yajña* is better than *karma*?

When a person says, 'It is better to be married than to be single,' or 'It is better to be single than to be married,' there is something better involved. But, here, it is not a matter of *jñāna-yajña*, being better than *karma* since absolute knowledge of oneself is beyond the range of comparison. It is not even the best. Comparisons are possible only when both things being compared are within the range of comparison.

Knowledge and *karma* are two different orders of reality. Knowledge deals with the absolute and *karma* is completely swallowed by that knowledge. Also, in terms of the result achieved, there is no possibility of comparison. The result achieved by *karma* is limited and that achieved by knowledge is limitlessness itself.

When I am limitless, where is the possibility of comparison? You can compare members of the same order of reality. You cannot compare an achievement belonging to one order of reality to that of another order of reality. Therefore, *karma* is one thing and *jñāna* is quite another. Yet, for want of a better expression, the word *śreyān,* superior, is used here. The beauty of this word is that, even though it is a comparative expression, it indicates *mokṣa*. By one kind of *yajña*, the *jñāna-yajña*, you get *mokṣa* and, by the other kind, the *dravya-yajña*, you do not.

Dravya-yajña can only give you a limited result that is other than yourself, either some external result or an internal result, called *antaḥ-karaṇa-śuddhi.* If you are a *karma-yogī*, a *mumukṣu*, you will gain *antaḥ-karaṇa-śuddhi,* which is useful for gaining knowledge. The various *yajña*s or religious disciplines you perform as a *karma-yogī* help you to perform the *jñāna-yajña*, the enquiry into the *śāstra*, properly. Enquiry is the direct means for gaining *samyag-darśana*, the clear vision, whereas the other *yajña*s simply help you in that enquiry.

The destruction of karma is total

Jñāna-yajña is said to be *śreyān*, superior, because knowledge destroys all *karma*s, meaning that *karma* in its entirety resolves in knowledge, *sarvaṁ karma akhilaṁ jñāne parisamāpyate. Akhilam*, with reference to *karma*, means that there is absolutely nothing left over after knowledge takes place. All *karma*s and everything connected with them are totally gone, without any trace of anything left behind.

Sarva is used here to indicate that all *karma*s go in the wake of knowledge. Sometimes, even when 'all' is said, there is something left over. For example, when you say, 'All the people at the beach are surfers' or 'All the people living in Beverly Hills are rich,' these statements are not really true. For instance, there are people such as the servants who are not rich in Beverly Hills. There are also those who, while living in big houses, have enormous debts, their liabilities being much greater than their assets.

Therefore, statements using the word 'all' are not always totally true. This word is more often used to indicate predominance, rather than an entirety wherein there is absolutely nothing left over. Recognising that the relative meaning of *sarva* may exclude some things, Kṛṣṇa uses the word *akhila* also in this verse. Since both of these words appear together *sarvam akhilam*, there is no doubt whatsoever that, what was meant here was *karma* in its entirety. And this *karma* resolves into knowledge, *jñāne-parisamāpyate*

There is nothing more to be gained

When you gain this knowledge, everything belongs to you. There is nothing more to be gained. There is a verse in the *Chāndogyopaniṣad*[30] that describes this totality by likening it to what happens in a game of dice. In ancient times during the

---

[30] यथा कृताय विजितायाधरेयाः संयन्त्येवमेनं सर्वं तदभिसमेति ।
यत्किञ्च प्रजाः साधु कुर्वन्ति यस्तद्वेद यत्स वेद स मयैतदुक्त इति ॥ (छान्दोग्योपनिषद् ४.१.४)

yathā kṛtāyavijitāyādhareyāḥ saṁyantyevamenaṁ sarvaṁ tadabhisameti
yatkiñca prajāḥ sādhu kurvanti yastadveda yatsa veda sa mayaitadukta iti
(*Chāndogyopaniṣad* 4.1.4)

game of dice, the four faces of the dice were called as follows– one, *kali;* two, *dvāpara;* three, *tretā* and four, *kṛta.* The *kṛta* was considered to be the winner. That is, when one threw the dice and he got the one with the number four, *kṛta* facing up, he was considered the winner. When the number four, *kṛta* wins then, in that winner all the other lower ones are included.

Similarly, when you gain this knowledge, you get the whole. Everything belongs to you. The idea here is that once you gain *mokṣa* there is no way of anyone or anything getting the better of you. You win all the way.

*Karma-phala*s can give you only limited happiness, *sukha,* whereas knowledge gives you absolute happiness, *paramānanda.* In *parama-ānanda,* even the little 'happinesses' are included, which is why Kṛṣṇa says that *karma* resolves in knowledge, *jñāne parisamāpyate.*

Another way of looking at this resolution is to see that, from the standpoint of the knowledge, *ātmā* is not subject to *karma.* Knowing this, all the *karma*s – *sañcita-karma, prārabdha-karma,* and *āgāmi-karma,* resolve into the knowledge. When I understand, 'I am not subject to *karma,*' it means that I am free from the accumulated *karma*s standing in my account and I am also free from new *karma*s because I am *akartā.* I am not subject to *prārabdha-karma* because I am *abhoktā;* I am not an enjoyer. *Prārabdha* is only for the *bhoktā,* the enjoyer. *Prārabdha* is only from the standpoint of the physical body, mind and senses. There is seemingly some action going on at that level due to *prārabdha,* but that is a different thing altogether; it has no effect on the *ātmā* whatsoever.

Verse 34

Kṛṣṇa explains how this knowledge can be accomplished

By saying that all religious disciplines, *karmas*, resolve into knowledge, Kṛṣṇa once again praises the knowledge. Even though Arjuna knew what he had to do to gain the knowledge and had already done it by asking Kṛṣṇa to teach him, in the next verse Kṛṣṇa confirms that Arjuna had done the right thing.

तद्विद्धि प्रणिपातेन परिप्रश्नेन सेवया ।
उपदेक्ष्यन्ति ते ज्ञानं ज्ञानिनस्तत्त्वदर्शिनः ॥ ३४ ॥

tadviddhi praṇipātena paripraśnena sevayā
upadekṣyanti te jñānaṁ jñāninastattvadarśinaḥ (34)

praṇipātena – by prostrating; *paripraśnena* – by asking proper questions; *sevayā* – by serving; *tat* – that; *viddhi* – understand; *jñāninaḥ* – the wise; *tattvadarśinaḥ* – those who have the vision of the truth; *te* – for you; *jñānam* – knowledge; *upadekṣyanti* – will teach

> Understand that (which is to be known) by prostrating (the wise), by asking proper questions, (and) by serving (them). Those wise persons, who have the vision of the truth, will teach you (this) knowledge.

Here, Kṛṣṇa explains how this knowledge can be accomplished, how the *jñāna-yajña* is to be conducted. Every *yajña* is in the form of a ritual and has certain stipulations such as – when it is to be performed, what kind of, and how many priests should participate, which materials to provide, who is to be paid what, and so on. These stipulations are elaborately detailed in the Veda.

For the *jñāna-yajña,* however, you require no priests, only a teacher. Nor is there a stipulated time for the *yajña,* which is nothing but your enquiry. When you find your teacher, when you are ready, then you begin. There is no question of 'when' here; there is only 'then.' There are no other considerations. It does not matter whether you enquire in the morning or in the evening, in summer or in winter; whether you enquire before or after you are married, or after your retirement. There are no such rules because knowledge is involved, and not *karma.*

Only for *karma,* for religious disciplines, are there such rules. For example, only married people can perform certain rituals. Without a wife, a man is not qualified to perform them. Further, a *brahmacārī* can perform certain rituals that a married man cannot perform. Like this, there are varieties of stipulations with reference to *karma* whereas for a *jñāna-yajña* there are only two.

Firstly, you must find a proper teacher. The next stipulation is that you must be proper. The propriety of the teacher and the student is all that really counts in *jñāna-yajña.* In this verse, Kṛṣṇa says, 'Understand that, *tad viddhi,*' meaning, 'Understand how this knowledge is to be gained, by what means it is to be gained.' Three other things were mentioned as the secondary means towards gaining this knowledge, *praṇipāta,* prostrating to the teacher, *paripraśna,* asking proper questions, and *sevā,* serving the teacher.

Significance of the act of prostration

The act of prostration does not mean that you are doing exercises. First, you have to find a teacher. Then, approaching the teacher, *ācāryam abhigamya*, you salute him or her. This is what is meant by *praṇipāta*, the literal meaning of which is 'falling down properly' that is, with the right attitude. This attitude is also called *namaskāra*, the intention of which is to show one's respect.

There are different forms of *praṇipāta*, falling down. One way is to bend down and touch the teacher's feet. Another is to place your hands together and bend your head slightly. Like this, there are varieties of *namaskāras*, one of which is called *aṣṭāṅga-namaskāra*, a *namaskāra* in which all the eight limbs – the head, chest, trunk, knees, hands, feet, the mind, and one's words – touch the ground.[31]

To touch the mind to the ground indicates that what you do with your body is to be backed by an attitude or feeling of respect. By words, also, one pays one's respect saying, 'O Bhagavan, I salute you.' Because one's whole body stretches out on the ground, this *namaskāra* is also called *dīrgha-namaskāra*, *dīrgha*, meaning 'long.'

Prostration implies a surrender on one's part. 'I want to learn and I have found a teacher. I therefore, approach the teacher with an attitude of surrender. I am ready to give up

---

[31] पद्भ्यां कराभ्यां जानुभ्याम् उरसा शिरसा दृशा । वचसा मनसा चैव प्रणामोऽष्टाङ्ग उच्यते ॥

padbhyāṁ karābhyāṁ jānubhyām urasā śirasā dṛśā, vacasā manasā caiva praṇāmo'ṣṭāṅga ucyate my *ahaṅkāra*, ego, because I want to know.' This giving up is an important attitude and the *dīrgha-namaskāra* is a symbol of this particular disposition.

Proper questioning and service to the teacher

The second means for gaining the knowledge is proper questioning, *paripraśna*, asking appropriate questions at the right time, taking into consideration the context of what is being taught. We have seen such questions in our own enquiry into the *Gītā*. To name a few – What is this bondage, *ko'yaṁ bandhaḥ*? How has it come about, *kathaṁ bandhaḥ*? What is release from this bondage, how does it take place, *kathaṁ mokṣaḥ*?

Only when the bondage is clear, will *mokṣa* become clear. In response to such questions, the teacher will say, 'You require knowledge.' Then, you may ask, 'What is that knowledge, *ka vidyā*?' The teacher will reply, 'The knowledge, *vidyā* is opposed to ignorance, *avidyā*.' In this way, questions may arise and, whenever appropriate, they should be asked because the subject matter is something that must be understood. This type of questioning is what is meant by *paripraśna*.

The third means of gaining the knowledge, mentioned in this verse, is *sevā*, service to the teacher. Anything that can be done for the teacher is done. This is a very common aspect of the *guru-śiṣya* relationship while the student is gaining the knowledge. There is no other payment involved – no tuition fee, no charge for room, board, and so on. *Guru-sevā* is an attitude that is important for gaining the knowledge.

What happens when these three-fold means for gaining the knowledge are followed? The teachers, who have been won over by your devotion, your commitment to the knowledge, your seriousness, will teach you; they will give you the knowledge, *jñāninaḥ upadekṣyanti te jñānaṁ*. The word 'teachers' is put in the plural here either to refer to all teachers or for the sake of respect.

A teacher must have the vision

In order to bless you with this knowledge, the teachers have to be *jñānī*s; they have to know the *śāstra*. Because they themselves were exposed to the teaching, they also know the methodology of it; therefore, they will definitely teach you.

Such teachers must also be *tattvadarśī*s, those who have clear vision of the truth. Kṛṣṇa adds this word because there are those who know the *śāstra*, logic, grammar and so on, and who teach. But, because they still have some obstructions, *pratibandhaka*s, they do not see the vision very clearly. Thus, only those who know exactly what they teach are called *tattvadarśī*s, those who clearly see the truth about themselves, the world, and God, according to the *śāstra.*

Those who know the *śāstra* are not merely informed in terms of the words, but they also know the meaning of the words like, '*tat tvam asi*, you are that.' Thus, they are not the knowers of the words; they themselves personify the content of these words of the *śāstra*. Such people alone are called *tattvadarśī*s and, if they teach you, the teaching will do exactly what it is supposed to do.

The purpose of the teaching is to reveal, and not to advise. Advice is something meant for you to do, like when a doctor advises you to follow a particular treatment. It is purely advice, which you have to follow; in other words, it is *karma*. Whereas, if the same doctor teaches you medicine – how to diagnose a problem, what it is, how it happened, what treatment is to be given, why it is given, how it may affect the patient and so on – then it is knowledge; it is something to be understood.

Here, the intention is to reveal the nature of *ātmā*, the world, and God. This is what the teaching does. Only when the words come from a teacher who knows what he or she is talking about is the teaching able to accomplish what is intended. This is why this teaching cannot be successfully taught by everyone. The words themselves can put people on the right track. However, the words can create knowledge only when the person who teaches sees what the words are. When the words are spoken by one who is the meaning of these words, there is real teaching, *upadeśa*.

The description of a proper teacher given here by Kṛṣṇa is also the contention of the *śruti*. Only when a teacher is a *tattvadarśī*, one who has the clear vision of the truth, will the teaching be conclusive. Otherwise, your pursuit will not end; it will have to continue.

Verse 35

Gaining the clear vision, the ignorance-born-delusion is gone for good

यज्ज्ञात्वा न पुनर्मोहमेवं यास्यसि पाण्डव ।
येन भूतान्यशेषेण द्रक्ष्यस्यात्मन्यथो मयि ॥ ३५ ॥

yajjñātvā na punarmoham evaṁ yāsyasi pāṇḍava
yena bhūtānyaśeṣeṇa drakṣyasyātmanyatho mayi (35)

pāṇḍava – O Pāṇḍava (Arjuna)!; *yat jñātvā* – knowing which; *punaḥ* – again; *evam* – in this manner; *moham* – delusion; *na yāsyasi* – you will not get; *yena* – by which; *aśeṣeṇa* – all; *bhūtāni* – beings; *ātmani* – in yourself; *atho* – and; *mayi* – in me; *drakṣyasi* – you will see

> Gaining this knowledge (which was taught by them)[32] Pāṇḍava[33] (Arjuna)! You will not again be deluded in this manner (and) by this (knowledge) you will see all beings in yourself and in me.

The knowledge referred to in this verse is what is taught by the teachers described in the previous verse. Gaining that knowledge, *yat jñātvā*, the delusion you had about being a doer and an enjoyer will not return. I am a doer, *ahaṁ kartā*, I am an enjoyer, *ahaṁ bhoktā*, I am limited, I am a seeker, I am seeking knowledge, I am seeking *mokṣa* – all these delusions, *moha*s, that have been with you thus far, you will not gain again, *punar na yāsyasi*. Never again will you come under the spell of *moha*, Kṛṣṇa tells Arjuna, addressing him as Pāṇḍava, the son of Pāṇḍu.

How is it that this delusion does not return? Because delusion, *moha*, once gone, is gone for good. *Moha* means confusion born of self-ignorance. Once the cause for confusion, ignorance of the self, has been removed, you cannot commit the same mistake again. Previously, there was a mistake. But, if this

---

[32] *jñānī*s and *tattvadarśī*s mentioned in the previous verse.

[33] Son of Pāṇḍu

mistake is corrected removing the ignorance because of which the mistake was originally committed, how could you again be in the same situation? Unless ignorance comes back, it is not possible. And ignorance does not come back, like one way traffic! Therefore, ignorance, once removed, is gone for good. It goes, never to return.

Knowledge never goes

Knowledge, on the other hand, comes and never goes, which makes it impossible for ignorance to come back. Whatever ignorance you had before knowledge, is gone. For example, can you be ignorant of an apple for even a moment? You cannot be ignorant of an apple because it is something you already know. You cannot give up what you already know, even if someone asks you to, because ignorance is not something that ever comes back.

You may ask, 'If I were to have a brain haemorrhage or something, and lose all my knowledge and memory, would ignorance not come back?' No! Ignorance does not come back. The memory and other mental activity may be gone, but the self-ignorance you had before cannot come back because it had already gone; gone for good. 'Gone' means no more delusion, no more *karma* for you, which means that *saṁsāra* is also not there for you. All that is lost, if the mind ceases to function, is the capacity to enjoy the *jīvan-mukta* state. *Jīvan-mukta* means that, while living, one is free. When you are free inside, this freedom can be enjoyed through your body, mind and senses interacting with the world. But if you are in a coma, or some equivalent state, even if you are free inside, due to the absence of the interaction with the world on the part of the body, mind, and senses you will not be able to enjoy this freedom; nor will you have any problems of *saṁsāra*.

Once knowledge is gained, it is always gained, even though the physical body may or may not continue to function, just as computer software cannot function if the hardware is damaged. New hardware, of course, can usually be obtained. But here, once knowledge of *ātmā* is gained, there is no longer any *karma* to generate new hardware. Therefore, no new software is necessary either, *ātmā* now being in the form of Parameśvara. The *jīva* is gone. From the standpoint of the world, all there is now is Īśvara, the Lord. There is no longer the individual, you. The individual, the person has become Īśvara.

This is what is meant by 'gaining Īśvara, *īśvara-prāpti*.' If the *jīva* as an individual is not there, there is only Brahman. And with reference to the people who exist, what does that Brahman become? Īśvara, the cause of the world, *jagatkāraṇa*. Therefore, you are Īśvara. There being no more *jīvatva*, there is only *īśvaratva*. This is the contention presented in this verse.

Seeing everything in oneself

The knowledge that removes your previous delusion and prevents it from returning is described in one sentence here – the knowledge by which you will see all beings in yourself, *yena bhūtāni aśeṣeṇa drakṣyasi ātmani*. All beings, *bhūtāni*, means all living beings, without exception, *aśeṣeṇa*. Whatever being you come across, whatever you see, you will see in yourself alone, *ātmani eva drakṣyasi*. Why? Because the knower is yourself, knowledge is yourself, and the object of knowledge is also yourself.

Previously, you had this problem of *kartṛtva*, doership, in that, you took yourself, the *ātmā*, to be the *kartā*, the agent, of either knowing or doing. Because the *kartā* is always opposed to what it is related to, you were always different from the objects you related yourself to. Therefore, a subject-object division was a reality for you.

This duality, which was a reality before, is removed by eliminating the *kartṛtva*, doership, in the *ātmā*. Now I see the self as pure consciousness that is not involved in anything but, at the same time, nothing is separate from it. All that is there is *ātmā* which is Brahman, which is what Kṛṣṇa reveals here when he says, 'You will see all beings in yourself, *ātmani sarvāṇi bhūtāni drakṣyasi*.'

The consciousness that is conditioned by the knower, knowledge, and the object of knowledge is one consciousness alone, *caitanya*. The names and forms, *nāma-rūpa*, have no independent existence apart from this consciousness. The knower, known, knowledge conditioning is not separate from *caitanya*, the consciousness, because the existence of everything, *sat* is nothing but the existence of *caitanya*, consciousness.

Because there is no separation, Kṛṣṇa says here that, once knowledge has taken place, whatever you previously saw as existing separately, as different from yourself, you will see in yourself alone. It means, you are the whole. And not only will you see everything in yourself, you will see it all in Īśvara, the Lord also. 'Because you see everything in yourself, you will see everything in Me,' Kṛṣṇa says talking as Īśvara, the Lord. It means that between you and the Lord there is no difference.

If the Lord is both the efficient and material cause of everything, nothing is separate from the Lord. Therefore, the entire creation and everything in it is the Lord. This means that the five elements, *ākāśādi-bhūta*s are the Lord and everything in space being non-separate from the Lord, is also the Lord. So too your physical body, being included in the physical universe which is the form of the Lord, is the Lord, as are its physiological functions, the mind, and senses. Everything, then, is the Lord.

Because consciousness is never created it was always there, just as the Lord was. In fact, the Lord is consciousness, the *caitanya,* and as such, is not created. In other words, the Lord does not create himself, the *caitanya*. This Lord is consciousness that is the mind, the senses, and everything else. Given this fact, who is there? Only the Lord is there; there is no individual. All that is there, including the physical body, the physical universe, the mind, and the subtle universe, are all included in the Lord. What is left out is consciousness that is you. And consciousness that is you is the same consciousness that is the Lord.

The Lord is in essence uncreated consciousness; therefore, all that is there is the Lord. And what is created by the Lord is non-separate from the Lord. And what is not created by the Lord, consciousness, the Lord's essential nature, continues to be the Lord. All that is there is one whole that is the Lord. Therefore, you are not an individual separate from the Lord.

Or, we can look at this in another way. If you are not separate from the Lord, either the Lord alone exists or you alone exist. When you say the Lord alone exists, there is no you, no small 'I.' Either way, it is the same. Therefore, Kṛṣṇa says, 'You will see all beings in yourself and in Me.' There is no difference whatsoever between the *jīva*, the individual, and Īśvara, the Lord. This is the vision that is the knowledge itself.

Verse 36

Even the worst wrong-doer will cross with ease by the raft of knowledge

अपि चेदसि पापेभ्यः सर्वेभ्यः पापकृत्तमः ।
सर्वं ज्ञानप्लवेनैव वृजिनं सन्तरिष्यसि ॥ ३६ ॥

api ced asi pāpebhyaḥ sarvebhyaḥ pāpakṛttamaḥ
sarvaṁ jñānaplavenaiva vṛjinaṁ santariṣyasi (36)

api cet – even if; *asi* – you are; *sarvebhyaḥ pāpebhyaḥ* – among all sinners; *pāpakṛttamaḥ* – the worst sinner; *sarvam* – all; *vṛjinam* – sin; *jñāna-plavena* – by the raft of knowledge; *eva* – mere; *santariṣyasi* – you will cross with ease

Even if you are the worst sinner among all sinners, you will cross all sins with ease by the mere raft of knowledge.

Here, a question may arise as to how can I, who is limited in so many ways, hope to gain such knowledge? After all, the knowledge being discussed is no ordinary knowledge. It is the knowledge of the whole. It is the knowledge that I am the fullness, Brahman, that I am everything, the Lord.

To gain this knowledge seems to be a very tall order indeed! It is too big a lump for me to swallow. It is not even a lump; it is the whole thing!

If this is your problem, I would say that, because it is the whole, you need not swallow it at all; you need only to understand. If it were a matter of faith, you would definitely have to swallow it. Wherever faith is involved, you are not to enquire; it is simply to be swallowed! Here, however, there is nothing to be swallowed because it is the whole. Yet, you may say, 'But it is too big for me, Swamiji! You have no idea of all that I have done in my life! This knowledge is possible for the people who have lived a clean life, who have dotted all the 'i-s' and crossed all the 't-s' who have never crossed the bounds, who have always lived within the framework of what is to be done and what is to be avoided. You are addressing only those fortunate people who have not transgressed the structure of *dharma*. This knowledge is much too sacred for a sinner like me. Therefore, I do not see how I can ever qualify for it.'

There are many people who, because of the particular religious doctrines, have been exposed to, think of themselves as born sinners through no fault of their own. Since their birth was not an immaculate one, they are told that they have been born of sin and they accept it. And, after birth, of course they are sinners. If I am already a born sinner, what difference does it make if I commit a few more sins? Therefore, I did whatever I could do. I would have committed even more sins, no doubt, had there not been some obstacle or the other in my way. Because I was born with limitations and was unable to do certain things because of my love for or commitment to *dharma*, I could not commit the sins. If I had even the slightest chance to commit them, I would surely have done so. How, then, can you say that I am Īśvara? Do you expect me even to understand?

'Yes,' Kṛṣṇa says in this verse. It is the glory of the knowledge that even the greatest sinner can gain the vision of the identity between the Lord and the self. The word 'sinners' here refers to the people who do things that are not becoming and includes all types of sinners found in the world –bootleggers, drug pushers, hit men, small sinners, big time criminals, and so on. To make his point, Kṛṣṇa chooses the greatest sinner of them all, *pāpakṛttama* as the subject of this verse.

Such a person is in the midst of the ocean of sin that is called *sarvaṁ vṛjinaṁ* here, *vṛjina* meaning *pāpa* or sin. Even the greatest of sinners can cross this ocean of sin by a single raft, the raft of knowledge, *jñāna-plava*. This raft of knowledge is just one short statement, '*tat tvam asi*, you are that.' The meaning that these three words convey is the knowledge after all. And, by this raft of knowledge, even if you are the worst among the sinners, you can cross the entire ocean of sin, *vṛjinaṁ sarvaṁ santariṣyasi*.

However, you may ask, 'Will this crossing not take a long time and involve great difficulties?' Not at all. Effortlessly you shall cross because all you have to do is to wake up to the reality of *ātmā*, the self.

Suppose you dream that you have committed multiple murders and that you are caught. In the dream, you appeared before the judge and the jury, you were declared guilty, sentenced to death, and now you are about to be executed. This is the entire scenario in the dream for you. Now you wake up. What happens to all the sins you committed in the dream? By the raft of knowledge, by being awake to the fact that you are not the doer of the dream actions, you are rescued from the entire scene – the sins, the sentence, everything. None of it can affect you in any way.

Who was the doer of the dream actions, then? The doer was not you. It was someone else, someone who was ignorant. That, doership was something you imposed upon yourself and, therefore, all the problems of the doer were yours. Then, by falsifying the dreamer, you falsified the entire act of dreaming and the dream itself; everything that was done in the dream and the results born out of those actions. If the dreamer is real, you cannot falsify him or her. But, in the wake of the knowledge of the waker, the dreamer is resolved. In other words, the waker swallows the dreamer, along with the dream world, the dream actions, and the dream results.

Ātmā is never a sinner

Similarly, the waker thinks that he or she is the *kartā* now, but this *kartā* is also false. The one who is able to see the falseness of doership of the self is free from doership. Seeing the falseness is *jñāna*, the knowledge that releases you completely from all that was done by the false doer. *Ātmā* is not a sinner because it is not a *kartā*; *ātmā* is always pure, *śuddha,* free from all doership.

You may say that previously you were a sinner, but now you are a saint because the unbecoming actions you did in the past have been neutralised by good actions. But the status of being a sinner or a saint is in terms of doership alone. The *kartṛtva*, doership, is retained in both the sinner and the saint. When one says, 'I am a sinner,' or 'I am a saint,' both the statements have an equal implication of doership. Previously you were a sinner; now you are a saint. You have given up all the sinful activities and are now transformed. You have changed your ways and your lifestyle. But the *kartṛtva*, doership, is just as much there as it was when you were a sinner. The point here is that *ātmā*, 'you,' was never a sinner. Even when you thought you were a sinner, you were not a sinner.

Ātmā is more than a saint. It has always been pure, *śuddha*. *Ātmā* takes on no blemish at all because it has neither doership nor enjoyership, neither happiness nor sorrow. *Ātmā* is neither a liker nor a disliker. It has always been free, pure consciousness, *nitya-śuddha-buddha-mukta-svabhāvaḥ ātmā*. There is no action here. Where, then, is the question of even the worst of the sinners not being able to gain this knowledge?

Being a sinner, of course, is a problem. But, if you know you have been a sinner and your intention is to be rid of all the sins, then you require only *śraddhā*, faith, about which Kṛṣṇa talks a little later. In fact, you need not get rid of anything. You need only understand *ātmā* as already free from all sins.

This is why Kṛṣṇa says here, 'You will cross all sins by the raft of knowledge.' By saying this, Kṛṣṇa leaves no excuse for an escape. Even if you are a sinner, you have to strive. You cannot just say, 'I am a sinner,' and give up. With this knowledge, you can cross the entire ocean of sin.

This verse is in praise of the knowledge itself. Even the worst sinner among the sinners can be liberated without tears by knowledge. It is because the very idea of sin and all that it implies is dependent upon the notion, 'I am the doer, the *kartā*.' This notion of doership that is imputed to the self is the cause for all actions and their results. In the wake of knowledge, the *kartṛtva,* doership, is falsified. Thus, *karma-phala*s, the results of action, are likened to the ocean and knowledge is the raft by which you cross the ocean without effort because the self, *ātmā*, is already free.

Since *karma-phala* can only be neutralised by another *karma-phala*, how can this knowledge destroy the results of injurious, sinful actions? Is it not true that destruction of something can only be brought about by another having the same order of reality? For example, only a tangible object, like a bullet or sword can destroy another tangible object like a physical body. Knowledge does not destroy it. But this particular argument is not valid here; let us see why.

Upon enquiry, we find that the destruction of something belonging to a given order of reality can be brought about by shifting to a higher order of reality. For example, when the dreamer wakes up, everything that was done in the dream is destroyed. Therefore, destruction can take place by falsification. To falsify that which is false is knowledge. The false snake seen, instead of the rope, is destroyed in the wake of the knowledge of the rope. And, by destroying the snake in this way, the products of the vision of snake, fear and so on, are also destroyed.

Here, too, in the wake of knowledge, the notion of doership gets destroyed. In the next verse, Kṛṣṇa uses an illustration to prove this point.

Verse 37

The fire of knowledge reduces all actions to ashes

यथैधांसि समिद्धोऽग्निर्भस्मसात्कुरुतेऽर्जुन ।
ज्ञानाग्निः सर्वकर्माणि भस्मसात्कुरुते तथा ॥ ३७ ॥

yathaidhāṁsi samiddho'gnirbhasmasātkurute'rjuna
jñānāgniḥ sarvakarmāṇi bhasmasātkurute tathā (37)

arjuna – O Arjuna! *yathā* – just as; *samiddhaḥ* – well lighted; *agniḥ* – fire; *edhāṁsi* – wood; *bhasmasāt kurute* – reduces to ashes; *tathā* – so too; *jñānāgniḥ* – the fire of knowledge; *sarvakarmāṇi* – all actions; *bhasmasāt kurute* – reduces to ashes

Just as a well lighted fire reduces wood to ashes, so too, Arjuna! the fire of knowledge reduces all actions (results of actions) to ashes.

There are different kinds of fire. Even the flame of a matchstick is fire. A small flame, however, cannot destroy everything unless it becomes big. Until then, even a small breeze is its enemy. But, once it turns into a big fire, the wind becomes its friend.

This is true also with one's strength. If a man is weak, anyone can bully him, whereas if he is strong, everyone wishes to be his friend. If the fire is a huge conflagration, then all the wood, wet or dry, turns to ashes, *bhasmasāt bhavati*. Kṛṣṇa tells Arjuna here that, this is exactly what happens to all one's actions in the fire of knowledge. Like the wood in a fire, all action turns to ashes in the fire of knowledge, *jñāna-agni.*

Knowledge itself is the fire, which is the meaning of the word *jñāna-agni*, even though this compound is translated into English as 'fire of knowledge.' And what is the object of this burning to ashes? The object of burning is not the usual fuel like logs of wood, *edhāṁsi*. The fire of knowledge burns all one's actions to ashes, *karmāṇi bhasmasāt kurute*; *karmāṇi* meaning all *karma*s along with their *karma-phala*s.

Of course, when it is said that knowledge destroys all *karma*s like fire destroys wood, it is not meant that there is any actual burning involved. Knowledge does not 'burn' *karma* like fire burning wood, but it negates the doership and thereby all the *karma-phala*s.

'All *karma*s' means *sañcita-karma*, those that have not yet begun to manifest, those that were previously gathered and are still standing in your account like a fixed or term deposit, and *āgāmi-karma*, those that you gather in this life before the knowledge takes place. Both the *sañcita-karma* and *āgāmi-karma* are reduced to ashes by *jñāna-agni.*[34]

---

[34] Refer to Volume 3 - page 53 - for discussion on 'Karmas are inexhaustible.'

Prārabdha-karma exhausts itself

Only the *prārabdha-karma* is not destroyed by knowledge, in the sense that the physical body continues. A *jñānī* is the one who, while living, is liberated, *jīvan-mukta*. If the knowledge destroys *prārabdha-karma* also, the body, which is the product of *Prārabdha-karma*, would also be destroyed and there would be no *jñānī*! But we do not see this happening. Therefore, when it is said, 'all *karma, sarva-karmāṇi*' here, it excludes *prārabdha-karma*, the *karma* that has already begun fructifying with the birth of the body. This *karma* can only be exhausted by going through the experiences for which this physical body has come into being. Thus, day after day, one's *prārabdha-karma* is being exhausted, even in the case of a *jñānī*.

Chāndogyopaniṣad says, 'a *jñānī* continues to be here until he is released from this body. Then he becomes one with Brahman.'[35] As long as the physical body, mind and senses continue, the person lives here as a *jīvan-mukta*. With the death of the body, there is no *jīva* or *karma* to cause rebirth for the *jñānī*. There is no separation between the person, the Lord and the world. In this way, the apparent divisions, the seeming limitations, also disappear.

The *prārabdha-karma* of a *jñānī* continues until it gets exhausted, but the *karma*s gathered in this life prior to gaining the knowledge are all destroyed in the wake of knowledge.

---

[35] तस्य तावदेव चिरं यावन्न विमोक्ष्येऽथ संपत्स्य इति । (छान्दोग्योपनिषद् ४.१.४)

tasya tāvadeva ciraṁ yāvanna vimokṣye'tha sampatsya iti (*Chāndogyopaniṣad* 4.1.4)

And what about the *karma*s done after the knowledge is gained? With the knowledge, the *jñānī* does various *karma*s. These are *āgāmi-karma*s, which along with the *sañcita-karma*s gathered from countless previous births, get burnt to ashes, *sarva-karmāṇi-bhasmasāt-kurute*. In other words, all actions that had not yet begun bearing fruit before the knowledge took place are burnt in the fire that is knowledge and also those done after the knowledge, or along with the knowledge, because they are done without the notion of doership.

Verse 38

Kṛṣṇa says knowledge is the greatest purifier

> न हि ज्ञानेन सदृशं पवित्रमिह विद्यते ।
> तत्स्वयं योगसंसिद्धः कालेनात्मनि विन्दति ॥ ३८ ॥
>
> *na hi jñānena sadṛśaṁ pavitram iha vidyate*
> *tat svayaṁ yogasaṁsiddhaḥ kālenātmani vindati (38)*

hi – indeed; *iha* – in this world; *jñānena sadṛśam* – equivalent to knowledge; *pavitram* – that which purifies; *na vidyate* – does not exist; *kālena* – in time; *yoga-saṁsiddhaḥ* – one who has attained preparedness through *karma-yoga*; *ātmani* – in the mind; *svayam* – naturally; *tat* – that (knowledge); *vindati* – gains

> In this world, there is indeed no purifier equivalent to knowledge. One who has in time attained preparedness through *karma-yoga* naturally gains (knowledge) in the mind.

The word '*sadṛśa*' along with a noun in the third or instrumental case means 'equivalent to' in English. Thus, *jñānena sadṛśaṁ* means equivalent to knowledge in terms of its ability to purify. There are many means, like rituals, charities, prayer and so on, for self purification. But none of them equals knowledge, self-knowledge.

Prayer is a very important means for purifier no doubt. But it is not equal to knowledge. Only knowledge can destroy the *kartā.* The one who prays being the *kartā,* prayer cannot destroy the *kartā.* There is a person offering a prayer. Because prayer gives rise to a desirable result, it is also considered to be a purifier. But there is nothing that purifies like self-knowledge. Prayer can lead you to the knowledge of what is, but it is that knowledge alone that releases you completely, even from the need of prayer.

Prayer implies some impurity or imperfection, *aśuddhi,* on your part. The sense of limitation, bondage, and helplessness is a form of *aśuddhi,* because of which prayer emerges from you. This sense of helplessness is centred on the *kartā,* the doer, the one who prays. The greatest result of prayer is knowledge, which is the best purifier because it eliminates all sense of helplessness by releasing you from the very notion that you are imperfect, subject to various forms of limitation. Self-knowledge releases you totally from doership and sorrow.

Preparedness through yoga

In the *Gītā,* the word '*yoga*' is generally used in the sense of *karma-yoga,* and occasionally in the sense of *jñāna-yoga,* depending on the context. Here, *yoga* as a means for gaining success in one's pursuit of knowledge means *karma-yoga.*

One who has succeeded in becoming eligible for the knowledge, who has gained the preparedness of the mind to make him or her competent to receive the knowledge is called *yoga-saṁsiddhaḥ* in this verse. Such a person has gained *antaḥ-karaṇa-śuddhi*, purification of the mind, meaning that the mind of the person is steady and enjoys a certain freedom from *rāga-dveṣa*s.

The accomplishment of this kind of mind requires time. It can happen immediately or it can take time. The expression 'in time,' *kālena* here does not necessarily imply a long time; it only means some time. Therefore, if you ask, 'Swamiji, how long will I have to do *karma-yoga*?' I cannot give you a specific period of time. I cannot say, for example, 'Practise *karma-yoga* for three years and *jñāna-yoga* for four years.' The expression 'in time' does not have such a meaning here because we are not producing anything. For instance, if there is production involved in baking cookies, I can say, 'Mix the ingredients together and bake for twenty minutes at 350° Fahrenheit. Then, the cookies will be ready.' The exact time can be stated only when something new is being produced, or when something is happening that can be predicted in terms of time.

Here, however, nothing new is to be created. Since you are already Brahman, where is the question of time? If you ask when you will get Brahman there is no answer possible because you 'are' Brahman. And if you do not know that you are Brahman, you had better know. And when will you know? When you are ready. Then, the next question is, 'When will that be?'

All you need to do now is to live your life with the right attitude and pursue knowledge. In this way, gain of the knowledge will take care of itself; in time, you will gain it, naturally, because what you are trying to gain is already there. You do not have to create any thing.

Where does the knowledge take place? Knowledge takes place where it always takes place, in the mind, in the *buddhi, ātmani*. Here, the word '*ātmani*' is not intended to convey its usual meaning, namely, 'in the self,' because that is not where knowledge takes place. This knowledge of the self is like any knowledge, and it takes place in the *buddhi, ātmani* – in the mind, that is prepared.

Verse 39

Commitment to mokṣa along with śraddhā, one gains absolute peace

Kṛṣṇa describes what else is required for gaining this knowledge and what is accomplished by the knowledge:

श्रद्धावाँल्लभते ज्ञानं तत्परः संयतेन्द्रियः ।
ज्ञानं लब्ध्वा परां शान्तिमचिरेणाधिगच्छति ॥ ३९ ॥

śraddhāvān labhate jñānaṁ tatparaḥ saṁyatendriyaḥ
jñānaṁ labdhvā parāṁ śāntim acireṇādhigacchati (39)

śraddhāvān – one who has faith (in the *śāstra* and in the words of the teacher); *tatparaḥ* – one who is committed to that (knowledge); *saṁyatendriyaḥ* – the one who is master of one's senses; *jñānam* – knowledge; *labhate* – gains; *jñānam* –

knowledge; *labdhvā* – having gained; *acireṇa* – immediately; *paraṁ śāntim* – absolute peace; *adhigacchati* – gains

> One who has faith (in the *śāstra* and in the words of the teacher), who is committed to that (knowledge) and who is master of one's senses gains the knowledge. Having gained the knowledge, one immediately gains absolute peace.

This is an important and oft-quoted verse of the *Gītā*, '*śraddhāvān labhate jñānaṁ*, one who has faith in the *śāstra* gains the knowledge.' Śaṅkara introduces it by saying, 'The verse points out the means by which this knowledge is gained without fail.' Knowledge will definitely take place when the appropriate means is present. And what is that means, because of which one will definitely gain the knowledge?

First, one must have *śraddhā*, faith, in the *śāstra* and in the words of the teacher. Gaining the knowledge is dependent upon this *śraddhā* because of which the *śāstra* is looked upon as a *pramāṇa*, a means of knowledge.

Without *śraddhā* in the *śāstra*, one cannot look upon it as a *pramāṇa*. *Pramāṇa* means that which is instrumental in gaining *pramā*, knowledge, and should not create doubts. Any doubt has to be converted into *pramā,* ascertained knowledge. The motivation to enquire further in order to convert a doubt or contradiction into *pramā,* which is non-contradictory, is created by the attitude called *śraddhā.* Therefore, to gain the knowledge, the *śāstra* must be looked upon as a means of knowledge; only then can it deliver the goods.

By adding two more qualifications, this verse also reveals that *śraddhā* alone is not enough. Faith in the *śāstra* may be there, but there are people who are slow starters, meaning they do not have the necessary commitment. Perhaps, they do not see the benefit of this knowledge or they may not have discerned the problem of life. For whatever reason, there may be those who have *śraddhā* in the *śāstra* but do not have the necessary commitment. When there is no commitment backing up one's faith in the *śāstra*, the approach or attitude of the person towards the pursuit will be lukewarm.

What does commitment mean here? There is commitment when I recognise that I must have this knowledge, that there is nothing else that is important to me, and that I am prepared to burn all my boats. The person who has this kind of commitment to the knowledge is called *tatpara* in this verse, *para* meaning one who is committed to.

Other than knowledge, there is no way to gain this freedom. You do not become free from mortality; you already are immortal. The freedom is only in terms of knowing that you are immortal.

It is possible for a person to be *tatpara* in that the person is committed to liberation, but he or she may not have *śraddhā* in the *śāstra*. Between liberation and the *śāstra*, there is a relation, a *sambandha*; one is *sādhana,* the means, and the other is *sādhya*, the end. In order to gain liberation, *mokṣa*, you go to the *śāstra*, for which you require *śraddhā*. You need to know that the *śāstra* is the means of knowledge whereby you will gain the knowledge that is liberation.

Śraddhā may be there without *tatparatva,* commitment, and *tatparatva* may be there without *śraddhā*. If both *śraddhā* and commitment are there, the person looks upon the teaching as a means to freedom, *mokṣa*, and also has a love for that freedom.

Both *śraddhā* and commitment may be there, but the person may still not make it. Why? Because, his or her mind is not together with reference to the senses and their pursuits. Dissipation and distraction, therefore, stand in the person's way of gaining the knowledge. So, one more requirement is given here, *saṁyatendriya*, one whose sense organs, meaning sense pursuits, are under control. This means that you do not propitiate your fancies, that you are not controlled by fancies. If you always go by your fancies, you will find no time for anything, even for something you have a great love for. *Saṁyatendriya* here means one whose mind is steady. When such a person also has *śraddhā* in the *śāstra* and is committed to *mokṣa*, he or she will definitely gain the knowledge.

Relative śānti and absolute śānti

What happens when this knowledge is gained? The person who gains this knowledge immediately gains absolute peace, *parāṁ śāntim acireṇa adhigacchati.* This *śānti* is not the kind of peace or truce that exists between two bouts of conflict. It is the peace that is one's essential nature.

Peace is usually understood to be a state of the mind as opposed to agitation that is also a state of the mind. You generally take yourself to be silent when actually the mind is silent. And therefore, you think the self is agitated when actually it is the mind that is agitated. But the peace referred to here is not a state of mind. It is rather the nature of the self, which is always silent, *śānta,* regardless of the state of mind. A *śānti* for which one does not depend upon the condition of the mind is called *parā. Parā- śānti* does not call for a non-thinking mind because it is not opposed to thinking.

Here we see two types of *śānti*. One is the *śānti,* tranquillity that is gained through *yoga*. By *karma-yoga,* one can gain certain tranquillity that is purely a condition of the mind. Being a condition of the mind, this *śānti* is subject to change. This type of *śānti* is also a necessity and is indicated by *saṁyatendriyatva,* mastery of the sense organs.

A person who enjoys the *śānti* gained by *karma-yoga* gains another *śānti* too, the absolute *śānti,* through knowledge. This is what is called *parā-śānti*. In spite of what the mind thinks, the person knows, 'I am *śānta* meaning that at the level of 'I,' there is freedom – freedom from *aśānti* because the person recognises that *ātmā* is always *śānta.* This recognition gives rise to *parā- śānti.*

The peace discussed in this verse is your very nature, *svarūpa-bhūta-śānti*. And, in the wake of knowledge, it is gained *acireṇa,* immediately, *na cireṇa,* not after a time. The person gains this *śānti,* which is *mokṣa,* because of the knowledge of the self that is *śānta*. And what is the distance in terms of time between knowledge and *mokṣa*? There is no distance between them because knowledge is the means and *mokṣa* is the end, just as there is no distance, no interval of time, between eating food and appeasing hunger. In the wake of one, the other takes place. In the wake of knowledge, there is liberation. This, then, is the meaning of the word, *acireṇa – na cireṇa,* immediately.

The order involved in gaining this knowledge

In his commentary of this verse, Śaṅkara clarifies the order involved in gaining this knowledge. First, there is *śraddhā* in the *śāstra* as a means of knowledge. Then, as a result of this *śraddhā*, a commitment arises that causes a person to give up everything and pursue the knowledge by approaching a teacher with the proper attitude. One who approaches the *guru* has both *śraddhā* in the *śāstra* as the means of knowledge and commitment to the knowledge. In addition, the person must also have the sense organs under control. These three factors being there, the knowledge will definitely be gained.

Śaṅkara also comments here on the three aspects of outward expressions of *śraddhā* towards the teacher that we saw in verse 34 of this chapter – *praṇipāta,* prostration, *paripraśna,* proper questioning, and *sevā,* service. Because these are external, they can be exhibited even without sufficient *śraddhā.* You can always put on an act. Just because you are smiling does not mean there is a smile inside. You may be crying at that time, but as soon as someone approaches you, you can wash your face quickly and smilingly say, 'Hello, how are you?'

In the same way, prostrating to the teacher, asking questions, and even the service you perform to the teacher may be nothing more than an act. Therefore, Śaṅkara says that outward expression is not a guarantee for knowledge because it can be false.

Therefore, without *śraddhā*, the prostration, questioning, and service are not enough. Only when *śraddhā* is there, does one's outward expression become a means for gaining the knowledge.

Thus, in this verse, Kṛṣṇa presents the positive aspect of *śraddhā* by telling Arjuna that a *śraddhāvān* gains knowledge. In the next verse, he presents the negative aspect by stating what happens to one who does not have *śraddhā*.

Verse 40

The one devoid of śraddhā – in the śāstra and guru – perishes

अज्ञश्चाश्रद्दधानश्च संशयात्मा विनश्यति ।
नायं लोकोऽस्ति न परो न सुखं संशयात्मनः ॥ ४० ॥

ajñaścāśraddadhānaśca saṁśayātmā vinaśyati
nāyaṁ loko'sti na paro na sukhaṁ saṁśayātmanaḥ (40)

ajñaḥ – one who has no discrimination; *ca* – and; *aśraddadhānaḥ* – one who has no faith (in the *śāstra* and the teacher); *ca* – and; *saṁśayātmā* – one who has a doubting mind; *vinaśyati* – perishes; *saṁśayātmanaḥ* – for the one with a doubting mind; *ayaṁ lokaḥ* – this world; *na asti* – is not there; *na paraḥ* – nor (the world) beyond; *na sukham* – nor happiness

> One who has no discrimination, and who has no faith (in the *śāstra* and the teacher), and one who has a doubting mind perishes. Because, for the one with a doubting mind, this world is not there, nor the world beyond, nor happiness.

Ajña here means *avivekī*, one who does not have discrimination. Śaṅkara clarifies this point here by saying that *ajña* means *anātmajña,* one who does not know *ātmā,* one who does not have *ātma-anātma-viveka,* discrimination between the self and non-self.

Almost everyone is an *anātmajña.* If the *anātmajña* has *śraddhā* in what the *śāstra* says, he or she has some hope. Such a person knows what is right and wrong and can follow his or her own *dharma* by performing the *nitya-naimittika-karmas,* enjoined by the *śāstra.* By living in this way, *viveka* will eventually be gained, and knowledge also.

Because of *śraddhā,* the non-discriminative ignorant person can become discriminating. And once there is discrimination, *viveka,* there will be *vairāgya,* detachment or objectivity, because of which the person will have the desire for liberation, *mumukṣutva.* This desire for liberation will lead to the enquiry whereby the knowledge is gained and, along with it, *parā-śānti.* In this way, the person who has *śraddhā* gains this world as well as the other.

The problem comes when the person who is an *ajña* is also *aśraddadhāna.* Not only does the person not have discrimination, he or she has no *śraddhā* either. Such a person cannot even give benefit of doubt to *śāstra.* But, disbelief is not based on reason. How can you prove there is no heaven, for example? You can neither prove its existence nor disprove it. How can you conclude something is right or wrong unless you make an enquiry, for which you must have some *śraddhā*? No enquiry is made if *śraddhā* is not there.

However, people who have no faith in the *śāstra* may have faith in themselves or in other people. They may also have faith in money or in power. This kind of faith will give these people something, at least. If a person has faith in the world, he can gain some happiness and security. The world does offer some *sukha* to such a person. And for the person who trusts his or her abilities and has faith in the efficacy of the various means and ends available to explore and use, definitely there are opportunities to pick up some *sukha.* Such a person is deprived of the other world, but he does gain this world.

The main problem presented in this verse is doubt, *saṁśaya.* One who is a doubter is called *saṁśayātmā,* the word *ātmā* meaning, the mind, *antaḥ-karaṇa,* in this context. Doubt can exist only in the mind.

About the *saṁśayātmā,* Kṛṣṇa says, 'Neither this world, nor the world beyond, nor happiness, is there for the doubter.' In his commentary, Śaṅkara explains that both the non-discriminative person and the one who has no *śraddhā*, perish, meaning, they go from death to death. But such people are not as badly off as the *saṁśayātmā* who has no *śraddhā* in the *śāstra*. He or she does not believe in the existence of *puṇya* and *pāpa* and so does not care to follow *dharma*. Therefore, he or she is deprived of the world hereafter.

The *saṁśayātmā* cannot gain happiness in this world. Such a person cannot even get married! He or she always asks, 'Will I be able to make a success of it? I doubt it.' And even if the person does get married, how long will the marriage last when one always doubts the other person? Every phone call becomes a matter for doubt, even if it is only a telephone operator on the other end! Like this, the *saṁśayātmā* is not only a tragedy to himself, but also to everyone else around. Thus, Kṛṣṇa says that this world is not there for the doubting person; nor is there the world beyond, nor any happiness here.

While knowledge of *ātmā* is not possible without *śraddhā*, a person who has faith in something other than the *śāstra* can get something out of life. But the *saṁśayātmā* has no trust whatsoever – in the scriptures, in other people, or even in oneself! Therefore, even this world is not there for the person, *ayaṁ lokaḥ nāsti*. This world, that is, whatever one can get from one's life is also not there for the *saṁśayātmā*.

Verse 41

The one who has these three qualifications is not bound by actions

योगसंन्यस्तकर्माणं ज्ञानसञ्छिन्नसंशयम् ।
आत्मवन्तं न कर्माणि निबध्नन्ति धनञ्जय ॥ ४१ ॥

yogasannyastakarmāṇaṁ jñānasañchinnasaṁśayam
ātmavantaṁ na karmāṇi nibadhnanti dhanañjaya (41)

dhanañjaya – O Arjuna!; *karmāṇi* – actions; *yoga-sannyasta-karmāṇam* – the one who has renounced action through *yoga*; *jñāna-sañchinna-saṁśayam* – the one whose doubts have been completely severed by knowledge; *ātmavantam* – the one who is together; *na nibadhnanti* – do not bind

> Dhanañjaya (Arjuna)! Actions do not bind the one who has renounced action through *yoga*, whose doubts have been completely severed by knowledge (and) the one who is together.

Kṛṣṇa addresses Arjuna as Dhanañjaya here, meaning one who has earned a number of titles and all kinds of wealth. The actions, *karmāṇi* referred to in this verse include all types of actions, proper and improper acts, Vedic rituals, and all worldly activities. None of them, Kṛṣṇa tells Arjuna, bind the person, *karmāṇi na nibadhnanti.*

Who is the one not bound by actions? Three qualifications are given here for such a person – *yoga-sannyasta-karmā, jñāna-sañchinna-saṁśaya,* and *ātmavān.*

Yoga sannyasta karmā

Śaṅkara explains *yoga-sannyasta-karmā* as one who has given up *karma* through *yoga* characterised by the clear vision of reality. In other words, through the knowledge of the true nature of the self.

Yoga refers to *jñāna-yoga* here. But the word is also used to include *karma-yoga,* since, in order to gain the knowledge, one should have lived a life of *karma-yoga.* Thus, *yoga-sannyasta-karmā* is the one who has given up all actions through knowledge. Such a person is a *jñānī,* one who sees *akarma* in *karma,* as we saw in verse 18 of this chapter.

A *yoga-sannyasta-karmā* is different from a *sannyasta-karmā.* A *sannyasta-karmā* is one who is a *sannyāsī,* who has given up all duties by will, in order to pursue knowledge. A *yoga-sannyasta-karmā,* on the other hand, is the one who on account of the knowledge of the self as *akartā* knows he or she is not the doer, and is therefore, not bound by any action whatsoever. The knowledge that one is not the doer distinguishes the *yoga-sannyasta-karmā* from a mere *sannyasta-karmā.*

Jñāna-sañchinna-saṁśaya

The second qualification is freedom from doubt. The person is described as a *jñāna-sañchinna-saṁśaya*, one whose doubts have been completely severed by the knowledge. In his commentary, Śaṅkara poses the question, 'How did the person become a *yoga-sannyasta-karmā*?' and replies, 'By knowledge.' He then describes this knowledge, this *yoga*, as the vision of the identity between oneself and the Lord, the vision that completely destroys all one's doubts. And what doubts are these? One may doubt whether fullness is really the nature of oneself, or if *ātmā* is eternal and *anātmā* non-eternal? Is there a connection between *ātmā* and *anātmā*? If so, what kind of a connection? Is there division or identity between the individual and Īśvara, the Lord? These are the doubts that arise.

The one who is free from all doubts knows that *ātmā* is real, *satya* and *anātmā* is unreal or false, *mithyā*. When the person has no doubt whatsoever about this fact, there is knowledge, not faith. Faith in the *śāstra* as a *pramāṇa* is required only until knowledge takes place.

With reference to heaven and so on, mentioned by the *śāstra*, the statements are not verifiable here. Therefore, existence of heaven remains a faith for you till death. If there is a heaven, you will go there, provided you have done whatever is to be done to get there according to the *śāstra*. But, what is to be understood here is that this heaven going is purely faith, and as such is not verifiable while in this body.

When it comes to Vedanta, however, knowledge is involved, not faith. Here we are talking about the self, the self-evident 'I.' 'I am' is self-evident, and hence I do not need the *śāstra* to tell me that 'I am' and that 'I exist'. The *śāstra* is required only to correct the erroneous notions or conclusions that I have about myself.

That 'I am' is a self-evident fact; it is not a conclusion, whereas 'I am a *saṁsārī*' is a conclusion. This conclusion is purely notional, and is absent when I am asleep, is absent between two thoughts, is absent in a moment of joy, and is falsified in the wake of the knowledge. I do not need to verify that 'I am' and that 'I exist.' I need to only eliminate the doubts and the errors about myself. The *śāstra* enables me do this.

The removal of error is what is *ātma-jñāna,* knowledge of the identity of the self with Īśvara. And the one whose doubts have been removed by this knowledge is called *jñāna-sañchinna-saṁśaya*.

Ātmavān

The third qualification mentioned is *ātmavān,* which explains how the removal of doubt and error is achieved. The *ātmavān* is a *yogī,* one who has the body-mind-sense complex under control. *Ātmā* here refers to one's physical body, mind, and senses, and the one who has control over them is called *ātmavān.*

Although everyone has a body, mind and senses, not everyone has control over them. Instead, the person is generally under their control and is therefore, *anātmavān*. For the *anātmavān*, it is the body, etc., that determines whether he is happy.

If the body puts on extra weight, becomes ill, or ages, the person thinks that he or she is finished. In this way, the body is said to control the person when there is a lack of maturity.

A person who is mature has the body-mind-sense complex with him. Such a person is a *yogī*. Before knowledge, he was a *yogī*, a *karma-yogī*, and after gaining the knowledge, the person continues to be a *yogī*. Kṛṣṇa quietly mentions *ātmavān* here to emphasise what he said in verse 39 of this chapter. There, he referred to someone who has mastery over the senses, *saṁyatendriya*; here he calls the person *ātmavān*.

In his commentary of this verse, Śaṅkara equates the word *ātmavān* to *apramatta*, meaning one who has no *pramāda*, no laziness, no indifference, no dullness, or no lack of alertness; in other words, a person who is together.

Yoga-sannyasta-karmā is the real *sannyāsī*. This person has given up all the *karmas*, not necessarily by renouncing them, but by the knowledge, 'I am *akartā*.' In this way, no action binds the person by producing unseen results, *puṇya* or *pāpa*. Because of the knowledge, whatever would have accrued to the doer simply resolves because doership is not there.

Knowing that the self is not the doer, the *jñānī* appears to perform *karma* based on *prārabdha*. Because the body-mind-sense complex is there, situations present themselves and actions take place, which, however, do not bind the person. Kṛṣṇa keeps saying throughout the *Gītā* that actions can only bind the one who takes the self to be the doer. When there is no doership, actions cannot bind. Even though the person appears to be engaged in action, he or she performs no action, *naiva kiñcit karoti*. This is because of the knowledge of non-action in action, *karmaṇi akarma darśana*, all of which we have seen before.

Verse 42

Kṛṣṇa concludes

Now after explaining all this Kṛṣṇa concludes the chapter by urging Arjuna to take to action with an attitude of *karma-yoga*, which will lead him to knowledge.

तस्मादज्ञानसम्भूतं हृत्स्थं ज्ञानासिनात्मनः ।
छित्त्वैनं संशयं योगमातिष्ठोत्तिष्ठ भारत ॥ ४२ ॥

tasmādajñānasambhūtaṁ hṛtsthaṁ jñānāsinātmanaḥ
chittvainaṁ saṁśayaṁ yogamātiṣṭhottiṣṭha bhārata (42)

tasmāt – therefore; *ajñānasambhūtam* – born of ignorance (lack of discrimination); *hṛtstham* – rooted in the mind; *enam* – this; *ātmanaḥ* – about the self; *saṁśayam* – doubt; *jñāna-asinā* – by the sword of knowledge; *chittvā* – slaying; *yogam* – *karma-yoga* (leading to knowledge); *ātiṣṭha* – take to (follow); *bhārata* – O Bhārata! (Arjuna)!; *uttiṣṭha* – get up

> Therefore, Bhārata (Arjuna)! slaying with the sword of knowledge this doubt about the self, which is born of ignorance, which is rooted in the mind, get up (and) take to *yoga* (*karma-yoga*).

In this verse, Kṛṣṇa addresses Arjuna as Bhārata, meaning one who is born in the family of Bharata, and asks him to stand up and take to the life of *yoga*. Here, *yoga* means *karma-yoga* which leads to *jñāna*, knowledge. When one lives a life of *karma-yoga*, the knowledge will face no obstruction. Therefore, Kṛṣṇa says to Arjuna, 'You have been listening to me all this time. Now, take to *karma-yoga*, through which you will gain the knowledge that is liberation.' In other words, since you should live a life of *karma-yoga* for a length of time while pursuing *jñāna*, do it, *yogam ātiṣṭha*.

We have seen that a person does not become a *sannyāsī* just by giving up all duties, even though there is a lifestyle called *sannyāsa*. A *sannyāsī*, in the primary sense, is one who gives up all activities by knowledge, by knowing that he is not the doer of action. Thus, Kṛṣṇa uses the word, 'therefore, *tasmāt*' here. Kṛṣṇa says, 'Therefore, take to *karma-yoga*, so that you can gain the knowledge that will enable you to become a *sannyāsī*, the one whose doubts have been slain by knowledge, *jñāna-sañchinna-saṁśaya*, and who has renounced all activities through the *yoga* that is knowledge.' Having given up the doership, *kartṛtva*, the *sannyāsī* performs no action in terms of knowledge even though the person apparently does action.

Kṛṣṇa has already told Arjuna in verse 39 of this chapter that he had to destroy whatever doubts he had. He did this by describing the *saṁśayātmā*, a person who doubts himself, the *śāstra*, and everything else. Such a person, Kṛṣṇa said, perishes, meaning that he destroys the self. Therefore, in the present verse, he tells Arjuna that the doubt in his heart, born of ignorance, must be slain.

Doubt is an enemy that resides in the mind

Ignorance, *ajñāna* results in lack of discrimination, *aviveka*. One's doubt about the self is born of ignorance and lack of discrimination. Therefore, Kṛṣṇa says, 'And where is this doubt, this enemy that can destroy you? Arjuna, this enemy is not outside of you, unlike Duryodhana who is outside of you. This enemy, Mr. Doubt, is inside you, in your heart; it is *hṛtstha*, in your mind. The doubt, *saṁśaya* has entered into your mind and is rooted there.'

Doubt is born because of your own lack of discrimination. It is not born of simple ignorance of facts but is born of lack of discrimination. Absence of discrimination here is absence of *ātma-anātma-viveka*, which means that there is no *vicāra*, enquiry, about life and therefore, everything is subject to doubt.

Doubts can be about anything, but the doubt referred to here is about oneself and this doubt is to be slain. But to slay something one requires a sword; the sword in this context is in the form of knowledge. By this sword of knowledge, one should destroy doubt about oneself, the doubt that is in the mind, born of ignorance and non-discrimination.

Slay the doubt with the sword of knowledge

To clarify Kṛṣṇa's point, Śaṅkara defines *jñāna* in his commentary as the clear vision that destroys defects such as sorrow, delusion and so on. 'Clear vision' here refers to the discrimination, *viveka*, between *ātmā* and *anātmā*, the real and the unreal. Knowledge alone is the sword that can destroy all of one's defects, *doṣa*s such as, *śoka*, sorrow; *moha*, delusion; *rāga-dveṣa*s, likes and dislikes; *krodha*, anger, and so on.

Because the doubt is in your own heart, born of your lack of discrimination between the real and the unreal, you alone can destroy it. Your doubt does not belong to anyone else, even though others may have the same doubt. What is meant here is that the doubt that is in your heart, in your mind, born of your self-ignorance, can only be slain by your gaining self-knowledge. And this knowledge can only be gained by first taking to the life of *karma-yoga*. '*Ātmanaḥ*,' here with reference to doubt, does not have the usual sense of the genitive or possessive case here, that is, it does not mean 'one's own, *svasya*,' since Kṛṣṇa says that the doubt is in one's own heart, *hṛtstha*. Therefore, the expression, '*ātmanaḥ saṁśayaṁ*' means a doubt whose subject matter is *ātmā* and not one's own doubt, For example, the expression, 'knowledge of the *Gītā*,' is also in the genitive case, but it does not have the sense of possession that 'the book of Rāma,' meaning 'Rāma's book,' has. In other words, it does not mean 'the *Gītā*'s knowledge' in that the knowledge does not belong to the *Gītā*. Rather, 'knowledge of the *Gītā*' means the knowledge for which the *Gītā* is the subject matter, just as 'knowledge of Electronics' means the knowledge for which Electronics is the subject matter. In these examples and in the use of '*ātmanaḥ*' in this verse, the genitive case is used in the sense of object, *karma*, rather than to indicate possession. This usage, which is called *karmaṇi ṣaṣṭhī* is common to many languages, including English and Sanskrit.

Therefore, *ātmanaḥ jñānam* means knowledge of the *ātmā*, knowledge for which the subject matter is *ātmā*. Similarly, *ātmanaḥ saṁśayaṁ*, doubt about the *ātmā*, means a doubt for which the *ātmā* is the object, *viṣaya*.

Doubts about the self create all kinds of problems; therefore, it should be put to rest. This doubt can only be put to rest by slaying it with the sword of knowledge, for which you must take to *karma-yoga*. Therefore, Kṛṣṇa says, '*uttiṣṭha yogam ātiṣṭha*, come on, stand up, Arjuna!'

Śaṅkara also explains that the doubt being discussed is that which is the cause for one's own destruction, following up on what Kṛṣṇa has said in verse 39 of this chapter – the one who doubts, perishes. For the doubter, *saṁśayātmā,* there is neither this world nor any other; nor is there any happiness for the person.

Since doubt is the cause for your own destruction, you should not allow it to remain in your heart. Only by gaining self-knowledge can you destroy it. For this you must live a life of *karma-yoga* and pursue the knowledge that completely destroys the doubt. Therefore, with *śraddhā,* you should take to *yoga* and pursue knowledge.

Jñāna-karma sannyāsa-yoga

This fourth chapter is called *jñāna-karma sannyāsa-yoga* because its subject matter, *yoga,* is *sannyāsa,* the renunciation, of *karma,* action, through *jñāna,* knowledge. *Sannyāsa* here is not in terms of the lifestyle of renunciation of all duties to pursue this knowledge. *Sannyāsa* here means giving up actions by knowledge that the self is not the doer. With this knowledge, one performs no action even when action appears to take place, *kurvannapi na karoti*. The one who is able to see non-action in action has given up *karma*s because there is no longer any doership for the person.

In this chapter, we saw that by the knowledge of *ātmā* as a non-doer, *akartā, karma* is given up. When doership, *kartṛtva,* resolves in the wake of knowledge, action, *karma,* along with everything connected with action, the *kārakas*, also resolves. They are sublated, negated, in terms of reality. The *kārakas*, you may recall, are denoted by the six grammatical declensions, excluding the genitive case. They are the *kartā*, the agent; *karma,* the object; *karaṇa* the means or instrument; *apādāna,* the source from where the action is produced, and *adhikaraṇa,* the location of the action.

When the knowledge is gained, the *kartā* or the agent of action is understood to be *mithyā*. The agent of action being *mithyā*, the action itself is *mithyā*, the instrument and purpose of action are *mithyā,* from where the actions takes place is *mithyā*, and the location of the action is also *mithyā*. In fact, everything becomes *mithyā* for the person who has the vision of non-action in action.

As mentioned earlier, the word '*yoga*' in the title of the *Gītā* chapters means subject matter. The first chapter was called *arjuna-viṣāda yoga,* indicating that the subject matter was Arjuna's sorrow. To take *yoga* in its usual sense would be absurd since no one wants to practise sorrow![36]

Similarly, the second chapter, entitled *sāṅkhya-yoga* is a chapter having knowledge, *sāṅkhya* or *jñāna,* as its subject matter. The third chapter has *karma* as its subject matter.

---

[36] *arjuna-viṣāda-yoga* is to be taken as, *arjunasya viṣādaḥ eva yogaḥ, viṣayaḥ yasya* – a chapter for which the subject matter, *viṣaya,* is Arjuna's sorrow.

Here, in the fourth chapter, the subject matter is the giving up of *karma* by knowledge. Kṛṣṇa completed this chapter by telling Arjuna to stand up and take to *karma-yoga* in order to ultimately gain the knowledge.

The fourth chapter ends with the same words, given below, like other chapters in the *Gītā*, the meaning of which we have already seen.

ॐ तत्सत्।

इति श्रीमद्भगवद्गीतासूपनिषत्सु ब्रह्मविद्यायां योगशास्त्रे श्रीकृष्णार्जुन-
संवादे ज्ञानकर्मसंन्यासयोगो नाम चतुर्थोऽध्यायः ॥ ४ ॥

oṁ tat sat.

iti śrīmadbhagavadgītāsūpaniṣatsu brahma-vidyāyāṁ yogaśāstre śrīkṛṣṇārjunasaṁvāde jñāna-karma-sannyāsa-yogo nāma caturtho'dhyāyaḥ (4)

Om, Brahman, is the only reality. Thus ends the fourth chapter called *jñāna-karma sannyāsa-yoga* – having the topic of renunciation of actions through knowledge – in the *Bhagavadgītā* which is in the form of a dialogue between Śrī Kṛṣṇa and Arjuna, which is the essence of the *Upaniṣads*, whose subject matter is both knowledge of Brahman and *yoga*.

Chapter 5

संन्यास-योगः

Sannyāsa-yogaḥ

Topic of renunciation

Introduction

The fourth chapter concluded with Kṛṣṇa's advice to Arjuna, 'Stand up and take to *karma-yoga*.' It means Arjuna could not run off to the Himalayas to take up the lifestyle of a *sannyāsī*. He was advised to take to the lifestyle of a *karma-yogī* and pursue knowledge.

With the last statement of the fourth chapter the *Gītā* seemed to be over. Arjuna had already been told about *karma-yoga*. Now, he was to destroy his doubts by the sword of knowledge and take to *karma-yoga*, a means to knowledge. So for Kṛṣṇa, the teaching was over, but in Arjuna's mind, it was not. In fact, what Kṛṣṇa had said moved Arjuna to ask one more question.

Many of Arjuna's questions, although phrased differently, are essentially the same in that they relate to whether he should pursue *sannyāsa* or *karma-yoga*. He wants to know which one is better. Because he still has a doubt at the end of the fourth chapter, he asks a question that marks the beginning of the fifth chapter. His question is really a doubt, a doubt about *sannyāsa* and *karma*.

Śaṅkara introduces the fifth chapter in great detail, explaining the reason for Arjuna's question. Throughout the fourth chapter, Kṛṣṇa talked about knowledge in such a way that Arjuna found it contradictory when he was told that he should follow *karma-yoga*. Kṛṣṇa said that because of knowledge the wise person sees non-action in action and described this person as one who has renounced action through knowledge. A number of verses also talked about total renunciation, *jñāna-karma-sannyāsa,* the renunciation of *karma* by knowledge. But after all this, Kṛṣṇa said, 'Take to *karma-yoga, yogam ātiṣṭha.*'

In Arjuna's mind, there is a contradiction here. He thinks, 'If knowledge is the ultimate end, and, once having gained it, *karma* is given up, is it not more expedient for me to seek knowledge straightaway instead of doing *karma* while seeking knowledge?' If renunciation of action is the main emphasis and this renunciation has to take place by knowledge, why not take to a lifestyle of *sannyāsa* that is meant for gaining that knowledge? Arjuna's question is both obvious and understandable, given what he understood so far from Kṛṣṇa's teaching.

We have seen that there are two types of *sannyāsa* accepted by the *śāstra*. One type Kṛṣṇa talked about was renunciation of action through knowledge. This type of *sannyāsa* is called *vidvat-sannyāsa,* the *sannyāsa* of a *vidvān*, one who has the knowledge that the self is not the doer. And by taking to the lifestyle of *sannyāsa,* the *vidvān* releases himself from the duties enjoined by the *śāstra*. The other is the *sannyāsa* as a lifestyle where one renounces duties in order to pursue knowledge. This is called *vividiṣā-sannyāsa*.

If the wise person does not adopt the lifestyle of *sannyāsa*, continuing to remain as a householder, he or she performs the enjoined duties so as to set an example for the society. It is not proper for one who is a householder to give up the duties that are to be done. However, for the *jñānī* there is a choice; he or she can take to *sannyāsa*, renouncing the duties.

In this way, the *jñānī* can give up activities or continue them. Even when engaged in activity, one really performs no activity. Kṛṣṇa talked about these two types of *jñānī*s, the one who is engaged in activity and still free from actions,[1] and the one who is engaged only in minimum activity necessary to sustain the body.[2]

Vidvat-sannyāsa, the *sannyāsa* wherein a person gives up activities because one has the knowledge, means that the person is a *sannyāsī* with all that *sannyāsa* implies. The person wears orange robes, has no family or societal connections, and no job. Such a person who knows, 'I perform no action even if action is performed,' is a *karma-sannyāsī* in life and by knowledge too. Within and without, he or she is a *jñāna-karma-sannyāsī*.

The *vidvat-sannyāsī* has nothing to accomplish by performing Vedic rituals, or any other action for that matter. Earlier in the *Gītā* it was said that for a *jñānī* to perform rituals enjoined by the Veda is as useful as the well water is when the well is under water because the whole area is flooded.[3]

---

1 *Gītā* 4.20

2 *Gītā* 4.21

3 *Gītā* 2.46

Such a person can give up the duties and walk away, taking to a life of *vidvat-sannyāsa*

There is no choice between knowledge and karma-yoga

Given this definition of *vidvat-sannyāsa*, meaning *sannyāsa* with knowledge, is there any choice possible between *jñāna-karma-sannyāsa* and *karma-yoga?* There is no choice possible here because one is a means and the other is the end. It is like choosing between enrolling in a doctoral program at a university and getting a Ph.D. Unless you enrol in a doctoral program you cannot get a Ph.D. Where then is the choice?

Between *karma-yoga*, which is the means, and *jñāna-karma-sannyāsa*, which is the end, there is no choice. There can be a choice only between the two lifestyles, *karma-yoga* and *vividiṣā-sannyāsa*. This distinction made by the *śāstra* is very important and should be understood well because there is a lot of confusion about it in the modern tradition of Vedanta. We must know that *vidvat-sannyāsa* is not open to choice; it is something that happens as a result of knowledge.

Jñāna-karma-sannyāsa is the end, whether the person is a *sannyāsī* in lifestyle or not. A *jñāna-karma-sannyāsī* may be a person like King Janaka who ruled a kingdom. He was not a *sannyāsī* in terms of lifestyle. Nevertheless, he was a *jñāna-karma-sannyāsī*. As a ruler and politician he had daily activities to perform. However, in spite of all the royal activities he was engaged in, he performed no action because he knew he was not a doer. Therefore, he was a *jñāna-karma-sannyāsī*, even though he did not follow the lifestyle of a *sannyāsī*. Choice is available between *karma-yoga* and *vividiṣā-sannyāsa*, both of which are lifestyles. And Kṛṣṇa made it very clear that Arjuna should choose *karma-yoga*.

Arjuna's confusion about sannyāsa

When Arjuna expressed a desire to be a *sannyāsī*, he meant it in the sense of the lifestyle only. Thinking that *karma* was fraught with problems, he wanted to live the lifestyle of a *sannyāsī*. He knew he was not a *jñānī*, he did not have the knowledge, and so he knew he should be pursuing it. And to do this, what better lifestyle was there than that of a *sannyāsī*?

This was the thinking that prompted Arjuna's question, 'O Lord! Which of these two – *sannyāsa* or *karma-yoga*, is better? Which one should I choose? If I have understood you correctly, you are saying that *karma* is limited and so, *karma* cannot liberate me. Although you say that *karma-yoga* is for *antaḥ- karaṇa-śuddhi*, you also say that there is nothing equal to knowledge as a purifier. Therefore, I should gain this knowledge for which *sannyāsa* seems to be the better course. Furthermore, you have been praising the renunciation of action. If renunciation of action is the final end, why should I not give up my duties right now? This definitely seems to be a more straightforward and appropriate way to gain the knowledge.'

To Arjuna what Kṛṣṇa was recommending seemed to be an unnecessarily cumbersome way to proceed. First, you perform actions and then, later, you discover that you are not the doer! You perform *karma* and then you have to release yourself from *karma-phala*. Hence, to give up *karma* and pursue knowledge seemed more appropriate.

'As the end, so the means,' Arjuna thinks. If the end is renunciation of action, the means should also be renunciation of action. Why should you perform activities in order to discover yourself to be free from activities? Based on what Arjuna had understood from listening to Kṛṣṇa words, he feels that Kṛṣṇa had a great value for knowledge and a value for *sannyāsa* 'You say that liberation is *sannyāsa* why, then, do you ask me to pursue *karma-yoga*?' This is Arjuna's plea.

Arjuna wants to understand everything before he decides what he should do. Therefore, he keeps asking the same question. At the beginning of the third chapter, Arjuna had said, 'O Lord, if it is your contention that knowledge is better than action, why then do you engage me in this terrible action?' Because Arjuna asked this question, Kṛṣṇa continued to teach. Now two chapters later, at the beginning of the fifth chapter, Arjuna again asks essentially the same question, although he puts it differently, as we shall see in this chapter. The same question is asked at the beginning of the twelfth chapter and again in the eighteenth chapter in a slightly different form.

Arjuna is confused because Kṛṣṇa has praised both *sannyāsa* and *karma-yoga*. And having praised *sannyāsa* Kṛṣṇa said to him, 'Take to *yoga* – *yogam ātiṣṭha*.' Therefore, Arjuna wants Kṛṣṇa to indicate which of the two is better, *sannyāsa* or *karma-yoga*, since the same result could not be gained from both.

Verse 1

Arjuna's question

अर्जुन उवाच ।
संन्यासं कर्मणां कृष्ण पुनर्योगं च शंससि ।
यच्छ्रेय एतयोरेकं तन्मे ब्रूहि सुनिश्चितम् ॥ १ ॥

arjuna uvāca
sannyāsaṁ karmaṇāṁ kṛṣṇa punaryogaṁ ca śaṁsasi
yacchreya etayorekaṁ tanme brūhi suniścitam (1)

arjunaḥ – Arjuna; *uvāca* – said;
kṛṣṇa – O Kṛṣṇa!; *karmaṇāṁ sannyāsam* – renunciation of actions; *punaḥ* – again (also); *yogaṁ ca* – and *karma-yoga*; *śaṁsasi* – you praise; *etayoḥ* – of these two; *yat* – that which; *śreyaḥ* – better; *tat ekam* – that one; *suniścitam* – definitely; *me brūhi* – tell me

Arjuna said:

Kṛṣṇa! You praise renunciation of action and also *karma-yoga*. Tell me definitely that which is the better of the two.

Once again, Arjuna raises the same doubt. In the last chapter Kṛṣṇa continued to praise the renunciation of activities and ended by praising the person who gives up actions through knowledge.[4] Therefore, in Arjuna's mind, Kṛṣṇa was clearly advocating *sannyāsa*. Why then was the Lord telling him to take to a life of *karma-yoga*?

---

[4] *Gītā* 4.41

Kṛṣṇa was in fact praising renunciation of activities through *jñāna-karma-sannyāsa,* knowledge. He said that *karma* resolves in this knowledge.[5] However, Arjuna understood it to be the praise of *karma-sannyāsa,* which is a lifestyle wherein one is free from the obligation of having to perform the rituals enjoined by the Veda and other obligatory duties. So, Arjuna understands that the renunciation of action is proper and that Kṛṣṇa is enjoining *sannyāsa* as a means of knowledge. What confuses Arjuna is that Kṛṣṇa is also praising *karma-yoga.* At one and the same time, Kṛṣṇa seems to be praising renunciation and performance of action!

Which is better – *sannyāsa* or *karma-yoga*?

Since *mokṣa* means the knowledge of *akarma* in *karma,* meaning one should see the *akartā,* non doer, in the *kartā,* doer, Arjuna wants to pursue that knowledge. Being very clear as to what is to be done, renunciation of action seems to be the right thing to do, especially since the knowledge, 'I am *akartā*' is the renunciation of activities. Arjuna thinks, 'Why, should I perform actions and then try to discover the *akarma* in them?' It seems so much more logical to him to renounce action.

In *sannyāsa,* role playing being minimal, minimum action is involved. Whereas, in *karma-yoga* roles are many and so are the actions. To be a son or daughter, husband or wife, father or mother, citizen, neighbour, a friend, implies activities and duties that have to be performed. *Karma-yoga* means that the activities and duties involved in the varieties of roles one plays

---

[5] *Gītā* 4.33

are to be done properly and at the right time. This is what is meant by proper attitude, the attitude of *yoga*. If, however, one takes to *sannyāsa*, there is only one role, that of the disciple and, later perhaps, that of the *guru*. There is no other role for the *sannyāsī*, meaning there are no other duties. The person is released from familial and social duties, thereby reducing the number of roles. Role reduction is what is accomplished by the lifestyle of *sannyāsa*, the roles having been reduced to one. This role reducing lifestyle, *sannyāsa*, seems to Arjuna to be the most appropriate one for gaining *mokṣa*. And Kṛṣṇa was definitely praising it by praising the renunciation of action by knowledge.

Whatever Kṛṣṇa praises, Arjuna thinks he should follow. But Kṛṣṇa was praising both renunciation and performance of action. Kṛṣṇa had said there was nothing like knowledge for gaining *mokṣa*. He was definitely praising it by praising the renunciation of action by knowledge.[6] And having praised knowledge in this way, told Arjuna to take to *yoga*.[7]

Arjuna feels that Kṛṣṇa was contradicting himself by praising the renunciation of activity while asking him to perform activity. The advice does not seem appropriate. But, Arjuna knows that Kṛṣṇa knows better. Therefore, he expresses his doubt. Is the renunciation of action better or the performance of action? Which of these two, *sannyāsa* or *karma-yoga* is better?

By 'better' Arjuna means the one that would give him *mokṣa*, *śreyas*. Knowing that renunciation and performance of

---

[6] *Gītā* 4.38

[7] *Gītā* 4.42

action could not yield the same result, he wants to know which one would lead him to *mokṣa*. His doubt, then, is centred on which one he should follow. Both are good, but if one is better than the other, meaning one is a means to *mokṣa*, and the other is not, then Arjuna wants to follow the better of the two.

Both renunciation of action and the performance of action cannot be pursued at the same time. They are opposed to each other. One cannot simultaneously renounce activities and do them also. And since they are contradictory, he cannot even follow each of them partially – a little bit of *sannyāsa* and a little bit of *karma-yoga*. Just as fasting and eating cannot be followed by the same person at the same time, so too, *sannyāsa* and *karma-yoga*, being opposites, cannot be followed by the same person at the same time. Therefore, Arjuna again asks Kṛṣṇa to clarify as to which of the two is better.

Verse 2

Kṛṣṇa responds – action as yoga is better than renunciation of action

श्रीभगवानुवाच ।
संन्यासः कर्मयोगश्च निःश्रेयसकरावुभौ ।
तयोस्तु कर्मसंन्यासात्कर्मयोगो विशिष्यते ॥ २ ॥

śrībhagavān uvāca
sannyāsaḥ karmayogaśca niḥśreyasakarāvubhau
tayostu karmasannyāsāt karmayogo viśiṣyate (2)

śrībhagavān – Śrī Bhagavān (Lord Kṛṣṇa); *uvāca* – said; *sannyāsaḥ* – renunciation (of action); *karma-yogaḥ ca* – and the performance of action as *yoga*; *ubhau niśśreyasa-karau* – both lead to liberation; *tayoḥ tu* – but of these two; *karma-sannyāsāt* – than renunciation of action; *karma-yogaḥ* – performance of action as *yoga*; *viśiṣyate* – is better

Śrī Bhagavān said:

Both renunciation (of action) and performance of action as *yoga* lead to liberation. But, of these two, the performance of action as *yoga* is better than renunciation of action.

We have seen that, though the word *śreyas* means 'better,' it also means *mokṣa*. *Niśreyasa* means the same. And what leads to *mokṣa*? Kṛṣṇa responds to Arjuna's question by saying that both *sannyāsa* and *karma-yoga* lead to *mokṣa*.

For Arjuna, it is an either or situation. Either *sannyāsa* can do it or *karma-yoga*, but not both. For Kṛṣṇa, however, there is no either or; both *sannyāsa* and *karma-yoga* lead to *mokṣa*.

The problem here does not have a simple either-or solution. But to appreciate this fact requires that both *sannyāsa* and *karma-yoga* be properly understood. In each lifestyle, there are advantages and disadvantages, depending on the qualifications of the person. One lifestyle may be advantageous to one person, while the other may be advantageous to another.

Both lifestyles have an equal status because both are *sādhanas*, means. So, between these two lifestyles, *sannyāsa* and *karma-yoga*, there is a choice. But Kṛṣṇa is not praising *sannyāsa* as a lifestyle; he merely states that there was such a lifestyle. Nor does he ever say that *sannyāsa* as a lifestyle is preferable to *karma-yoga*. He praises *sannyāsa* only as an end to be gained.

At the beginning of the third chapter, Kṛṣṇa said that there were two lifestyles, *jñāna-yoga* and *karma-yoga*.[8] *Jñāna-yoga* is characterised by the pursuit of knowledge alone and *karma-yoga* combines the pursuit of knowledge with *karma*. In the verse presently under study, Kṛṣṇa again refers to these two lifestyles as being equal. Since both of them are means, what else could he do? Even though Arjuna wants to know only one of them, Kṛṣṇa has to teach both. Therefore, once again, Kṛṣṇa seems to be confusing him.

It is wonderful if you understand Kṛṣṇa's statement, 'Both renunciation and *karma-yoga* lead to *mokṣa*,' but it can be exasperating if you do not understand it. If both *sannyāsa* and *karma-yoga* lead you to *mokṣa*, you may also prefer *sannyāsa*, as Arjuna did. It is like being told that to reach a place, there are two routes. One route requires you to walk half a mile and the other route requires you to walk five miles. Which one are you likely to choose? You will no doubt choose the easier of the two, because we always go for the easiest way to do anything.

Similarly, if both *sannyāsa* and *karma-yoga* lead you to *mokṣa*, you will choose the easier. And which is the easier? At first glance, it looks as though *sannyāsa*, doing nothing or doing

---

[8] *Gītā* 3.2

very little, is easier. But, in fact, *sannyāsa* is definitely the more difficult of the two if you are not ready for it. Kṛṣṇa makes it very clear in this verse that performing action is better than giving it up.

Renunciation of action means that one should be able to be with oneself. One should be happy with oneself, for which one requires preparation, which is why Kṛṣṇa says here that *karma-yoga* is better than renunciation. It does not mean, however, that no one should take *sannyāsa*. It simply means that *sannyāsa* is difficult, and therefore, one should be ready for it, as Kṛṣṇa makes clear later on. *Karma-yoga* actually paves the way to *sannyāsa*.

Here, Kṛṣṇa is saying that *karma-yoga* is better than a mere life of *sannyāsa*, without the necessary preparation. He explains why this is so in the next verse.

Verse 3

The one who is free from the opposites is released from bondage

ज्ञेयः स नित्यसंन्यासी यो न द्वेष्टि न काङ्क्षति ।
निर्द्वन्द्वो हि महाबाहो सुखं बन्धात्प्रमुच्यते ॥ ३ ॥

jñeyaḥ sa nityasannyāsī yo na dveṣṭi na kāṅkṣati
nirdvandvo hi mahābāho sukhaṁ bandhātpramucyate (3)

yaḥ – the one who; *na dveṣṭi* – does not hate; *na kāṅkṣati* – does not long (for anything); *saḥ* – that person; *nityasannyāsī* – always a renunciate; *jñeyaḥ* – should be known as; *mahābāho* – O mighty armed (Arjuna)!; *hi* – indeed; *nirdvandvaḥ* – free from the opposites (likes and dislikes); *bandhāt* – from bondage; *sukham* – effortlessly; *pramucyate* – is released

> The person who neither hates nor longs (for anything) should be known as always a renunciate, Arjuna, the mighty armed! One who is free from the opposites (likes and dislikes) is indeed effortlessly released from bondage.

We saw that, in answer to Arjuna's question, whether *sannyāsa* leads to *mokṣa* or *karma-yoga* leads to *mokṣa*, Kṛṣṇa said that both lead to *mokṣa*. If you have the knowledge, you already are a *sannyāsī*. If you are not a *jñānī*, there is a choice in that there are two lifestyles for pursuing the knowledge. Having said this, Kṛṣṇa hints at the difficulties inherent in merely giving up action, *karma-sannyāsa* without the necessary preparation, and says that *karma-yoga* is preferable.

To say that *karma-yoga* is better than *karma-sannyāsa* is strictly from the standpoint of one's qualifications, since both are means for *mokṣa* alone. The *karma-yogī* and the *karma-sannyāsī* are both *mumukṣus;* they both desire liberation, freedom. The only difference is that the *karma-yogī* has duties to perform and the *sannyāsī* does not. And, if one has no duties to perform, one should be able to live with oneself and pursue knowledge to the exclusion of everything else, which takes certain preparedness. This is why Kṛṣṇa says that *karma-yoga* is better than simply giving up action.

Kṛṣṇa's definition of a sannyāsī

Kṛṣṇa wants Arjuna to understand what *sannyāsa* means. You do not become a *sannyāsī* simply by giving up action, even though by your appearance people may look upon you as one. You are not a *sannyāsī* if the inner preparedness or maturity that characterises a *sannyāsī* is not there.

The external symbols, like wearing the orange cloth, may be of some psychological help to the person who takes to the lifestyle of *sannyāsa* in order to pursue knowledge. Combined with the discipline of the lifestyle itself, external symbols can help the person bring about the inner changes necessary to prepare the mind for knowledge. These external factors are an advantage if the person is ready for this lifestyle, but if the person is not ready, such a lifestyle can become a decided disadvantage.

So, without *jñāna* or at least certain preparedness, *sannyāsa* can be a real problem. You need not have complete knowledge, but some insight and a cheerful disposition are definitely required. If this is not there, *sannyāsa* is definitely a problem. The person is neither in the world where he or she can work things out nor is he or she in the world of *sannyāsī*s. The person is somewhere in between – a *sannyāsī* without a field in which to polish oneself.

Under such circumstances, *sannyāsa* becomes an onerous responsibility, one that the person is not really able to fulfil. This is why Kṛṣṇa says that *karma-yoga* is better than simply giving up action. By merely changing your lifestyle, you do not become a *sannyāsī*. Whereas a person who neither hates nor longs for things is to be understood as a *sannyāsī*.

An adjective, '*nitya*,' is also added to the *sannyāsī*. *Nitya-sannyāsī* does not mean eternal *sannyās*. Rather, the *nitya-sannyāsī* is one who is a *sannyāsī* always, as opposed to the person who is sometimes a *sannyāsī* and sometimes not. This 'sometime *sannyāsī*' is called *kādācitka-sannyāsī*.

With reference to certain things, everyone is a *nitya-sannyāsī*. And, with reference to everything for a certain period of time, everyone is a *kādācitka-sannyāsī*. For example, with reference to balloons, spinning tops, and Barbie dolls, you are a *nitya-sannyāsī*. In fact, with reference to many things you loved once, without which you could not live because they were so important to you, and which you have completely grown out of, you are a *nitya-sannyāsī*. You did not give up these things; you simply grew out of them.

If you had given them up, you would still be attached to them. But, if you have grown out of them, you no longer think about them, let alone talk about your having given them up. If a man says that he has given up a title and a job, for example, it is because the person has only given them up. He has not grown out of them; a taste or a value for what has been given up remains in the mind, which is why the person talks about them.

No one ever says, 'I gave away the garbage the day before yesterday.' You simply leave the garbage out and forget about it. If, however, you keep talking about the garbage, then you still have a value for it. Similarly, when anyone talks about what one has given up, it means that the person still has a value for it. Whereas, you do not say, 'I have given up spinning tops, balloons, and dolls,' because you have grown out of them. If you have only given them up, you will be afraid to face them because they still remain as tempting factors in your life. Being tempting objects, you are not free from desire for them and therefore, you cannot face what you have only given up. Naturally, then, you have to keep away from them to protect yourself from them. If, however, you have grown out of them, you have neither hatred nor longing for them.

So, with reference to a number of things, you are a *nitya-sannyāsī* but with reference to other things, you are not a *sannyāsī* at all. As long as there are things without which you cannot live, you cannot call yourself a *sannyāsī* because there are things that still bind you and upon which you depend for your sense of well being. Even though you are a *sannyāsī* with reference to a few things, and not a *sannyāsī* with reference to other things, I cannot call you a *nitya-sannyāsī*. *Nitya-sannyāsī* refers to a person who is a *sannyāsī* in all situations. If this is not the case, then you are a *kādācitka-sannyāsī* only – meaning that you are a *sannyāsī* whenever you confront certain things; otherwise, you are not.

The nitya-sannyāsī

There are also times when you can be a *sannyāsī* with reference to everything – moments when you are totally free, when you do not need anything. For instance, in your seat of meditation, you may feel that you are everything. At such times, you do not need anything other than yourself; you are *pūrṇa*, full. You can experience a total contentment with yourself, which is *sannyāsa*.

You are definitely a *sannyāsī* whenever you are happy. The world does not seem to have anything to demand your attention, which is exactly what is meant by *sannyāsa*. There is no longing or hatred, no *rāga* or *dveṣa*. At that moment you are a totally free person, a *sannyāsī*. Everyone is a *sannyāsī* in this way, occasionally, with reference to everything. But, being only for the moment, this is *kādācitka-sannyāsa*, not *nitya-sannyāsa*.

Who is a *nitya-sannyāsī*? The one who neither hates nor longs for anything. One can long to avoid things and also to have things. Both are longings. However, when one wants to avoid things, we do not call it longing; we call it *dveṣa*, hatred or dislike.

A *sannyāsī* is not bound by *rāga-dveṣa*s, that is, he or she is not under the spell of likes and dislikes. Only such a person can be a *nitya-sannyāsī*. To be free from *rāga-dveṣa* with reference to everything means one is not affected by the presence or absence of a given thing. One is not overwhelmed or afraid in the presence of something, and one does not miss something when it is not there.

Sannyāsa will not work if it is an escape

Sannyāsa is not merely giving up duties. It is very easy to give up your duties, especially those that are cumbersome and difficult. In fact, your tendency is to avoid them! You always want to escape from any situation that is painful or difficult to handle. Therefore, *sannyāsa* can become an escape.

You do not become strong by escaping situations; only by facing them do you become strong. By escaping, you become necessarily weak. You may think you have avoided something but, in fact, what has really happened is that you have lost something, your strength. Escape means you have yielded to the enormity of the problem. By running away from the problem, no matter how enormous it is, you become weaker. Escape has another disadvantage in that in the future you will find it necessary to run away from lesser problems. With each escape, you lose the strength you would have gained by remaining and facing the problem, for you become stronger with every problem you face, whether you are successful or not.

Kṛṣṇa wants Arjuna to know that one does not really grow by running away from duties, however painful they may be. Nor does one become a *sannyāsī*, in the real sense. In fact, giving up the duties that are to be done, *kevala-karma-sannyāsa* is exactly what is not to be done! Only the person who neither dislikes nor longs for anything is a *sannyāsī*.

According to Śaṅkara, a *nitya-sannyāsī* can be understood in an absolute as well as in a relative sense. Relatively, Śaṅkara explains a *nitya-sannyāsī* as a *karma-yogī*, one who may have *rāga-dveṣa*s, but who does not come under their spell. In an absolute sense, a *nitya-sannyāsī* is one who has self-knowledge and is therefore totally free from *rāga-dveṣa*s.

If you are afraid of *karma* and you choose *sannyāsa* as a lifestyle in order to avoid it, then you are definitely under the spell of your *rāga-dveṣa*s. A *sannyāsī* is one who is not under their spell. The fear of *karma* is *dveṣa* and the love for *sannyāsa* is *rāga*. If *sannyāsa* is an object of your *rāga*, it will not work for you. As a *karma-yogī*, however, you have an opportunity to release yourself from the spell of *rāga-dveṣa*s.

By living a life of a *karma-yogī*, you allow your *rāga-dveṣa*s to manifest themselves and, at the same time, you are able to manage them effectively. The ability to remain free from their spell is what makes you a *karma-yogī*, which is why *karma-yoga* is referred to as *buddhi-yoga*, the *yoga* of attitude, in the second chapter. There, *buddhi* means a particular attitude towards what is to be done, what is not to be done, and also towards the result of action.

Towards the result of action, there is *prasāda-buddhi*, an attitude wherein whatever comes is looked upon as *prasāda*, gift from the Lord. With reference to action itself, you conform to *dharma*, which is looked upon as Īśvara. This is called *īśvara-arpaṇa-buddhi*, an attitude of offering your action to the Lord. These two attitudes, namely, *prasāda-buddhi*, and *īśvara-arpaṇa-buddhi*, constitute *karma-yoga*. This attitude, maintained in the midst of activities, makes you a *karma-yogī* and frees you from the spell of your *rāga-dveṣa*s.

There is no problem once you are a *sannyāsī*, even relatively. But, until then, you need to live a life of a *karma-yogī*. This is why Kṛṣṇa describes a *nitya-sannyāsī* in this verse, as *nirdvandva*, one who is free of the pairs of opposites. 'Opposites' here stands for *rāga-dveṣa*s, success-failure, pleasant and unpleasant situations, and so on. Such situations are *dvandva*s, opposites. These *dvandva*s are always there, and because of your *rāga-dveṣa*s they can bind you.

Mastery over likes and dislikes

The world does not bind you nor do the events that take place. What binds you is only your *rāga-dveṣa*s, *dvandva*s.

All the opposites can be reduced to *rāga-dveṣa*s, and therefore, one who is free from the hold of *rāga-dveṣa*s is *nirdvandva*.

In fact, even the opposites themselves do not really bind you; they are simply facts of life. Not getting what you want is always in terms of your *rāga*, that is, certain situations are not in keeping with your likes. You want something to happen which may not happen; instead, the opposite may happen. It is the very nature, the order of things, not because the world is too much or your *rāga-dveṣa*s are bad, but simply because that is how it is. Since you are not omniscient, you are not free from *rāga-dveṣa*s, and since you are not omnipotent, they will often remain unfulfilled. If you were almighty, all powerful, then you could fulfil all your *rāga-dveṣa*s, but you are not.

The only way out, then, is to have mastery over your *rāga-dveṣa*s. To the extent you have such mastery, to that extent you will have mastery over your life, over the world. Management of your emotional life, spiritual life, in fact everything, can be narrowed down to the management of these two, *rāga* and *dveṣa*. This is why the psychology of the entire *gītā-śāstra* is based on *rāga-dveṣa*s.

So, in order to be a *jñānī*, in order to gain *mokṣa*, freedom from bondage, you must be a *nitya-sannyāsī*. A *nitya-sannyāsī* is either a *jñānī* or an accomplished *karma-yogī*. An accomplished *karma-yogī* is a *sannyāsī*. Anyone who has the maturity, who is not in the hands of *rāga-dveṣa*s, is a *sannyāsī*, whether he or she has the external symbols. This is the person who is fit to be released from bondage.

Kṛṣṇa also says here that, for such a person, the release is effortless, *sukhaṁ pramucyate*. If a person is ready, mature, and not in the hands of *rāga-dveṣa*s, there is nothing that can deny him or her the knowledge; therefore, the release from bondage is indeed effortless. *Sukham* can also be translated as 'happily' here. Happily, the person is released from bondage if one is prepared.

Mokṣa is the only aim of the karma-yogī

A *karmī* is interested in *karma-phala*s, which are many and varied, and for which the person performs a variety of actions. However if the *karmī* becomes a *karma-yogī*, he or she will not be doing these actions for heaven, power, wealth, or something else, because the person has no interest in such things. The *karma-yogī* is interested only in *mokṣa*.

A person who does not have *mokṣa* as the only end cannot be a *karma-yogī*. He or she is only a *karmī*, also known as *karmaṭha*, one who is interested in various ends that action can provide. The person who is interested in heaven is not a *karma-yogī*, even though he or she may think that heaven is the same as *mokṣa*, because it promises certain security and pleasure. Such a person is not a *karma-yogī* but an *artha-kāma-kāmī*, one who desires security and pleasure.

Who, then, is a *karma-yogī*? The one who goes about doing various actions that are to be done purely for his or her own *antaḥ-karaṇa-śuddhi*, the preparation of the mind that is required in order to be freed from *rāga-dveṣa*s. Fulfilment of *rāga-dveṣa*s is not the criterion for a *karma-yogī*. His or her motive is rather to gain mastery over *rāga-dveṣa*s.

In fact, *antaḥ-karaṇa-śuddhi* is itself a kind of *mokṣa*, freedom from the hold of *rāga-dveṣas*. It is the first *mokṣa*. Then, freedom from the sense of bondage, from *ajñāna*, is the ultimate *mokṣa*. One is of the nature of maturity and the other of the nature of *jñāna*, knowledge. Maturity itself is an accomplishment, for which one takes to a life of *karma-yoga* and then one gains knowledge.

Giving up and performing activity can only have the same end in view, *mokṣa*. One person gives up action and gains *mokṣa* while the other continues his or her activities and gains *mokṣa*. But, how can this be? Should there not be a difference in what is accomplished when the means are different? Surely, there should be a different result when one performs actions, and when one does not. This was Arjuna's thinking.

Kṛṣṇa addresses Arjuna's doubt from the standpoint of the *phala*, result.

Verses 4&5

Mokṣa is the end for both karma-yoga and sannyāsa

साङ्ख्ययोगौ पृथग्बालाः प्रवदन्ति न पण्डिताः ।
एकमप्यास्थितः सम्यगुभयोर्विन्दते फलम् ॥ ४ ॥

sāṅkhyayogau pṛthagbālāḥ pravadanti na paṇḍitāḥ
ekam apyāsthitaḥ samyagubhayorvindate phalam (4)

bālāḥ – children (those who do not know); *sāṅkhyayogau* – knowledge and *karma-yoga; pṛthak* – are different; *pravadanti* – argue; *na paṇḍitāḥ* – not the wise; *ekam api* – even one; *samyak* –

properly; *āsthitaḥ* – the one who follows; *ubhayoḥ* – of both; *phalam* – result; *vindate* – gains

> Children (those who do not know), (but) not the wise, argue that knowledge and *karma-yoga* are different. The person who follows even one (of the two) properly, gains the result of both.

By nature, of course, *sannyāsa* and *karma-yoga* are different, one implying the renunciation and the other the performance of activity. Here, Kṛṣṇa brings in the word '*sāṅkhya*' in the place of *sannyāsa*, the reason for which we shall see later. In the compound '*sāṅkhya-yogau*,' *sāṅkhya* means knowledge and *yoga* means *karma-yoga*. People argue that knowledge and *yoga* are different, meaning that they are not only different in nature, but their results are also different.

Who argues in this way? Kṛṣṇa refers to such people here as children, *bālāḥ*, meaning those who do not know. Such people have studied the *śāstra* and know what it says, but do not know what it means. Like children, they repeat what they have heard without understanding. The child having been told by his father that money is dangerous, keeps repeating the statement, 'Money is dangerous.' But he does not know why. He does not know that his father means that money, if not handled properly, is dangerous. There is always some truth in such statements, but the child does not know the meaning even though he may constantly repeat his father's words. In the same manner these people repeat the words of the *śāstra* without knowing what they mean.

Sannyāsa, meaning renunciation of action, is not the means to *mokṣa*, nor is *karma-yoga*. *Jñāna* alone is the means. Only by knowledge is *mokṣa* gained. There is no other way because the bondage from which *mokṣa* is sought is ignorance. To gain this knowledge you need a *pramāṇa*, a means of knowledge. Therefore, whatever you follow, knowledge is common.

Separate paths are not mentioned anywhere in the *śāstra*. All that is mentioned are only two *niṣṭhā*s, lifestyles – *pravṛtti*, the pursuit of activities called *karma-yoga*, and *nivṛtti*, the giving up of activity, that is, *sannyāsa* or *jñāna-yoga*. This is all the *śāstra* talks about and both of these lifestyles are meant for *mokṣa*.

Earlier in this chapter, Kṛṣṇa said that *karma-yoga* is preferable to *sannyāsa*.[9] Knowing this to be the case for a person who is not ready for *sannyāsa*, Kṛṣṇa wants the seeker to play it safe.

Kṛṣṇa says whether you follow *sannyāsa* or *karma-yoga*, the result is the same provided, of course, you follow it properly. The two lifestyles do not yield different results. The result is one and the same, *mokṣa*.

By following a life of *karma-yoga*, which means performance of duties and pursuit of knowledge, you first gain *antaḥ-karaṇa-śuddhi* and then knowledge. And, by following a life of *sannyāsa*, which is pursuit of knowledge, you gain the same end. In other words, what can be gained by *sannyāsa* can also be gained by

---

[9] *Gītā* 5.2

living a life of *karma-yoga*. However, *sannyāsa* deprives you the field necessary for polishing yourself, whereas *karma-yoga* provides you with factors which, by rubbing up against, enable you to become polished in the process. This is the difference between the two and which is why Kṛṣṇa says that *karma-yoga* is preferable to simply giving up the duties.

Why does Kṛṣṇa use the word '*sāṅkhya*' instead of *sannyāsa* in this verse? At the beginning of the chapter, Arjuna asked Kṛṣṇa to tell him which would give him *mokṣa, sannyāsa* or *karma-yoga*. Kṛṣṇa responded in the second verse by saying that *sannyāsa* and *karma-yoga* both result in *mokṣa*. He followed this up in the third verse by pointing out that the person to be known as a *sannyāsī* was one who had no hatred or longing for anything.

But here, in the fourth verse, Kṛṣṇa replaces the word *sannyāsa* with *sāṅkhya*. It means for Kṛṣṇa *sāṅkhya* and *sannyāsa* are one and the same. *Sāṅkhya* means 'that which is very well unfolded by Vedanta.' In other words it is *brahma-jñāna*, the knowledge of identity between Brahman and *ātmā*. The *śāstra* unfolds this knowledge. Therefore, *sāṅkhya* means *brahma-jñāna*, which is also the meaning of the word *sannyāsa* in the primary sense.

Arjuna wants to know which of the two, *sannyāsa* or *karma-yoga*, is better, and Kṛṣṇa begins talking about *sāṅkhya* and *yoga*. Śaṅkara confirms in his commentary to this verse that this is not something new that Kṛṣṇa is introducing. In fact, Kṛṣṇa had already used the word *sāṅkhya* in the third chapter when he described the two lifestyles given by him, one of which was the pursuit of knowledge for the *sannyāsī*. In the present verse, he uses the word again, the context having been made very clear in the previous two verses by his use of the word *sannyāsa*. So, *sāṅkhya* here means the same as *sannyāsa*. It also fits into the metre of this particular verse easier than *sannyāsa* because it has one syllable less.

By using the word *sāṅkhya* instead of *sannyāsa*, Kṛṣṇa is quietly telling Arjuna that *sannyāsa* is the pursuit of knowledge and that it is common to both *karma-yoga* and *sannyāsa* Both of them produce the same result, *mokṣa*. All one has to do is follow one of them properly.

One can be either a *karma-yogī* or a *sannyāsī*, but *mokṣa* is the result of *jñāna* alone. Therefore, both the *sannyāsī* and the *karma-yogī* have to pursue knowledge. No one becomes liberated simply by taking to a life of *sannyāsa* or by remaining a *karma-yogī*. Only by knowledge does one become liberated. There is no choice here at all. The choice is only between *sannyāsa* and *karma-yoga* as a lifestyle. That is what Kṛṣṇa means here when he says that by following either one properly, the result achieved is the same.

यत्साङ्ख्यैः प्राप्यते स्थानं तद्योगैरपि गम्यते ।
एकं साङ्ख्यं च योगं च यः पश्यति स पश्यति ॥ ५ ॥

yatsāṅkhyaiḥ prāpyate sthānaṁ tadyogairapi gamyate
ekaṁ sāṅkhyaṁ ca yogaṁ ca yaḥ paśyati sa paśyati (5)

sāṅkhyaiḥ – by the *sannyāsīs*; *yat sthānam* – which end (*mokṣa*); *prāpyate* – is gained; *yogaiḥ api* – by the *karma-yogīs* also; *tat* – that (end); *gamyate* – is reached; *yaḥ* – the one who; *sāṅkhyaṁ ca* – knowledge; *yogaṁ ca* – and *yoga* (*karma-yoga*); *ekam* – as one; *paśyati* – sees; *saḥ* – he; *paśyati* – sees (the truth)

> The end (*mokṣa*) that is gained by the *sannyāsins* is also reached by the *karma-yogins*. The one who sees knowledge and *karma-yoga* as one, that person (alone) sees (the truth).

The knowledge, which is *mokṣa*, gained by the *sannyāsīs*, is also the *mokṣa* reached by the *karma-yogīs* in time. First, they gain *antaḥ-karaṇa-śuddhi*, a pure mind, and then they gain knowledge. *Sthāna* means place or end. Here the end is the knowledge that is *mokṣa* for both the *sannyāsī* and the *karma-yogī*.

The use of the words 'gained, *prāpyate*' and 'reached, *gamyate*' denotes a small difference here – the difference in the degree of preparedness of the *sannyāsī* and the *karma-yogī*. What is *prāpyate*, accomplished, by the *sannyāsī* is *gamyate*, reached, by the *karma-yogī* in time, meaning when his or her mind has been properly prepared by living a life of *karma-yoga*. This is the only difference.

The *karma-yogī* lives a life of *karma-yoga* and gains the knowledge, either by becoming a *sannyāsī* or while still remaining a *karma-yogī*. Either way, the person can gain knowledge. Even when knowledge takes place, one can become a *sannyāsī* or continue to remain as a *karma-yogī*, like King Janaka did. The one who understands this clearly is a *paṇḍita*, wise person, whereas the others are *bālas*, children, who do not see clearly, even though they have studied the *śāstra*. One person may renounce activities, looking upon renunciation as more desirable than *karma-yoga*, while another may perform action and look upon it as more desirable than *sannyāsa*. Thus, we have these two groups of people, one group insisting that you must renounce and the other group advocating that you must do *karma*. In fact, neither group knows the truth.

There are those who, analysing the *Gītā* in their own way, have tried to prove that the *Gītā* advocates *karma* only, that the performance of *karma* alone produces *mokṣa*, and that it does not talk about *sannyāsa* at all. This is an error and it creates problems for others as well. Kṛṣṇa has said very clearly that there are two lifestyles in this world.[10] So, it is difficult to understand how anyone can interpret the *Gītā* to mean that *karma* alone produces *mokṣa*. But they do – being prejudiced, being committed to the hard and fast conclusions they have made before even studying the *Gītā*. This is why we need to analyse if what they advocate is true. And to do so, we need to look into the *Gītā* and see what it actually does say.

To first make a conclusion and then look into the *Gītā* to support your conclusion is not *pramāṇa-vicāra*, enquiry. It is merely your own interpretation. *Pramāṇa-vicāra* is to see what the *Gītā* really says; for this, you need to be highly objective. When you think, 'Because I have *śraddhā* in the *Gītā*, I want to know what it says,' it is called *pramāṇa-vicāra*.

---

[10] *Gītā* 3.3

Sannyāsa only looks easier

Here, Kṛṣṇa says that the person who sees *sannyāsa* and *karma-yoga* are one is the one who really sees. It means that both are equal.

'If both are equal, I will take *sannyāsa* because it is easier than *karma*. *Karma-yoga* means I have so many duties to perform, whereas *sannyāsa* seems to be free from problems. In *karma-yoga*, I have to get up early in the morning, take a bath, and do the required rituals and prayers. The duties involved in a life of *karma-yoga* are endless; and in Arjuna's case, it can even amount to killing people! *Sannyāsa* definitely seems easier. I have no duties and therefore, no problems!' This may have been Arjuna's thinking, and therefore, Kṛṣṇa goes on to tell him that knowledge is difficult to gain without the proper preparation, which a life of *karma-yoga* provides. This is what we see in the next verse.

Verse 6

The necessity of living a life of karma-yoga

संन्यासस्तु महाबाहो दुःखमाप्तुमयोगतः ।
योगयुक्तो मुनिर्ब्रह्म नचिरेणाधिगच्छति ॥ ६ ॥

sannyāsastu mahābāho duḥkham āptum ayogataḥ
yogayukto munirbrahma nacireṇādhigacchati (6)

mahābāho – O mighty armed (Arjuna)!; *ayogataḥ* – without *karma-yoga*; *sannyāsaḥ* – renunciation of action; *āptum* – to accomplish; *duḥkham* – difficult; *tu* – whereas; *yoga-yuktaḥ* – committed to a life of *karma-yoga*; *muniḥ* – one who is capable of reasoning; *na cireṇa* – (not after a long time) quickly; *brahma* – Brahman; *adhigacchati* – gains

> Renunciation of action, Arjuna, the mighty armed! is difficult to accomplish without *karma-yoga*. Whereas, one who is committed to a life of *karma-yoga* and is capable of reasoning, gains Brahman quickly.

Although both *sannyāsa* and *karma-yoga* are the means to knowledge, without *yoga*, it is not easy to live the life of *sannyāsa*, let alone gain knowledge. This is what Kṛṣṇa is telling Arjuna here.

If you take the word *sannyāsa* to mean knowledge, it is certainly difficult to gain *sannyāsa* without *karma-yoga*, which is essential for *antaḥ-karaṇa-śuddhi*, purification of the mind. Without *antaḥ-karaṇa-śuddhi*, you cannot gain knowledge; you cannot even live a life of *sannyāsa*. Thus, *karma-yoga* is the means to accomplish *sannyāsa* both in terms of lifestyle as well as knowledge.

Whether a person takes to a life of *sannyāsa*, the person acquires certain qualities of a *sannyāsī* if he lives a life of *karma-yoga*. However, people under the spell of *rāga-dveṣa* will find it very difficult to live a life of *sannyāsa*. Such people sometimes take to *sannyāsa* simply because they are disenchanted with life, being unable to fulfil their *rāga-dveṣa*s. Impelled as they are by their *rāga-dveṣa*s, they continue to be frustrated. Even as a *sannyāsī*, the person may have to deal with the mind if *rāga-dveṣa*s have not been resolved; therefore, he has a lot to do in addition to *guru-sevā*, serving the *guru*. It is strictly with reference to one's *rāga-dveṣa*s that the two lifestyles are given and choice exists only in terms of these two lifestyles.

Suppose you go to a *guru* with many *rāga-dveṣa*s in your mind. If you are lucky, the *guru* who knows the subject matter perhaps can help you neutralise them. By serving the *guru* and following his instructions, you can gain *antaḥ-karaṇa-śuddhi*. What Kṛṣṇa points out here is that, without *karma-yoga*, *sannyāsa* is not easy to accomplish. He does not say it is impossible, but he does say it is difficult to accomplish *sannyāsa* without the preparation of *karma-yoga* – *duḥkham āptum ayogataḥ*.

You cannot become a *sannyāsī* by will, by just deciding to do so. You need to be endowed with *karma-yoga*, *yoga-yukta*, meaning that you need to live a life of *karma-yoga*. One who is endowed with *yoga* is one who can understand and analyse what is being said. Such a person is a *muniḥ*, one who can understand and who gains Brahman, *muniḥ brahma adhigacchati*.

Nyāsa means renunciation and *sannyāsa* means perfect or total renunciation, a renunciation with maturity. *Sannyāsa*, *sāṅkhya*, and Brahman have the same meaning. Knowledge of Brahman is *sāṅkhya*, which is also called *sannyāsa*. And *sannyāsa* is also called *brahma*, which is gained by the *yoga-yukta*, the one endowed with *yoga*, and who is a *muni*. Such a person gains Brahman, otherwise referred to as *sannyāsa*, knowledge of Brahman.

Adhigacchati means 'goes to' or 'gains.' And when does the person gain Brahman? *Na cireṇa*, not after a long time. Once a person has the maturity on account of *karma-yoga*, it does not take time for the person to gain Brahman. How this is so, is explained in the next verse.

Verse 7

Kṛṣṇa presents a natural order of how one gains this knowledge

योगयुक्तो विशुद्धात्मा विजितात्मा जितेन्द्रियः ।
सर्वभूतात्मभूतात्मा कुर्वन्नपि न लिप्यते ॥ ७ ॥

yogayukto viśuddhātmā vijitātmā jitendriyaḥ
sarvabhūtātmabhūtātmā kurvannapi na lipyate (7)

yoga-yuktaḥ – one who has committed to a life of *karma-yoga; viśuddhātmā* – one who has a purified mind; *vijitātmā* – one who has mastered the body (organs of action); *jitendriyaḥ* – one whose sense organs are under control; *sarva-bhūta-ātmabhūta-ātmā* – one who knows oneself to be the self in all beings; *kurvan api* – even while doing (actions); *na lipyate* – is not affected

> One whose mind is purified by being committed to a life of *karma-yoga*, who has mastered the body and the sense organs, and who knows oneself to be the self in all beings, (such a person) is not affected even while doing (actions).

In this verse, Lord Kṛṣṇa tells Arjuna in detail how one gains this knowledge and, at the same time, explains the meaning of the expression, *na cireṇa*. It takes time to gain the necessary maturity of the mind, and this maturity is the result of living a life of *karma-yoga*. Once this maturity is gained, not much time passes before the knowledge is gained, *na cireṇa adhigacchati*.

A natural order is presented in this verse. Lord Kṛṣṇa begins by saying that the person under discussion has the discipline of *karma-yoga*. As a result of that, the person becomes a *viśuddha-ātmā*, one whose *ātmā*, mind, is *viśuddha*, pure. Here, *ātmā* refers to the mind and so, *viśuddha ātmā* means one whose mind is free from the spell of *rāga-dveṣa*s.

Next, the person acquires a control of the physical body, meaning the organs of action, and also control of the organs of perception; such a person is a *vijitātmā*. The word *ātmā* in *vijita-ātmā* refers to the body, which has the ability to move and is therefore, synonymous with the organs of action. The movements and actions of the physical body must also be properly integrated. Therefore, the *karma-yogī* is one who not only has his senses under control but also the organs of action.

To have the control of the organs of action is possible only when one's mind is pure, when it is no longer under the spell of *rāga-dveṣa*s. Thus, there is an order presented here, a natural order that is very beautiful. Having the discipline of *karma-yoga*, the mind is pure and, therefore, the body, mind, and senses are under one's control. Such a person then becomes the one who knows oneself as the self in all beings and is called *sarvabhūta-ātmabhūta-ātmā*. *Sarva* means 'all' and *bhūta* means 'beings.' And who are these beings? Every being, from Brahmaji to a mosquito – all of them. It means that one's self is the self of all beings and that there is no other self or anything else apart from the self.

Previously, the person knew the self as separate from every other self, but now the person knows the self to be the one who is the self of all beings. It means that the self is one non-dual self, the truth of all beings. Everything else being *anātmā*, this is the only self, the non-dual self, there is.

The self does not become non-dual by any process. It is only by knowledge that the self is discovered to be non-dual. By knowledge, the person discovers the fact that he or she is the non-dual self, which is the self in all. In the wake of this knowledge, the person comes to be called *sarvabhūta-ātmabhūta-ātmā*; he or she performs no action even though appearing to do so, being free from the sense of doership. Such a person performs *karma* according to one's *prārabdha* for the welfare of the world or just to sustain the body, but one is not tainted, stained or affected by the result of the *karma* in any manner, *kurvan api na lipyate*.

The person who knows that the self is the self of all, cannot have a sense of doership. The self performs no action whatsoever because it is all pervasive. Even though appearing to perform actions, the wise person is free from the notion of doership and is, therefore, not affected by *karma*. This is exactly what Kṛṣṇa said in the fourth chapter – the person who sees non-action in action and action in non-action is wise among people and has done all that is to be done.[11] This is the knowledge, *sannyāsa*, accomplished by the wise who is *sarvabhūta-ātmabhūta-ātmā*.

That the *ātmā* in all beings is one's own *ātmā* is a fact, but previously the person did not know it. Once this knowledge takes place, one is no longer tainted or affected in any way by

---

[11] *Ġītā* 4.18

the performance of action. One finds oneself free of *karma* even while performing it.

Where, then, is the question of the wise giving up *karma*? Only when you are affected by *karma* does the question of giving it up arise. In that case, even if you give up *karma*, you will still be affected by it. In other words, if you are not doing the *karma* that you should be doing, you will be doing something else. That is why the lifestyle of *sannyāsa* is only appropriate if one is ready for it; otherwise it is difficult. Kṛṣṇa tells Arjuna here that only when action is given up through knowledge is there real *sannyāsa*, wherein one knows that one performs no action even while doing actions, *kurvan api na karoti*.

Verses 8&9

Kṛṣṇa explains, 'not doing in spite of doing'

नैव किञ्चित्करोमीति युक्तो मन्येत तत्त्ववित् ।
पश्यञ्शृण्वन्स्पृशञ्जिघ्रन्नश्नन्गच्छन्स्वपञ्श्वसन् ॥ ८ ॥

प्रलपन्विसृजन्गृह्णन्नुन्मिषन्निमिषन्नपि ।
इन्द्रियाणीन्द्रियार्थेषु वर्तन्त इति धारयन् ॥ ९ ॥

naiva kiñcitkaromīti yukto manyeta tattvavit
paśyañśṛṇvan spṛśañjighrannaśnan gacchan
svapañśvasan (8)
pralapan visṛjan gṛhṇannunmiṣan nimiṣannapi
indriyāṇīndriyārtheṣu vartanta iti dhārayan (9)

yuktaḥ – the one who is together; *tattvavit* – one who knows the truth; *paśyan* – seeing; *śṛṇvan* – hearing; *spṛśan* – touching; *jighran* – smelling; *aśnan* – eating; *gacchan* – walking; *svapan* –

sleeping; *śvasan* – breathing; *pralapan* – talking; *visṛjan* – releasing; *gṛhṇan* – grasping; *unmiṣan* – opening (the eyes); *nimiṣan* – closing (the eyes); *api* – even (while); *indriyāṇi* – the organs; *indriyārtheṣu* – in their objects; *vartante* – are engaged; *iti* – thus; *dhārayan* – knowing (full well); *kiñcit* – anything; *na eva karomi* – I do not do at all; *iti* – thus; *manyeta* – would think (thinks)

> The one who is together, who knows the truth, thinks, 'I do not do anything at all,' even while seeing, hearing, touching, smelling, eating, walking, sleeping, breathing...
>
> ...talking, releasing, grasping, opening and closing the eyes, (the person) knowing (full well that) the organs are engaged in their objects.

In these two verses, Kṛṣṇa continues to describe the person who is a *sarvabhūta-ātmabhūta-ātmā*. It is not that such a person has done away with actions; rather, he or she is not affected by them in any way. The word '*kurvan*, doing,' in the previous verse is in the present continuous tense, meaning that, while doing action, the *sarvabhūta-ātmabhūta-ātmā* is not affected by the action or its result.

How can a person who performs action not be affected by the result of the action? Whether the person likes the result, the law of karma slaps it on him or her. Does Kṛṣṇa really mean that the person who has self-knowledge is not affected by the results of action? Yes, because the one does not look upon oneself as the *kartā*, doer, and is therefore, not affected by the result. Kṛṣṇa explains this in these two verses, giving number of examples of the various actions that such a person performs.

Paśyan, seeing; *śṛṇvan*, hearing; *spṛśan*, touching; *jighran*, smelling; *aśnan*, eating; *gacchan*, walking; *svapan*, sleeping; *śvasan*, breathing; *pralapan*, talking; *visṛjan*, releasing; *gṛhṇan*, grasping; *unmiṣan*, opening the eyes; and *nimiṣan*, closing the eyes. Thus the word '*kurvan*' of the previous verse is explained elaborately in the above manner in this verse.

Actions can be either voluntary or involuntary. Or they can be both, like breathing and opening and closing the eyelids. The activities mentioned in this verse stand for both voluntary and involuntary actions.

Each sense organ and organ of action has its own function to perform, its own purpose to serve. For example, the eyes see, the ears hear, and the legs walk. And the one who knows this is described here as *yukta, tattvavit*. *Tattvavit* means the knower of the truth of oneself and *yukta* means *samāhita*, a person who is together. So, the same person who was previously referred to as *yoga-yukta* and *sarvabhūta-ātmabhūta-ātmā* is called *yukta* and *tattvavit* here.

The person who is together, who knows the truth of *ātmā*, knows the self to be one who performs no action. He knows, '*naiva kiñcit karomi*, I do not do anything.' Unless a person is a *yukta*, together, he or she cannot be a *tattvavit*, wise. Therefore, the words *yukta* and *tattvavit* are used here to describe the wise person.

Kṛṣṇa is not giving a mandate here

Lord Kṛṣṇa is not giving a mandate to Arjuna, as the mood of the verb '*manyeta*' here might suggest. He is not saying, 'You must look upon yourself as one who performs no action.'

What he is saying is that a person who is *yukta* and *tattvavit* does not consider, *na manyate,* the self to be the performer of any action. Rather, the person knows, 'I perform no action.'

Is this because there is no action performed by the person? No, even while appearing to perform all these actions, seeing, hearing, touching, and so on, the person knows that it is the sense organs and organs of action which are engaging themselves in their own spheres of activity, *indriyārtheṣu vartante.* And, knowing this very well, *dhārayan,* what does the person think while doing these actions? '*Naiva kiñcit karomi,* I perform no action whatsoever.'

So the *aham, ātmā,* is *akartā* and performs no action. The person does not have the notion of doership in the self, meaning that one does not look upon the self as a doer. The *tattvavit* understands that the sense organs and organs of action are simply doing their jobs. In the next verse, the *karma-yogī* is again discussed.

Verse 10

How one's action can become an offering to Īśvara

ब्रह्मण्याधाय कर्माणि सङ्गं त्यक्त्वा करोति यः ।
लिप्यते न स पापेन पद्मपत्रमिवाम्भसा ॥ १० ॥

brahmaṇyādhāya karmāṇi saṅgaṁ tyaktvā karoti yaḥ
lipyate na sa pāpena padmapatram ivāmbhasā (10)

yaḥ – the one who; *saṅgam* – attachment; *tyaktvā* – giving up; *karmāṇi* – actions; *brahmaṇi* – unto Brahman; *ādhāya* – offering (one's actions) *karoti* – performs; *saḥ* – he; *padmapatram ambhasā iva* – just as the leaf of a lotus (does not get wet) by water; *pāpena* – by sin; *na lipyate* – is not affected

> The one who performs actions, giving up attachment, offering (one's actions) unto Brahman, is not affected by sin, just as the leaf of a lotus (does not get wet) by water.

Here, *karmāṇi* refers to actions not only enjoined by the Veda but other actions as well. And how are these actions to be performed? *Saṅgaṁ tyaktvā*, giving up attachment for the results of one's actions and *brahmaṇi ādhāya*, offering the actions to Īśvara, the Lord. From this we understand that it is the *karma-yogī* who is being discussed here.

When a *karma-yogī* offers his or her actions to the Lord, it implies giving up one's attachment. Here a question may arise, 'How can I offer my actions unto Īśvara? I am walking, talking, seeing, hearing, and doing various things. How can I offer these actions unto the Lord? I can understand that placing flowers or fruit at the altar of the Lord is an offering, but how can all these actions be an offering? When I am cooking, cleaning the floor or washing the dishes, how does this action become an offering to the Lord?

Actions become offerings when Īśvara is looked upon as *dharma*.

We have already seen how one's actions can become offerings.[12] It is a crucial point in terms of understanding

---

[12] Refer to Gītā 2.47 (Volume 2– page 237)

karma-yoga and *dharma*. We have seen that *dharma* is two-fold, *sāmānya-dharma* and *viśeṣa-dharma*. *Sāmānya-dharma* is a term used to denote universal values such as not hurting others, not stealing, not doing things that we do not want others to do to us.

The other kind of *dharma*, *viśeṣa-dharma*, which is born out of *sāmānya-dharma*, refers to what you have to do in a given situation, given the role you are playing. Every role has a script and that script becomes *viśeṣa-dharma*, which is governed by *sāmānya-dharma*. Both *sāmānya-dharma* and *viśeṣa-dharma* are Īśvara. Only when Īśvara is looked upon as *dharma* can there be an attitude of offering your actions unto the Lord. Only then will it work. Otherwise, performing one's actions becomes Īśvara's mandate which you have to obey. Of course, you can take what is being said here as a mandate and follow it, or you can look upon *dharma* itself as Īśvara, which is how it is presented in the *Gītā*.

We will see in the eighteenth chapter how Īśvara and *dharma* are non-separate, the creation being pervaded by Īśvara, *yena sarvam idaṁ tatam*.[13] Since the Lord is both the material and the maker, the creation is non-separate from the creator. Any natural order is part of the creation, and not created by some individual; it is universal – universal *dharma*.

In the eighteenth chapter, Lord Kṛṣṇa says that your action becomes a worship of the Lord when you perform your duty, *sva-karma*, the action that is to be done by you at a given

---

[13] *Gītā* 18.46

time and place.[14] By doing this, *antaḥ-karaṇa-śuddhi* is gained. By living a life of *karma-yoga antaḥ-karaṇa-śuddhi* takes place, after which knowledge can be gained. This is what is meant by *karma-yoga*.

What we call *dharma* is to be looked upon as Īśvara; then, offering actions to the Lord is possible. Even if you look upon *dharma* as the mandate of Īśvara, there is no problem. But a mandate implies a master servant situation, wherein the faithful, obedient servant goes about doing what is to be done without necessarily knowing why, simply because it is the mandate of the master. The servant's will is surrendered to the will of mandator, the master. In the same manner, the individual may surrender his or her will to the Lord, which is also *īśvara-arpaṇa-buddhi*.

A karma-yogī is a devotee

So, either you take *dharma* as a mandate or you take it as Īśvara. Either way, this awareness of Īśvara makes you a devotee. A devotee is one who is aware that *dharma* or the mandate is non-separate from Īśvara. Only such people are devotees; they alone can be *karma-yogī*s.

A *karma-yogī* is a devotee. What is commonly called *bhakti-yoga* is actually *karma-yoga*, because only a devotee can perform actions as an offering to the Lord. So, the *karma-yogī* performs an action saying, 'I perform this action for the sake of Īśvara – meaning according to his mandate, his order. I happen to be

---

[14] *Gītā* 18.46

in this situation and this is to be done. Let it be *arpaṇa*, an offering, to the Lord.' In his commentary of this verse, Śaṅkara equates this attitude to that of a servant who goes about doing various actions for the sake of the master.

The expression, 'For the sake of Īśvara' is further qualified in the verse by the words, '*saṅgaṁ tyaktvā*.' *Saṅga* means attachment, implying that the person is impelled or dictated by likes and dislikes. And *tyaktvā* means giving up. When you are impelled by likes and dislikes, you are performing action for your own sake. Whereas, if you sacrifice your likes and dislikes and perform action with the awareness of *dharma*, then you are doing it for the sake of Īśvara.

You have no problem if what you have to do for the sake of Īśvara happens to be in agreement with your *rāga* and what you should not do happens to be in agreement with your *dveṣa*. Then you are a *bhakta* and your actions become spontaneous. Only when your *rāga-dveṣa*s are against *dharma* does the conflict arise. So, what does a *karma-yogī* do? He or she conforms to *dharma*, even though it may be unpleasant. In this way, the action of a *karma-yogī* becomes an offering to Īśvara.

Verse 11

The purpose and the kinds of action that a karma-yogī engages in

कायेन मनसा बुद्ध्या केवलैरिन्द्रियैरपि ।
योगिनः कर्म कुर्वन्ति सङ्गं त्यक्त्वात्मशुद्धये ॥ ११ ॥

kāyena manasā buddhyā kevalairindriyairapi
yoginaḥ karma kurvanti saṅgaṁ tyaktvātmaśuddhaye (11)

yoginaḥ – *karma-yogī*s; *saṅgam* – attachment; *tyaktvā* – giving up; *ātmaśuddhaye* – for the purification of the mind; *kevalaiḥ* – purely (without being impelled by likes and dislikes); *kāyena* – with the body; *manasā* – with the mind; *buddhyā* – with the intellect; *indriyaḥ api* – and also by the senses; *karma* – action; *kurvanti* – perform

> Giving up attachment, *karma-yogī*s perform action purely (without being impelled by likes and dislikes) with the body, mind, intellect, and also by the senses, for the purification of the mind.

In this verse, we see what the *karma-yogī*s do, how they do it, and why they do it. A *karma-yogī* performs action by using his or her instruments or means, *karaṇa*s, the physical body, the mind, senses, and the intellect.

Since everyone performs actions using the body, mind, senses, and intellect, why does Kṛṣṇa say here that the *karma-yogī* performs actions in this way? The *karma-yogī* does exactly what others do with only one difference – giving up attachment, *saṅgaṁ tyaktvā*. Both the *avivekī*, a person without discrimination, and the *vivekī*, *karma-yogī*, may appear to perform action in a similar way, but the *vivekī* does it having given up attachment to the results of action.

We have already seen what giving up attachment means. One's actions are offered to the Lord without the mind being dictated by *rāga-dveṣa*s. This is the reason why the adjective '*kevalaiḥ*' is used here. *Kevalaiḥ* means 'purely,' without likes and dislikes. This attitude is called *īśvara-arpaṇa-buddhi*. With *īśvara-arpaṇa-buddhi*, the *yogī* performs actions. Giving up attachment also means that the results of one's actions are taken as *prasāda*, a gift from the Lord. Actions are done in keeping with *dharma*, which is Īśvara. This is how actions are performed by the *karma-yogī*.

And what do *karma-yogī*s get out of performing action in this way? They perform action purely for *antaḥ-karaṇa-śuddhi*, for purifying the mind, *ātma śuddhaye*, nothing more. They do not perform action for their pleasure and security as the *avivekī*s do. This is the only difference.

Between the *karma-yogī* and the *jñānī*, there is one more difference. The *jñānī* does not have the notion of doership. The *jñānī* knows that the self is not the doer; he knows very clearly that he performs no action whatsoever. All that is happening when an action takes place is that the sense organs are engaged in their respective fields. So, the difference between the *jñānī* and the *karma-yogī* is that *jñānī* does not have the sense of doership whereas the *karma-yogī* does. But the *karma-yogī* has the proper attitude, *īśvara-arpaṇa-buddhi*, the awareness of Īśvara; so he or she gains *antaḥ-karaṇa-śuddhi*.

Because *karma-yogī*s are *mumukṣu*s, they perform actions as a means for *mokṣa* just as *sannyāsī*s do, whereas those who are not *mumukṣu*s perform actions for the sake of results. *Karma-yoga* is primarily for purifying the mind so that self-knowledge can be gained, but it is not a direct means for *mokṣa*. This is why it is said that perform action for the sake of *antaḥ-karaṇa-śuddhi*, which prepares the mind for knowledge.

Verse 12

The meaning of 'purification of mind'

युक्तः कर्मफलं त्यक्त्वा शान्तिमाप्नोति नैष्ठिकीम् ।
अयुक्तः कामकारेण फले सक्तो निबध्यते ॥ १२ ॥

yuktaḥ karmaphalaṁ tyaktvā śāntim āpnoti naiṣṭhikīm
ayuktaḥ kāmakāreṇa phale sakto nibadhyate (12)

yuktaḥ – the one who is endowed with (*karma-yoga*); *karmaphalam* – the result of action; *tyaktvā* – giving up; *naiṣṭhikīm* – born of a commitment to a life of *karma-yoga; śāntim* – composure; *āpnoti* – gains; *ayuktaḥ* – the one who is not committed to a life of *karma-yoga; kāma-kāreṇa* – led by desire; *phale saktaḥ* – (being) attached to the result (of action); *nibadhyate* – is bound

> The one who is endowed with (*karma-yoga*), giving up the result of action, gains a composure born of a commitment to a life of *karma-yoga*. (Whereas) the one who is not committed to a life of *karma-yoga*, led by desire, is bound, (being) attached to the result (of action).

In this verse, Lord Kṛṣṇa explains the meaning of 'purification of the mind.' Such a mind is what is implied here by the word *śānti*, meaning composure. To the extent that one has a pure mind, to that extent is his or her degree of composure.

Śānti is gained because of the freedom from *rāga-dveṣa* that is gained by living a life of *karma-yoga*. *Prasāda-buddhi* is an attitude wherein there is a glad acceptance of whatever comes. Whatever comes now and whatever has happened before are taken gladly, cheerfully. It means that nothing is taken personally, either as 'something that has happened to me or something that I have accomplished.' And this is only possible when there is *prasāda-buddhi*. The *karma-yogī* does not impute to the self all the omissions and commissions of the past. And, with reference to the present, whatever happens is taken as *prasāda*. He or she is not dictated by *rāga-dveṣa*s.

Being in harmony with the order that is Īśvara

As long as your likes and dislikes dictate your activities, you are bound to have problems of frustration, anger, and so on. Because of the pressure of *rāga-dveṣa*s, such problems cannot be avoided. Whereas, if you have *īśvara-arpaṇa-buddhi*, devotion to the Lord or an awareness of the Lord as *dharma*, you are in harmony with the Lord, which is why there is always a sense of relief when you do something that is right. There is a satisfaction because you are not rubbing against the law. You know what is right and, if it is done, you find you are in harmony. There is no conflict. This absence of conflict is *śānti*. On the other hand, if you go against *dharma* in order to fulfil your *rāga-dveṣa*s, *aśānti*, conflict, will result.

The *yukta* referred to in this verse is the *karma-yogī* who performs action in accordance with the *dharma* of Īśvara or *dharma* that is Īśvara. We saw how, if *dharma* is taken as Īśvara's mandate, there is a master servant relationship, wherein you become the servant and the Lord is the master. You just do what you have to do, and what is expected of you, given the situation in which you are placed. In this way, there is conformity to the natural order, Īśvara's order, which gives you *śānti*.

If you look upon *dharma* as Īśvara, which is how *dharma* is presented in the *Gītā* you become a contributor. As an individual you are endowed with the means of action like hands and legs, and with these you participate. You are not a mere witness; you are an active participant in the creation, which itself is Īśvara's order. In keeping with the order, there is a huge offering, *yajña* going on, and you contribute to it through active participation. This active participation is nothing but doing what is to be done by you when it is to be done. If something is to be done by you right now, and you do it for Īśvara and not just for fulfilling your *rāga-dveṣa*s, you enjoy an attitude that gives you composure. You give up the results of your action in the sense that there is no reaction on your part, whatever be the result. You simply accept the *karma-phala* as *prasāda*.

Since action is not done for the fulfilment of *rāga-dveṣa*s, there is no attachment to the actions and their results. The *karma-yogī* does not desire that a given thing should happen or that some other thing should not happen. The person does not impose this kind of pressure on himself or herself. This pressure is something that you can happily be without since it is always possible that what you wish should happen may not happen, and what you do not want to happen can certainly happen. The only way to deal with such happenings is to have the attitude that whatever happens is acceptable. Otherwise, you will always have to cope with a sense of failure because, to use the vernacular, you do not call all the shots. Since you do not call all the shots, you had better accept things as they are and do what you can do.

This is the attitude of a *karma-yogī* who says, 'I perform action for Īśvara.' And, with this attitude, *buddhyā*, having given up the results of action, the person gains composure, *śāntim āpnoti*. This is what is meant by *antaḥ-karaṇa-śuddhi*, purification of the mind. *Antaḥ-karaṇa-śuddhi* is nothing but *śānti*, an inner leisure because there is a glad acceptance of what is.

If you do not accept your past, for example, who is going to suffer? Whether anyone else accepts your past, you need to accept it because you are the one who suffers if you do not. Of course, there may be people who do not accept your past, for whom there is no forgiveness for the wrong doings of others; at least you accept it. The glad acceptance of the past, whatever it is, brings about *śānti*.

Karma-yoga is not a technique

There is no technique involved in gaining this *śānti*. If it were born of a technique, it would not last long because any technique wears out. Either the technique becomes monotonous or it becomes inadequate in itself to significantly change you, the person. Techniques can be useful, but they cannot change the person. A restless person continues to be restless; an angry person continues to be angry.

Just as a technique will not give you the kind of *śānti* being discussed in this verse, so too, situations cannot give it to you. It is because the situation itself changes or it eventually becomes monotonous. In either case, *śānti* is lost. For instance, when you go to a beautiful beach, you become happy, a state of mind that is also *śānti*. But this happiness depends entirely upon the situation. How long will you be able to enjoy the sand and so on unless, of course, you are a beach bum? Even a beach bum cannot be that happy when there is no surf.

What happens here is similar to the principle of diminishing utility in the economics of Adam Smith. When you are hungry, food is very valuable but when you are not hungry, it is no more as valuable. As the utility of the food diminishes, so does your value for it. Every situational *śānti* is governed in the same way.

Karma-yoga is not a technique, like *prāṇāyāma*, for instance. *Prāṇāyāma* can give you certain *śānti*, which you can utilise to understand yourself and your mind. It is a useful discipline, but it cannot give you the *śānti* being discussed here because you cannot do *prāṇāyāma* all the time.

Unlike a technique or a discipline, *karma-yoga* is not a particular action. There is no particular situation in which you follow *karma-yoga*. *Karma-yoga* is your life and, as a *karma yogī*, you are a devotee, whose devotion is not spasmodic. It is not something that comes every now and then, and goes away. A person who has *īśvara-arpaṇa-buddhi* is one who is abidingly devoted to Īśvara, taking things as they come. And when such a person performs action, he or she conforms to *dharma*. This awareness of Īśvara is what brings about the change in the person.

Relative śānti and svarūpa śānti

Naiṣṭhikīm śānti, a composure born of *niṣṭhā*, a commitment, can be understood either as relative composure or absolute composure, depending upon the interpretation of the word *niṣṭhā*. *Niṣṭhā* can be *yoga-niṣṭhā*, commitment to a life of *karma-yoga*, or it can be *jñāna-niṣṭhā*, abidance in knowledge. The *śānti* born of *yoga-niṣṭhā* will be a relative *śānti*, wherein there is a degree of composure that helps you gain the knowledge. Because of the purity of the *antaḥ-karaṇa*, characterised by a relative degree of *śānti*, the person gains *jñāna-niṣṭhā* as a result of which the person gains absolute *śānti*, *parā śānti*. So, there is an order here – *yoga-niṣṭha-śānti*, followed by *jñāna-niṣṭha-śānti*.

Śaṅkara explains this order in his commentary of the verse. First, there is *śānti* gained by *antaḥ-karaṇa-śuddhi* or *sattva-śuddhi*, *sattva* being another word for *antaḥ-karaṇa*, the mind. When one has *sattva-śuddhi*, as a result of which self-knowledge is gained, there is *ātma-jñāna-prāpti*. When knowledge is gained, there is *sarva-karma-sannyāsa*, renunciation of *karmas*. *Ātmā* being free from the sense of doership, the person knows, 'I perform no action.' This renunciation of action by knowledge is, in fact, *jñāna-niṣṭhā*. And the one who has this knowledge of the *ātmā* has *svarūpa-śānti*.

There being two *niṣṭhās*, both are pointed out here as the basis for *śānti*–the *śānti* born of knowledge and *śānti* born of *karma-yoga*. One is relative *śānti* and the other, *svarūpa śānti*, is absolute *śānti*, *parā śānti*. Just as there is relative *ānanda*, happiness, and the *ānanda* that is the very nature of *ātmā*, the *svarūpa-ānanda*. *Svarūpa-ānanda* is your nature, that is you are free from limitations, you are fullness itself, you are the whole. And relative *ānanda* is the experiential happiness dependent upon the disposition of the mind. *Antaḥ-karaṇa-śuddhi* results in relative *śānti*, whereas *jñāna*, knowledge, gives you the *svarūpa-śānti*, the *śānti*, that is your nature.

Between gaining the relative *śānti* that comes from a life of *karma-yoga* and gaining *śānti* that is the *svarūpa* of oneself, several stages mentioned in verse 7 of this chapter have already occurred–*viśuddha-ātmā*, *vijitātmā*, and so on. It was also said that the wise man was *sarvabhūta-ātmabhūta-ātmā*, the one who knows the self as the self in all beings. This knowledge has to take place to convert the relative *śānti* to *svarūpa-śānti*.

One who is not endowed with karma-yoga remains bound

The second half of this verse is an example of how the *Gītā* sometimes states the positive, followed by the negative, in order to emphasise the positive. The first line reveals what happens when a person is committed to a life of *karma-yoga*. To emphasise the value of *karma-yoga*, the second line of this verse tells what happens when a person does not follow this lifestyle. Such a person is referred to as *ayukta* here, one who is not endowed with *karma-yoga*.

The *ayukta* performs *karma* as dictated by *rāga-dveṣa*s, rather than for the sake of Īśvara. He performs *karma* to fulfil his likes and dislikes and not because of any consideration for the natural order. Thus, the *ayukta* performs action only for his own sake and fails to recognise the cosmic ecology, the divine ecology, the order that is there. This person is completely oblivious to the fact that there is an order, a *dharma*, and performs action strictly to fulfil his *kāma*, desires. Because of the commitment to *kāma*, that is *rāga-dveṣa*s, the person is committed to the *karma-phala*s, results of action, rather than to *dharma* that is Īśvara.

We have two opposing situations, actions performed for one's own sake to fulfil one's *rāga-dveṣa*s, and actions performed for *loka-saṅgrahārtham*, for the sake of the world, or for the sake of Īśvara.

When a person is dictated by *rāga-dveṣa*s, consideration for right and wrong is set aside. The *ayukta* remains bound, *nibadhyate* to *karma* and *karma-phala*, to *puṇya* and *pāpa*, and therefore, to the cycle of birth and death. Even in this life, let alone in future lives, the person is bound by *sukha-duḥkha*, being tossed from one to the other all the time as the barometer of the mood goes up and down. Today, the person is up and tomorrow he is down. Deflation and inflation are always there because the ego is so huge, so obese, that it inflates and deflates constantly. Therefore, Kṛṣṇa says to Arjuna here, 'May you become a *karma-yogī*. Once you become a *karma-yogī*, you will gain the *śānti* that will lead you to *jñāna-niṣṭhā*.'

Verse 13

Kṛṣṇa explains jñāna-niṣṭhā

सर्वकर्माणि मनसा संन्यस्यास्ते सुखं वशी ।
नवद्वारे पुरे देही नैव कुर्वन्न कारयन् ॥ १३ ॥

sarvakarmāṇi manasā sannyasyāste sukhaṁ vaśī
navadvāre pure dehī naiva kurvan na kārayan (13)

vaśī – one who is self-controlled; *dehī* – the indweller of the physical body; *manasā* – mentally (by knowledge); *sarvakarmāṇi* – all actions; *sannyasya* – having renounced; *navadvāre pure* – in the nine-gated city (the body); *eva* – indeed; *na kurvan* – not performing action; *na kārayan* – nor causing (others) to act; *sukham* – happily; *āste* – remains

> The indweller of the physical body, the one who is self-controlled, having renounced all actions mentally (by knowledge), remains happily in the nine-gated city (the body) neither performing action, nor causing (others) to act.

Here, *jñāna-niṣṭhā* is discussed by presenting the *sannyāsī* who has renounced all actions by knowledge.

We have seen previously the two meanings of *sannyāsa* – one being the renunciation of action by will when a person takes to a life of *sannyāsa* and the other being renunciation of action by knowledge. The latter *sannyāsa*, renunciation of all action by knowledge, is the one discussed in this verse. Since this knowledge takes place in the mind, the word '*manas*,' mind, is used here in the sense of knowledge. Mentally, one gives up *karmas*. How? By knowledge. Therefore, *manasā* means *jñānena*, by knowledge, by knowing *ātmā*, 'I,' performs no action.

The person who has this knowledge is called *vaśī* here, one who has his personality together. *Vaśa* means control. Bringing power such as money or kingdom under your control is called *vaśīkaraṇa*. What you can have under your control is your body, mind, and senses. In fact, there is nothing else in your *vaśa*, not even your child. Otherwise, the child would always do as you say, which is not what happens. Therefore, only your own body, mind and senses can be in your control and the person in whose control these are, is *vaśī*.

The master of the nine-gated city

A *jñānī* is naturally a *vaśī* and in this verse, is also referred to as *dehī*, one who dwells in the *deha*, physical body. Kṛṣṇa says here that the one who has everything under control, the *dehī*, indweller of the body, having given up all actions by knowledge, remains happily in the nine-gated city, *nava-dvāre pure*. This nine gated city is the physical body that has nine apertures or gates – the two sockets of the eyes, two nostrils, two ears, a mouth, and the two lower apertures for rejection make a total of nine. And in this nine-gated city, the *jñānī* remains happily.

Here, one can raise an objection. Since everyone dwells in the physical body, why does Kṛṣṇa make a point of saying that the *jñānī* alone dwells in the body? The reason is that people do not know that they are dwelling in the body. If you ask them where they are located, they will say, 'I live in this city, in this area, on this street, in this building, in this apartment,' and so on. They see themselves located somewhere, but no one says, 'I am seated in my body.' They take the body to be the self and the body is seated somewhere; and so, they think the self is located in that place. The ignorant do not know that the body is the place where the self dwells, and that the body is not the self.

To make it clear that the body is not the self, Lord Kṛṣṇa describes the body here as a nine-gated city in which the person,the self, dwells. The wise man knows, 'I am not the body; I dwell in the body.' This is why giving up all action, knowing that action is nothing but the sense organs being engaged in their respective fields, the *jñānī* says, 'I perform no action,' and remains happily in the body.

The *jñānī* knows that he or she does no work. And, if one does not do any work, how can one get worked up about anything? Therefore, for the *jñānī*, there is no problem; he or she simply remains happily, *sukham āste*. People think that they would be happy if they did not have work. But, in fact, no one works at all because the self is actionless. The wise man knows this and, therefore, work is not a burden for him at all.

We saw in the third chapter how no one can completely give up all action, *na hi kaścit kṣaṇamapi jātu tiṣṭhati akarmakṛt*.[14] Even in deep sleep, certain involuntary activities are going on. In the eighteenth chapter also, Kṛṣṇa would say that it is not possible for one who has a physical body to give up all actions entirely – *na hi dehabhṛtā śakyaṁ tyaktuṁ karmāṇi aśeṣataḥ*.[15] As long as the person is alive, some action will go on.

Why then does Kṛṣṇa say here that actions are given up by the *jñānī*? If it is not possible to give up actions completely, how does the *jñānī* renounce all actions? This verse tells us that they are given up mentally, *manasā sannyasya*. The word '*manasā*' makes it clear that renunciation by knowledge is what is meant here, the knowledge that *ātmā*, 'I,' performs no action whatsoever.

---

[14] *Gītā* 3.5
[15] *Gītā* 18.11

We may think that *ātmā* itself does not perform action but perhaps it makes the mind, the intellect, and so on, perform action. But *ātmā* neither performs actions, *na karoti* nor directs, the body, the senses, the mind or the intellect to perform action, *na kārayati*. This is saying that the *jñānī* has renounced action by knowledge. And with this knowledge the *jñānī* abides in the happiness, fullness, that is his or her nature.

In a walled city, there would always be a *svāmī*, king, or master of the various activities going on inside the city. The wise person is also called a *svāmī* because he or she is the master of the body, mind and senses. This *svāmī* dwells in the body, the nine gated city, and remains happily, *sukham āste* because he or she does not identify with the body, mind and senses.

The *svāmī* understands that physical body-mind-sense complex is a *pura*, city, and that he is the *pura-svāmī*, the master of the city, performing no action. This person does not have the problems that a king has because he knows that *ātmā* neither performs action nor causes others to perform action. Kṛṣṇa said the same thing in the second chapter when he told Arjuna that the one who knows the *ātmā* kills no one nor causes anyone to kill.[16] Such a person performs no action whatsoever, either directly or indirectly.

The nature of *ātmā* is consciousness, it performs no action. At the same time, no action is possible without the *ātmā*. Thus, there is no seer without *ātmā*, but *ātmā* is not the seer; there is no hearer without *ātmā*, but *ātmā* is not the hearer.

---

[16] *Gītā* 2.21

Knowing this is what is meant by *manasā sannyasya*, renouncing mentally, in terms of knowledge. Seeing, I perform no action of seeing; hearing, I perform no action of hearing; thinking, I perform no action of thinking.

Ātmā, 'I,' never performs any action. *Ātmā* never performed action before, nor does *ātmā* perform action now. Previously, one did not know it, and now one does. Knowing this fact, one is free from any doing.

Verse 14

Knowing that ātmā performs no action – one is free from any doing

न कर्तृत्वं न कर्माणि लोकस्य सृजति प्रभुः ।
न कर्मफलसंयोगं स्वभावस्तु प्रवर्तते ॥ १४ ॥

na kartṛtvaṁ na karmāṇi lokasya sṛjati prabhuḥ
na karmaphalasaṁyogaṁ svabhāvastu pravartate (14)

prabhuḥ – the one who is self effulgent (*ātmā*); *lokasya* – for any person; *kartṛtvam* – doership; *na sṛjati* – does not create; *na karmāṇi (sṛjati)* – nor (does he create) actions; *na karma-phala-saṁyogam (sṛjati)* – nor the connection with the results of action; *tu* – but; *svabhāvaḥ* – one's own nature; *pravartate* – leads to action

Ātmā creates neither doership nor action for any person nor the connection with the results of action. But one's own nature leads to action.

In this verse, we are told why the wise person can remain happily in the physical body. Existence cannot be established unless there is consciousness. The self-existent, self effulgent *ātmā* is called *prabhu* here. This *prabhu, kartṛtva na sṛjati lokasya,* does not create doership for the person. *Ātmā* does not issue order to anyone, and therefore does not create doership in anyone.

Doership can be created in you if someone orders you, 'Please do this!' and you do it. *Ātmā* does not ask anyone to do anything, nor does it ask the mind, the intellect, or the memory to do, to think, to decide. It does not say, 'Come on, recollect! Get depressed! Get angry! Learn Vedanta!' It does not issue such orders to anyone. It is not the cause of doership within oneself, nor is it the cause of anyone else's doership.

The person who knows this was described in the previous verse as a *vaśī*, meaning master, one who is seated happily inside the nine gated city, the physical body, just as a king sits in his walled city with many gates. There is, however, as in all illustrations, a defect in this comparison between a king and a *vaśī*. Even though others do the work, yet the king is the *kartā*, doer. He sits on his throne wearing a crown and wields the royal sceptre of power.

The question now is, is *ātmā* also a doer, like a king? Is *ātmā* seated in its inner chambers ordering the mind, intellect, and so on, to do various actions? If so, *ātmā* would also be a *kartā*, doer. In response to this question, Lord Kṛṣṇa says that *ātmā* does not create or cause doership, *kartṛtvaṁ na sṛjati,* meaning that even indirectly *ātmā* is not involved in doing anything.

A question may arise here. 'While I can understand that *ātmā* is not a doer, is it not the *ātma* that makes the mind and senses function? Even the *śruti* describes *ātmā* as *śrotrasya śrotram*, ear of the ear, *manaso manaḥ*, mind of the mind, *cakṣuṣaścakṣuḥ*, eye of the eye, and so on. Since *ātmā* is said to be behind all the functions, does *ātmā* not order all of them?' Kṛṣṇa says here, 'No, it is not so.'

Ātmā does not create karma

Ātmā does not create any action, *karmāṇi na sṛjati*, meaning that *ātmā* performs no action, *karmāṇi na karoti*. Thus, *na sṛjati*, 'does not create,' is understood as *na karoti*, 'does not do.' *Ātmā* does not perform action directly or indirectly.

If we translate the word '*karmāṇi*' in its grammatical sense, then the phrase, *karmāṇi na sṛjati* means that *ātmā* does not create objects. '*Karma*' in grammar means the object of a verb such as chariot, pot, house, and so on. These are called objects in terms of action. For instance, when you say, 'He makes a pot,' 'She bakes a cake,' 'The children eat food,' the objects like pot, cake, food, etc., are not created by *ātmā*. *Ātmā* neither performs actions nor creates objects, *karmāṇi na sṛjati*. So, the word *karmāṇi* here can be understood as the object of an action as well as the action itself.

Ātmā also does not create karma-phala saṁyogam

Since the results of action are accrued to the *kartā*, the doer, Kṛṣṇa also says that *ātmā* does not create this connection between the result of an action and the doer, *na karma-phala saṁyogaṁ sṛjati*. The results of action are in keeping with the laws of Īśvara, but here we are talking about Īśvara's *svarūpa*, which is also *ātmā*, the self. Since *ātmā* neither creates doership nor objects, it also does not create the connection between one's action and the results of action.

If *ātmā* does not do anything, who is it that does all this? Kṛṣṇa says, *svabhāvastu pravartate*, one's own nature engages itself. We saw this in verse 9 of this chapter when Kṛṣṇa said, 'The sense organs engage themselves in the sense objects.' The sense organs are *svabhāva*. The eyes see, the ears hear, the mind thinks, the intellect decides, and so on.

Due to lack of discrimination, one superimposes these activities on *ātmā*, which is why one thinks, 'I am the doer,' 'I am the thinker,' and so on. Since people do not know that there is this superimposition, Kṛṣṇa discusses it in the next verse.

Verse 15

People are deluded because knowledge is covered by ignorance

नादत्ते कस्यचित्पापं न चैव सुकृतं विभुः ।
अज्ञानेनावृतं ज्ञानं तेन मुह्यन्ति जन्तवः ॥ १५ ॥

nādatte kasyacit pāpaṁ na caiva sukṛtaṁ vibhuḥ
ajñānenāvṛtaṁ jñānaṁ tena muhyanti jantavaḥ (15)

vibhuḥ – the all-pervasive (*ātmā*); *kasyacit* – of anyone; *pāpam* – *pāpa*; *na ādatte* – does not take; *sukṛtam* – *puṇya*; *ca na eva* – and indeed not; *ajñānena* – by ignorance; *jñānam* – knowledge; *āvṛtam* – is covered; *tena* – due to that (ignorance); *jantavaḥ* – people; *muhyanti* – are deluded

The *ātmā* takes neither *pāpa* nor *puṇya* of anyone. Knowledge is covered by ignorance and due to that (ignorance) people are deluded.

It was said earlier that *ātmā* does not create the connection between one's actions and the results. This is being explained here by saying that *ātmā* does not take on *puṇya* or *pāpa* because *ātmā* does not have *bhoktṛtva*, enjoyership. It is one luminous self that lights up the *antaḥ-karaṇa*. *Ātmā* is called *dṛṣṭa*, seer, because seeing cannot take place without *ātmā* but in reality *ātmā* is the very *svarūpa* of the seer, and not the seer in the primary sense. The seer is *ātmā* but *ātmā* is not the seer. *Ātmā*'s nature is *caitanya*, pure consciousness, which is why it is referred to as the ear of the ear, the eye of the eye, and so on. Therefore, there is no connection between *ātmā* and the results of action; neither *puṇya* nor *pāpa* of anyone is taken by *ātmā*

If this is so, why do people think, 'I am the doer, I am the enjoyer, I am performing this ritual for this reason,' and so on? There is nothing wrong with performing action to invoke the grace of the Lord. It is to be done, as long as you do not understand *ātmā*. Once you have the knowledge of the true nature of *ātmā* such action is not necessary. Presently, this knowledge is covered by ignorance, *ajñānena āvṛtam*. The very fact that you do not know *ātmā* is not a doer means there is ignorance. Since *jñāna*, knowledge, can only take place in your mind, not knowing *ātmā* means your mind is covered by ignorance.

Here *jñāna* can be taken to mean either discriminative knowledge of *ātmā* and *anātmā*, or the mind. We can say either the mind is covered by ignorance or the discriminative knowledge is covered by ignorance, the idea being that knowledge is never created, it is only covered.

Human beings are deluded because the discriminative knowledge of *ātmā* is covered by ignorance. And what is the *moha*, delusion, here? 'I am a doer. I will do this. I will get this result. I will go to heaven. I will accomplish this by doing that,' and so on, all of which is because knowledge is covered by ignorance.

Verse 16

When ignorance is removed the self is revealed as Brahman

ज्ञानेन तु तदज्ञानं येषां नाशितमात्मनः ।
तेषामादित्यवज्ज्ञानं प्रकाशयति तत्परम् ॥ १६ ॥

jñānena tu tadajñānaṁ yeṣāṁ nāśitam ātmanaḥ
teṣām ādityavajjñānaṁ prakāśayati tatparam (16)

tu – whereas; *ātmanaḥ* – of the self; *jñānena* – by knowledge; *yeṣām* – whose; *tat* – that; *ajjñānam* – ignorance; *nāśitam* – is destroyed; *teṣām* – for them; *jñānam* – knowledge; *ādityavat* – like the sun; *tat param* – (the self as) that Brahman; *prakāśayati* – reveals

> Whereas for those whose ignorance of the self is destroyed by knowledge, the knowledge reveals (the self as) that Brahman, like the sun (reveals objects previously covered in darkness).

Ajñāna, ignorance, here is not the absence of knowledge, but is that which is opposed to knowledge. Ignorance exists only until it is removed by knowledge. The word '*ajñāna*' is not to be interpreted as absence of knowledge, because *abhāva*, absence, cannot cause problems; only *bhāva*, presence of something, can cause problems. Therefore, *ajñāna* is not *jñāna-abhāva*, absence of knowledge. Ignorance is opposed to knowledge and, because it causes problems, ignorance is a very crucial issue. Because it is opposed to knowledge, ignorance has a status of existence as long as it lasts. However, in the wake of knowledge, it cannot exist at all. Therefore, ignorance can rule the roost only until another rooster, knowledge, takes its place.

When does ignorance go?

Just as darkness is there until light comes in, so too, ignorance will be there until knowledge comes. This is what Kṛṣṇa means when he says, 'Ignorance of the self is destroyed by knowledge.'

Ignorance has *bhāva*, an existence, and therefore causes error and problems. For example, ignorance of the rope causes the error of a snake which causes fear. In dream too, ignorance of the waker on the part of the dreamer causes problems like a millionaire dreaming that he is a beggar and vice versa.

By what knowledge is this ignorance destroyed? Just as ignorance of a pot can only be destroyed by knowledge of the pot, and not by knowledge of cloth, so too, ignorance of *ātmā* can only be destroyed by knowledge of *ātmā*.

For whom is this ignorance of the self destroyed? The knowledge that the self is Brahman takes place in the minds of those who were ignorant. Kṛṣṇa likens this knowledge to the sun. As the sun rises, darkness rolls away. And not only does the sun cause the darkness to roll away, it also lights up everything there is. As the sun rises in the eastern sky, the darkness rolls away and the objects that previously were not visible now come to be lighted. Like the sun, self-knowledge destroys self-ignorance and reveals the self as Brahman, *tatparam prakāśayati*, a fact that was previouslynot known.

The analogy here between knowledge and the sun must be understood properly; otherwise, this verse can be very confusing. It is not that knowledge lights up the self that you can then see. Rather, knowledge destroys the ignorance you had about the self and reveals a fact that was unknown to you–the fact that you are Brahman. Knowledge does not light up the self; the self itself is the light. Knowledge destroys the ignorance and reveals the nature of the self.

This knowledge is *vṛtti-jñāna. Vṛtti* means thought. Here the *vṛtti* is, '*ahaṁ brahma asmi*, I am Brahman.' This *vṛtti* takes place in the mind, and is what is meant by the knowledge that destroys ignorance of the self, revealing the truth about the self being Brahman. 'I am Brahman' is the truth of all truths, the ultimate truth, *tattva*, that one comes to recognise by this knowledge born of the teaching of the *śāstra*.

Verses 17-21

Kṛṣṇa describes those who recognise the fact that ātmā is Brahman

तद्बुद्धयस्तदात्मानस्तन्निष्ठास्तत्परायणाः ।
गच्छन्त्यपुनरावृत्तिं ज्ञाननिर्धूतकल्मषाः ॥ १७ ॥

tadbuddhayastadātmānastanniṣṭhāstatparāyaṇāḥ
gacchantyapunarāvṛttiṁ jñānanirdhūtakalmaṣāḥ (17)

tadbuddhayaḥ – those whose intellect is awake to that (Brahman); *tadātmānaḥ* – those for whom the self is that (Brahman); *tanniṣṭhāḥ* – those who are committed only to that (Brahman); *tatparāyaṇāḥ* – those for whom the ultimate end is that (Brahman); *jñāna-nirdhūta-kalmaṣāḥ* – those whose impurities have been destroyed by knowledge; *apunarāvṛttim* – a state from which there is no return; *gacchanti* – they attain

> Those whose intellect is awake to that (Brahman), for whom the self is that (Brahman), who are committed only to that (Brahman), for whom the ultimate end is that (Brahman which is already accomplished), whose impurities have been destroyed by knowledge – they attain a state from which there is no return.

In the previous verse, Kṛṣṇa said that knowledge reveals the truth that *ātmā* is Brahman. That Brahman is the meaning of the pronoun '*tat*, that,' occurring in the compound words in the present verse, *tadbuddhayaḥ tadātmānaḥ tanniṣṭhāḥ* and *tatparāyaṇāḥ*.[17]

Because of this knowledge, the wise become *tadbuddhayaḥ*, *tadātmānaḥ*, *tanniṣṭhāḥ*, and *tatparāyaṇāḥ*. All of their impurities are destroyed by this knowledge and, when they go, meaning when they die, they do not return again. There is an order to be noted here, as we shall see by analysing these compounds one by one.

---

[17] यत् परं ज्ञानं प्रकाशितं (तत् ब्रह्म)
तस्मिन् गता बुद्धिः येषां ते तद् बुद्धयः। तद् एव परं ब्रह्म आत्मा येषां ते तदात्मानः।
निष्ठा = अभिनिवेशः = तात्पर्यम् = सर्वाणि कर्माणि सन्न्यस्य ब्रह्मणि एव अवस्थानम् येषां ते तन्निष्ठाः। तद् (ब्रह्म) एव परम् अयनम् = परा गतिः येषां भवति ते तत्परायणाः (शंकर भाष्यम्)

Tadbuddhis for whom the self is Brahman

*Tadbuddhi*s are those whose *buddhi* is in Brahman, meaning that the *buddhi* is awake to the knowledge of *ātmā* being Brahman. In Brahman, their *buddhi* is rooted. Previously the *buddhi* was awake only to *anātmā*, the *ahaṅkāra*, ego, or I notion. When the *buddhi* is awake only to *anātmā*, it is always concerned with *artha*, securities, and pleasure, *kāma* because the 'I' always feels small and has to be boosted up. Only then can the person feel good. Everything is centred on feeling good and that is necessarily dependent upon a number of external physical and psychological factors. Therefore, the *ahaṅkāra* always holds on to these factors, which are *anātmā*s.

However, for the *tadbuddhi*s, those who are awake to Brahman, whose *buddhi* is in Brahman, everything is Brahman alone. The *buddhi* is Brahman, the mind is Brahman, the body is Brahman; everything is Brahman alone. Therefore, the *buddhi* is never away from Brahman. Go where it will, the *buddhi* is always in Brahman alone.

Why are these people called *tadbuddhi*s? Because, for them *ātmā* is Brahman, they are *tadātmā*s. Previously the body, mind, intellect, memory, and so on were *ātmā*. History was *ātmā*, biology was *ātmā*. Even the hair and skin were *ātmā*, 'I am blonde, I am black and so on.' Money was *ātmā*, body's physiological system was *ātmā*, even time and nationality were *ātmā* – I am rich, I am poor, I am restless, I am sad, I am young, I am old, I am an American, Indian and so on. These are some of the many notions people have about *ātmā*.

Do not make the mistake of thinking that these I notions together constitute *ātmā* because some are contradictory. Each has its problems. For example, when you say, 'I am an Indian,' there is a problem and when you say, 'I am an American,' there is another problem. If you take the sense organs to be the *ātmā*, there is the problem of requiring reading glasses because you cannot see well, or having to have everything repeated to you three times because you cannot hear well! Since most of the memories are not pleasant or interesting, memory also is a problem. Everything is limited in some way or the other and therefore, taking any of these to be *ātmā* is a problem.

Everyone has this problem of placing the I-notion somewhere. One says, 'This is I,' with reference to the body, mind, etc. This verse says that for the wise, the notion, 'This is I' is totally negated and the 'I' is recognised as pure consciousness, that which is not limited in anyway, and which is the truth and the basis of the entire *jagat*. The *jagat* is understood as *mithyā* by this person, *mithyā* being that which is dependent on *satya*, while *satya* is self-existent.

Only the self can be self-existent. Nothing else is self-existent. And for whom the self, the 'I,' is Brahman are called *tadātmanaḥ*.

Tanniṣṭhas are committed to Brahman

Niṣṭhā means commitment, as we have seen in our study of the third chapter. A *japa-niṣṭha* is one who is committed to the practice of *japa*, and a *tapo-niṣṭha* is committed to the practice of spiritual or religious disciplines called *tapas*. A *yoga-niṣṭha* is committed to the eight-fold discipline called *aṣṭāṅga yoga*. So, there are many forms of *niṣṭhā*s, commitments. This verse refers to those who are committed to Brahman alone.

For the *tanniṣṭha*s, Brahman is what counts because all there is, is Brahman, for them, there is nothing else to be counted. Having this knowledge, there is nothing more for them to accomplish. If there were something more for them to accomplish, their *niṣṭhā*, commitment, would shift. Perhaps they would do *japa* for a while, and then their *niṣṭhā* would shift to something else. Such a shift in commitment does not happen for the *tanniṣṭha*s whose commitment is to Brahman alone. It means their knowledge of *ātmā* is firm; it is no longer shaky. They have neither vagueness nor any more problems to solve with reference to the self, and therefore, nothing further to accomplish.

Tatparāyaṇas are those whose ultimate end is Brahman

Having become *tanniṣṭha*s, *brahma-niṣṭha*s, what else remains for these people to do? Whether they do or not do anything, it is the same for them because they have already gained the ultimate end that is Brahman. *Parāyaṇa* means the ultimate end, the real home. For whom the ultimate end is Brahman, *tat*, are called *tatparāyaṇa*s.

Knowing Brahman as *ātmā* is the goal they have to accomplish. Now that they have this knowledge, there is no more goal. This is what Kṛṣṇa meant earlier when he said, 'The one who sees Brahman in everything attains Brahman, is Brahman.'

People have different goals such as *artha,* security *kāma,* pleasures, either here or in the hereafter like heaven and so on. But, for the wise, there is no goal other than Brahman, which they already are. Because they are *tadbuddhayaḥ, tadātmānaḥ,* and *tanniṣṭhāḥ,* they are *tatparāyaṇāḥ.* It means that their goal is accomplished; there is nothing more to be done.

Jñāna-nirdhūta-kalmaṣas are jīvan-muktas

Kṛṣṇa then describes these people as *jñāna-nirdhūta-kalmaṣa*s, those whose *kalmaṣa*s, impurities, have been removed, *nirdhūta* by knowledge, *jñānena.* What are these impurities that have been removed? Likes and dislikes, ignorance and error, *puṇya* and *pāpa,* happiness and unhappiness, all of which are referred to here as *kalmaṣa,* impurities. These impurities are removed by knowledge.

When such people go, meaning when they die, they do not come back, that is, they are not born again, *apunarāvṛttiṁ gacchanti.* And while living, they are already *tadbuddhayaḥ, tadātmānaḥ, tanniṣṭhāḥ,* and *tatparāyaṇāḥ.*

*Jñāna-nirdhūta-kalmaṣa*s are *jīvan-mukta*s, people who are liberated while living. They cannot become bound again when they die, because there is no 'they.' They are Brahman and Brahman does not come and go, let alone come back. For such people, there is no more duality; there is only Brahman who is Īśvara and the world. Those who know the self as Brahman gain an end from which there is no return, *apunarāvṛttiṁ gacchanti;* there is no longer any connection to another physical body.

How do these people, whose self-ignorance is destroyed, see the truth? Do they see the world differently from those who are ignorant?

Such wise people see Brahman everywhere and in everything

विद्याविनयसम्पन्ने ब्राह्मणे गवि हस्तिनि ।
शुनि चैव श्वपाके च पण्डिताः समदर्शिनः ॥ १८ ॥

vidyāvinayasampanne brāhmaṇe gavi hastini
śuni caiva śvapāke ca paṇḍitāḥ samadarśinaḥ (18)

vidyā-vinaya-sampanne – in one who is endowed with knowledge and humility; *brāhmaṇe* – in a *brāhmaṇa*; *gavi* – in a cow; *hastini* – in an elephant; *śuni ca* – and in a dog; *śvapāke ca* – and (even) in a dog-eater; *paṇḍitāḥ* – wise people; *eva* – indeed; *samadarśinaḥ* – (are) those who see the same (Brahman)

Wise people are indeed those who see the same (Brahman) in a *brāhmaṇa* who is endowed with knowledge and humility, in a cow, in an elephant, in a dog, and (even) in a dog eater.

In this verse, Kṛṣṇa says that wise people become *samadarśī*s. They see the same Brahman, *sama*, which is not subject to change in everything. It means they are able to recognise Brahman everywhere, as that which is not affected or stained in any way by *puṇya* or *pāpa* or by different types of impressions, *saṁskāra*s, be they conscious or unconscious. They know everyone to be Brahman that remains untouched by *karma*s and *karma-phala*s because it remains always the same, unaffected by any change whatsoever.

Brahman remains the same, unstained by anything, eternally pure, and is never involved in any way, at any time. Remaining uninvolved itself, Brahman is that without which no involvement is possible. This is the beauty of Brahman which is *ātmā*, the self. Those who see this *sama*, Brahman, everywhere and in everything, are called *samadarśī*s.

To make this point, Kṛṣṇa points out few instances in which the wise see the *sama*, Brahman. The first is a *brāhmaṇa*, described here as a *vidyā-vinaya-sampanna*, one who is endowed with both knowledge and humility. In such a *brāhmaṇa*, the wise person sees the same Brahman as he or she sees in a cow, elephant, a dog, and even in a dog eater.

From childhood onwards, a *brāhmaṇa* is brought up in a religious way and lives according to the rules and stipulations set out for *brāhmaṇa*s in the Veda. Such a person therefore, has devotion, a prayerful mind, knowledge, and humility. Naturally, such a person also has good *saṁskāra*s and a relatively happy mind free of emotional problems. Because this person is endowed with knowledge and humility, his or her actions are always good, thereby creating a lot of *puṇya* for the person. Is the *brāhmaṇa-ātmā* affected by good *saṁskāra*s? 'No,' Kṛṣṇa says here.

A cow, an elephant, and a dog, on the other hand, have no *saṁskāra*s whatsoever, neither good nor bad. They behave according to the particular programme governing the species to which they belong. Yet, there is a difference between a cow and an elephant, for example, in terms of qualities–*sattva*, *rajas* and *tamas*. The cow is not a lazy animal; it does not have a predominance of *tamas*. It has some *sattva* and a lot of *rajas* in that it is active. An elephant, however, even though a very intelligent animal, has more *tamas* because it moves slowly. And a water buffalo has much more *tamas*. Dolphins and whales seem to have more *sattva*, intelligence, as evident by the manner in which they respond to people, as compared to many other animals. So, there are differences in qualities in different animals. Here, Kṛṣṇa probably mentions the dog in order to bring in the dog eater, a person considered to be despicable.

In all of them, the *brāhmaṇa*, the cow, the elephant, the dog, and the dog eater, the wise see one *ātmā*. And what is that *ātmā*? *Sama-ātmā*, *ātmā* that is never subject to change and, therefore, unaffected by either good or bad *saṁskāra*s. Nor is *ātmā* affected by any of the *guṇa*s, qualities or attributes, *sattva*, *rajas* and *tamas*, even though it is the basis for all of them. *Ātmā* is the truth of all of them; without *ātmā* none of them can exist. However, *ātmā* is free from all of them. This *ātmā*, Brahman, is the same in all. If *ātmā* could be affected in any way, then the dog-*ātmā* would be different from the elephant *ātmā* and so on. When the dog bends its head, *ātmā* will also bend! If this is your understanding, you may think that when you were born, your *ātmā* was innocent and now *ātmā* has become wild, sad, and so on. You may also think that you are all of these, and that they cannot be removed. To correct such thinking, Kṛṣṇa makes it clear that *ātmā* is always *śuddha*, pure.

The wise people, called *paṇḍita*s here, are those who see Brahman, which is not subject to modification, in everyone and everything. Because they have this vision, these *paṇḍitas* are more than scholars. Therefore, they are also called *samadarśīs*.

Those who have this vision of sameness are free from birth and death

इहैव तैर्जितः सर्गो येषां साम्ये स्थितं मनः ।
निर्दोषं हि समं ब्रह्म तस्माद् ब्रह्मणि ते स्थिताः ॥ १९ ॥

ihaiva tairjitaḥ sargo yeṣāṁ sāmye sthitaṁ manaḥ
]nirdoṣaṁ hi samaṁ brahma tasmād brahmaṇi
te sthitāḥ (19)

yeṣām – whose; *manaḥ* – mind; *sāmye* – in that which is the same in everything (in Brahman); *sthitam* – is rooted; *iha eva* – here itself (in this life); *taiḥ* – by those (wise people); *sargaḥ* – the cycle of birth and death (*saṁsāra*); *jitaḥ* – is won over; *hi* – because; *nirdoṣam* – free from any defect; *brahma* – Brahman; *samam* – is the same; *tasmāt* – therefore; *te* – they; *brahmaṇi* – in Brahman; *sthitāḥ* – abide

The cycle of birth and death (*saṁsāra*) is won over here itself (in this life) by those whose mind is rooted in that which is the same in everything (that is in Brahman). Since Brahman, that is free from any defect, is (always) the same, they (the wise people) abide in Brahman.

We have seen how those who have knowledge of *ātmā* being Brahman are free from doership and enjoyership caused by ignorance and error. Their self-ignorance and everything caused by it has been destroyed in the wake of knowledge. Their minds are awake to *ātmā* being Brahman, being free from any sense of limitation. They know they are free because, for them, the 'I' is Brahman alone. There is no longer any doubt or error and nothing more remains to be accomplished.

Such people see Brahman in everyone and everything, from the most exalted to the lowliest. How? Because they know that there is only one *ātmā* in all beings and that *ātmā* is their own self. They know that *ātmā* is not affected by anything that happens to the body, mind, or senses, whether it is the *ātmā* of a respected *brāhmaṇa* or the *ātmā* of a dog eater.

Ātmā is one, whole, limitless, and is manifest in every intellect, just as there is one whole space present in every stomach. Just as you find the all-pervasive space wherever you go, so too is consciousness everywhere. Consciousness is not limited by time and space. Consciousness is always there in any place; all movement takes place in consciousness. *Ātmā* is consciousness and those who know this are *samadarśī*s; they recognise *ātmā* that is the same in all beings.

The mind has to be prepared

The wise do not take *ātmā* as a limited entity, knowing that it is all pervasive and unaffected. The body or the nature of even a dog eater does not affect *ātmā*, or anything the person does, but the ignorant do not recognise this fact. If a wise person were to teach a dog eater, what would he teach him? Would he say, 'Your *ātmā* is impure because you have been eating dogs?' *Ātmā* is ever pure and so, a wise person cannot make such a statement. All he can teach is '*tat tvam asi*,' regardless of whether the listener is an angel, a god, or a dog eater. And how can one say, *tat tvam asi,* unless the self happens to be *tat,* the self of everything?

Ātmā is the truth of everything; it is always the same. It does not undergo any change, which is why the wise can share his or her vision with anyone. The question, of course, remains whether the listener will be able to understand the teaching. He or she may require some polishing, for which we have various disciplines. First, the dog may be removed from the dog eater's diet so that the person can become more sensitive, and it may be followed by other disciplines such as prayer. Only when the mind of the listener has been prepared, can the knowledge take place.

None of the preparations being discussed here are to purify the *ātmā*. It is only to prepare the person's mind to recognise that *ātmā* has always been pure. There is no other purpose for such a preparation. It is not preparation for *ātmā* but a preparation for the mind. Nor does this preparation have anything to do with changing the cells of a person's physical body. The preparation has only to do with the person's mind. The mind has to be prepared and that is all we try to do.

Another point that Śaṅkara clarifies in his introduction to this verse is that when Kṛṣṇa says that the wise see same *ātmā* in everyone, it does not mean that he treats everyone equally. Suppose a person looks upon a *brāhmaṇa* and a dog eater as equals, placing them on the same pedestal, so to speak. Can you say that such a person has the vision of the same, Brahman, in all? Not necessarily; the person may be ignorant, not wise.

What needs to be understood here is that it is not that the wise do not perceive a dog eater as a dog-eater; of course, they do. What Kṛṣṇa says here is that they recognise one *ātmā* in everyone and everything – one self that is the self, the truth of all. These are the people being discussed in this verse; they alone are *samadarśīs* referred to in the previous verse.

The word '*sarga*' means birth and implies the cycle of births and deaths called *saṁsāra*, the life of becoming that the ignorant are caught up in. The *saṁsāra* is now *jita*, won over, by the wise, which means that there is no future birth for them. The winning over takes place while one is alive, in this body, in this life, at this time, right now, here, *iha eva*. These people have gained a victory over this life of becoming through knowledge, thereby proving that such a victory is indeed possible.

Kṛṣṇa describes the mind of those who gain this victory, as *sthita*, being established or steady, in that which has sameness, *sāmye*, that which does not undergo any change whatsoever is Brahman.

Ātmā is consciousness – free from attributes

Not being subject to time, Brahman undergoes no change whatsoever. Brahman has no qualities and therefore, there is nothing that can undergo change. For example, a substance has its own peculiar attributes. By adding or taking away the attributes, the substance undergoes a change. Even if the substance is left alone, in the course of time its attributes undergo changes. Thus, it always goes on changing.

That which does not undergo any change whatsoever is *ātmā* which is Brahman. Even space disappears in sleep, but not Brahman. Not being subject to change, there is no death for the *ātmā*. *Ātmā* neither dies nor does it cause anything to die. Death is only for a substance that obtains within time.

If you analyse *ātmā*, it is only *caitanya*, consciousness. The analysis itself is possible because of your being conscious of your mind, senses, body, this world, and other people, with reference to which you take yourelf to be a separate entity, which is not true. In fact, anything you objectify is *anātmā*; *ātmā* is the only one that is self-evident.

Even time is evident to the self-evident *ātmā*. Time does not objectify consciousness; rather, in your consciousness there is the concept of time. Anything other than *ātmā*, being totally dependent upon *ātmā* for its existence, is *mithyā*. And *ātmā*, that is self-existent, is *satya*, the truth of everything. Not being bound by time, *satya-ātmā* is not subject to change or death; it always remains the same. Therefore, in this verse, *ātmā* is called *sāmya*, meaning that the self is in everything and yet is not affected by *puṇya-pāpa* or the qualities of *sattva*, *rajas*, and *tamas*.

For whom is this *sāmya*, the *ātmā*? Certainly not for the one who is affected. Suppose you take yourself as one who possesses good qualities of a *brāhmaṇa*, can you sit beside a dog-eater and watch him eat, even if the food is nicely served and the table, beautifully decorated with flowers and so on? Of course not. Being a humble *brāhmaṇa*, you will surely shrink and want to leave immediately.

If you are *ātmā* that enjoys the attributes of scholarship and so on, and another *ātmā* has the attributes of ignorance and error, then definitely each *ātmā* is different. But the wise people, *paṇḍitas*, *samadarśīs*, have the vision of the self that is the same in all, unaffected by anything and everything that happens to be done by anyone.

Mokṣa is not after death

For those whose minds are awake to this *ātmā*, *saṁsāra*, the life of becoming, is no more, even while they are alive, here, *iha eva* in this body. It means that *mokṣa*, freedom, is not after death. How can knowledge of *ātmā* happen after death? All you do after death is travel. If you spend your life meditating on Brahman as the cause of everything, praying to that Brahman and so on, without understanding that you are Brahman, then you may go to *brahma-loka*, the heaven considered to be the greatest of all the heavens.

Please do not ask me if there is a *brahma-loka*. I cannot prove that there is, and you cannot prove that there is not. Therefore, let us simply assume that *brahma-loka* is, and that you, having lived a life of devotion to Īśvara, will go there and live with Brahmaji for some time. There you will enjoy peace and whatever happiness *brahma-loka* has to offer. Eventually, Brahmaji may even decide to teach you. What will he teach? He can teach only '*tat tvam asi*,' exactly what you were taught before when you were here in this life! Now Brahmaji is teaching you and you understand. You are liberated by the knowledge. And when does this liberation take place? Only now, always now.

There is no after death *mokṣa*. If there is survival after death, there is only travel, not *mokṣa*. *Mokṣa* gained by being taught by Brahmaji, is also not after-death *mokṣa*. *Mokṣa* is not an event in time; it is an accomplished fact. *Ātmā* is ever *mukta*, liberated. If bondage were real, even God could not remove it because it would be a reality, God's own reality. Nor can God remove a bondage that is false because it is not there. No one can remove something that does not exist, not even God. God can only teach and make you understand that there is no bondage.

Ātmā is sinless, pure

Kṛṣṇa also describes *samaṁ brahma* in this verse as *nirdoṣam*. *Doṣa* means a defect or blemish. Ultimately, any attribute or quality is a *doṣa*, and it exists because it can only belong to a substance. Substance is always *anitya*, non-eternal. Therefore, *nirdoṣa* means free from any defect, from any attribute, such as mortality, division, and so on.

For those people who do not know the true nature of *ātmā*, *ātmā*, is taken to have attributes, defects such as dog eating, and so on. When you say that a dog eater is a sinner, what do you mean? A sinner means one who has committed sins and therefore, the sins are sticking to the person. Who is this person? Is the physical body the sinner? Are the senses or the mind the sinner?

The body itself cannot perform any action, and therefore, it cannot be taken as the sinner. The senses are only instruments; they are not sinners either. Similarly, the mind is not a sinner;

it too is an instrument, a means. Who then, is a sinner? *Ātmā* is the sinner. When you condemn a person as a sinner, you are condemning *ātmā* as the sinner, because you look upon *ātmā* as one who possesses attributes or defects. Then, anything you do as though sticks to the *ātmā* and *ātmā* is taken as *doṣavān*, defective. It means that *ātmā* is already *doṣavān* and keeps gathering more *doṣas*. *Ātmā* is equivalent to a substance, like any other substance with a nucleus, and attracts varieties of seen and unseen results in the form of *puṇya* and *pāpa*. All of this sticks to *ātmā* for those who are deluded, who do not know that *ātmā* is always pure and, therefore, never affected by *puṇya* and *pāpa*. *Ātmā* is not affected in any way whatsoever by the *doṣa* you impute to it.

Since Brahman, which is *ātmā*, is *nirdoṣa*, it is *sama*, always the same, even when the self is taken to be a sinner and so on. *Sama* means *eka*, one. Brahman does not undergo any change; it is always one, the same. And in Brahman alone, the wise people ever remain rooted, *sāmye brahmaṇi sthitāḥ*. They remain rooted because they are Brahman, *ātmā* being Brahman. *Brahmaṇi te sthitāḥ* means that the wise are non-separate from Brahman.

Previously, due to *aviveka*, lack of discrimination, not knowing the true nature of *ātmā*, they thought *ātmā* was subject to *puṇya* and *pāpa*, meaning subject to defect, *doṣa*. Therefore, everyone appeared different –'I have my own *puṇya-pāpa* and you have yours.' Each one comes with his or her baggage, collects additional baggage, and leaves the world taking only the subtle baggage with him or her. Just as one throws away useless baggage and takes only what is important, the subtle baggage called *puṇya* and *pāpa* is carried to the next birth.

Even if you do not want to, you have to carry your *puṇya-pāpa* baggage with you, because it is the law. As long as you look upon yourself as the receptacle for *puṇya-pāpa*, assuming doership, there will be this connection with *karma*. When there is the notion, 'I am the doer,' due to *aviveka*, you are bound. By *viveka*, you come to recognise that the self is Brahman now and always. Such people are Brahman and there is no question of re-birth. They never return, *gacchanti apunarāvṛttim*. To remain in Brahman means they are Brahman. Therefore, there is no question of their taking another birth.

Ātmā is not born and does not die

You may say here that, while it is very pleasant to think of yourself as eternal, you do not like the idea of not coming back. It is because you want to survive, which is every mortal's desire. Survival being the original instinct, no one wants death and so one thinks he or she has to survive. 'I want to survive' is a part of the original problem.

If you want to survive here, naturally you also want to survive after death. The scriptures say that you will survive, a point that you are very much interested in. And if you are told that after realising Brahman you will again come back, that you will be born with this self-knowledge and you will enjoy this world, that too is very interesting. Or, if you are told that, after gaining this knowledge here, you will have increasing layers of happiness, you can enjoy that possibility.

Perhaps you will have a different type of body, X-ray eyes, better ears, and so on. If you are told all this, and similar things, you will definitely find it interesting.

The problem here is that you think you are imperfect. 'I am imperfect' is a conclusion you have made and because of that, there is a love for getting something later. This is the problem of the *saṁsārīs*. Therefore, they say, 'Swamiji, I do not like the idea of not coming back. I want to return.' For the *saṁsārīs*, I can definitely say, 'Do not worry, you will come back. Who told you, you will not be reborn? Just do not ask me how you will be born because there are so many possibilities! You may be born as an angel or as a cockroach. But, definitely, you will return!'

Whereas, for the wise, no such thing happens. Knowing they are Brahman, the wise are established in Brahman, *brahmaṇi sthitāḥ*, meaning they are non-separate from Brahman. There is no cause for fear.

The original fear is the fear of death. But *ātmā*, the self, just is; it is not born and it does not die. The problem is that you think you are subject to mortality, imperfections, and attributes. That you are subject to *doṣa* is the original problem. As long as you think, 'I,' the *ātmā* has attributes or defects, there are problems. *Ātmā* being subject to time is a *doṣa*. *Ātmā* being subject to imperfection is a *doṣa*. *Ātmā* being subject to sorrow is a *doṣa*. *Ātmā* being subject to limitation is a *doṣa*. *Ātmā* being subject to birth and death is a *doṣa*. *Ātmā* being subject to *puṇya-pāpa*, doership, and enjoyership is a *doṣa*. As long as you look upon *ātmā* as a *doṣavān*, there is no way of getting rid of the *doṣa*s. Even if you remove one *doṣa*, another will arise.

There is nothing to be afraid of

Therefore, Kṛṣṇa makes it very clear here that because *ātmā* is *nirdoṣa,* free from defect, it is *sama,* Brahman. Knowing this, the wise are Brahman. There is no *jīva* left anymore to come back. Remaining in Brahman, they have won over the cycle of birth and death, that is *mokṣa,* liberation. They are liberated right now and, after the death of the present body, there is no coming back.

Does this mean they completely disappear? They cannot disappear because what exists is *satya-ātmā* alone. What disappears is the false, and the truth alone remains. *Ātmā* is *satya-brahma* and Brahman is Īśvara, the cause of the world. You are Brahman and as Īśvara, you are *jagat-kāraṇa.* All there is, is Īśvara, there being no other entity. This is the truth.

You are Īśvara even now. Who says you are not? '*Tat tvam asi*' means 'You are Īśvara'– from the standpoint of the self. The self, *ātmā,* is Īśvara. When what is, is Īśvara you do not lose anything by being Īśvara. There is no birth and death. What, then, is there to be afraid of?

How a wise person would respond to situations

न प्रहृष्येत्प्रियं प्राप्य नोद्विजेत्प्राप्य चाप्रियम् ।
स्थिरबुद्धिरसम्मूढो ब्रह्मविद् ब्रह्मणि स्थितः ॥ २० ॥

na prahṛṣyet priyaṁ prāpya nodvijet prāpya cāpriyam
sthirabuddhirasammūḍho brahmavid brahmaṇi sthitaḥ (20)

brahmavit – one who knows Brahman; *brahmaṇi* – in Brahman; *sthitaḥ* – established; *sthirabuddhiḥ* – one whose knowledge is firm; *asammūḍhaḥ* – one who is free from delusion; *priyam* – that which is desirable; *prāpya* – gaining; *na prahṛṣyet* – would (does) not rejoice over; *apriyaṁ ca* – and that which is not likeable; *prāpya* – gaining; *na udvijet* – would (does) not resent

> The one who knows Brahman, who is established in Brahman, whose knowledge is firm, and who is free from delusion, would not rejoice over gaining that which is desirable nor would he resent gaining that which is not likeable.

In this verse, Kṛṣṇa continues his discussion of the person who has the vision of the self, *ātmā*, as that which never undergoes any change, that which is always *sama*, same. Such people were referred to as *samadarśinaḥ* in verse 18 because they see this sameness, this *ātmā*, in everyone and everything – in a *brāhmaṇa*, a cow, an elephant, a dog, and even in a dog eater. It is not that they see everyone and everything as equal but, rather, they see *ātmā*, the self, in everyone that undergoes no change. It is a very important distinction that needs to be clearly understood.

Here, in this verse, we are told how such a wise person would respond to situations, both *priya* and *apriya*, desirable and undesirable. Examples have already been given – a *brāhmaṇa*, one who has knowledge and humility, *vidyā-vinayavān*, and a dog eater, *śvapāka*, respectively. The wise person is called *sthira-buddhi* in this verse, which we shall discuss later.

There is no mandate intended here

Gaining something desirable, *priyaṁ prāpya*, the *sthira-buddhi* does not rejoice, *na prahṛṣyet*. The form of the verb used here, *prahṛṣyet*, generally implies a mandate, 'May the wise person not rejoice. May he or she not become elated.' But is this really a mandate? Kṛṣṇa is not cautioning the wise here. He is not saying, 'Be very careful! You are a knower of Brahman and, if you rejoice or get upset, your knowledge may be disturbed. So, do not get elated or troubled by anything!' Since there is no question of a wise person becoming elated or troubled, Kṛṣṇa's statement, 'May one not become elated bythe desirable and troubled by the undesirable!' is not a mandate.

Whenever this kind of statement comes up in the *Gītā*, there is a conversion to be made because it is not Kṛṣṇa's intention to mandate behaviour here or to set down rules. The words as they are, however, accomplish something in that they are quiet statements for those who want to become wise, *brahmavits*, because they imply that, by following *karma-yoga*, the mind will become prepared for gaining knowledge. But, with reference to the person who already has knowledge, the sentence, '*na prahṛṣyet*, may he or she not rejoice,' should be translated as '*na prahṛṣyati*, he or she does not rejoice.' Similarly, '*na udvijet*, may he or she not get upset,' is to be taken as, '*na udvijate*, he or she does not get upset.' This is the intended meaning here.

What Kṛṣṇa is saying here is that if a person is wise, he or she does not get elated when confronted by desirable situations.

Nor does such a person get upset by undesirable situations, *apriyaṁ prāpya ca*. This response to situations is quite unlike how others usually behave. When something desirable comes along, you become so elated; you hit the ceiling, to use the vernacular. And if it is something undesirable, you hit the ground, rolling around moaning and groaning about your lot. In this way, your responses are like the ups and downs of a yo-yo because anyone who is subject to elation is also subject to the anti climaxes that come in its wake.

The wise person, on the other hand, is disturbed neither by the desirable nor the undesirable, *na prahṛṣyet priyaṁ prāpya na udvijet prāpya ca apriyam*. The person does not become elated or dejected. One is happy with the desirable and not unhappy with the undesirable, which does not mean that the wise person is happy with the undesirable! What is meant is that one is not unhappy with the undesirable and is not elated by the desirable. For the wise person there is only fullness, his or her own fullness. Such a person's fullness does not depend upon situations because he or she is *sthira-buddhi*, one whose knowledge of *ātmā*, the self, is firm.

The wise person's knowledge is steady

In his commentary of this verse, Śaṅkara defines *sthira-buddhi* as one who knows firmly the one unchanging *ātmā*, free of attributes, in all beings.[18] Such a person's knowledge, *buddhi* is steady, *sthira*, meaning that it is firm, clear. Therefore, the

---

[18] सर्वभूतेषु एकः समः निर्दोषः आत्मा इति स्थिरा निर्विचिकित्सा बुद्धिः यस्य सः स्थिरबुद्धिः ।
(शङ्कर भाष्यम्)

person is called *sthira-buddhi*. The word *sthira* is defined here because you may think that, like a steady, well rooted tree, if you shake the knowledge it may become uprooted. In fact, steady knowledge cannot be shaken whcih is why it is *sthirā*, steady. In his definition of *sthira-buddhi*, Śaṅkara, adds a word, *nirvicikitsā*. *Vicikitsā* means doubt and *nirvicikitsā* means that which is free from doubt.

Steady knowledge is firm knowledge, knowledge that is free from all doubt and vagueness. The one who has this doubt-free knowledge is called *sthira-buddhi*, one whose knowledge is totally firm, free from doubt. When one's knowledge is absolutely doubt-free, the person is free from any *moha*, delusion. There is no delusion whatsoever about *ātmā*. The person does not take *ātmā* as the *kartā*, doer, or as the *bhoktā* enjoyer, nor does the person think that *ātmā* is something that is located in some place, which is different from everything else. Such a person is called *asammūḍha* here. There is no Brahman other than *ātmā*.

The person is *asammūḍha* because he or she is a *brahmavit*, one who knows Brahman. The one who knows *ātmā* is an *ātmavit* and he is a *brahmavit*, the one who knows Brahman. The one who knows *ātmā* is a *brahmavit*, and the one who knows Brahman is an *ātmavit* because there is no Brahman other than *ātmā*. *Ātmā* is Brahman; therefore, one who knows *ātmā* is a *brahmavit*. And being a *brahmavit*, the person is said to be established in Brahman alone, *brahmaṇi eva sthitaḥ*.

The knowledge of Brahman is not something one can lose because it is oneself. Thus the one who knows Brahman abides in Brahman. Knowing Brahman is not a matter for memory.

Memory is something that one collects about an object. Here, the person was ignorant about the nature of *ātmā* and ignorance is no longer there now. Because the self is always there, there is no question of forgetting the self. The person who knows Brahman is Brahman, and he or she remains in Brahman. Even after death the person is Brahman. The entire meaning, then, is expressed by this one short sentence, *sthira-buddhiḥ, asammūḍhaḥ brahmavit brahmaṇi sthitaḥ*.

The happiness of such people does not wane

बाह्यस्पर्शेष्वसक्तात्मा विन्दत्यात्मनि यत्सुखम् ।
स ब्रह्मयोगयुक्तात्मा सुखमक्षयमश्नुते ॥ २१ ॥

bāhyasparśeṣvasaktātmā vindatyātmani yatsukham
sa brahmayogayuktātmā sukham akṣayam aśnute (21)

bāhya-sparśeṣu – with reference to external (sense) objects that contact (the sense organs); *asakta-ātmā* – one whose mind is not attached; *ātmani* – in oneself; *sukham* – (limited) happiness; *vindati* – gains; *saḥ* – he (or she); *brahma-yoga-yukta-ātmā* (*cet*) – if his mind is endowed with the knowledge of Brahman; *tat sukhaṁ yat akṣayam* – happiness that does not wane; *aśnute* – gains

> The one whose mind is not attached to the external (sense) objects, gains (limited) happiness in oneself, whereas, if his mind is endowed with the knowledge of Brahman, he gains that happiness that does not wane.

This verse can be interpreted in two ways. First, we will see how Śaṅkara explains it. Then we will see the other interpretation. *Bāhya-sparśa* refers to external objects that come into contact with the sense organs. This compound is resolved by Śaṅkara as *bāhyāśca te sparśāśca*, meaning they are external, *bāhyas*, and they come into contact with the sense organs, *sparśas*. Generally, *sparśa* is used only in the sense of touch; that which is experienced by the sense of touch is called *sparśa*. Extending this meaning, any object that a person comes in contact with is *sparśa*.

The sense objects such as sound, etc., are *sparśas* and they are external; therefore, they are *bāhya-sparśas*. *Śabdādayaḥ*, sound, etc., include all sounds, forms, touch, taste, and smell. And, with reference to these external objects, *bāhya-sparśeṣu*, the person is *asakta-ātmā*. That is, his or her mind, *ātmā*, is uninvolved, *asakta* with any of them, meaning that the person's mind is not hooked by them. In other words, the fancies of the mind do not bother the person. The one whose mind is not carried away by such fancies with reference to external sense objects is therefore, described in this verse in two words, *bāhya-sparśeṣu, asakta-ātmā*.

Freedom from longing

Śaṅkara expresses this *bāhya-sparśeṣu asakta-ātmā* as one who is free from longing with reference to the sense objects, as *viśayeṣu prīti-varjita*, a person who does not miss the external objects. This being so, the person gains the happiness that is in the *ātmā*, *ātmani yat sukhaṁ tat vindate*. *Ātmā* here means *sat-cit-ānanda-ātmā*.

Happiness, *sukha* has to be mentioned in this way because people generally think that the objects themselves give them *sukha*. But the wise person is also happy, without objects being instrumental in any way. If a wise man is not elated by objects, how does he become happy? He is happy because any happiness is with himself.

Sukha is the very *svarūpa*, nature of *ātmā*. *Sukha* really means fullness here, fullness being *ātmā*'s nature. This *sukha*, fullness, is gained by the *jñānī* who knows that *ātmā* is not affected by the external objects that come into contact with the sense organs. He or she gains *sukha* that obtains in the *ātmā*, which is the person's *svarūpa*.

How do we know that the person being discussed here is wise? The next line points this out, along with the context provided by the previous verse. The person is referred to as *brahma-yoga-yukta-ātmā*. *Brahma-yoga* is the recognition of *ātmā* being Brahman. This recognition itself is the *yoga*. *Yukta*, in this compound, means 'endowed with.' Thus, the one endowed with the knowledge of Brahman is *brahma-yoga-yukta* and the one whose mind is endowed with, or resolved in the knowledge of Brahman is *brahma-yoga-yukta-ātmā*, *ātmā* meaning the mind, *antaḥ-karaṇa*, here. This is the person who gains the happiness that is oneself, *brahma-yoga-yukta-ātmā ātmani*, in oneself, *sukhaṁ vindate*.

Relative and absolute sukha

A question might now be asked, 'How much *sukha* is there in *ātmā*? There may be just a bit of happiness, like even the happiness you get from eating ice cream. Such happiness comes, but it also goes. For a *brahma-yoga-yukta-ātmā,* is this the kind of *sukha* that is there in the *ātmā*? 'No!' says Kṛṣṇa. The *sukha* in the *ātmā* is *sukha* that does not wane, *sukham akṣayam aśnute.* There is a song, the theme of which is that if you give love away, it will grow. In other words, it does not get spent or die. Similarly here, the *sukha* in the *ātmā* is a *sukha* that is not dependent upon any situation, *sukham akṣayam;* it is your *svarūpa.*

This verse can also be looked at as a description of two different people by taking the two lines separately. The first line describes the *karma-yogī* who is not carried away by fancies, *bāhya-sparśeṣu asakta-ātmā* and the second line describes the *jñānī* who is endowed with the knowledge of Brahman, *brahma-yoga yukta-ātmā.* If we look at the verse in this way, we see that there are two types of *sukha* mentioned here.

A person who does not depend on any external object or situation for his or her happiness – whether he or she lives the lifestyle of a *sannyāsī* or a *karma-yogī* – has an attitude, cheerfulness and contentment with whatever there is. And, because of this attitude, the person gains a greater degree of *sukha* than a person who is entirely dependent upon the presence of desirables and the absence of undesirables. The latter person's *sukha* is definitely going to be more short lived when compared to the *sukha* of a person who is not dependent on situations. For example, one may like tofu, but it may not be served in the way one wants it. One may like it as it is and it may even come to one as fried tofu. Therefore, there are comparable degrees of *sukha* that people get, and the world over it is same. Generally, people are dependent for their *sukha* upon desirable things coming and undesirable things staying away.

The sukha of maturity

Suppose there is a person who, because of an inner maturity, is able to find happiness, cheerfulness, in doing what he or she can do. Such a person definitely gains some *sukha*. Because of a prayerful attitude, the person picks up *sukha* that is not totally dependent upon his or her *rāga-dveṣa*s. Instead, it depends upon the person's sense of satisfaction. This is the person who begins to discover that there are things that are to be done and enjoys doing them as an offering to the Lord, *īśvara-arpaṇa-buddhyā*. Because the person is courting the Lord, so to speak, he or she will naturally discover certain joy. And, because of this love or cheerfulness that the person enjoys, one is not held by *rāga-dveṣa*s.

The freer you are from your *rāga-dveṣa*s, the more you can enjoy small things. Even the stars will be enjoyable to you. There are many things in life you can enjoy without fulfilling your likes and dislikes. Thus, the person who is *bāhya-sparśeṣu-asakta-ātmā* gains *sukha* in the mind. Even if the person gives up something, one does not really miss it and, again, there is *sukha*, a *sukha* which is limited but definitely better than the *sukha* enjoyed by the person who is totally dependent on one's *rāga-dveṣa*s.

The *sukha* of the person who is committed to *rāga-dveṣa*s is going to be very limited and is not going to be lasting.

Whereas, the one who is not in the hands of *rāga-dveṣa*s, whether a *karma-yogī* or a *sannyāsī*, has a disposition because of which happiness is gained in oneself, *ātmani sukhaṁ vindati*. Here, *ātmani* should be taken as 'in oneself,' that is, in one's mind.

Now, what happens if this same person, the *bāhya-sparśeṣu asakta-ātmā*, becomes a *brahma-yoga-yukta-ātmā*? By withdrawing from the hold of *rāga-dveṣa*s, the person definitely gains some *sukha*. But when this same person becomes one with Brahman, when the person's mind is alive to the knowledge of Brahman, what *sukha* will the person gain? Such a person gains a *sukha* that does not wax or wane, the *sukha* that is the *svarūpa* of oneself.

We see in all of this an order. For one whose mind is not attached to external objects, there is some *sukha*, not because of the objects but because of the cheerfulness of the mind. This is due to *antaḥ-karaṇa-śuddhi*. And if such a person becomes a *brahma-yoga-yukta-ātmā*, the *sukha* gained will be one's very nature, limitless and eternal.

The significance of context

Thus, this verse can also be seen as reflecting this order. If Śaṅkara were here, I think he would agree with this latter interpretation, given that it holds with what was said before and what was said later. Whenever you interpret what is said differently from Śaṅkara's interpretation, you must see that it is contextually proper. Otherwise, anyone who knows what it is all about can easily prove you wrong. If, however, having understood the context properly, you are able to see another meaning, one that does not go against anything that is said and fits better into the context, you can present it and the tradition will accept it.

Śaṅkara himself often views a verse in two or three different ways, a practice the tradition allows, provided of course, it facilitates understanding without hurting what the *śāstra* says grammatically, contextually, and logically. Because the tradition thoroughly analyses the *śāstra* before giving its meaning, presenting any other meaning requires the utmost care and consideration in terms of what has been said before and what is said later. We shall see how this latter interpretation is upheld as we proceed.

Verse 22

Enjoyments are potential causes for sorrow

ये हि संस्पर्शजा भोगा दुःखयोनय एव ते ।
आद्यन्तवन्तः कौन्तेय न तेषु रमते बुधः ॥ २२ ॥

ye hi saṁsparśajā bhogā duḥkhayonaya eva te
ādyantavantaḥ kaunteya na teṣu ramate budhaḥ (22)

kaunteya – O son of Kuntī!; *hi* – because; *ye* – those which; *saṁsparśajāḥ* – are born of contact (between the sense organs and desirable objects); *bhogāḥ* – enjoyments; *te* – they; *duḥkha-yonayaḥ eva* – (are) the sources of pain alone; *ādi-antavantaḥ* – (and they) have a beginning and an end; *budhaḥ* – the wise person; *teṣu* – in them; *na ramate* – does not revel

Because those enjoyments that are born of contact (between the sense organs and desirable objects) are the sources of pain alone, and have a beginning and an end, Kaunteya (Arjuna)! the wise person does not revel in them.

Both the *bāhya-sparśeṣu asakta-ātmā* and the *brahma-yoga-yukta-ātmā* of the previous verse are again commented upon here. The objects contacted by the sense organs are called *saṁsparśa*s, *sparśa* meaning 'contact' as we have seen. Between the *indriya*s, sense organs, and the *iṣṭa-viṣaya*s, desirable objects, there is contact and because of that contact there is *sukha* called *bhoga* here, meaning enjoyment, a pleasant experience. These pleasant experiences are born out of sensory contact with desirable sense objects, *saṁsparśajāḥ bhogāḥ*.

Kṛṣṇa also says here that these enjoyments are the potential causes for sorrow, *duḥkha-yonayaḥ*. *Yoni* means womb. Therefore, enjoyments or pleasant experience, born of the contact between the sense organs and desirable objects, are the wombs or potential causes for *duḥkha*. They are sources of sorrow. Why? Because, even before gaining these pleasant experiences, there is *duḥkha* in that you have to work for them until you get them.

To bring a desirable object or pleasant experience into alignment with the sense organs is not an easy thing. If you want to see an object that is away from you, you either have to take yourself to the object or bring the object to you. If it is a mountain, you have to go to the mountain. If it is something else, you may be able to bring it to yourself. Either way, you have to work for coming into contact with it. You either have to come in contact with the object or it has to come in contact with you. This contact has to take place, which itself implies a lot of effort on your part. And this is only the beginning!

When the contact takes place, it must be proper; it must be desirable. The sight of a favourite dish may make you happy, but if, when you put it on your tongue, it is too hot, there is a problem. The sight of it was one contact, which was desirable, and the contact the food made with your tongue was another, which was undesirable. Thus, to ensure that the contact is proper and desirable is not always easy.

Desirable experiences cannot last

How long the desirable contact can last is another problem. The process of experiencing an object itself may exhaust the object and then you will miss the contact. Or, you yourself may become tired and therefore unable to continue the contact. The attitude or the mood to enjoy also goes away and, again, you lose the contact. Whether due to change of mood, the sense organs becoming tired, or the object no longer being available, you always find that this kind of happiness is only temporary, if not momentary. And when it goes, it leaves you high and dry; it leaves you unhappy.

We see that, before gaining enjoyments there is *duḥkha*. And after you get them you spend your time thinking, 'I am going to lose this happiness.' Finally when they are over, there is more *duḥkha*. Again, you have to work for them.

Enjoyments are *duḥkha-yoni*s, sources of sorrow, because they have a beginning, *ādi* and an end, *anta* – they are called *ādi-antavantaḥ* in this verse. A desirable contact is the beginning; the end is when the desirable contact is no longer available. It means that these *bhoga*s are *anitya*, not lasting; they are non-eternal.

The person who understands the limited nature of such enjoyments is called *budhaḥ* in this verse. *Budha* means *vivekī*–*budha* can be taken either to mean a discriminative person or a wise person. In his commentary on this verse, Śaṅkara defines *budha* in the latter sense, one who understands the real nature, the truth, of oneself, *avagata-paramārtha-tattvaḥ*.

Since a *vivekī* understands the limitations of ordinary happiness, he or she goes after *akṣaya-sukha*, the happiness that does not wane, which is why the person was called *bāhya-sparśeṣu asakta-ātmā*, one who is not carried away by the mind's fancies for external objects. Because of the person's discrimination, he or she becomes *bāhya-sparśeṣu asakta-ātmā*.

Enjoying a natural cheerfulness, this person, the *karma-yogī*, goes about doing only what is to be done, not bound by anything. The *karma-yogī* may enjoy certain objects, but he or she is not bothered by any of them. This *karma-yogī*, on becoming a *brahma-yoga-yukta-ātmā*, one who is endowed with the knowledge of *ātmā* as Brahman, gains the happiness that does not wane.

Giving oneself to one's desires

In his introduction to the next verse, Śaṅkara points out that desire or longing for enjoyments is opposed to serious enquiry into oneself, an enquiry that requires certain maturity. A person who wants to understand *ātmā*, Brahman, the ultimate, and who, at the same time, wants to go to discos will have no time for such an enquiry. First, the mind of such a person has to be fixed up, but one will not have any time for that either. The person is acting out of the likes and dislikes in his or her mind and not dealing with them directly. Only when you begin to deal with your likes and dislikes do you become a serious person, an enquirer and a seeker.

You may have hundred problems, but as long as you are ready to deal with them, there is no real problem at all. The person, who deals with his or her problems, already has certain maturity and the problems of such a person will resolve in time. But, for the person who is given to the problems themselves, where is the chance for him or her to deal with them? Giving oneself to one's desires is the real problem and, as Śaṅkara says, is opposed to the pursuit of liberation, *mokṣa – kāmaḥ śreyomārga-pratipakṣī*. This problem is one that is the most difficult to deal with.

Śaṅkara continues, being controlled by *kāma*s, desires, is considered to be the most difficult problem, because it becomes the cause for that which you do not want, *duḥkha* in all of its many forms. For example, if you lose your health due to over indulgence of certain desires, you will also lose your money and a variety of other things in the process. Or, losing your money, you may lose your health! And these *kāma*s, in the form of *rāga-dveṣa*s, are not easy to eliminate, *durnivāra*; in other words, they are difficult to get in hand.

Verse 23

An extra effort is required to bring about an antidote for kāma

शक्नोतीहैव यः सोढुं प्राक् शरीरविमोक्षणात् ।
कामक्रोधोद्भवं वेगं स युक्तः स सुखी नरः ॥ २३ ॥

śaknotīhaiva yaḥ soḍhuṁ prāk śarīravimokṣaṇāt
kāmakrodhodbhavaṁ vegaṁ sa yuktaḥ sa sukhī naraḥ (23)

yaḥ – the one who; *prāk śarīra-vimokṣaṇāt* – before release from the body; *kāma-krodha-udbhavam* – born of anger and desire; *vegam* – the force; *iha eva* – here itself (in this world); *soḍhum* – to master; *śaknoti* – is able; *saḥ* – he (or she); *yuktaḥ* – (is) a *karma-yogī; saḥ* – he or (she); *sukhī naraḥ* – is a happy person

The one who is able to master the force born of anger and desire here (in this world) before release from the body is a *karma-yogī*. He (or she) indeed is a happy person.

Here, Kṛṣṇa is saying that you do not control *kāma* and *krodha*, desire and anger; rather, you knock off the *kāma-krodha-udbhavaṁ vegam*, the force born of *kāma* and *krodha* First, you should know how to take care of *vega*, the force; then you can take care of the desire, anger, and the pain that become the cause for that force. Behind every pain, there is an expectation, and unfulfilled expectation leads to anger, as we have seen. *Kāma* and *krodha* have certain sting; by taking care of the force born of them you remove their sting. So, you have to pay attention to *kāma* and *krodha*.

The entire psychology of the *Gītā* is in terms of *rāga*s and *dveṣa*s, the management of your likes and dislikes. By managing likes and dislikes, a normal person can overcome any psychological problems that he or she may have. Such problems are natural. That you are angry is normal. That you have desires is normal. That you are subject to pain is also normal. This normal psychology is dealt with by the *Gītā* in terms of likes and dislikes.

Kāma, desire, is a common word for both *rāga* and *dveṣa*. *Kāma* is purely a want. The thought process through which you desire an object, an end, is called *kāma*. The desire can be either to gain something, *rāga*, or to avoid something, *dveṣa*; to retain something gained, or to get rid of something that you already have. *Kāma* produces certain force and symptoms which are indicative of the virulence of desire. If these symptoms were not there, you would not know whether the *kāma* was a binding desire or a non-binding desire.

If one has a desire that is not fulfilled and one does not get upset in the process, then that desire is not a binding desire. We are not dealing with non-binding desires here; we are dealing only with those that produce *vega*, force. This *vega* is the outcome of desire and is something that indicates the virulence or the intensity of *kāma* as well as *krodha* that results if the desire is not fulfilled. The *vega* described here by the expression, *kāma-krodha-udbhavaṁ vegam*, the force that is released by or born of *kāma* and *krodha*, is the ultimate object to be mastered.

Another important expression used in this verse is *prāk śarīra-vimokṣaṇāt*. *Prāk* means 'before,' *vimokṣaṇa* means 'release,' and *śarīra* is the physical body. Therefore, the expression means, before release from the physical body. Before one dies away, then, one is able to master, *soḍhuṁ śaknoti*, this force born of *kāma* and *krodha*. Kṛṣṇa mentions this for two reasons, the first one being that if a person is able to accomplish this before he or she dies, then the person is a mature human being, *nara*. And, because one is mature, having mastered one's mind, the person is happy, *saḥ sukhī*.

It seems to me that human life is divided into two activities – one is to gather all sorts of nonsense as a child and the other is to learn how to manage them all. Somewhere along the way, you are able to realise that what you had gathered as a child has nothing to do with what you are now. Only the person who realises this and then addresses the problems that arise can be called *nara*. Until then, the person is still a child.

Therefore, I would say, that if a person is able to master the force born of desire and anger, he or she has made it as an adult human being. I would say that he is a *sukhī* and also a *karma-yogī* because to master the *vega* of *kāma-krodha* requires certain attitude.

Maturity also implies expressing your free will in its highest form, meaning that you can voluntarily appreciate and offer prayer. Prayer and a prayerful attitude are the expressions of a mature will. In fact, they are based on will alone. No one is driven to prayer. You are driven to swear, to cry, and to do varieties of things, but you can never be driven to prayer. Even if you pray in a moment of distress, the will is expressing in its highest form.

In the act of prayer, you do not see the one to whom you pray. Īśvara is nowhere around. All you see are the contending forces that you have to deal with. Therefore, if in the process of living, a person is able to appreciate an Īśvara and offer a prayer to him, that person becomes a *karma-yogī*. Without this, the *kāma-krodha-udbhavaṁ vegam* is not easy to master. This particular religious conversion, as it were, has to take place in the person and is what is implied here by the word *yukta*, meaning *yogī*. And this *karma-yogī*, this mature person who is able to master the force born of desire and anger, is a happy person, *sa sukhī naraḥ*.

Karma-yoga and knowledge reflect an order

In the previous verse we saw that this person does not get carried away by the mind's fancies, knowing them to be the sources of pain and sorrow. A person who is carried away by such fancies is one who is subject to *kāma*, to one's *rāga-dveṣa*s. Such a person cannot get the happiness that a *yogī* can get.

There is an order involved here, meaning that everyone has to become a *karma-yogī* first. The knowledge will then take care of itself. And when does all this take place? In this life itself, *iha eva*, as we saw in the nineteenth verse, and also at any time until death, until one is released from the physical body. While living, until death, the *yogī* who is yet to be a *jñānī* must have this particular capacity, this mastery of *kāma* and *krodha*. You cannot simply say, 'I have already mastered my *kāma* and *krodha*,' and then sit back and think they will not come back. They will come back. There is no such thing as,

'One day, I mastered them; therefore, they will not come back.' This is not one day problem that you deal with for once. It is something that has to be dealt with everyday, until death as Śaṅkara makes it clear here.

We have already seen that, in terms of knowledge, liberation or *mokṣa* can happen at any time in your life, even in old age.[19] This is another meaning for the expression *prāk śarīra-vimokṣaṇāt*, at any time, while living here in this world, in this physical body, this knowledge can be accomplished by a mature human being.

The force of kāma and krodha continues until death

In his commentary to this verse, Śaṅkara emphasises 'until death' meaning to make it clear that the *vega* force, released by *kāma* and *krodha*, by your *rāga-dveṣas*, operates throughout your lifetime, until death, just as the force of hunger and thirst does. For the living person, this *vega* definitely takes place. It is not something that happens one day and goes away the next. And what is its cause? The causes are endless, Śaṅkara says, *ananta-nimittavān hi saḥ vegaḥ*.

What makes you angry? There are countless situations that can cause anger. Therefore, there is no end to the force, *vega*, that is born of desire and anger. In certain situations, there will be no force, whereas in other situations, the *vega* will be there in various degrees and the *kāma-krodha* from which this force comes can be virulent indeed!

---

[19] *antakāle'pi brahmanirvāṇamṛcchati* (*Gītā* 2.72)

Necessity for alertness

Until you see something you may not have *kāma* at all. But once it has been sighted, *kāma* is there. Similarly, there can be *kāma* with reference to what is heard. Thus, you find that *kāma* can take place at any time, which is why Śaṅkara describes *vega* as that for which the cause is endless. Therefore, in terms of tackling or mastering the force born of *kāma-krodha*, you must be alert; you should not relax. It does not mean that you should become tense; it simply means that you should not become indifferent. And, from the standpoint of one who is a *yogī* and not a *jñānī*, this alertness must continue until death.

As we have seen previously, *kāma* refers to both *rāga-dveṣa*s. Here, the emphasis is mainly on *rāga*, that which is desired by you. Within the scope of your sense perception, an object is seen or heard. You may have experienced the object before as something desirable and therefore you remember it. When you experience this object, it becomes the cause for your happiness and is therefore desirable to you. Then you long for it. This longing is like thirst, a thirst for objects that make you happy. The longing itself is called *kāma*. All desires are not the *kāma*s that we discuss here, only those which are binding.

Krodha is born of your seeing or remembering something that is opposed to your desire, opposed to your longing, causing you pain. Naturally, between *kāma*, desire, and, *krodha*, anger, certain pain is involved. Anger would not come unless there was pain in between.

When your expectation is not fulfilled, there is pain, and what you consider to be the obstruction or cause of the pain becomes the object of your anger. Thus, *kāma* itself, causing pain, dislike, and hatred, turns into what we call a 'locked up' anger, *krodha*. The force that arises out of this *kāma-krodha*, referred to in this verse as *kāma-krodha-udbhavaṁ vegam* is what needs to be mastered.

How do you know there is a force? Śaṅkara gives few interesting indications of its existence. When you hear or see something that you find so desirable, you long for it. What happens? Your hair stands on end, *romāñcana*, your eyes open wide, *prahṛṣṭa-netratva*, and your mouth is agape, *prahṛṣṭa-vadanatva*. Śaṅkara says, these are the symptoms of the force of *kāma*.

Each culture has its own way of expressing *kāma* and this expression takes many forms. Naturally, you express the force of your desires according to your culture. How you express also depends on how cultured you are.

Śaṅkara also gives few symptoms of the force of *krodha*–*gātra-prakampa*, shaking of the body; *prasveda*, sweating; *rakta-netra*, bloodshot eyes and *sandaṣṭa-auṣṭhapuṭatva*, biting the lips. Other symptoms of the force arising out of anger are shouting, screaming, heavy breathing, and so on. When the force of *kāma-krodha* is there, you are no longer in charge; the force itself is in charge. This is the force that is to be mastered, the methods for which were already pointed out in the third chapter, where Kṛṣṇa talked about *karma-yoga*. In fact, this self-mastery is mentioned all over the *Gītā*.

Self-mastery comes with living a disciplined life

Self mastery comes with living a disciplined life, having a sound value structure that includes prayer and a prayerful attitude, *prasāda-buddhi,* all of which we have seen. This attitude is based on glad acceptance of what is, living in conformity with the order of *dharma,* and appreciating this order as Īśvara. If you live in this way, you find that *kāma-krodha-vega* loses its sting. Even if anger comes, you are not overcome by it. Only in this way do you become one who has self mastery, one who is a *yogī.*

As a *yogī,* you are in charge and, therefore, you are a cheerful person, *sukhī.* Otherwise, you will have a yo yo life wherein the *vega* takes care of you. Under the spell of *vega,* you are likely to do anything because you are no longer rational. Whatever wisdom or culture you have becomes useless when the *vega* born of your desire and anger is in charge. Whereas one who is able to address this problem, who can withstand this force, is a *nara,* a mature human being.

Problems must be addressed

People do not address this problem, and for the most part suffer under the force of *kāma-krodha* for their entire lifetime. They live a life of *vega* and then they die. They do not even have a chance to address the problem. But everything does seem to happen finally for the good in that there seems to be a new awareness in the society today. For instance, alcoholism has been causing problems that people were not really aware of until fairly recently. But now, it is understood that everyone who lives or has lived in a house where alcohol is used, is affected. And, because of this realisation, a huge movement has resulted, a brand new wave that is not an ordinary one, in which it is commonly accepted that there is no way of resolving these problems without addressing them directly. And to do this, it is also accepted that there must be a programme of conversion through prayer and religion.

A better society may be the natural outcome of this particular awareness alone because those who go through this programme of conversion, and experience the changes that such a programme implies, will become saintly people. These people will be sensitive to the problems of others. They will be people who do not harm others and who are very understanding and mutually helpful to each other. Having come through their own problems, they understand the problems of others; they know what pain is and why others behave the way they do. Perhaps, then, we are in for a new society, because of alcohol!

Addressing the problem is the main point here. That you have a problem is not important because you are not responsible for it. It has all been picked up over a period of time. You did not go out looking for your problems because you wanted to have problems. Rather, they are problems that you happened to pick up. But you must address them here, while living in this life, in this physical body, before you die, *prāk śarīra-vimokṣaṇāt*.

First, you pick up problems and then you solve them. It seems to be how growth is. You create hurdles and then try to jump over them. That is the fun of it all. Life is like a hurdle race.

The race itself is fun, but when you create hurdles and then try to jump over them, it makes the race even more fun. Because you have free will, this situation is inevitable. The creation, the world, is like what it is, because it cannot be any better right now. If you were already programmed, that is, without free will, there would be no human being, at all. Nor would there be *Gītā* or any further evolution. To be a human being implies free will. And once free will is given to you, then wisdom is something that has to be gathered by you; in other words, by free will.

Everyone is given innocence first. Then, while innocent, you gather problems. But you will also become mature. Enough experiences, pain and sorrow is given to you so that you can become an adult. So, you find that the person who addresses the problem becomes a happy person. This person alone is a true human being, a *karma-yogī*, who is ready to take the next step, meaning that the person's mind is prepared for self-knowledge.

Verse 24

The one who has this knowledge revels in oneself

योऽन्तः सुखोऽन्तरारामस्तथान्तर्ज्योतिरेव यः ।
स योगी ब्रह्मनिर्वाणं ब्रह्मभूतोऽधिगच्छति ॥ २४ ॥

yo'ntaḥ sukho'ntarārāmastathāntarjyotireva yaḥ
sa yogī brahmanirvāṇaṁ brahmabhūto'dhigacchati (24)

yaḥ – the one who; *antaḥ sukhaḥ* – whose fulfillment is in oneself; *antar-ārāmaḥ* – who revels in oneself; *tathā* – so too; *yaḥ* – the one; *antar-jyotiḥ* – whose mind is awake to oneself; *saḥ yogī* – that wise person; *eva* – alone; *brahmabhūtaḥ* – being the one whose self is Brahman; *brahma-nirvāṇām* – the freedom which is Brahman; *adhigacchati* – gains

> The one whose fulfilment is in oneself, the one who revels in oneself, the one whose mind is awake to oneself, that wise person alone, whose self is Brahman, gains the freedom which is Brahman.

In the previous verse, Kṛṣṇa talked about the *karma-yogī*, *sukhī*, the happy, cheerful person. Here, we have three beautiful words to describe the wise person, one who has the knowledge of *ātmā* being Brahman, *antaḥ-sukhaḥ*, *antar-ārāmaḥ*, and *antar-jyotiḥ*, the meanings for which we shall see now.

The *antaḥ-sukha* is one for whom fulfilment is in oneself alone. What kind of self? The self that is *sat-cit-ānanda-ātmā* that is Brahman. Generally, people look to situations for their happiness, which is why they have problems, which have been already pointed out. We also saw that the *karma-yogī*, because of his or her attitude, enjoys certain *sukha*. Here, knowing *ātmā*, the person finds fulfilment in oneself.

Where else can you find fulfilment in fact? Because 'I am fullness, I am fulfilled.' You cannot say, 'I am fulfilled because I am married, because I have a son, because I have this job, because I have this or that.' If you think your fulfilment depends on such things, you will definitely find yourself in trouble sooner or later. The one who is fulfilled is one for whom fulfilment is centred on the knowledge of 'I.' That 'I' is fulfilment in itself.

It is fullness; it does not lack anything whatsoever. It is free from any notion, free from doership, free from any sense of limitation or imperfection. All that is there is pure consciousness, which is fullness, which is whole. The person who is truly fulfilled with this knowledge of oneself is called *antaḥ-sukha* here.

Because this person is *antaḥ-sukha*, he or she revels in the self. The word 'revel' here is used in the sense of play. People generally require lot of playthings to keep themselves in good humour, like skating rinks, theatres, or a pack of cards. Because you have to amuse yourself, you are always doing something. Here Kṛṣṇa says that the wise man amuses himself by himself. Nothing else is required to amuse the person. He is amused all the time! With eyes open or closed, he is amused. And, when he looks at his mind, he is definitely amused. Even the wise man has memories, but instead of getting into them, he is simply amused by them.

The mind itself is like an amusement park; you require no one or nothing else to thrill you. Your own mind provides different amusements, musings, and thrillers, too! It has music and talk shows also. Because a wise man is amused in himself by himself, he is called *antar-ārāma* here.

Finally, the wise person is called *antar-jyotiḥ*, meaning 'mind' here. *Jyotiḥ* usually means 'light.' Like light, the mind illumines objects for you to see. Therefore, it is called *jyotiḥ*. In addition to illumining objects, the mind is also awake to the self, the self that puts up the seeming show of division. In dream, you are the dreamer, the dreaming, and the objects dreamt.

In waking, it is the same. The seer or the knower is the self; the sight, the thought, is the self; and the objects of the thought, the seen, is the same self alone. The consciousness that is the self is the same knower consciousness.

All-knowledge implies consciousness. Every thought is consciousness and the object of thought is not separate from this consciousness, which is the existence, *sat* of everything. This knower-known-knowledge difference is purely a show, a good show. And the one whose mind is awake to this *ātmā*, who is aware of the self, is called *antar-jyotiḥ*.

The wise person, also referred to as *yogī* in this verse, is said to be one who is in the form of Brahman, *brahma-bhūtaḥ*, meaning one whose *ātmā* is Brahman, the one whose *ātmā* is no more separate from Brahman, whose very self is Brahman. And what does this wise person gain? *Mokṣa*, liberation, *brahma-nirvāṇa*. *Brahma-nirvāṇa* means *brahma-nirvṛti* or *brahma-ānanda*, otherwise called *mokṣa*.

The one who is *antaḥ-sukha*, *antar-ārāma*, and *antar-jyoti* being one whose self is Brahman, *brahma-bhūta*, gains *mokṣa*, freedom from a sense of limitation and bondage. The self that is Brahman is understood by this person; therefore, the person is Brahman.

And who is this person?

From verse 22 of this chapter onwards, Lord Kṛṣṇa has started summing up his description of a *sannyāsī* as a person who is *sarva-karma-sannyāsī*, the one who renounces different forms of action, not literally, but by knowledge.

Kṛṣṇa used the same word, *brahma-nirvāṇa*, in the last verse of the second chapter; the person whose self is in Brahman is not deluded and, being established in Brahman, even at the end of one's life, gains liberation.[20]

Such a person is called *brahma-bhūta* in the present verse, one whose *ātmā* is Brahman, free from doership and enjoyership. The person gains *brahma-nirvāṇa*, which is *mokṣa*. Because the word '*nirvāṇa*' alone is sometimes understood as some kind of void, we use the word *brahma-nirvāṇa*. *Nirvāṇa* means *ānanda*, freedom from everything; in other words, the limitlessness that is one's own nature.

Verses 25&26

Summary of a sarva-karma-sannyāsī

लभन्ते ब्रह्मनिर्वाणमृषयः क्षीणकल्मषाः ।
छिन्नद्वैधा यतात्मानः सर्वभूतहिते रताः ॥ २५ ॥

labhante brahmanirvāṇam ṛṣayaḥ kṣīṇakalmaṣāḥ
chinnadvaidhā yatātmānaḥ sarvabhūtahite ratāḥ (25)

kṣīṇakalmaṣāḥ – those whose impurities have been destroyed; *chinnadvaidhāḥ* – those whose doubts have been resolved; *yata-ātmānaḥ* – those who have self-mastery; *sarvabhūtahite ratāḥ* – those who are happily engaged in the good of all beings; *ṛṣayaḥ* – sages; *brahma-nirvāṇam* – liberation; *labhante* – gain

---

[20] *Gītā* 2.72

Sages whose impurities have been destroyed, whose doubts have been resolved, who have self-mastery (and) who are happily engaged in the good of all beings, gain liberation.

In the previous verse, Kṛṣṇa described the person who has already gained *mokṣa,* using the words, *antaḥ-sukha, antar-ārāma* and *antar-jyotiḥ.* Such people are also the subject of this present verse. They are called *ṛṣi*s, which is generally translated as sages.

For some people, the word *ṛṣi* brings to mind an old man with matted hair, a long white beard, and long finger nails, practising extreme forms of austerities. In reality, the word *ṛṣi* has two meanings, the one who keeps moving, *aṭati,* who does not get caught up in any one place or situation and, the one who knows, *jānāti.* In the present context, the latter meaning applies. All the teachers in the Vedas are referred to as *ṛṣi*s. These are the people who gain *mokṣa.*

How does one become a sage?

How did they become *ṛṣi*s? Once again we find that Kṛṣṇa gives a complete description of the wise man within the verse itself. First of all, they are *kṣīṇa-kalmaṣāḥ,* those for whom impurities, *kalmaṣa,* is destroyed, *kṣīṇa.* Impurity here means one's *rāga-dveṣa*s. By living a life of *karma-yoga* and enquiry, the impurities are gone.

They are also described here as *sarva-bhūta-hite ratāḥ,* those who joyously engage themselves for the good of all beings. This is a very important qualification for the one who wants to gain knowledge. Afterwards, of course, acting in this way becomes natural to the person. Such people observe *ahiṁsā*, non-violence, with great alertness and sensitivity. They do not hurt other persons or beings in any way–by word, action, or even by thought. Infact, the vow of *ahiṁsā*, not to hurt another, is the main vow a person takes when he or she takes to a life of *sannyāsa*, which is why *sannyāsī*s give up all competitive activities. For, in order to win or compete in anything, injury to another person or living being is inevitable; it is inherent in competition of any kind. By taking the vow of *ahiṁsā*, the *sannyāsī* announces to all beings that they have nothing to fear from him or her.

The word '*yatātmānaḥ*,' in this verse, refers to those who have control or mastery over the organs of action and organs of perception. Such people are also *chinna-dvaidhas*. *Dvaidha* means *saṁśaya*, doubt, and *chinna* means resolved, removed, uprooted. For these people, the doubts are gone. In this pursuit, doubts can take many forms such as – is *ātmā* limitless or limited, is *ātmā* eternal or non-eternal, is *ātmā* one or many, is the individual, *jīva*, different from Īśvara, is the world real or unreal?

The wise are free from such doubts, which means a lot of enquiry has been done. The concepts have been carefully analysed and the knowledge has been freed of any possible doubts.

While the qualifications given in this verse are natural to a wise person, they are means or *sādhana*s for the one who wants to gain self-knowledge. Enjoying these virtues, people become *ṛṣi*s and gain the freedom they are seeking.

Further, Kṛṣṇa says:

कामक्रोधवियुक्तानां यतीनां यतचेतसाम् ।
अभितो ब्रह्मनिर्वाणं वर्तते विदितात्मनाम् ॥ २६ ॥

kāmakrodhaviyuktānāṁ yatīnāṁ yatacetasām
abhito brahmanirvāṇaṁ vartate viditātmanām (26)

Kāma-krodha-viyuktānām – for those who are free from desire and anger; *yata-cetasām* – for those whose mind is under control; *viditātmanām* – for those who know the self; *yatīnām* – for the *sannyāsīs*; *abhitaḥ* – both here and in the hereafter; *brahma-nirvāṇam* – liberation; *vartate* – there is

> For the *sannyāsī*s who are free from desire and anger, whose mind is under control, (and) who know the self, there is liberation, both here and in the hereafter.

Throughout the *Gītā* there is a repeated mention of *kāma* and *krodha* and the need to become free from them. Those who have freed themselves from *kāma-krodha* are referred to here as *kāma-krodha-viyuktāḥ*.

Kāma, as we have seen, is born of your *rāga-dveṣa*s, and *krodha* is born of desire; these two, hold people under their control. Those who have freed themselves from *kāma* and *krodha* are the subject of this verse. There are few more words in this verse qualifying those who are wise.

Yati means a person who is a *mumukṣu*, who has a desire for *mokṣa*. Such a person makes proper effort, which implies *yoga*. In common parlance, *yati* means a *sannyāsī* but, in its true sense, it includes the *karma-yogī* too. Anyone who is engaged in a well-directed pursuit or enquiry into the nature of oneself is a *mumukṣu* and therefore, a *yati* – whether the person lives the life of a *sannyāsī* or a *karma-yogī*.

Such a person who has his or her mind under control is called a *yata-cetas*. Because these people are also described here as *viditātmā*s, those who know the *ātmā*, in this compound the word *yata* indicates that they are *sarva-karma-sannyāsī*s, those who have given up actions in terms of knowledge of the actionless self. Such people are totally free from *kāma* and *krodha*, and are also free of actions because of the knowledge of *ātmā*.

If all that is required is knowledge of *ātmā*, why worry about *kāma* and *krodha*? Is it not a waste of time to get rid of desire and anger? Why not pursue *ātma-jñāna* straightaway? The answer is that unless *kāma-krodha* is addressed, you cannot know *ātmā*. Once again, then, what is implied here is the need for certain level of maturity and a commitment to self-knowledge.

Once the commitment is total, you will gain self-knowledge, you will be a *viditātmā*. Then there is nothing for you to worry about because knowing *ātmā* and gaining *mokṣa* are one and the same. Because of the knowledge of the self that is ever free, you are liberated.

The word '*abhitaḥ*,' in the verse is explained as *ubhayataḥ*, meaning 'in both ways.' Here, while living, there is *mokṣa* for these people and, later, in the hereafter, also there is *mokṣa*. Knowing you are free is the greatest freedom. While living you are liberated; you are free. This is one freedom. The second freedom is called 'after death' freedom, in that there is no coming back to this bondage because you are free, once and for all.

Some people worry about what happens after death, saying, 'I take so much effort and gain liberation here, but suppose I come back?' Any supposing with reference to coming back, having gained liberation by knowledge, is totally irrelevant. There must be a nucleus of some kind for any coming back. The nucleus is the *jīva*, the individual, and that is what is falsified. Who or what, then, is there to come back? Liberation having been gained, there is no one any more to come back. Thus, Kṛṣṇa says that in both ways, here and hereafter, those who know *ātmā* gain *mokṣa*. Although a two-fold *mokṣa* is talked about in terms of here and hereafter, in fact, there is only one *mokṣa* A two-fold *mokṣa* is mentioned only with reference to this question of coming back.

There are, on the other hand, people who are afraid that they will not be able to come back; they want to come back to this world. 'What for?' I ask. 'So that I can accomplish something more or do something better next time,' they say. It means they have already concluded that they are not going to make it in this life! First, let us take care of this life. Then the next life will take care of itself!

Introduction to meditation

There are two types of *sādhana* – *bahiraṅga-sādhana*, external means, and *antaraṅga-sādhana*, internal means. Doing *karma* is doing what is to be done by you with the right attitude and following proper values. In other words, *karma-yoga* is *bahiraṅga-sādhana*. *Dhyāna*, meditation, wherein the mind alone is involved, is *antaraṅga-sādhana*. It can be a prayer, contemplation, or any inner discipline, but it is purely internal. No limbs are involved, nor is the organ of speech. Therefore, one type of *sādhana* is external and the other is internal, both of which we should follow.

The external means, *bahiraṅga-sādhana*, take care of your likes and dislikes because these can only be worked out through your interactions with the external world. For gaining steadiness of mind and the composure necessary to gain self-knowledge, there is *antaraṅga-sādhana*, inner discipline of meditation, which is also very important. Thus, Kṛṣṇa first gives a brief account of *dhyāna-yoga*, meditation, in the next three verses and then discusses it at length in the next chapter.

Verses 27&28

Keeping the external world external

स्पर्शान्कृत्वा बहिर्बाह्यांश्चक्षुश्चैवान्तरे भ्रुवोः ।
प्राणापानौ समौ कृत्वा नासाभ्यन्तरचारिणौ ॥ २७ ॥

यतेन्द्रियमनोबुद्धिर्मुनिर्मोक्षपरायणः ।
विगतेच्छाभयक्रोधो यः सदा मुक्त एव सः ॥ २८ ॥

sparśān kṛtvā bahirbāhyāṁścakṣuścaivāntare bhruvoḥ
prāṇāpānau samau kṛtvā nāsābhyantaracāriṇau (27)

yatendriyamanobuddhirmunirmokṣaparāyaṇaḥ
vigatecchābhayakrodho yaḥ sadā mukta eva saḥ (28)

bāhyān – external; *sparśān* – objects; *bahiḥ kṛtvā* – keeping external; *ca* – and; *cakṣuḥ* – eye; *bhruvoḥ antare eva* (*kṛtvā*) – placing between the two eyebrows alone; *nāsābhyantaracāriṇau* – moving in the nostrils; *prāṇa-apānau* – exhalation and inhalation; *samau kṛtvā* – keeping them equal; *yaḥ muniḥ* – the contemplative person who; *yata-indriya-mano-buddhiḥ* – (is the) one who has mastered his (or her) organs of action, senses, mind and intellect; *mokṣaparāyaṇaḥ* – for whom *mokṣa* is the ultimate end; *vigata-icchā-bhaya-krodhaḥ* – who is free from desire, fear and anger; *saḥ* – that person; *sadā* – always; *muktaḥ* – is liberated; *eva* – indeed

> Keeping the external objects external, and the eyes between the two eyebrows (and closed), keeping the exhalation and inhalation that move in the nostrils equal, (rhythmic), the contemplative person, who has mastered his (or her) organs of action, senses, mind, and intellect, for whom *mokṣa* is the ultimate end, who is free from desire, fear, and anger, (that person) is always liberated indeed.

Here, Kṛṣṇa gives out small tips that would be of help in the preparation for meditation. We have already seen that anything that comes in contact with a sense organ is called *sparśa*, object. And because they are *bāhya*, external, to the body, they are called *bāhya-sparśa*. The sense organs are exposed to the sense objects, meaning the world. The eyes are exposed to colours and forms; the ears are exposed to sounds; the nose is exposed to smells; the tongue is exposed to tastes; and the sense of touch is exposed to the textures of various sense objects.

In his commentary, Śaṅkara explains that the sense objects, sound and so on, enter your mind through the gates of the sense organs, ears, and so on. In meditation, the external objects are to be kept outside, meaning you leave them alone for the time being. You simply stop thinking about them. You turn your mind to something else. You do not need to turn these sense objects away from yourself, nor do you have to turn away from them. You just have to leave them right where they are.

The sense objects enter your mind in the first place by your thinking about them. Therefore, you cannot blame the sense objects for being in your head. Śaṅkara said, do not think about them, and they will not be there. The sense objects are already external and by not dwelling on them, they remain external. This is how the sense objects are kept outside.

The eyes are generally kept closed. You can meditate with your eyes open, but keeping the eyes closed makes it easier for the mind to think about the object of meditation. If your eyes are open, your mind may wander to what is in front of you. Therefore, you close the eyes to eliminate distraction from a particular sense perception. The expression, '*cakṣuśca bhruvoḥ antare kṛtvā*' used in this verse, means, 'keeping the eyes between the eyebrows,' meaning that the eyeballs are kept inside the eyelids. In other words, the eyes are kept closed.

Watching the breath

Then, breathing is mentioned, *prāṇa-apānau samau kṛtvā, nāsābhyantaracāriṇau*. Here, *prāṇa* and *apāna* mean exhalation and inhalation, respectively. How is this breathing to be done?

Moving inside the nostrils, *nāsābhyantaracāriṇau*, the incoming air and the outgoing air should be kept rhythmic. By making the inhalation and exhalation rhythmic, you become conscious of the breathing process and, by watching the breath, the breathing becomes quiet, thereby relaxing the body and quietening the mind.

Doing this the person becomes one who has mastered the senses, organs of action, mind, and intellect, *yata-indriya-mano-buddhi*. This person is called *muni*, meaning one who has done *śravaṇa*, listening, and *manana* analysis. For the *muni*, *mokṣa* is the ultimate end; he is *mokṣa-pārāyaṇa*. The knowledge is relieved of any doubts and the person is freed from problems, meaning, he or she is always liberated.

Freedom from fear

There is one more qualification describing such a person that serves to repeat what has been said before, *vigata-icchā-bhaya-krodha*, meaning the person is free from desire, fear, and anger. Previously, Kṛṣṇa said that the wise person is freed from *kāma* and *krodha*. Here, he added one more word, *bhaya*, fear. The person is emotionally mature in the sense that he or she is not under the spell of desire, fear, or anger. Such a person is a *sannyāsī*. He or she is indeed liberated because of self-knowledge.

As an introduction to the next verse, Śaṅkara refers to the person who is totally committed to knowledge, meaning one who has done proper *śravaṇa* and *manana*, as *samāhita-citta*, meaning one whose mind is steady and well absorbed in oneself and who is more or less satisfied with oneself.

Kṛṣṇa concludes this chapter with the next verse revealing the identity between the individual, *jīva*, and Īśvara, the Lord, and what one gains knowing this identity.

Verse 29

Kṛṣṇa is talking as Īśvara

भोक्तारं यज्ञतपसां सर्वलोकमहेश्वरम् ।
सुहृदं सर्वभूतानां ज्ञात्वा मां शान्तिमृच्छति ॥ २९ ॥

bhoktāraṁ yajñatapasāṁ sarvalokamaheśvaram
suhṛdaṁ sarvabhūtānāṁ jñātvā māṁ śāntim ṛcchati (29)

yajñatapasā – of rituals and disciplines; *bhoktāram* – the sustainer; *sarvaloka-maheśvaram* – the Lord of all the worlds; *sarvabhūtānām* – of all beings; *suhṛdam* – friend; *mām* – me; *jñātvā* – knowing; *śāntim* – peace (liberation); *ṛcchati* – gains

Knowing me as the sustainer of rituals and disciplines, the Lord of all the worlds, friend of all beings, he (or she) gains peace (liberation).

Kṛṣṇa is talking here as Īśvara when he uses the word *mām*. He says, 'Knowing me, the person gains me, *jñātvā māṁ śāntim ṛcchati*.' Here gaining *śānti* means gaining Īśvara, that is, by understanding the identity between oneself and Īśvara, one becomes Īśvara, as we shall see.

Generally, by knowing something, you do not become that thing. By knowing it, you only know it. It can become an object of your desire. You can appreciate it, but you cannot become the object. Here, Kṛṣṇa says that by knowing him, the absolute *śānti*, peace, that is your nature, is gained.

Śānti that is centred on yourself, that is your *svarūpa,* is gained by knowing me. Now, who is this me? Is it Kṛṣṇa, the son of Devakī? No, the verse says 'Me,' the sustainer of rituals and disciplines, the Lord of all worlds, and the friend of all beings.

The word '*yajña*' in the compound *yajña-tapas* stands for actions that are performed by you, as well as the rituals enjoined by the Vedas. *Tapas* refers to all forms of meditation and discipline. There are, of course, many forms of exercise that can also be considered disciplines, such as jogging, walking, cycling, and so on. There is, however, an important difference here. For example, *yogāsana*s are much more than exercise; they are a form of prayer. For every *āsana* there is a *devatā*. Originally, every *āsana* was performed as a prayer to its presiding *devatā*. So, there is a prayerful attitude involved on the part of the person. Only prayerful disciplines are called *tapas*.

The one who sustains the *yajña*s and who enjoys them is a *bhoktā*. Who is the one who enjoys these results? The *kartā*, doer, *bhoktā*, the enjoyer, the *jīva*, in other words. But then it is said here that the *bhoktā* is the Lord of all worlds.

The word 'Maheśvara' is an important word because Īśvara can be used in a relative sense too. Any boss can be considered Īśvara, as can a king or *devatā;* in their own domains they are Īśvara. Thus, anyone who is lord in his or her domain can be called Īśvara. However, when the word Maheśvara is used, any chance of a local person being mistaken for Īśvara is eliminated. Maheśvara means one who does not have a superior or an equal. The two words, *mahat* and Īśvara, are in apposition with each other, meaning that they enjoy the same status. They both qualify the same object; they reveal the same object. The object they reveal is *mahān*, one without equal; Īśvara, the Lord, is the Maheśvara of all worlds, worlds here including all living beings.

The one who is the Lord of all worlds is the *kartā*, the doer, and he is the *bhoktā*, the enjoyer of the *karma*s. When a ritual is performed there is always a doer involved, who is Īśvara, and also a deity involved, who is also Īśvara. Thus, the *kartā* is Īśvara, the *devatā* is Īśvara, and the enjoyer of the results of the *karma* is also Īśvara, meaning there is no *jīva* at all. The one who is *kartā* and *bhoktā* is Parameśvara alone. The one who enjoys the results of action is Parameśvara and the one who performs the action is also Parameśvara. It means that *kartṛtva*, doership, and *bhoktṛtva*, enjoyership, are false.

The word '*mām*' in this verse is also qualified by the expression *suhṛdaṁ sarva-bhūtānām*, the friend of all beings. A friend is someone who helps you. Help can be extended for a number of reasons. Someone may help you because he or she expects something from you in return. It is generally the case. A return can be in any form – simple thanks or some other expression of gratitude, or it may be a nice feeling you receive from being able to help someone – all of which is related to ego. Some parents, even when their children are grown up, like to be asked for help now and then so that they can still have the feeling of being parents, of helping their children. When they are asked for help, they feel they are wanted. It is one kind of help.

There is also the help that is given without the person expecting any kind of result. Without much introduction or without there being any friendship or affection involved, you may help someone out of sheer empathy. One who gives such help, even to a stranger, without expecting any type of return, is a *suhṛd*, different from a mere *mitra*, friend.

We all need a friend who will be able to do things for us. Due to friendship, *sneha*, affection, then, one's help is extended. This kind of friend is a *mitra*, whereas *suhṛd* is one who extends his or her help without even knowing the person or expecting any result. The Lord is also called a *suhṛd*. He is a friend to all beings, *suhṛd sarva-bhūtānām* and *karma-phala-dātā*, the giver of fruits of action. We perform actions and he gives the result without getting involved. His nature is to give according to what we do.

If you want to think, you can. If you want to sleep, you can. If you want to daydream, you can. He never says, 'No!' Sometimes even your own mind will say, 'No!' If you want to think, the mind may say, 'No, let us go to sleep!' If you want to eat, the stomach says, 'No, I cannot eat anymore!' If you want to walk, the legs may say, 'No, we have had enough!' The liver, the kidneys, and so on, say, 'No.' So everyone says, 'No' sometime or the other except *ātmā*. Even if you say, 'I want to keep the ignorance going,' *ātmā* will say, 'No problem!' It simply illumines the ignorance.

Ultimately, Nārāyaṇa is the end that all human beings seek. Knowing Nārāyaṇa, meaning Īśvara, '*mām*, me' in this verse, the person gains *śānti*. *Śānti* here does not mean simple peace. It is the point where all forms of *saṁsāra* resolve. It is the *śānti* that amounts to the resolution of *saṁsāra*, of doership and enjoyership.

Ātmā is not opposed to anything; it is unopposed to everything. But it does not mean that *ātmā* is a 'yes man!' A 'yes man' says 'yes' only when it is convenient, when it serves his ends. Here, 'yes' is absolute. Why is it so? *Ātmā* is that without which no action is possible, no enjoyment of the results of action is possible. Therefore, the enjoyer is nothing but Parameśvara, whereas Parameśvara is not the enjoyer. Parameśvara is not the doer, but the doer is Parameśvara. B is A, but A is not B.

The teaching, that is self-knowledge, is for the *jīva*, the doer and enjoyer alone, and the *jīva* is Parameśvara. Thus there is an equation between *jīva* and Īśvara. By understanding this equation and by appreciating the identity that obtains between *jīva*, the individual, and Īśvara, the Lord, the person gains *śānti*, *śāntiṁ ṛcchati*, gains *śānti*, which is the resolution of *saṁsāra*. The result of this knowledge of the identity between *jīva* and Īśvara is what is called *mokṣa*. This *mokṣa*, this *śānti* is gained by one who has self-knowledge.

The following is always the conclusion that we have seen at the end of each of the four chapters that have gone by.

ॐ तत्सत् ।

इति श्रीमद्भगवद्गीतासूपनिषत्सु ब्रह्मविद्यायां योगशास्त्रे श्रीकृष्णार्जुन-
संवादे संन्यास-योगो नाम पञ्चमोऽध्यायः ॥ ५ ॥

oṁ tat sat.

iti śrīmadbhagavadgītāsūpaniṣatsu brahma-vidyāyāṁ yogaśāstre śrīkṛṣṇārjunasaṁvāde sannyāsa-yogo nāma pañcamo'dhyāyaḥ (5)

Om, Brahman, is the only reality. '*oṁ tat sat*' as we have seen before, is a statement made at the end of the teaching, meaning, 'That alone is Brahman.' *Om* is the name for Brahman, Parameśvara, the Lord. That Brahman alone is *satya*. The *kartā* is not *satya*; *karma* is not *satya*, *karma-phala* is not *satya*; the *karma-phala bhoktā* is not *satya*; the *devatā* is not *satya;* the world is not *satya;* the body is not *satya;* the mind is not *satya*. But Brahman alone is *satya*. All of them are Brahman, but Brahman is none of them.

Then what is *satya*? *Om* alone is *satya*. That Parameśvara, *paraṁ-brahma*, the cause of the world, *jagat-kāraṇa*, the cause of everything is *satya*. Therefore, the effect becomes *mithyā*. If the effect is *mithyā*, the causal state is also *mithyā*, whereas the *svarūpa*, the essence of the cause, is *satya*. For example, clay is the cause for the pot. The pot being *mithyā*, the causal state for the clay is also *mithyā* because, if you look into the clay, there is no cause; there is only clay. Thus, the cause and the effect are equally *mithyā* and the *svarūpa*, the essence of the cause, is *satya*. Everything else being *mithyā, om* that is *Brahman, jagat-kāraṇa*, is *satya*.

When all is said and done it is all *oṁ tat sat*.

Thus ends the fifth chapter called *sannyāsa-yoga* – having the topic of renunciation – in the *Bhagavadgītā* which is in the form of a dialogue between Śrī Kṛṣṇa and Arjuna, which is the essence of the *Upaniṣads*, whose subject matter is both knowledge of Brahman and *yoga*.

Alphabetical index of verses

Text	Chapter	Verse	Vol	Page
daṇḍo damayatām asmi	10	38	6	426
dambho darpo'bhimānaśca	16	04	8	176
daṁṣṭrākarālāni ca te mukhāni	11	25	7	53
dātavyam iti yaddānam	17	20	8	271
divi sūryasahasrasya	11	12	7	25
divyamālyāmbaradharam	11	11	7	24
duḥkham ityeva yatkarma	18	08	9	35
duḥkheṣvanudvignamanāḥ	02	56	2	324
dūreṇa hyavaraṁ karma	02	49	2	287
dṛṣṭvā tu pāṇḍavānīkam	01	02	1	176
dṛṣṭvedaṁ mānuṣaṁ rūpam	11	51	7	101
devadvijaguruprājñapūjanaṁ	17	14	8	252
devān bhāvayatānena	03	11	3	76
dehī nityam avadhyo'yam	02	30	2	178
dehino'smin yathā dehe	02	13	2	62
daivam evāpare yajñam	04	25	4	208
daivī hyeṣā guṇamayī	07	14	5	351
daivī sampadvimokṣāya	16	05	8	180
doṣairetaiḥ kulaghnānām	01	43	1	238
dyāvāpṛthivyoridam antaraṁ hi	11	20	7	40
dyūtaṁ chalayatām asmi	10	36	6	422

Books by Swami Dayananda Saraswati

Public Talk Series :

1. Living Intelligently
2. Successful Living
3. Need for Cognitive Change
4. Discovering Love
5. The Value of Values
6. Vedic View and Way of Life

Upaniṣad Series :

7. Muṇḍakopaniṣad
8. Kenopaniṣad

Prakaraṇa Series :

9. Tattvabodhaḥ

Text Translation Series :

10. Śrīmad Bhagavad Gītā
    (Text with roman transliteration and English translation)
11. Śrī Rudram
    (Text in Sanskrit with transliteration, word-to-word and verse meaning along with an elaborate commentary in English)

Stotra Series :

12. Dīpārādhanā
13. Prayer Guide
    (With explanations of several Mantras, Stotras, Kirtans and Religious Festivals)

Moments with Oneself Series :

14. Freedom from Helplessness
15. Living versus Getting On
16. Insights
17. Action and Reaction
18. Fundamental Problem
19. Problem is You, Solution is You
20. Purpose of Prayer
21. Vedanta 24x7
22. Freedom
23. Crisis Management
24. Surrender and Freedom
25. The Need for Personal Reorganisation
26. Freedom in Relationship
27. Stress-free Living
28. Om Namo Bhagavate Vāsudevāya
29. Yoga of Objectivity

Bhagavad Gītā

30. Bhagavad Gītā Home Study Course (Hardbound - 9 Volumes)

Meditation Series :

31. Morning Meditation Prayers
32. What is Meditation?

Essays :

33. Do all Religions have the same goal?
34. Conversion is Violence
35. Gurupūrṇimā
36. Dānam
37. Japa
38. Can We?
39. Moments with Krishna
40. Teaching Tradition of Advaita Vedanta
41. Compositions of Swami Dayananda Saraswati

Exploring Vedanta Series : (*vākyavicāra*)

42. śraddhā bhakti dhyāna yogād avaihi ātmānaṁ ced vijānīyāt

Books translated in other languages and in English based on Swami Dayananda Saraswati's Original Exposition

Tamil

43. Veeduthorum Gitopadesam (9 Volumes)
    (Bhagavad Gītā Home Study Course)
44. Dānam

Kannada

45. Mane maneyalli Adhyayana (7 Volumes)
    (Bhagavad Gītā Home Study Course)

46. Vedanta Pravesike

Malayalam

47. Muṇḍakopaniṣad

Hindi

48. Ghar baithe Gītā Vivecan (Vol 1)
(Bhagavad Gītā Home Study Course)
49. Antardṛṣṭi (Insights)
50. Vedanta 24X7
51. Kriya aur Pratikriya (Action and Reaction)

English

52. The Jungian Myth and Advaita Vedanta
53. The Vedantic Self and the Jungian Psyche
54. Salutations to Rudra
55. Without a Second

Biography

56. Swami Dayananda Saraswati
Contributions & Writings
(Smt. Sheela Balalji)

Distributed in India & worldwide by
MOTILAL BANARSIDASS - NEW DELHI
Tel : 011 - 2385 8335 / 2385 1985 / 2385 2747

Also available at :

ARSHA VIDYA RESEARCH
AND PUBLICATION TRUST
32 / 4 Sir Desika Road
Mylapore Chennai 600 004
Telefax : 044 - 2499 7131
Email : avrandpt@gmail.com
Website : www.avrpt.com

ARSHA VIDYA GURUKULAM
Anaikatti P.O.
Coimbatore 641 108
Ph : 0422 - 2657001
Fax : 0422 - 2657002
Email : office@arshavidya.in
Website : www.arshavidya.in

ARSHA VIDYA GURUKULAM
P.O.Box 1059. Pennsylvania
PA 18353, USA
Ph : 001-570-992-2339
Email : avp@epix.net
Website : www.arshavidya.org

SWAMI DAYANANDA ASHRAM
Purani Jhadi, P.B.No. 30
Rishikesh, Uttaranchal 249 201
Telefax : 0135 - 2430769
Email : ashrambookstore@yahoo.com
Website : www.dayananda.org

Other leading Book Stores:

Chennai:	**044**
Motilal Banarsidass	24982315
Giri Trading	2495 1966
Higginbothams	2851 3519
Pustak Bharati	2461 1345
Theosophical Publishing House	2446 6613 / 2491 1338
The Odessey	43910300
Bengaluru:	**080**
Gangarams	2558 1617 / 2558 1618
Sapna Book House	4011 4455 / 4045 5999
Strand Bookstall	2558 2222, 25580000
Vedanta Book House	2650 7590
Coimbatore:	**0422**
Guru Smruti	948677 3793
Giri Trading	2541523

PTO

Trivandrum:	**0471**
Prabhus Bookhouse	2478 397 / 2473 496
Kozhikode:	**0495**
Ganga Bookhouse	6521262
Mumbai:	**022**
Chetana Bookhouse	2285 1243 / 2285 3412
Strand Bookstall	2266 1994 / 2266 1719/ 2261 4613
Giri Trading	2414 3140

Made in the USA
Las Vegas, NV
10 August 2023

75924600R00260